Bestr Isidore Charles Tirard

Albuminuria and Bright's Disease

Bestr Isidore Charles Tirard

Albuminuria and Bright's Disease

ISBN/EAN: 9783337155391

Printed in Europe, USA, Canada, Australia, Japan

Cover: Foto ©ninafisch / pixelio.de

More available books at **www.hansebooks.com**

ALBUMINURIA

AND

BRIGHT'S DISEASE

BY

NESTOR TIRARD, M.D., F.R.C.P.

PHYSICIAN TO KING'S COLLEGE HOSPITAL AND SENIOR PHYSICIAN TO THE EVELINA
HOSPITAL FOR SICK CHILDREN; PROFESSOR OF MATERIA MEDICA AND
THERAPEUTICS AT KING'S COLLEGE; EXAMINER IN MATERIA MEDICA TO
THE CONJOINT BOARD OF ENGLAND, FORMERLY EXAMINER AT THE
UNIVERSITY OF LONDON AND AT THE VICTORIA UNIVERSITY;
AUTHOR OF 'DIPHTHERIA AND ANTITOXIN'

WITH ORIGINAL ILLUSTRATIONS

LONDON
SMITH, ELDER, & CO., 15 WATERLOO PLACE
1899

CONTENTS

CHAPTER		PAGE
	INTRODUCTORY—STRUCTURE, FUNCTIONS, TESTS	1
I.	ALBUMINURIA—*a*. EXTRA-RENAL ; *b*. RENAL	25
II.	HÆMATURIA	57
III.	HÆMOGLOBINURIA—CHYLURIA	71
IV.	RENAL CASTS	83
V.	ACUTE NEPHRITIS	92
VI.	SCARLATINAL NEPHRITIS	116
VII.	CHRONIC NEPHRITIS	137
VIII.	CIRRHOSIS OF THE KIDNEY	180
IX.	PUERPERAL ALBUMINURIA, NEPHRITIS AND ECLAMPSIA	222
X.	RETINAL CHANGES IN BRIGHT'S DISEASE	237
XI.	LARDACEOUS DISEASE OF THE KIDNEY	245
XII.	CONGESTION OF THE KIDNEY, RENAL EMBOLISM	261
XIII.	RENAL CALCULUS	276
XIV.	HYDRO-NEPHROSIS, CONSECUTIVE CIRRHOSIS, SUPPURATIVE NEPHRITIS	281
XV.	URÆMIA	299
XVI.	GENERAL DIAGNOSIS OF ALBUMINURIA	320
XVII.	GENERAL PROGNOSIS OF ALBUMINURIA	331
	INDEX TO AUTHORS	339
	GENERAL INDEX	343

LIST OF ILLUSTRATIONS

PLATE
I. TRANSVERSE SECTION OF TUBULES AFTER TYPHOID FEVER WITH ALBUMINURIA . . . . *to face p.* 44

II. SECTION OF CORTICAL PORTION OF KIDNEY IN CHRONIC NEPHRITIS, DURING A SUBACUTE ATTACK . . . . „ 62

III. SECTION OF TUBULES IN ACUTE NEPHRITIS, SHOWING EPITHELIAL CHANGES . . . . „ 96

IV. SECTION OF KIDNEY IN ACUTE NEPHRITIS (GLOMERULO-NEPHRITIS) . . . . „ 120

V. SECTION OF KIDNEY IN CHRONIC NEPHRITIS, SHOWING PERI-CAPSULITIS AND ENDO-CAPSULITIS . . . „ 142

VI. SECTION OF KIDNEY IN CHRONIC NEPHRITIS, SHOWING CAST IN A TUBE . . . . „ 144

VII. SECTION OF FIBROUS AREA IN CIRRHOSIS OF THE KIDNEY „ 186

VIII. OBLIQUE SECTION OF A SMALL ARTERY IN CIRRHOSIS OF THE KIDNEY . . . . „ 188

IX. SECTION OF TUBES IN CIRRHOSIS OF THE KIDNEY . . „ 190

X. ALBUMINURIC RETINITIS, LEFT EYE, ERECT IMAGE . . „ 238

XI. ALBUMINURIC RETINITIS, LEFT EYE, ERECT IMAGE . . „ 240

XII. ALBUMINURIC AND DIABETIC NEURO-RETINITIS . . . „ 242

XIII. RETINAL CHANGES THREE YEARS AFTER ACUTE ALBUMINURIC RETINITIS . . . . „ 244

XIV. SECTION OF LARDACEOUS KIDNEY, IN AN EARLY STAGE . „ 248

XV. PULSE TRACINGS WITH ALBUMINURIA . . „ 326

ALBUMINURIA AND BRIGHT'S DISEASE

INTRODUCTORY

OBJECTION may be taken to the title of this book on the ground that it is lacking in scientific precision, inasmuch as albuminuria is not a true disease, but a condition which may or may not be associated with definite pathological changes, while Bright's disease includes a number of conditions which present at least one definite change in common, viz. that of an acute or chronic disease of the kidney. Practically, however, it is found that by many authors the terms so frequently associated are regarded as almost synonymous; indeed, one writer goes so far as to state that, 'to avoid wearisome reiteration,' he employs sometimes one and sometimes the other term. The natural tendency of modern days is to react against the somewhat narrow limits that were applied to both terms within a few years of Bright's publication of his researches, and to allow that many forms of albuminuria occur independently of structural renal changes. One of the fundamental propositions formulated by Sir George Johnson is that Bright's disease is not merely a local malady, but a disease of constitutional origin; and that the proximate cause of the renal disease is in all probability a morbid condition of the blood. This generalisation, which is doubtless correct, appears to justify me in linking, for the purpose of description and investigation, the conditions of albuminuria and Bright's disease. The disease of the kidney is not, in the latter, the true starting point.

The intimate connection between albuminous urine and morbid alterations in the structure of the kidneys was first demonstrated by Dr. Richard Bright, who, in 1827, in the first volume of his 'Reports of Medical Cases,' gave numerous coloured drawings of the morbid appearances of the kidney. He was certainly the first to connect definite renal changes with dropsy and albuminuria. The presence of albumin in the urine had been discovered by Cotugno, whose observations were published in Vienna in 1770; it was also discovered by Blackall of Exeter, that albuminous urine was frequently associated with dropsy. Blackall, however, thought that the re-absorption and elimination of dropsical fluid were responsible for the appearance of albumin in the urine. Dr. W. C. Wells, in 1792, described definite renal changes; he described the kidneys as remarkably hard, and the definite thickening of the cortex in cases which had been marked by albuminuria during life, but he failed to establish any connection between the renal change and the albuminuria. The frequent association of the three conditions, renal changes, dropsy, and albuminuria, having been formulated by Dr. Richard Bright, a name for the newly discovered disease was sought, and the terms suggested by Rayer and Christison, 'nephrite albumineuse' and 'granular degeneration,' having been found open to grave objections, it became customary to employ the name of the discoverer as a general term for the conditions he described. The term 'Bright's disease' was speedily adopted almost universally, but it has involved certain difficulties. In the first place it appears to assume that all the conditions he described are different stages or phases of a disease, resulting from a single morbid process. A second difficulty is the need of a satisfactory definition; Sir George Johnson thinks that the best definition of 'Bright's disease' is the following: 'a generic term indicating several forms of acute and chronic disease of the kidney, usually associated with albumin in the urine, and frequently with dropsy and with various secondary diseases resulting from deterioration of the blood.' This definition is certainly fairly free from objection, since it allows that Bright's disease may occasionally exist without albuminuria, and that dropsy also does not form an essential or invariable feature. One of the chief difficulties, however, connected with the term 'Bright's disease' is that it has been so readily caught up by the non-medical world, and that it appears to be regarded amongst the laity as synonymous with albuminuria. This is much to be regretted, as it frequently causes needless alarm and depression when at some casual examination the presence of albumin in the urine has been detected. It cannot be too often insisted that albuminuria is frequently symptomatic, that it may occur in the course of heart disease, diphtheria, erysipelas, and other diseases, and that on the contrary it may occasionally be met with under the various conditions which have been conveniently grouped under the heading of 'Functional Albuminuria'—conditions which are, so far as our present knowledge extends, not associated with any existing renal changes, and are not always, if ever, followed by true kidney disease at a later period.

General Work of the Kidney

This work being intended chiefly for clinical purposes and for those familiar with the general structure of the kidneys, it is unnecessary to enter at length into details of their anatomy, position, or connection with the bladder, facts which are too well known to need description here.

Passing on, therefore, to the work of the kidney, we find that it consists of two chief functions: (1) the true secretion, and (2) a function which is nearly allied to simple filtration. The true secreting work of the kidney is performed by the glandular epithelium which lines the convoluted portions of the tubules. Various organic substances—urea, uric acid, and a certain proportion of the solids of the urine—are separated from the blood by the secreting cells of these tubules; while the filtration or diffusion of fluid appears to be performed by the tufts of capillaries within the Malpighian capsules. Without a doubt the capillaries within the glomeruli are submitted to a high blood pressure, and reference has often been made to the smallness of the efferent vessels as an indication of one possible cause of the high pressure within the Malpighian tuft. This explanation, however, scarcely seems conclusive. The efferent vessel is certainly smaller than the afferent, but this possibly may be the result of the work of the Malpighian tuft rather than its cause. Undoubtedly a small efferent vessel, if its walls were rigid, would give rise to high blood pressure within the

Malpighian tuft, but it appears to be equally probable that the efferent vessel is small as the result of the filtration from the Malpighian capillaries. The efferent vessel has less fluid to carry than the afferent, and therefore it is not necessary that it should be so large.

In all probability some salts pass through the Malpighian tuft, together with water, as, for example, the inorganic crystalline salts, which doubtless readily diffuse through the membrane.

The presence of a layer of flattened epithelium over the capillary tuft has been said to prevent to a large extent the albuminous constituents of the blood from passing away with the water, and this contention has derived some support from experiment. If the renal arteries are ligatured for a short time, this epithelial coating becomes injured, and the urine is found to be albuminous. It has been sometimes asserted that even in health, albumin is constantly added to the fluid, which is filtered through or diffused through the glomerulus; and the general absence of albumin from the urine has been attributed to re-absorption of albumin within the tubules.

The twofold sources of the constituents of the urine have long been recognised, and numerous experiments tend to show the correctness of the theory above enunciated. Undoubtedly, when the epithelium of the convoluted tubes becomes injured by disease, the excretory power of the kidney is impaired, and the interference in function is found to affect the organic substances, rather than the water and inorganic salts. In other words, in chronic kidney disease, while the amount of urea and uric acid is largely reduced, the amount of urine passed is frequently slightly in excess of the normal quantity. The diminution of the organic constituents of the urine is the natural result of the alteration of the secreting epithelial cells, but the alteration in the quantity of urine is not so easily explained. When the vessels of the kidney are engorged, either as part of an acute inflammatory process or in consequence of interference with the circulation owing to chronic disease of the heart or the lungs, the amount of urine is commonly much reduced. With less blood passing through the renal capillaries in a given time, less fluid is withdrawn from them. When, on the other hand, the pressure within the renal vessels is increased, as, for instance, from hypertrophy of the arterioles in chronic kidney disease, an increased filtration is favoured, and the daily amount of fluid excreted is commonly greater than in the healthy state.

These clinical deductions, in support of the twofold nature of the work of the Malpighian capillaries and of the convoluted tubes, are in close accordance with the results of experimental investigations upon the healthy kidney. Though such experiments are, in many instances, difficult to perform, it has been stated, for example, from the experimental side that Ribbert has succeeded in extirpating the medullary substance of the kidney while leaving the cortical part intact, and that when he collected the urine which passed through the Malpighian bodies only, before reaching the looped tubules, he found that it was far more watery than that which was secreted by the entire kidney. Although the details of this experiment seem almost incredible, it has been freely quoted by numerous authors. The theory receives more satisfactory confirmation from the changes in the urine associated with the relative insignificance of the tubules of the kidney. Hufner has observed that among fishes, frogs, tortoises, birds, and mammals the tubes are long or short according as the animal requires water to be re-absorbed in each case. By experimenting with sulphindigotate of soda, Heidenhain has shown that when injected into the blood, after section of the medulla, this substance was taken up by the cells of the convoluted tubules, and by these only, so that they became blue. It has further been stated by Heidenhain, Bowman, and von Wittich that crystals of urates can be seen within the epithelial cells. Nussbaum experimented upon frogs and newts to show that urea was also excreted by these cells; and he found that sugar and peptone injected into the circulation pass into the urine of a kidney when intact, but not when the renal artery is tied. On the other hand, he found that urea was excreted only when the circulation among the tubules was intact, and he further asserted that water was excreted in two ways by the kidney, both by the glomeruli and by the epithelial cells.

With regard to the influence of nerves on the secretion of the kidney, it may be stated that dilatation of the branches of the renal arteries produced through the influence of the vasomotor nerves will cause increase of pressure within the glomeruli, and will result in the passage of an increased quantity of urine. When the pressure is increased by other conditions—such as, for instance, by an increase in the force or in the frequency of the heart's beat, by an increase in the volume of the blood, or by a constriction of small vessels independently of those of the kidney—the result is seen again in an increased quantity of water. On the other hand, whenever the pressure within the glomeruli is diminished, it is associated with a diminution in the amount of urine excreted. While, therefore, both clinically and experimentally, it may be regarded as certain that the nitrogenous elements are separated by the epithelium in the convoluted tubes, and that the water and inorganic salts come from the Malpighian tufts, it must be admitted that two points yet remain doubtful. First, whether any fluid passes into the convoluted tubes through the epithelial cells in company with the nitrogenous elements; and secondly, whether, as has been asserted, there is a normal outflow of albumin from the Malpighian tufts, with re-absorption of the albumin by the cells in the tubules. For the elucidation of these two points further observations and experiments are necessary. The constituents resulting from this twofold work of the kidney must now be considered.

CONSTITUENTS OF URINE.—The following classification of the constituents of normal urine is taken from Hoppe-Seyler's 'Physiologische Chemie':

1. Urea and related bodies: uric acid, allantoin, oxaluric acid, xanthin, guanin, creatin, creatinin, thio-cyanic acid.
2. Fatty non-nitrogenous bodies: fatty acids of the series $C_nH_{2n}O_2$: oxalic acid, lactic acid, glycerin-phosphoric acid; also inosit.
3. Aromatic substances: the ether-sulpho-acids of phenol, cresol, pyrocatechin (catechol), indoxyl, scatoxyl; also hippuric acid, cyanuric acid, paraoxyphenylacetic acid, parahydrocumaric acid, &c.
4. Inorganic salts: chloride of potassium and chloride of sodium, sulphate of potassium, phosphate of sodium, calcium and magnesium phosphate, soluble silicic

acid, ammonia combinations, calcium carbonate, &c. (Traces of iron and nitric and nitrous acids may also be present.)

The chief gases of the urine are nitrogen and carbonic acid, although small quantities of peroxide of hydrogen and sulphuretted hydrogen are occasionally present.

In the case of certain diseases the following abnormal constituents may also be met with: Serum-albumin and other proteids, hæmoglobin, met-hæmoglobin, bile-pigments, bile-acids, abnormal urinary pigments, leucin and tyrosin, oxymandel acid, grape sugar, milk sugar, glycuronic acid, fats, lecithin, cholesterin, cystin, constituents derived from food or drugs, and microscopic elements like blood corpuscles, urinary casts, and renal epithelium.

The amount of the constituents present in normal urine is represented in the following tables quoted from Yvon, Berlioz, and Parkes:

	Male	Female
Volume per diem	1,360 c.c.	1,100 c.c.
Specific gravity	1·0225 ,,	1·0215 ,,
Urea (per litre)	21·5 grams	19·0 grams
,, (per diem)	26·5 ,,	20·5 ,,
Uric acid (per litre)	0·5 ,,	0·55 ,,
,, ,, (per diem)	0·6 ,,	0·57 ,,
Phosphoric acid (per litre)	2·5 ,,	2·4 ,,
,, ,, (per diem)	3·2 ,,	2·6 ,,

	By an average man of 66 kilos	Per 1 kilogram of body weight
Water	1,500·000 grams	23·0000 grams
Total solids	72·000 ,,	1·1000 ,,
Urea	33·180 ,,	·5000 ,,
Uric acid	·555 ,,	·0084 ,,
Hippuric acid	·400 ,,	·0060 ,,
Creatinin	·910 ,,	·0140 ,,
Pigment and other substances	10·000 ,,	·1510 ,,
Sulphuric acid	2·012 ,,	·0305 ,,
Phosphoric acid	3·164 ,,	·0480 ,,
Chlorine	7·000 (8·21),,	·1260 ,,
Ammonia	·770 ,,	
Potassium	2·500 ,,	
Sodium	11·090 ,,	
Calcium	·260 ,,	
Magnesium	·207 ,,	

It may be helpful to summarise here the principal tests for the more important normal constituents of the urine.

In all cases, if the urine is opaque it should be filtered before applying the following tests; if it contains albumen, this should be completely precipitated by nitric or picric acid, and the precipitate should be removed by filtration.

Chlorides.—The urine is first acidulated with two or three drops of nitric acid, and one or two drops of solution of nitrate of silver are then added. A white precipitate, which is insoluble after the addition of more nitric acid but soluble in ammonia, indicates the presence of chlorides; the density of the precipitate is proportionate to the amount of chlorides present. In performing this test the preliminary addition of nitric acid is essential, as otherwise the precipitate might be due to the interaction of phosphates and nitrate of silver.

Phosphates.—If the urine is warmed after being made alkaline by the addition of solution of ammonia, or of caustic potash, a white flocculent precipitate is formed, which is soluble in acetic acid or in nitric acid. When the urine is alkaline or neutral, it may be turbid with phosphates when it is passed, or it may become turbid on being heated, even without the addition of ammonia or caustic potash. This turbidity is, however, at once cleared by the addition of a little acetic or nitric acid, and this test serves to differentiate the precipitate of phosphates from that of albumen.

Sulphates.—After acidulation with hydrochloric acid, the addition of a solution of barium chloride produces a white precipitate, insoluble in nitric acid. Unless hydrochloric acid is first added, phosphates and carbonates will be precipitated by barium chloride.

Urea.—This may be obtained in a crystalline form by evaporating the urine to a third of its original bulk, and then adding either nitric acid or oxalic acid, when urea nitrate or oxalate is formed. With an alkaline solution of hypobromite of sodium, or hypochlorite of calcium, urea is decomposed and nitrogen is evolved; these solutions are employed for the estimation of the amount of urea, and ureometers of various shapes have been devised; but the principle is the same in all—viz. the accurate measurement of the amount of nitrogen obtained by mixing known quantities of the reagent and of urine. Unless the test solution of hypobromite of sodium or hypochlorite of calcium contains an excess of alkali, the decomposition of urea is attended by the evolution of carbonic acid gas, mixed with the nitrogen. It is customary to prepare 15 c.c. of hypobromite solution when required, by mixing bromine 1·3 c.c. with caustic soda solution (1 in 25) 13·7 c.c.; the mixture is made in the open air on account of the extremely unpleasant fumes of bromine.

When crystals of urea have been melted by heat and subsequently dissolved in water, they give the well-known biuret reaction—a deep purple or rose-red colour—on adding a few drops of caustic soda or of caustic potash, and a drop of solution of copper sulphate.

Uric acid.—This is commonly recognised by the characteristic form of the crystals, and by their dark red colour when obtained direct from the urine. These microscopic crystals may separate after mixing urine with five per cent. of hydrochloric acid and allowing the mixture to stand for twenty-four hours, or they may be produced more conveniently by placing a small quantity of urine in a watch-glass and acidifying with acetic acid; if a thread is now placed in the mixture it will, at the end of twenty-four hours, be found to have collected upon it some of the characteristic crystals. Turbidity of the urine due to the deposition of urates, or to deposits of uric acid or urates, may be readily recognised by the ease with which it is cleared when the urine is warmed.

Urates or uric acid will also form characteristic reactions with the Murexide test and with Schiff's test. The former consists in evaporating to dryness, on a white porcelain dish, a mixture of nitric acid and either concentrated urine or the crystalline deposit. A yellow or reddish-yellow deposit is left, and, when cold, this is changed to a purplish red on the addition of a drop of ammonia. On the subsequent addition of caustic potash the colour is changed to a purplish blue. A violet colour, which disappears upon heating, is produced when caustic potash or caustic soda is used without the previous employment of ammonia. Schiff's test consists in dissolving the crystals of uric acid in the smallest possible quantity of solution of sodium carbonate, and placing a drop of the solution on a piece of filter paper moistened with solution of silver nitrate, when a greyish or black spot of metallic silver appears. Fehling's solution or copper sulphate and caustic potash may be reduced, with the formation of a reddish precipitate, on being boiled with urine in which uric acid or urates are present in relatively large amount. This result might be mistaken for sugar, which may, however, be identified by the picric acid and potash test.

For tests for the other constituents of urine, such as creatinin, hippuric acid, &c., as well as for detailed descriptions of quantitative estimation, the reader is referred to Dr. MacMunn's excellent work on the 'Clinical Chemistry of the Urine,' and to Professor Halliburton's 'Handbook of Physiological Chemistry.'

General Physical Characters of the Urine; Tests for Albumen

The nature of the urine varies constantly, even in a healthy condition; it varies with alterations of habit of the individual, with the quantity of liquid taken and the nature of the liquid, with the amount of exercise, with variations of temperature; and, as might be expected, these changes are still more marked with any deviations from the healthy state.

Quantity.—With regard to quantity, although the average amount may be reckoned as fifty ounces, exercise, which will increase the work of the skin or the loss of water by means of the lungs, will necessarily diminish the quantity passed by the kidneys in the twenty-four hours. On the other hand, the amount may be increased rapidly by alterations in the quantity of liquid taken, some forms of liquid acting especially as stimulant diuretics. Cold and certain emotional conditions may also cause an increased elimination, but in the healthy condition these variations are scarcely worth considering; in disease, however, we find that a good deal may be learned from a consideration of the absolute number of ounces passed daily. For example, in fevers the amount passed is less during the time the temperature is high. In some forms of chronic Bright's disease, notably with lardaceous disease, the quantity may be increased, as it is also usually in both forms of diabetes, although it is by no means uncommon to find that in the early stage of saccharine diabetes the quantity remains normal, or is only slightly increased. With any acute congestive disease of the kidney, or with any condition which produces renal engorgement, the amount passed may be considerably reduced. Thus, in the early stage of acute nephritis occurring after scarlet fever, the daily amount passed may be as low as from ten to fifteen ounces. Even in chronic Bright's disease, when an acute congestion is superadded to the chronic affection, it is found that the amount passed immediately falls. These variations in amount, as they frequently afford indications of the nature of the eliminative work of the kidney, will perhaps be more properly dealt with in detail under the heading of the respective diseases. In rare cases twenty-four hours or more may elapse without any excretion, and in such cases the urine is said to be *suppressed*. These cases sometimes occur in the course of acute nephritis; they have also been described as occurring after diphtheria, and they are sometimes met with in the course of hysterical attacks, although in this last condition polyuria is more frequent than anuria.

Colour.—Generally the colour of the urine will be found to fall under one of the following headings, which comprise the so-called 'Vogel's scale':

1. Pale yellow
2. Bright yellow
3. Yellow
4. Reddish-yellow
5. Yellowish-red
6. Red
7. Brownish-red
8. Reddish-brown
9. Brownish-black

Although in the healthy condition the urine is usually amber coloured, the colour is to a great extent dependent on the quantity; that is to say, as a general rule the larger the quantity the lighter the colour, this variation being of course one of mere dilution. But the colour is also subject to variations which may result either from the influence of drugs, or from the presence of some abnormal constituents. Thus, for instance, the colour may be darkened very much during the administration of rhubarb, or during the use of santonin, the deepening of colour in the latter being most marked when the urine is alkaline.

Senna also sometimes produces a brownish discoloration, and logwood may cause a reddish tinge. When carbolic acid has been applied to a large surface, or when it has been taken internally in over doses through inadvertence or design, the urine frequently becomes a dark olive colour, which has been attributed to the presence in the urine of hydrochinon. This discoloration is so well known that it is frequently regarded as an indication of carbolic acid poisoning. Other forms of poisoning are sometimes associated with alterations in colour; thus in poisoning by arseniuretted hydrogen a black discoloration has been produced, while creosote and the external application of tar can also produce very dark or almost black urine. The alterations of tint produced by drugs or poisons may also be due to the presence of blood-colouring matter. Thus in some cases of malarial poisoning the blood-colouring matter is liberated from the corpuscles and added to the urine; and the same result may occasionally follow the administration of salicylates or the use of some of the newer antipyretics, especially those derived from the aniline series. The appearance when bile pigment is present will vary considerably with the cause of the jaundice. When due to chronic obstructive disease, as in cancer of the liver affecting the transverse fissure, or from tumour arising from the head of the pancreas, or in the neighbourhood of the pylorus, pressing upon the common bile duct, the colour is usually dark green, sometimes with a reddish tinge. Bile pigment in the urine may be readily detected by allowing a few drops of nitric acid to mingle with a few drops of the urine on a white porcelain plate, when a play of colours becomes manifest, passing from violet to green and red, and speedily fading. The presence of blood corpuscles can be mostly recognised by the dusky, reddish-brown tint of the urine, which is seen in acute nephritis and in acute congestive affections of the kidney; while, on the other hand, in chronic forms of kidney disease the colour of the urine becomes very much lighter and paler, owing to the reduction in the eliminative work performed by the kidney. The pale urine of chronic Bright's disease and the pale urine of diabetes are of much the same tint; but in the former case the colour is due to absence of pigment, while in the latter it is due to dilution.

The colour of the urine is frequently curiously modified when it contains small quantities of pus or muco-pus from vesical irritation. The urine is then generally light in colour, and has a peculiar semiopacity which, under some conditions, almost suggests fluorescence.

Persistent froth.—A frequent peculiarity of albuminous urine is the formation of a somewhat persistent froth after the vessel containing it has been shaken. This has been noted by Dr. Lauder Brunton, and it is a characteristic which is often very valuable as a side indication of albuminuria. As a rule, this condition is only noticeable when the amount of albumin present is relatively large.

Turbidity or cloudiness.—An opaque appearance of the urine may be due to a variety of causes. Sometimes it is opaque when passed, and the opacity is then usually due to the precipitation of phosphates owing to the urine being neutral or slightly alkaline. This turbidity is commonly white and chalky. On the other hand, it may become opaque on standing, when the turbidity may be due either to urates or phosphates, to the former when they are present in excess or when there is abnormal condensation of the urine. When the opacity is due to urates, the deposit which gradually forms is usually reddish in tint, and small quantities when heated in a test-tube speedily become clear, especially if the urates present are diluted by the addition of a little water. If the opacity is due to phosphates, the deposit formed is usually paler in colour and perhaps even white, and the deposition of phosphates on standing is mostly the result of change in the reaction of the urine owing to the formation of ammoniacal compounds. In this case, when a small quantity of the deposit is heated in a test-tube and even diluted, the opacity tends to increase rather than to diminish, and the liquid can only be cleared by the addition of a few drops of nitric acid. The presence of pus or muco-pus may also cause the appearance of cloudiness, especially if the urine has been allowed to stand. As in the last case, the deposit is white, but the urine is usually somewhat more alkaline, especially if much muco-pus is present. When the cloudiness is due to pus, a thick, creamy, yellowish-white deposit speedily falls to the bottom of the vessel. In these cases a clear appearance is only produced on boiling the liquid with an equal part of caustic potash, when, although the general tint clears, a ropy precipitate entangling air bubbles speedily forms.

When blood is present the urine also becomes opaque, the tint and opacity varying necessarily with the amount of blood. Sometimes the colour is merely rendered slightly darker than usual, while at others the urine becomes deep brownish-red. In moderate cases of hæmaturia the presence of blood may be recognised by a pale reddish-brown cloud forming at the lower part of the vessel, and the existence of blood may be proved by the blue colour which results on mixing the urine with tincture of guaiacum and ozonic ether. This test may be performed either in a test-tube, or more conveniently on blotting-paper or white linen. In the latter case a drop of the suspected urine is removed with a pipette from the lower part of the vessel and put on the blotting-paper, and drops of the tincture of guaiacum and ozonic ether are allowed gently to run together. If blood is present, a bright blue line speedily forms along the line of junction.

Turbidity of the urine may in rare cases result from the passage of oil globules, as in the condition termed *chyluria*, which will be referred to in greater detail later. Urine that has been kept for any length of time invariably becomes turbid, owing to a change in its reaction and to the development of micro-organisms.

In examining urine it is always necessary to note not only the nature of the deposit, but the character of the supernatant fluid. Occasionally erroneous deductions may be drawn if attention is confined to the deposit only. Small quantities of albumin may be overlooked, especially if urates are present in large amount.

Specific gravity.—With regard to the specific gravity, this varies within somewhat wide limits. In the condition of health the usual range extends from 1015 to 1025, but the specific gravity may rise above or fall below these numbers as the result of numerous conditions. Obviously a large quantity of liquid taken by the mouth may cause a great reduction in the specific gravity of the urine, and this reduction is most marked when the liquid has been taken fasting. A single observation of the specific gravity as a rule affords very little reliable information, since the density is subject to such great variations that it is only when the specific gravity is persistently above the normal, or below the normal, that any stress can be laid upon this fact. Sometimes, independently of alterations in the time at which the specimen has been passed, the specific gravity will fall very much below the normal point owing to nervousness. It is by no means uncommon in insurance work to find that young men of a neurotic type will pass water of a very low specific gravity, although there may be nothing beyond the nervousness incidental to the examination to give rise to this abnormality. So, too, after hysterical attacks in women the specific gravity is, as a rule, considerably reduced. On the other hand, prolonged fasting may cause an increase in the density of the urine, and a similar increase may be due to concentration owing to the reduction in the amount passed through some form of disease, or it may result from the presence of some abnormal constituent. If there has been much drain of liquid from the system, such as would result from copious perspiration or profuse diarrhœa, the specific gravity is likely to rise. The colour of the urine usually affords some indication of the amount of stress which it is legitimate to place upon the specific gravity. Thus, if the colour is pale and the specific gravity is high, in all likelihood the specific gravity is due to the presence of some abnormal constituent, most probably sugar; but, on the other hand, if the colour is pale and the specific gravity is low, it is by no means a proof that an abnormal constituent is not likely to be present. For instance, in some cases of advanced kidney disease these conditions exist, although a relatively large amount of albumin may be present. In febrile conditions the specific gravity is usually high, and this is in part due to a diminution in the quantity of water; but it is also largely the consequence of an increase in the amount of solids present, since in these conditions there is a definite increase of urea, uric acid, and other salts eliminated. It is obvious that when we know the total quantity passed in the day and its mean specific gravity it is perfectly easy to calculate the total amount of solids passed in the twenty-four hours; but, in endeavouring to estimate the amount of solids, care must be taken not to draw wrong conclusions from a single observation of the specific gravity. It may be mentioned in passing that the specific gravity does not vary materially with the amount of albumin present. In some forms of chronic kidney trouble, when a large amount of albumin is being passed, the specific gravity is low owing to the eliminative work of the kidney being very much reduced by disease; while, on the other hand, in acute nephritis, when again a large quantity of albumin is being passed, the specific gravity will be high owing to the diminished amount of urine passed. Sir Andrew Clark described, under the term 'renal inadequacy' ('Brit. Med. Jour.' 1884), a class of cases in which, although the kidney presented no alteration of structure, it was unable to produce a perfectly healthy urine. In these cases the urine is low in density and deficient in solid constituents, principally in urea and its congeners. He considered that persons who have this renal inadequacy are characterised by (1) a curious inability to repair damage done to them either by accident or disease; (2) not only do they repair damage slowly, but they are peculiarly vulnerable; (3) there is uncertainty as to the result of the performance of an ordinary surgical operation upon them.

Reaction.—In health the urine is generally acid, owing to the presence of acid salts, phosphates and urates, and also to some extent from free acids, lactic, oxalic, acetic, &c.; but the degree of acidity varies considerably with the food that has been taken, with the administration of medicines, and with deviations from health. With measles there is commonly considerable diminution in the degree of acidity. In many healthy persons the urine may become neutral or even alkaline for two or three hours after heavy meals, and to this condition the name of *alkaline tide* has been applied. Sir William Roberts, amongst others, has investigated this condition somewhat closely, and finds that the effect of dinner is not perceptible until the second hour after that meal, and that during the succeeding three hours the alkaline tide runs in its greatest strength. At the end of the sixth hour the tide has generally turned and the acid reaction has been restored. Sir William Roberts attributes the alkalinity after food to fixed alkali and not to ammonia; he found that the urine was generally rich in earthy and alkaline phosphates, and mostly it was somewhat turbid from the precipitation of earthy phosphates. He thinks that the occurrence of the *alkaline tide* after meals is mainly due to the entrance of newly digested food into the blood, rather than to the withdrawal of acid from the blood into the stomach, and he supports this idea by noting that the acidity of the urine does not suffer depression for an hour or two after food has been taken into the stomach, nor, in fact, until the meal has been in great part absorbed.

With medicinal substances it is far more easy to render the urine alkaline than to increase its acidity. Benzoic acid and salicylic acid are credited with causing an increased acidity: the former by its conversion into hippuric acid, the latter into salicyluric acid. Very large doses of citric and tartaric acid, as well as of citrates and tartrates, may also increase the acidity, while moderate doses of the same drugs render the urine more alkaline. Cinnamic acid by its conversion into hippuric acid will also increase the acidity. In diseased conditions it is sometimes desirable to increase the acidity of the urine, or to convert alkaline urine into acid urine, and for these purposes benzoic acid or ammonium benzoate are most commonly employed. Most of the alkaline salts are capable of rendering the urine alkaline if given in sufficiently large doses, or, if given in smaller doses, they will reduce the acidity of the urine. All salts of potassium, sodium, lithium, and calcium may be used for these purposes. The citrates, tartrates, and acetates of potassium, sodium, and lithium increase the alkalinity by their conversion into carbonates; on the other hand, ammonium salts, which are so commonly alkaline, are found to possess very little power of rendering the urine alkaline, and this has been attributed to the decomposition within the body of the ammonium radical, with the probable increased formation of urea.

Most of the above salts which possess the power of rendering the urine alkaline, also increase the total quantity of liquid passed, and they prevent the deposition of solids in the crystalline form in the urine; hence they are very commonly employed when uric acid or acid urates tend to crystallise. or when these substances are present in excessive quantities. Lithium compounds appear to be the most active, and from the lower atomic weight of lithium a smaller quantity of this drug will be sufficient to render a large amount of uric acid soluble.

Odour.—The characteristic odour of the urine may be intensified by the addition of mineral acids. When undergoing decomposition an ammoniacal odour is usually present; hence, to a certain extent, the odour may be an indication of the reaction. Under the influence of certain drugs or foods the odour may be considerably modified: thus asparagus, cubebs, and copaiba modify the characteristic odour, while turpentine is said to produce an odour of violets. Diabetic urine has mostly a faint sweetish odour (somewhat like that of chloroform), which may occasionally be increased when diabetic coma is impending. The odour is also modified considerably by the presence of blood, but, as a test, the odour is of little value as compared with the colour or with chemical reactions.

Tests for albumin.—Under different conditions of disease various forms of albumin exist in the urine, and the following may be enumerated: (1) Serum albumin, the form which is most commonly present in the blood serum; (2) serum globulin, or paraglobulin, which is frequently present with serum albumin, although its proportion varies; (3) peptone, which has been described as occurring after the absorption of inflammatory effusions; (4) pro-peptone, or albumoses, intermediate in constitution between proteids and peptones; (5) acid albumin, or syntonin, the result of the action of acids upon albumin, which is sometimes found in natural conditions; (6) alkali albumin, produced by the action of alkalies upon albumin and occasionally found in the urine; (7) hæmoglobin, the red colouring matter of the red corpuscles, found in hæmaturia and hæmoglobinuria, also after poisoning with arseniuretted hydrogen, or salicylic acid, after transfusion and other conditions; (8) fibrin, found in cases of hæmaturia; (9) mucin, an albuminoid substance, a constituent of mucus; this is added to the urine after its secretion in the kidney, being derived from the urinary tract; (10) lardacein, said to be occasionally present in renal casts.

Most of the tests which have been employed in the recognition of albumin in the urine apply chiefly to serum albumin and serum globulin. The tests for albumin are almost endless, and with few exceptions they depend upon the coagulation of the albumin either by heat or by the addition of some reagent. When a small quantity of urine is heated, the serum albumin and serum globulin coagulate at a temperature much below the boiling point. The opacity thus produced might, therefore, be confused with that resulting when earthy phosphates are present in excess; the precipitate in the latter case may, however, be dissolved, so as to form a clear solution, by the addition of a drop or two of nitric acid. On this account, therefore, the test of heat alone is rarely employed; sometimes a few drops of acetic acid or nitric acid are added before heating the urine so as to prevent the precipitation of phosphates, but if the acid is added in excess the albumin is converted into acid albumin, which no longer precipitates with heat. Unless the urine is acid, or is acidulated with a small quantity of acetic acid or nitric acid, the heat test alone is not to be trusted. When the urine is alkaline, although it may contain a relatively large amount of albumin, it will often show no indication of opacity on boiling the upper layer. It is important to remember this source of fallacy, especially when patients are taking alkalies. In a case recently under my care at King's College Hospital the urine remained perfectly clear after boiling, though the addition of a few drops of nitric acid sufficed to bring down a dense cloud. When the urine is highly alkaline it may be necessary to add far more than the regulation 'two or three drops'; nitric acid must be added until the alkalinity is distinctly overcome. In my opinion, this possible source of error forms a strong objection to the routine employment of the heat test, since, unless its importance is fully appreciated, it must inevitably lead to the non-detection of albumin, even when a large proportion is present.

The turbidity due to precipitation of phosphates by heat has already been referred to; this is most likely to occur when the urine is alkaline, neutral, or very slightly acid. This precipitate can scarcely be mistaken for that due to albumin, since it clears up speedily on the addition of a small quantity of acetic or nitric acid. A test that is rather more useful, although perhaps not so precise, consists of the addition of cold nitric acid so as to form a layer below the albuminous urine, when a white coagulum is formed at the line of junction of the fluids. In performing this test it is sometimes recommended that the acid should be put in the test-tube first, and the urine gently floated on to the surface of the acid. When performed in this way a very sharply defined line of opacity is produced, but if the amount of albumin present is very small the line is sometimes narrow and indistinct. I have generally found that for small proportions of albumin it is better to put the urine in the tube first and to allow the acid subsequently to trickle down the side of the tube; the ring of opacity thus produced is usually wider and more evident, even though perhaps not quite so opaque. Occasionally, when testing with cold nitric acid, a very faint cloud of opacity makes its appearance in the upper or middle part of the column of urine, instead of at the line of contact of the two fluids; this haze might be mistaken for one produced by albumin, but it is really due to the presence of mucin, which is only precipitated in very dilute nitric acid. It may be readily distinguished if the acid has been added with sufficient care, so as to produce a sharply defined line of contact. Other objections to this test are that it may produce an opaque zone with urates, with urea, and with resinous substances. The zone with urates can be readily dissolved by heat; the ring of opacity with urea consists of crystalline plates which, by their structure, can be easily recognised.

In distinguishing the turbidity due to urates from that due to albumin, Sir William Roberts says that albumin begins to coagulate immediately above the stratum of acid, and that the turbidity spreads upwards, while with urates the opacity first appears at or near the surface of the urine and spreads downwards. This distinction, although frequently true, is not invariable. I have often seen the opacity commence immediately above the level of the acid; sometimes the irregularity of the upper level of opacity serves to indicate the probable nature of the precipitate; occasionally cloud-like films wreathe upwards through the urine like rising mists above a Swiss valley; sometimes, commencing in this way, the whole of the urine in the upper part of the tube becomes opaque. When this occurs I have always found that slight heat cautiously applied to the upper part of the tube, without disturbing the lower layer of acid, is sufficient to restore the original transparency. I have only met with these possible sources of fallacy when dealing with urine concentrated by free perspiration, by diarrhœa, or by rise of temperature, and the results have been most striking when testing urine immediately after it has been passed, as in insurance work. Urine examined later, under such circumstances, will probably be opaque before the application of any tests, owing to the deposition of urates in an amorphous form as the urine cools.

Before leaving the cold nitric acid test, it may be well to enjoin caution in adding the acid, so that the two liquids should not mix freely. When poured in quickly and carelessly, an acid albuminate may be formed and dissolved in the excess of acid so that no line of opacity may result, even though a fairly large amount of albumin may be present.

Picric acid was largely recommended by the late Sir George Johnson; this test consists in adding an equal quantity of a saturated solution of picric acid to the urine and subsequently boiling. With the addition of the picric acid, if albumin is present in any form, the mixture becomes opaque, and this opacity is rendered more evident on boiling the solutions. It has been objected that picric acid gives precipitates with peptones and with alkaloids such as quinine, but these readily dissolve on heating.

Sir William Roberts recommends the employment of acidulated brine composed of a saturated solution of common salt, acidulated with 1 per cent. of strong hydrochloric acid. This acts upon all varieties of albumin, but has not come into general use.

Trichloracetic acid has been recommended, and in my hands has given good results, always indicating the presence of minute traces of albumin, but sometimes also apparently forming a crystalline line of opacity, possibly with urates. This acid has the advantage of being of high specific gravity in the liquid state, but it is often employed in the form of crystals. If used in the solid state, a crystal is dropped into the test-tube, and, after liquefaction, gives a very sharply defined line of separation from the urine, in which any opacity is readily apparent. Dr. D. M. Reese [1] states that trichloracetic acid precipitates not only

[1] *Brit. Med. Journ.*, March 22, 1890.

the albumin ordinarily found in the urine, but also an albumin occasionally present, which is dissolved by acetic acid. In fourteen out of eighty-seven different specimens of urine he obtained a precipitate with trichloracetic acid and not with nitric or picric acids, or heat and acetic acid. His paper is of special interest, since in eleven of these fourteen cases granular, epithelial, or hyaline casts were found, and in three of these eleven cases the necropsy showed distinct changes in the kidneys. Dr. C. F. Heywood [1] speaks of this test as being in some respects without a rival, since for clinical use nothing else known is so handy, quick, and decisive. Although I have formed a high opinion of the value of this test in the ready detection of minute traces of albumin, I am convinced that, with the cold nitric acid test, it shares the danger of giving fallacious results when the urine is rich in urates. On three recent occasions both these tests have at once given the appearance of a dense precipitate of albumin, and on microscopic examination the zone of opacity was found to consist of numerous minute crystals of urates. In each case the urine was highly concentrated, the opacity disappeared on heating the test-tube, and reappeared on subsequent cooling; while when the urine was heated and diluted no precipitates were obtained with either test. I venture to lay some stress upon these occasional results with the cold nitric acid test and with trichloracetic acid, since I think it is probable that they may explain some of the supposed cases of 'albuminuria' which are unexpectedly met with in insurance work, more particularly when hot weather or other passing conditions have led to unusual concentration of the urine. In doubtful cases it is always advisable not to trust to a single test, and also to repeat the tests after moderate dilution of the specimen.

Salicylsulphonic acid has been recommended for the precipitation of albumin, and it is said that the reaction is not affected by the presence of urea and uric acid, peptones, or glucose. Of other tests that have been employed it may be sufficient to mention metaphosphoric acid, ferrocyanide of potassium, tungstate of soda, potassio-mercuric iodide, and ammonium sulphate. Fehling's solution generally gives a reddish-brown or mauve

[1] Merck's *Bulletin*, Feb. 1891.

colour in the presence of serum albumin, while it gives a rose-pink with peptones and pro-peptones. This reaction has been termed the Biuret reaction.

The cold nitric acid test, the test of boiling with the subsequent addition of a few drops of nitric acid, and the test with picric acid are those which are most commonly employed, as being easy or sufficiently accurate for all practical purposes. The test-pellets devised by Dr. Pavy and the test-papers by Dr. Oliver are frequently convenient for testing urine away from the consulting room, but they are scarcely to be trusted if only a slight reaction is given.

The estimation of the amount of albumin passed by a patient usually involves a somewhat lengthy process, but if the specimen of urine be allowed to subside after it has been boiled with the addition of acid, a rough calculation may be made from the height at which the precipitate stands in the test-tube. The method which is commonly employed is that described by Esbach, in which a specially graduated tube is used, the markings upon the tube indicating the quantity of urine tested and the amount of the reagent employed. The reagent consists of a mixture of picric and citric acids, and the urine is previously diluted, if necessary, until the specific gravity is not above 1010. After the mixture of the solutions, the fluids are set aside to stand for twenty-four hours, and at the end of that time the amount of coagulum indicates the number of grammes per litre. Esbach's method is not always easy to perform; very slight changes of temperature may sometimes influence the extent to which the precipitated albumin will 'settle,' and at the end of twenty-four hours the albumin is often found in a curdy, flocculent state at the upper level of the fluid instead of at the bottom of the tube.

Another method which has been suggested consists in the use of tannic acid to precipitate the albumin, and the suspension of the precipitate in the urine by means of mucilage. After being diluted with water the mixture is poured into a graduated vessel, and placed over a white surface on which black lines are drawn. The amount necessary to obscure the lines will be in inverse ratio to the quantity of albumin in the urine, and the quantity can be easily estimated by the employment of a suitably graduated burette. In spite of its ingenuity, this method does not appear preferable to that of Esbach, and although advocated in 1889 it has not passed into general use. More accurate results may be obtained by the separation, drying, and weighing of the albumin, but this process is lengthy and difficult. Sir William Roberts's dilution process is based upon the fact that when urine is diluted with water, it is found that, after a certain stage, opacity with nitric acid only appears between thirty and forty-five seconds after the fluids have come together. Esbach's method is probably the most satisfactory, and gives results which correspond closely with those of drying and weighing.

For further details concerning the accurate quantitative estimation of albumin, the reader is referred to text-books dealing purely with clinical chemistry.

CHAPTER I

ALBUMINURIA

FROM a clinical aspect it will be well to regard the subject of albuminuria as divisible into two broad classes:

(*A*). Extra-renal, false, or accidental albuminuria.

(*B*). Renal, or true albuminuria.

In the former the albumin is not derived from the renal vessels, but is, from some cause, mixed with the urine after it has been secreted; and in these cases, although albumin is readily detected, sometimes in large amount, it affords no indication of renal disease. Under the heading of 'Renal, or True Albuminuria,' it is proposed to consider all those cases in which the albumin is added to the urine during its secretion, and is derived mainly, if not entirely, from the renal vessels. The importance of the symptom varies greatly with the cause; sometimes it denotes grave disease of the kidney, of an acute or chronic character; sometimes it is an indication of disease in other parts of the body, affecting the circulation through the kidney; sometimes it serves as a warning of some physiological error of life, the removal of which is speedily followed by the disappearance of the danger signal.

All forms of classification of renal, or true albuminuria, are open to objection. Many have been attempted and in turn cast aside. It is practically impossible to classify the varieties according to their frequency, their permanent character, or even their importance. Ideas of frequency depend largely upon the class of individuals examined and upon the tests employed; general practitioners, hospital physicians, and medical officers of assurance companies and others, who are in the habit of examining the urine of presumably healthy individuals, would probably differ widely if questioned regarding the relative frequency of the different forms of renal albuminuria. Then, again, with reference to the permanency of the symptom, it is generally recognised that in many of the most chronic forms of kidney disease, albumin may frequently be absent for weeks or months, just as in many forms of functional albuminuria. It is still more hopeless to attempt to group varieties of renal albuminuria according to their importance, partly on account of insufficient data, and partly on account of the extreme difficulty of assessing their relative prognostic value. While conscious of many objections to the classification which has been adopted in the following pages, it has been selected as being the most intelligible and useful. In all probability, several of the groups overlap; thus it is not easy to indicate a sharp boundary between the dietetic and oxaluric groups, and it may be safely asserted that many cases of albuminuria, which at their commencement have been correctly placed in one category, may, at a later stage, have to be relegated to another. The following classification of renal forms of albuminuria must therefore be regarded as convenient merely and provisional.

(B). Renal, or True Albuminuria

1. Without definite structural change of renal tissue.
   (a) *Mechanical* causes affecting the blood pressure within the kidney, as diseases of the heart, the lungs, and other viscera, or overstrain of renal vessels from muscular exercise.
   (b) *Hæmatogenous changes*, as from anæmia, toxic influences, febrile conditions, pregnancy, syphilis, or dietetic causes (which may lead to oxaluric or lithæmic changes).
   (c) Functional, intermittent, and cyclic forms, which, together with the albuminuria of adolescence, may result from alterations of blood pressure or from hæmatogenous changes.
2. With definite structural change of renal tissue.

The appearance of albuminuria as a symptom of numerous diseases of the kidney which are marked by structural changes, as with Acute Nephritis, Chronic Nephritis, Renal Cirrhosis, Consecutive Cirrhosis, Puerperal Nephritis, Lardaceous Disease, and other conditions, is dealt with in detail under these respective headings. It may be sufficient to mention here that the amount of albumin affords very little indication of the severity of these different diseases—it may often be extremely small, or albumin may even be absent for a time, in diseases with almost hopeless prognosis. The modifications in the amount of albumin, the quantity of urine, the specific gravity, and the proportion of the normal constituents of the urine, will be fully considered in dealing with the indications of each disease.

(*A*). EXTRA RENAL, FALSE, OR ACCIDENTAL ALBUMINURIA

In this group the urine, as it is excreted by the kidney, is to be regarded as normal, the addition of albumin resulting from some accidental cause after the urine has left the kidney. This cause is commonly the addition of blood or of pus. The presence of blood may be due to the irritation of some part of the urinary tract by a calculus; a renal calculus may thus give rise to blood, and consequently to albumin in varying amount, according to the site it occupies; if lying in the pelvis of the kidney, and not subjected to changes of locality, the amount of blood is generally small. On the other hand, if the calculus has been dislocated from its position of quiescence and lodged in the infundibulum, or passed onwards to the ureter, the amount of blood increases greatly, even though the total quantity of urine may be for the time diminished. The occurrence of hæmaturia as an indication of vesical calculus is too well known and too surgical in character to require more than a passing mention. Hæmaturia which results from the presence of malignant or villous growths in the bladder will fall into the same surgical category, though it frequently comes first under the notice of the physician; it is usually to be distinguished from that due to calculus by the absence of the characteristic radiating pain. It may also be noted that it is, as a rule, more irregular in its appearance and disappearance. The urine may, without warning and without apparent cause, suddenly be found to be dark, smoky, or opaque with blood, and a few hours later it may have regained its normal appearance, even though the presence of blood and of albumin may still be demonstrated by appropriate tests. Many such cases have come under my observation, some occurring in young women, some in elderly men. Until the precise cause is recognised they always give rise to much anxiety, and, indeed, even after the cause has been clearly ascertained, the prognosis depends largely upon the age and general condition. As illustrations I may mention three cases that have lately been under my notice. Two occurred in young women. In the first case, the presence of small traces of blood and albumin in the urine had been noted for some months, and the urine had repeatedly been examined microscopically, oxalates in abundance and a few altered blood corpuscles being the only abnormalities detected. Without other warning, and with no accompanying symptoms, the urine was one day found to be highly blood tinged; it rapidly cleared in colour, and then again, although the patient was kept in bed, returned to a dark reddish-brown, and, after a few days of oscillation, resumed its normal condition, when she passed from observation. Similar changes occurred in the second patient, but in this case we were more fortunate in convincing her of the advisability of a thorough examination of the bladder; a villous growth was detected and removed, and she made a speedy recovery. In the third case, an elderly clergyman, a malignant tumour was found to be the cause of the hæmaturia, but the patient's age and general condition rendered an operation inexpedient.

When the albuminuria is dependent upon some inflammatory or ulcerative changes leading to the formation of pus, the urine is more or less turbid, since cellular elements are present in addition to pus serum, and the former are insoluble in water. The serum is mostly albuminous, and does not differ materially from the blood serum. Unless the degree of inflammation is severe, the amount of albumin is generally comparatively small. The microscopic appearance of the pus corpuscles varies with the condition of the urine. When the urine is acid the corpuscles may be either globular or amœboid. If it is alkaline, or of low specific gravity, the corpuscles swell to twice or thrice their usual size, and the nuclei become more evident. It may sometimes, especially in cases of candidates for life assurance, be very important to be certain that the albuminuria is due to pus alone; this is often extremely difficult, though an opinion may be broadly based on the results of a microscopic examination. The true cause may be sometimes ascertained by noting the degree of admixture of the pus with the urine. If it is due to urethral irritation, the urine which is first passed is more turbid, and contains more albumin than that passed towards the end of micturition. As a rule, however, very valuable information may be gathered from an examination of the meatus or the linen.

Purulent catarrh of the bladder may cause a suspicion of true albuminuria, but it may be distinguished by the physical properties of the urine, which usually has an ammoniacal odour, and is either alkaline when it is passed, or speedily becomes so, owing to rapid decomposition. Microscopically the sediment is found to contain pus corpuscles, vesical epithelium, crystals of triple phosphate, and bacteria.

Pyelitis is sufficiently common to require special attention; though, as a rule, the clinical features are so distinct that there is little possibility of error. In advanced cases there is usually more or less pain and tenderness in the loins, and a tumour may occasionally be detected. Sometimes, but not always, there is a history of renal colic or of hæmaturia; there is usually a certain amount of pyrexia, and the course of the symptoms may be interrupted by rigors. The quantity of pus present in the urine may show great variations, but the urine often retains an acid reaction which helps to distinguish the case from purulent catarrh of the bladder; while the absence of casts in the acid urine will help to free the kidneys from suspicion of glandular changes.

Prostatic and spermatic albuminuria have been described. In the former, which may result from chronic inflammatory conditions of the prostate, the presence of prostatic cylinders, amyloid bodies, and Böttcher's crystals may aid the diagnosis. The addition of spermatic fluid is stated to cause a copious precipitate with picric acid, which is dissolved by heat, but no change ensues with heat alone, nitric acid, or ferrocyanide of potassium solution with citric acid. On these grounds it seems safe to conclude that this precipitate, which is certainly uncommon, does not result from the presence of serum albumin.

In dealing with cases of albuminuria in females, the

possibility of contamination by the menstrual flow must be kept in mind, and it is well also to inquire about leucorrhœa. Either of these conditions would obviously be sufficient to give rise to albumin in the urine, and the utmost care therefore is necessary before a more serious condition is credited with its causation.

From the above it will be seen that in cases of extra renal, false, or accidental albuminuria the quantity of albumin, although it may occasionally assist diagnosis, yet plays a relatively unimportant part. The disease giving rise to this condition requires to be recognised, and the treatment, which is frequently of a surgical nature, does not call for further consideration here.

(B). RENAL, OR TRUE ALBUMINURIA

1. *Without Definite Structural Change of Renal Tissue*

(*a*) *Mechanical causes which influence the blood pressure within the kidney.*—If extra pressure is exerted through the general venous circulation as a result of valvular disease of the heart, or as a result of dilatation of the right side of the heart, whether consecutive to emphysema or to other chronic affections of the lungs, the result is frequently seen in the appearance of a varying amount of albumin in the urine. Under such conditions the quantity of urine that is passed is sometimes small in amount; it is frequently dark coloured, of a high specific gravity, deposits urates and contains a large proportion of urea; the leading characteristic which separates this form of albuminuria from others connected with definite disease of the kidney lies in the great variation in the amount of albumin passed from day to day. Sometimes under treatment, and sometimes as the result of rest in bed, the albumin may totally disappear for a short time; while if the obstruction to the circulation is increased by an extension of the original disease, the effect is frequently speedily seen in an increase of the albuminuria.

Amongst the conditions which produce albuminuria in this way may be mentioned obstruction of the renal veins occurring independently of any disease affecting the general circulation. Bartels records a case of this nature where the obstruction was due to obliteration of the inferior vena cava above the openings of the renal veins. When the pressure within the peritoneal cavity is increased by the presence of ascitic fluid, or by the rapid growth of abdominal, ovarian, aneurysmal, or malignant tumours, and perhaps sometimes from rapid increase in the size of the pregnant uterus, albuminuria, which is undoubtedly due to pressure on the inferior vena cava or on the renal veins, may frequently result; in many such cases the dependence of the albuminuria on the conditions named is only rendered certain if it decreases as pressure from these conditions is lessened.

Amongst other ways in which similar venous congestion and albuminuria may be brought about, may be mentioned insufficiency of the tricuspid valve, which so often results from mitral disease; and compression exerted upon the abdominal or thoracic cava by tumours, or by deformities of the chest due to spinal curvature, or by large accumulations of pleuritic fluid. Intermittent albuminuria, as a result of the temporary resistance to the free movement of the blood through the kidney, is well shown in an interesting case which is reported by Falkenheim.[1] A man, fifty years of age, was admitted to hospital with a large splenic tumour. While he was under observation it was found that albumin appeared intermittently in his water, and it was further ascertained that the urine which was excreted while he was up was free from albumin, and that which was passed while he was in bed was albuminous. It was soon shown that the position in bed had also an important influence; after lying upon his right side or on his back there was only a trace of albumin, but the urine which was secreted when lying partly or completely on his left side was highly albuminous. After lying on his face, or partly on his face and partly on the right side, there was no trace of albumin. Falkenheim further found that when the urine was albuminous the left testicle became swollen; hence he inferred that both conditions were the result of pressure of the posterior border of the splenic tumour upon the renal vein beyond the point at which it is joined by

[1] *Deutsch. Archiv für klin. Med.*, September 1884.

the spermatic vein. These clinical facts agree entirely with the results of experimental compression of the renal vein. Compression lasting from seven to twelve minutes has caused the urine secreted during that time to be highly albuminous.

Sir J. Grainger Stewart remarks that the greater the backward pressure of the systemic veins the more pronounced is the albuminuria. He also draws attention to Ludwig's statement that when the renal vein is closed, the capillaries round the tubules become over-filled, and hence he considers that the transudation of albumin is not so much from the Malpighian tufts as from the capillaries which surround the tubules. He further supports these observations by the effects produced by the administration of digitalis to patients with albuminuria who are suffering from heart disease. Under this treatment the quantity of urine rises, and the albumin at the same time frequently diminishes. He explains the diuresis by the increase of pressure within the Malpighian tufts, and points out that this would necessarily be associated with increase of albumin if the capillary loops of the Malpighian tufts were at fault.

Muscular exercise.—The influence of muscular exercise in the production of temporary albuminuria has often received attention. Edlefsen noticed transient albuminuria after exertion in three healthy but anæmic men. Leube examined the urine of a large number of healthy soldiers in the morning and found it normal, but after a long march or severe exercise in the summer months he found albuminuria in 16 per cent. The amount detected was always small, and never exceeded 1 per cent., and casts and blood corpuscles were absent. It is highly probable that the explanation of these interesting cases is to be found in variations of blood pressure, and this view is supported by a curious observation by Dr. W. W. Keen—viz. that in one such case, while albuminuria was always induced by slight exercise, it was absent when the patient was kept in bed, and was also absent after from forty to fifty minutes' massage thoroughly applied.

Dr. Griswold, of New York, relates the following case which curiously illustrates the effect of exercise in producing albuminuria. The urine of a gentleman, who appeared before the medical examiner of an insurance company in the afternoon, was found to contain much albumin, and his proposal was rejected. The following month he was examined for another company, and the urine was then found to be normal. On narrating his previous experience, the urine was twice examined at intervals of a week: the first specimen was entirely free from both albumin and casts; the second was distinctly albuminous and abounded in hyaline, fatty, and granular casts. It was then ascertained that just before the last examination he had had a boxing lesson, as had also been the case before the examination for the other company. That this was no accidental coincidence was subsequently proved by repeated examinations of the water passed before and after boxing lessons. Albumin and casts were found in every specimen examined after undergoing the muscular exertion. A fact of great interest in this case was the character of the casts, which are described as being always hyaline, and sometimes granular as well. This would seem to show that it does not take so long for hyaline casts to form as has generally been supposed.

Interference in the circulation through the renal arteries may sometimes cause albuminuria. Thus, for example, when the circulation through certain areas is arrested by the presence of an embolic plug detached from the valves of the heart, the congestion in the surrounding vessels is commonly associated with the appearance of albumin or of blood in the urine. It is well known that an embolus constantly gives rise to engorgement of the neighbouring vessels, and this engorgement necessarily leads to transudation of albumin.

It is highly probable that the albuminuria and hæmaturia which are so commonly met with as complications of purpura and scurvy must be attributed to a rupture of capillaries similar to that which occurs beneath the skin or on mucous membranes. So that amongst these mechanical causes we see that the symptom may be produced through veins, arteries, or capillaries.

(b) *Hæmatogenous causes.*—Another group of causes may be classified as hæmatogenous, where the condition results from some change within the blood. Sir William Gull stated that he not unfrequently noticed albumin in the urine of anæmic young girls about the time of puberty. This condition I have often met with amongst children in the out-patient department, but it has not appeared to be so common as the albuminuria dependent upon errors in diet which occurs so frequently in young children.

Fagge states that anæmia leading to deficient blood supply through the renal arteries, as in cholera, is to be considered a cause of albuminuria, and in support of this view he quotes Bartels and Cohnheim, who regard the albuminuria as the result of the ischæmia which exists during the state of collapse; and he further lays stress on the fact that the renal affection of cholera appears never to form the starting point of chronic Bright's disease. Cohnheim maintains that this albuminuria is precisely analogous to that which can be produced experimentally by temporary obstruction of the circulation through the renal artery—a condition which may last for hours or even days after the obstruction is removed.

Some of the toxic agents which influence the secretion of the kidney may probably produce albuminuria by altering the composition of the blood. Thus, the albuminuria and hæmaturia which occur after the administration of many of the newer antipyretics may be explained in this way. Antipyrine, phenacetin, pyrodin, and many others of the coal-tar derivatives produce this symptom by disorganising the red blood corpuscles, and there is some probability that the hæmaturia which occasionally follows the administration of certain anæsthetics, especially of chloroform, should be attributed to the same cause. In 1876 M. Bouchard found that the inhalation of air mixed with chloroform-vapour caused an intense albuminuria and hæmaturia, although the amount inhaled might be too small to produce either sleep or anæsthesia. This albuminuria he regarded as toxic, though he was uncertain as to the exact method of action: the drug might either influence the glandular elements at the time of elimination, or, if carried to the nerve centres by the blood, it might there affect the parts presiding over the nutrition and circulation of the kidney. Similar experiments by MM. Ferrier and Patin have confirmed these observations; but M. Ferrier is disposed to attribute the albuminuria to a certain tendency to asphyxia produced by the chloroform. The albuminuria which sometimes accompanies the late stages of diabetes might perhaps be grouped under this heading, since although in some cases it may be due to acute inflammation of the kidney, or to some nervous influence affecting the vessels of the kidney, yet in all probability the symptom may also result from the changes in the blood.

In some cases of malaria it is possible, as Germain See remarked, that hæmatogenous albuminuria may depend on alteration of the blood and the production of a more diffusible form of albumin. Irritation of the kidney by toxic agents which act as renal irritants will often produce albuminuria. Thus, in poisoning by metals or caustic poisons, by lead, mercury, phosphorus, cantharides, or turpentine, hæmaturia or albuminuria are frequently noted. Sometimes these toxic forms of albuminuria may be regarded as hæmatogenous, as in the case of poisoning with phosphorus; more commonly their influence is mainly irritative and exerted through modifications of the vascular system. The danger of producing albuminuria, or of increasing a pre-existent albuminuria, should be remembered in prescribing any of these drugs. Under these circumstances the albumin is almost invariably accompanied by blood, and the history of the employment of an irritant is sufficiently clear for the symptom not to give rise to any uncertainty of diagnosis.

Ollivier[1] demonstrated causal connection between albuminuria and lead poisoning. He found that dogs, rabbits, and guinea-pigs when poisoned with repeated doses of carbonate of lead invariably passed albuminous urine, and that their kidneys exhibited signs of incipient organic disease. These observations were confirmed clinically by himself, and by Lancereaux and Danjoy. Ollivier inferred that the existence of lead in the kidneys induced an organic lesion of these organs, and that the albuminuria was the consequence of that lesion.

Neurotic albuminuria.—A form of neurotic albuminuria has been described, and it is certain that in many cases this classification would be a convenience. I have often noticed a faint cloud of albumin when candidates for life assurance have had nervous diuresis before presenting themselves for examination, and I have also found the same condition amongst young men who are being physically examined for appointments. In many such cases reference to the medical attendants has shown that

[1] *Archives Générales*, 1868, ii. pp. 530 and 709.

the albuminuria was absolutely transient; it occurred only on the one day of nerve strain or excitement and not subsequently, when the individual was kept under close observation. In other cases, especially amongst very neurotic women, the albumin may be observed to come and go in an irregular fashion, and in these cases chronic renal disease can only be excluded by the absence of any other symptoms of renal trouble. Some cases associated with long continued nervous strain or business worry may fall into this category, but it is possible that many should be placed rather in the group of oxaluric or lithæmic cases. It is extremely difficult to differentiate such cases of long continued albuminuria due to nerve strain from true cases of chronic nephritis; indeed, it seems probable that many gradually pass from the functional to the organic group. An acute neurotic albuminuria may be of little moment, but an albuminuria, often repeated and prolonged, even though associated with distinctly neurotic symptoms, must always be regarded with suspicion and anxiety.

The explanation of neurotic albuminuria probably lies in diminished vaso-motor tone affecting the vessels of the kidney, the inhibiting influence of the higher centres being partially arrested during the discharge of nerve force in other directions. Possibly the cases of slight albuminuria in young men who have been working hard for competitive examinations may belong to the neurotic group; but very often, although the neurotic element is distinctly present, these cases may find a truer solution on reference to the digestive system. The prolonged sedentary application may have been followed by constipation and digestive disturbance, and this is the more likely if the idea of the need of large quantities of food has been accompanied by the desire to save time by hurrying over meals.

This classification of neurotic albuminuria may frequently be misleading, and cases originally placed in this group may later have to be put under another heading. I have notes of a case of albuminuria from supposed overstrain in preparing for a competitive examination, showing that the amount of albumin discovered at the time of the physical examination was so slight that the candidate was given the benefit of the doubt, and passed by a very high medical authority. Two years later, when he had not been working particularly hard, this gentleman came under my observation, and was then found to be anæmic, and to have a high-tension pulse, with accentuation of the heart sounds at the base ; these indications and the examination of his water, with the low specific gravity and fairly large quantity of albumin, left me in no doubt that he was suffering from chronic kidney mischief.

The association of albuminuria with diseases of the nervous system is not common, and the connection is not easily traced. Bernard produced polyuria with albuminuria by irritating the floor of the fourth ventricle above the site of the diabetic puncture. Section of the spinal cord in rabbits below the seventh cervical vertebra is followed by a like result. Laschkewitsch has seen it produced in man by an injury to the spinal cord by a pistol-ball which entered the spinal canal between the third and fourth dorsal vertebræ. Effusion of blood into the kidney and albuminuria have also followed section of the vaso-motor nerves of the kidney by Von Wittich, Ludwig, and Hermann. It does not appear, however, very probable that albuminuria often results from central nervous lesion. Grainger Stewart only gives six cases out of 450 where the connection appeared to bear any causal relationship—two cases of epilepsy, two of exophthalmic goître, one of infantile paralysis, and one of multiple sclerosis. So far as albuminuria appears with diseases of the spinal cord, it seems mostly to be the result of catarrh of the bladder rather than of secondary renal changes. The converse, the production of nervous symptoms as the result of chronic albuminuria, constituting Bright's disease, is extremely common. The frequent association of hemiplegia and of the renal headache merely requires mention here ; they will be dealt with together with other nervous symptoms among the sequelæ of Bright's disease.

Albuminuria has been met with in cases of concussion of the brain, in tetanus, delirium tremens, and epilepsy, but in such cases it is not easy to ascertain whether it is a consequence or a cause ; thus, before leading to delirium tremens, alcohol may have induced chronic Bright's disease, and epileptiform convulsions associated with albuminuria should always lead to a suspicion of uræmia rather than of epilepsy.

Febrile albuminuria.—A large number of cases with high temperature frequently present albuminuria. Though when the disease appears to be dependent on some definite toxic organism, albuminuria may appear without any very great rise of temperature, yet sometimes it appears to be associated rather with the height of the temperature than with the presence of any infective material. It is undoubtedly very convenient to classify a form of 'febrile albuminuria' where the term does not necessarily imply the existence of any acute or chronic renal change.

When albuminuria occurs in the course of scarlet fever it is frequently, although not always, an indication of nephritis; but it is well to bear in mind that for a short time small quantities of albumin may sometimes occur during the early stage of scarlet fever. The initial or early albuminuria of scarlet fever occurs in about a third of the cases, and may make its appearance during the first few days; its occurrence is generally associated either with unusual severity of throat symptoms, or with a high temperature. Except as an accompaniment of other severe symptoms, this early albuminuria is of small importance, though sometimes it gradually leads on to late albuminuria, or true scarlatinal nephritis, as the primary urgent symptoms subside. Scarlatinal nephritis most commonly commences after the end of the first week of the fever—generally in the course of the second or third week—but the risks of this complication are continued, in a minor degree, until fully six weeks from the onset. As will be seen later (*vide* 'Scarlatinal Nephritis'), the relative frequency of late albuminuria varies greatly in different epidemics of scarlet fever.

With diphtheria some albumin is present in a very large number of cases at the acute stage, but it is exceptional to find that the albumin is associated with blood-colouring matter, and it is also exceptional to find dropsy or uræmic symptoms, although suppression of urine may occur. Henoch states that he has never observed uræmia or anuria, and Fürbringer has only seen them on one occasion. I have elsewhere dealt with the subject of diphtheritic albuminuria in some detail;[1] but it may be well here to repeat that the albuminuria of diphtheria, although frequently associated with severe symptoms, is im-

[1] *Diphtheria and Antitoxin*, Longmans, 1896.

portant rather as an indication of the severity of the attack than on account of any renal symptoms or permanent renal affection that are likely to result. In such cases there is frequently a large amount of renal epithelium to be found in the sediment, red corpuscles may sometimes be met with, and renal casts are frequently present, and are usually more opaque than in cases of true kidney disease. If the diphtheria does not prove fatal from laryngeal or toxic symptoms, the albuminuria, even in severe cases, frequently passes away as the patient recovers, although in exceptional cases it may be some months before the last traces of albumin disappear.

Some authors recognise a form of diphtheritic nephritis, and consider that the engorgement of the kidney and the cloudy swelling of the epithelium, which are so frequently found after death, are to be regarded as indications of a form of true nephritis; but inasmuch as these changes do not appear to precede permanent alterations in the structure of the kidney, it may be well to discard this term in favour of diphtheritic albuminuria, which does not imply the presence, or at least the constant presence, of permanent renal changes.

In typhoid fever albuminuria may occur in the course of the second week—Murchison and others have noticed it in one-third of the cases—and some authors have endeavoured to attribute many of the so-called typhoid symptoms to nephritic changes. Sometimes in typhoid fever the albuminuria is associated with hæmaturia, which may continue up to the fourth week. Fürbringer states that he has seen cases accompanied by dropsy, but he qualifies this statement by saying that the intensity of the dropsy was always proportional to the severity of the fever, and he also says that in such cases the fever followed its normal course. It is quite exceptional for severe uræmic convulsions to occur in the course of typhoid fever, but when they occur the prognosis is invariably bad. Albuminuria has been stated to occur in from 68 per cent. to 88 per cent. of cases of typhus fever.

It is comparatively rare for albuminuria to be associated with measles, and there is some reason for suspecting that some of the cases which have been described under this heading were really cases of scarlatinal nephritis.

In the course of small-pox albuminuria sometimes occurs,

but it is generally associated with the presence of a large quantity of blood in the urine, which appears to be derived from the pelvis of the kidney.

Genuine hæmorrhagic nephritis, even with dropsy and fatal uræmia, has been shown to occur occasionally with chicken-pox, and some stress should perhaps be laid upon this fact, as the disease is frequently of so mild a type that the early symptoms of nephritis may be overlooked unless they are specially sought for.

With whooping-cough albuminuria is occasionally found, but it appears to be frequently associated either with rise of temperature owing to the development of some intercurrent disease, or else with frequent and violent paroxysms of cough, when, in all probability, the albuminuria must be regarded as due to alterations in blood pressure, rather than to febrile or toxic causes. The albuminuria of whooping-cough varies greatly from day to day, and it is comparatively rarely associated with hæmaturia. It does not produce any symptoms directly referable to renal changes, and although it is often associated with an anæmic and dropsical appearance of the face, this œdema is generally purely local, and is often to be seen independently of the occurrence of albuminuria. The puffiness round the eyes so often observed in pertussis appears to be only linked with albuminuria as results of a common cause, the distension of capillaries, and consequent effusion, during the severe paroxysms of cough.

Acute tonsillitis is sometimes associated with albuminuria, although not with the same frequency as diphtheria; hence when albuminuria occurs with any tonsillar affection it is more likely to favour a diagnosis of diphtheria than one of acute tonsillitis; and it is by no means uncommon to find that, in mild cases, the appearances are so uncertain that bacteriological investigations must be trusted to assist the diagnosis.

In the course of the different varieties of malarial fever, albuminuria of a hæmorrhagic form is extremely common. Kannenberg has described organisms as being present in the fresh urine in such cases, and he thinks that the origin of the illness is to be explained by these germs having affected the renal parenchyma. This explanation does not seem to be entirely satisfactory, since the albuminuria mostly occurs after sudden rises of temperature, and there appears to be no evidence that the organisms in the urine are increased during this period. Sir J. Grainger Stewart says that cases of albuminuria are often met with in those who have suffered from malarial poisoning, even although they have not had ague, and he thinks it is often associated with a degree of inflammation of the tubules, and attended by dropsy and the presence of a few tube casts. Professor Atkins [1] mentions a tubal and diffuse form of nephritis, as the result of malaria, and doubts whether the disease ever occurs primarily as purely interstitial nephritis. Whether the albuminuria is associated with temporary or permanent renal changes, or whether it is simply an accompaniment of the febrile state induced by the malignant poison, all observers are agreed that it should be treated with quinine or with arsenic, rather than by the ordinary measures directed primarily for the treatment of albuminuria or nephritis.

With croupous pneumonia, especially amongst children, albuminuria is frequent. It usually makes its appearance about the fourth day and continues until the eighth day, and its existence does not seem in any way to influence the course of the primary disease. Fürbringer's experience is that simple albuminuria is to be found in about one-third of all cases, but I believe that the percentage is really much higher amongst children. Inflammation of the glomeruli has been described in cases of pneumonia, but, for the cases that recover from the pneumonia, the prognosis is essentially favourable, so far as subsequent liability to kidney disease is concerned.

Erysipelas and acute rheumatism are also occasionally associated with albuminuria, but in these diseases this symptom appears to be entirely dependent upon the height of the temperature.

Symptoms of febrile albuminuria.—From the foregoing remarks it will be readily seen that the great majority of the forms of albuminuria at present under discussion have usually no symptoms which can be definitely attributed to the urinary change. It is true that in these cases the general condition of the patient is very often serious; that the temperature is very high and sometimes presents great variations; that the pulse

[1] *Amer. Journ. of the Med. Soc.*, July 1884.

may be quick, and that sometimes dyspnœa and collapse supervene; but most of these symptoms appear to depend rather upon the original illness than upon any renal disturbances. Cases have been described in which serious gastric symptoms and intestinal disturbances have formed the prelude to rigors, pains in the limbs, stoppage of urine, dropsy, and fatal uræmia, but these are quite exceptional.

Theoretical explanations of albuminuria in febrile diseases.—If it is difficult to describe the symptoms of albuminuria occurring in the course of febrile diseases, it is still more difficult to provide a theory which shall explain the occurrence of this condition. Gerhardt accepted a theory of abnormal processes of filtration under the influence of increased temperature. Another hypothesis is that the condition results from relaxation of the vascular walls owing to altered innervation, such relaxation allowing a more ready transudation of albumin into the urine. It has been proved experimentally that, in animals, a rapid increase of the body temperature can produce albuminuria, and it has been suggested that, under such circumstances, the albuminuria may be the result of increased blood pressure. Although there are some arguments in favour of this hypothesis, it must be observed that febrile albuminuria is often met with when the blood pressure is abnormally reduced owing to the weakening influence of continued high fever, or owing to weakness of the cardiac muscle. Hence pyrexial albuminuria is by some attributed to a depression of the blood pressure, to passive engorgement and retardation of the blood current in the glomeruli.

Attractive as it may appear to associate high temperature and albuminuria as cause and effect, both experimentally and clinically, the parallel is not found to hold constantly, since albuminuria may be found with the slightest degree of fever, and be occasionally absent when the fever is very high. According to Leyden and Eckstein, febrile albuminuria depends upon ' an abortive kind of acute nephritis,' and if this suggestion is accepted it would render unnecessary any further theories connected with alterations of the blood pressure, and it would open up the classification of a form of renal inflammation which should be styled 'toxic nephritis,' since the theory would suggest that the albuminuria results from elimination through the kidneys of a toxic agent due to the growth of specific micro-organisms. This explanation would account for the frequent absence of albuminuria in febrile affections which, so far as is known at present, do not depend upon an infectious organism; but, on the other hand, it appears to me to raise a new difficulty, since it does not in any way explain why albuminuria is not always met with in diseases which always depend upon the growths of micro-organisms. Thus, for example, in diphtheria, scarlet fever, and many other infectious diseases, albuminuria, though frequent, is not constant. It has been suggested that this symptom may depend upon the elimination of an increased quantity of urea in the course of fevers; but it is difficult to see how this should produce albuminuria, although it is easy to see how fallacious deductions might be drawn from careless testing, when the urine contains large quantities of urea, uric acid, or urates.

In the majority of cases of febrile albuminuria the anatomical appearances are not characteristic of any recognised form of nephritis, as might, indeed, be inferred from their classification with other forms of albuminuria without definite structural change of renal tissue. The appearances here described are not constant, although they occur with sufficient frequency to deserve mention. The anatomical appearances are usually confined to cloudy swelling of the epithelial cells of the urinary tubules. In some cases the kidney appears somewhat large, and it may occasionally be hyperæmic; in others, however, the kidney appears paler than usual, and, in addition to this anæmia, the kidney may appear actually smaller. Roy explains this contraction as the result of irritation of the central nervous system produced by infective blood. Sometimes, when the condition has been extreme, desquamation with formation of casts and hæmorrhages into the tubules may be found, but these definite changes are only met with in exceptional cases. On microscopical examination of the urine in cases of febrile albuminuria, hyaline casts are almost invariably present; blood corpuscles and renal epithelium may sometimes be found, and occasionally degenerated and granular casts. Fürbringer considers that febrile albuminuria, especially in diphtheria, gradually passes on, both anatomically and clinically, into genuine nephritis, but this is contrary to my own experience of the extreme frequency with which such cases permanently recover.

Albuminuria in pregnancy.—During pregnancy albuminuria occurs so frequently, and its connection with puerperal nephritis and with eclampsia is so close, that it has been deemed advisable to treat the subject in detail at a later page. It must be mentioned here, however, as there is no doubt that the albuminuria of pregnancy must be recognised as one of the varieties of true renal albuminuria, which is sometimes, although not always, unassociated with structural change of the kidney. Numerous theories of explanation have been formulated respecting this occurrence. Rayer thought it was due to hydræmia, which exists during pregnancy, and in support of this theory he referred to the experimental production of albuminuria by the injection of water into the veins of an animal. This experiment cannot be regarded as conclusive, since it simultaneously caused an augmentation of blood pressure within the renal vessels—a condition which might, in itself, produce albuminuria by over distension of the Malpighian tuft of capillaries. Claude Bernard, in view of the albuminuria caused by the injection of white of egg into the circulation, thought that in pregnancy a similar result might ensue from superalbuminosis. Others have held that it resulted from an increased blood pressure, either from compression of the aorta below the renal arteries, due to the growth of the gravid uterus, or by similar pressure upon the renal veins. A theory, which was at one time received with favour, attributed the symptoms to true renal disease, excited by obstruction to the flow of urine through the ureters, through pressure of the uterus. In addition to other objections, this theory wholly fails to explain the frequent rapid disappearance of albumin after parturition—a fact inconsistent with true nephritis from obstruction. Nervous influences due to communications between the uterine and renal plexus have been suggested, and more recently much attention has been paid to certain white infarcts, which are frequently found in the placenta of women who have had albuminuria. Colonies of bacteria have been found in these infarcts,[1] and injection of these germs into the veins of guinea-pigs and rabbits set up

[1] Ehrhardt and Favre, *Nouv. Arch. d'Obstét. et de Gynéc.*, Sept. 1890.

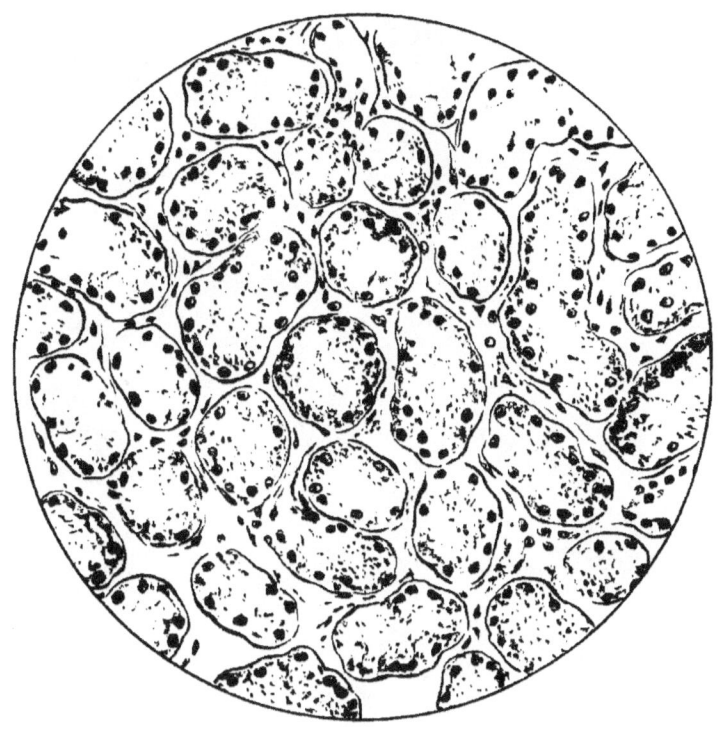

Transverse Section of Tubules, after Typhoid Fever, with Albuminuria. The epithelial cells are cloudy and swollen, the outlines are indefinite, the lumen of the tubules contain granular matter. The nuclei between the tubes have not undergone proliferation, and they appear to be only the normal nuclei of small vessels.

(*See page* 43.)

N. Tirard. Del.   Mintern Bros., imp.

parenchymatous nephritis. It has been suggested that these germs, in non-pregnant patients, produce leucorrhœa and other symptoms of chronic endometritis, while in pregnancy they lead to placental infarcts and nephritis. Although these observations are of considerable interest, they fail to account for the clinical fact of the frequent disappearance of albumin within twenty-four or forty-eight hours after delivery.

Albuminuria in syphilis.—Although syphilis is often associated with habits of life which may result either in the production of extra-renal or accidental albuminuria, or else in chronic renal cirrhosis, there are a certain number of cases in which it is difficult to attribute the albuminuria to either of these causes. From their clinical features, and especially from the readiness with which they yield to mercurial treatment, there appears to be no doubt that a form of syphilitic albuminuria, independent of renal structural change, must be recognised. During the early days of treatment it is always difficult to assign the albuminuria in any particular case to this cause, and even when the urine gives no further reaction some doubt may remain, since similar disappearance of albumin is of frequent occurrence in the course of renal cirrhosis. Dr. Oscar v. Petersen [1] published the results of an inquiry into the connection of syphilis with albuminuria and nephritis. He found renal lesions were present in thirty-four out of eighty-eight necropsies of syphilitic bodies, and he also ascertained that in thirty-six cases in which the fatal issue had been caused by syphilis, seven of the patients had succumbed mainly to chronic nephritis. This led him to examine the urine in two hundred consecutive cases of syphilis, all of which were treated by intramuscular injections of salicylate of mercury. The urine was examined by boiling and nitric acid, once after admission, and subsequently once a week, usually on the day after the mercurial injection. In fifty-five—*i.e.* 27·5 per cent. of all cases examined—albumin was found. In twenty-eight it was dependent on an accidental admixture of proteids from purulent balanitis, gonorrhœa, prostatitis, &c.; in nineteen it was transitory, and in seven there was a genuine permanent or syphilitic albuminuria. It is possible that some of these results might

[1] *Vratch*, No. 21, 1891.

be attributed to the salicylate treatment, since it is well known that salicylates may occasionally, when given in large doses, cause albuminuria, or even hæmaturia, of a transitory nature. The influence of mercury, on the other hand, is purely beneficial; its elimination by the kidney does not cause a genuine albuminuria, though the existence of nephritis in a syphilitic patient may often be inferred from the readiness with which sponginess of the gums appears under mercurial treatment. In spite of this, however, Dr. v. Petersen maintains that syphilitic albuminuria is rapidly cured by the use of mercurials.

Dietetic and digestive albuminuria.—The frequent association of albuminuria with serious diseases of the digestive system has long been recognised. It occurs under many conditions where tumours may be reasonably believed to cause an interference with the normal circulation of blood through the kidney. It has been observed occasionally in cases of cancer of the stomach or liver, and in connection with gastric catarrh, with chronic intestinal irritation associated with diarrhœa; it is also not uncommon in strangulated hernia and in other cases of intestinal obstruction.

Apart from these conditions, it has been encountered so often with milder disturbances of digestive functions that many authors recognise a form of dietetic or digestive albuminuria. Sir J. Grainger Stewart has found that the ingestion of food in many healthy people is followed by slight transient albuminuria, and he thinks it may be referred to altered blood pressure, or to altered chemical composition of the blood serum, or to both causes acting simultaneously. Dr. Stanley Rendall concludes that in such cases there is a true hæmatogenous albuminuria, produced by an alteration of the blood plasma and not by any change in the kidneys or their blood pressure; he thinks this alteration may be due to the introduction of an imperfect form of albumin into the blood current, resulting from some disorder in digestion or assimilation. Murchison, in view of the symptom being frequently intermittent or remittent, considered that it was due to hepatic derangement, independently of structural disease of the kidneys, but he also allowed that renal degeneration might follow as the result of continued elimination of products of faulty digestion through the kidneys

Experiment in this direction has given very conflicting results. In animals albuminuria has been shown to follow the injection of egg albumin into the veins or into the rectum, but authorities differ widely as to the effects obtained after the introduction of egg albumin into the stomach. In many cases the ingestion of raw eggs in succession has produced headache, sickness, and diarrhœa, and these symptoms have sometimes, but not always, been accompanied by albuminuria. On the other hand, I have found that this result appears occasionally to ensue after eating two or more cooked eggs, especially if hard boiled, and similar observations have been previously made by Claude Bernard and others. I have notes of several cases of young men, large eaters mostly, in whom I have observed this condition; in one it appeared to result from a habit of taking two meals only in the day, and of consuming large quantities of food on each occasion, and in this case diminution and distribution of food were speedily followed by the disappearance of albumin. The main feature of this class of cases is the small quantity of albumin passed and the variability of the condition of the water.

Other substances besides eggs, such as pastry, nuts, cheese, &c., are often credited with the production of albuminuria in healthy individuals, but the effect on the average man is so slight and so uncertain, that these albuminurias, if they exist, must be set down to idiosyncrasy. While in exceptional cases the nature of the food or some special idiosyncrasy produces albuminuria in otherwise healthy individuals, it is far more common to find this symptom result from defective digestion or imperfect metabolism, and it is accordingly convenient to subdivide some of these digestive albuminurias into (*a*) oxaluric, (*b*) gouty or lithæmic.

(*a*) *Oxaluric albuminuria.*—This is most common in early adult life, though it may occur in children and even in the aged. Sir Andrew Clark [1] considered that the majority of cases of albuminuria occurring in young men of from eighteen to thirty years of age fell into the group of oxaluric albuminuria.

This condition may be produced by a variety of circumstances. Grave errors in diet or defective digestion may lead

[1] *Brit. Med. Journ.*, Aug. 16, 1884.

to an increase in the amount of oxalates excreted, and it is possible that, owing to the sharp edges and corners of these oxalate crystals, they may scratch the mucous membrane and thus cause the appearance of albumin or blood in the urine. I have repeatedly found crystals of oxalates in cases where only a variable trace of albumin has been discovered, and where the quantity and specific gravity of the urine have not departed sufficiently from the normal conditions to allow of diagnosis of chronic renal affection.

This oxaluric albuminuria is extremely common, especially amongst young men, and in all probability it accounts for a very large number of the cases of slight albuminuria seen at insurance offices. In these the urine is of good colour, the specific gravity is frequently normal, and there are no vascular changes indicative of chronic renal affection. The frequency of oxaluric albuminuria may perhaps be often overlooked by the regular medical attendant, since persons suffering from it may not be troubled by any symptoms directing attention to the water, and, indeed, they rarely make any complaint of their health. Occasionally they may admit that they suffer from low spirits and lassitude, and sometimes they may confess to slight dyspeptic trouble, but unless they are also passing phosphates in excess they rarely appear to think much about their symptoms or to attach much importance to the condition, even when it has been pointed out.

(b) *Gouty or lithæmic albuminuria.*—Lithæmia may be the predisposing cause of a transient albuminuria at almost any age, while in patients advanced in years it may form the foundation of an albuminuria which, after commencing in an insidious irregular way, ultimately gives place to a permanent albuminuria with definite structural changes, changes which affect not only the kidney, but also the vascular system, and are indicative of chronic renal disease. In young children, however, especially in those who receive an insufficient supply of liquid and an over supply of solids, the urine may become highly concentrated, and may give evidence of an increase of urea as well as of the presence of varying amounts of albumin. In such cases the urine is high coloured and of relatively high specific gravity, and it may form a sandy deposit of urates which are readily recognised either on microscopic examination or on heating a small quantity of the deposit, when the urates will dissolve. Such cases of slight albuminuria may sometimes be met with in young adults who consume enormous quantities of meat, and it is readily amenable to a more rational dietary. This form of albuminuria is closely allied to the preceding, and it is generally a fleeting condition which passes off with an increased consumption of liquid or with a diminished supply of nitrogenous food.

During the early attacks of paroxysmal gout albuminuria is frequently absent, though it appears when the attacks occur with increasing frequency. At the commencement of a gouty attack there may be no albumin, but, according to Lecorché, it appears to have distinct relation to the excretion of uric acid, being present about the third or fourth day of the attack, and diminishing as the excretion of uric acid diminishes. The amount of albumin in these cases is usually small, and it indicates the inability of the kidneys to cope with the increased and altered work entailed by the gouty changes. Not only is there the increased metabolism associated with the pyrexia, but there may also be irritation of the tubular epithelium by the excess of uric acid to be eliminated. Such urinary changes are generally the precursors of more serious structural alterations in the kidney, although it is extremely difficult to decide the exact stage at which chronic renal affection must be diagnosed. The tubal catarrh may be excited by an acute attack of gout in kidneys which are already undergoing cirrhotic changes, and although it may pass off with the acute attack of gout, it will probably leave these changes somewhat more advanced than before. In cases of chronic gout some degree of albuminuria is common, and the urine usually presents the ordinary characters of interstitial nephritis. The amount of albumin is generally small and variable; it may disappear for long periods, and a diagnosis of Bright's disease is therefore scarcely justifiable; but frequently other changes in the urine, such as polyuria and low specific gravity, changes due to a deficient elimination of urea and salts, will form a sufficient justification for a diagnosis of chronic kidney disease. According to Virchow [1] the acute irritation of the

[1] *Berl. klin. Woch.*, No. 1, 1884.

urinary organs, accompanied by albuminuria which sometimes occurs in gouty persons, is not due to acute nephritis, but to a general purulent catarrh of the genito-urinary tract, excited by the excess of uric acid in the urine. In support of this view he narrated his personal experience in 1883. After suffering for some time with considerable urinary irritation, the urine containing pus, albumin, and tube casts, he was led to examine the urine more attentively. On adding acetic acid he was surprised to find the whole field covered with microscopic crystals of uric acid to an extent he had never seen before. He then took biborate of soda and Carlsbad water, and under this treatment the urinary trouble quickly subsided.

In this connection I may mention some similar observations which I recently made upon the urine of a gentleman, aged 72, who had at various times passed small concretions, though at the time when I examined his water he was free from any urinary pain. I found, however, that there was a faint cloud of albumin formed on the addition of cold nitric acid, the urine being of a specific gravity which varied from 1025 to 1030. The faint ring of opacity which first formed, speedily extended towards the upper part of the test-tube, and on examination of this zone of opacity it was found to be due to numerous minute colourless crystals of uric acid. When the urine was examined with trichloracetic acid similar reactions occurred, but in this case the crystals were somewhat larger, of a rosette form, and coloured. As the excess of uric acid disappeared under treatment, no trace of albumin could be found.

FUNCTIONAL, INTERMITTENT, AND CYCLIC FORMS OF ALBUMINURIA, TOGETHER WITH THE SO-CALLED ALBUMINURIA OF ADOLESCENCE

The above constitute the most debatable ground connected with albuminuria. It occasionally happens that every effort to trace the cause of albuminuria fails, and such cases have been sometimes regarded as 'physiological,' since no known pathological conditions can be found. The use of this term was vigorously contested by the late Sir George Johnson, who regarded the appearance of albumin as an indication of a departure from the healthy or physiological state. The term 'functional' is less open to objection; it only implies a departure from the normal condition of work, without attempting to account for the cause. The other terms, 'intermittent' and 'cyclic,' have largely lost their original limitations, and they might with equal propriety be employed in the description of many of the varieties of albuminuria already dealt with, as well as of some cases of chronic nephritis or cirrhosis. The term 'intermittent' merely indicates that sometimes, perhaps for days or weeks, albumin may be found, and that such attacks occur without any regularity, and are separated by intervals, of varying length, during which no trace of albumin can be detected. This sequence of events marks many cases of renal cirrhosis, and it is equally characteristic of the history of many diabetic cases.

The term 'cyclic albuminuria' was originally used to denote the presence of albumin for a certain period only, the urine during the remainder of the twenty-four hours being entirely free from albumin. Dr. Pavy, who described this form, thinks it may continue for weeks, months, or years without impairment of health. As a rule, casts are absent, but sugar has sometimes been detected, and crystals of oxalate of lime are mostly present. He states that he has observed sharp, unduly forcible cardiac impulse, but that the pulse was not hard and sustained, as in the early stages of Bright's disease. I think it is extremely probable that, under this heading, Dr. Pavy has grouped two or more well recognised types of albuminuria; some of the cases with crystals of oxalate of lime may perhaps belong more properly to the group of oxaluria, while those with the altered nature of the cardiac impulse may possibly be found, in their later history, to have been really premonitory indications of chronic nephritis or renal cirrhosis. Sir J. Grainger Stewart, in his interesting and valuable book on 'Albuminuria,' describes a 'paroxysmal' variety; and he illustrates his remarks by describing, as a typical case, the symptoms presented by a young woman who was admitted on account of acute illness. She had general malaise, some degree of fever and gastric catarrh, some puffiness of the face, but no dropsy. The urine was rather scanty, dark in colour, and loaded with albumin. It contained tube casts in great number, and of several varieties—epithelial, granular, and hyaline—and there were also some crystals of oxalate of lime. He compares this condition to paroxysmal hæmoglobinuria, and states that both may be brought on either by cold and wet, or sometimes by errors of diet and alcoholic intoxication. In considering the explanation of such cases he refers to the probable irritation of the kidney due to oxaluria, and thinks that if any alterations of blood pressure exist they are only a secondary element. I prefer not to accept this classification of paroxysmal albuminuria, for two reasons. In the first place, beyond the sudden onset, which necessarily attracts attention, there is nothing to differentiate such an attack from those already described under the heading of 'Oxaluric Albuminuria;' and secondly, because similar speedy improvement may often be witnessed in the course of cases of renal cirrhosis.

Another form is described by the same author as *simple persistent albuminuria*, and he summarises the features of this class in the following way: persistent presence of albumin, usually in small quantity, with few tube casts, and these mostly hyaline, without diminution of urea, increased vascular tension, cardiac hypertrophy or other consequence of renal malady, persisting for a period of months or years, and little influenced by diet or exercise. The relation between these transient forms of albuminuria and Bright's disease is perhaps comparable to that existing between a slight pulmonary hæmorrhage and phthisis. Such hæmorrhages are undoubtedly sometimes the precursors of phthisis, but, although they cause much anxiety, they are not necessarily followed by serious pulmonary changes.

Closely allied to the foregoing types stands the condition originally described by Dr. Moxon [1] as the albuminuria of adolescence, and spoken of by Sir William Roberts [2] as *albuminuria of adolescents, transient or physiological albuminuria.* According to Moxon, the symptom continues during a long period in a desultory and irregular way; the patient is out of condition, listless and languid, sleeps too much, and yet rises unrefreshed, is anæmic, and grey and sunken about the eyes. Disorders of digestion may often be noted, and yet at times the general health appears to be perfect. The amount of albumin varies

---

[1] *Guy's Hosp. Reports*, 1878, vol. xxiii. p. 233.
[2] *On Urinary and Renal Diseases*, p. 197.

greatly—mostly only a trace is present, but occasionally a dense thick ring may be obtained by the contact test. Even in the individual case the amount varies from day to day, and at different hours of the day. Some specimens, especially those passed before breakfast, may be quite normal, while albumin appears later in the day. Sometimes it is found only in the urine passed shortly after meals. Generally the urine is of good colour, and fairly high specific gravity; it may contain a large excess of urea, and frequently, on standing, it deposits urates and oxalates, and sometimes a few hyaline casts may be formed. The occurrence of casts is important, as it indicates that the albumin is derived from the capillaries of the Malpighian tuft, or from those of the convoluted tubes, instead of resulting from irritation of some portion of the genito-urinary tract and the later admixture of albumin. Dr. T. Morley Rooke [1] was the first to draw attention to the remarkable influence of rest in bed upon the albuminuria of adolescence. He found that the symptom was reduced, removed, or kept in abeyance when patients were kept in bed. Conversely, others have found the frequency of the symptoms greatly affected by muscular exercise. Leube [2] examined the urine of soldiers after a long march, and found albumin in the urine of 16 per cent. Dr. Clement Dukes [3] agreed that it sometimes followed excessive exertion, but found that it occurred after a sudden change of temperature, after mental emotion, and sometimes after an error in diet. At the same time he held that alterations in diet were very uncertain in their results: a patient who had no albuminuria when taking milk, might not be able to add a little bread to his diet; while one who had to limit his food in the strictest way so long as he was up and about, could eat and drink freely if kept to his bed.

In his latest writings upon the 'albuminuria of adolescence' Dr. Clement Dukes [4] protests against the employment of this term, which he considers inappropriate, since the malady is not exclusively one of adolescence. He is convinced that a considerable proportion of the cases which

---

[1] *Brit. Med. Journ.*, 1878, ii. p. 596.   [2] *Virch. Arch.*, 72, p. 145.
[3] *Brit. Med. Journ.*, 1878, ii. p. 794; and 1881, ii. p. 776.
[4] *Lancet*, December 12, 1891.

are ordinarily described under this term never recover, but progressively increase, and he suggests that the term 'early albuminuria' might be more correct. He thinks, however, that the only appropriate name would be one which should designate the actual state as a hyperæmic or an inflammatory change in the vascular system of the kidney, or hyperæmia depending upon a neurosis of the nervous supply (vaso-motor) to the vascular system of the kidney. As on many former occasions, he protests against calling this condition 'functional albuminuria,' since he holds that though like the early stage of any other disease it may be transient and recoverable, yet if the slight attacks be frequently repeated they tend to produce permanent organic mischief. His explanation of the condition is that in the early stages there is a 'congestive neurosis arising from a certain state of the vaso-motor nerves, which have lost control over the blood vessels of the kidneys.' He believes that a frequent or a chronic congestion must entail changes in the gland cells and eventually cause an 'interstitial plastic exudation,' which, pressing on the parenchyma, will eventually destroy the secreting tissue of the kidney, these changes ultimately producing the contracted or cirrhotic kidney. He maintains that it is incorrect to speak of 'cyclic albuminuria' in such cases, since it is solely the sudden transfer of the body from the horizontal to the vertical position which entails this cyclical character, owing to the alteration in the circulation. He holds that all cases of albuminuria, except, of course, those of acute nephritis, commence in this way. The albuminuria is present or absent only intermittently at first, but as the case advances it usually becomes confirmed. In short, his theory is that where the hyperæmia of the kidneys is severe the albuminuria is persistent in whatever position the body may be placed, whether at rest or not, and whatever diet may be taken; while if the hyperæmia be slight, from the cause having been trivial, or from a severe attack which is passing away, then the albuminuria only shows itself when the body assumes the vertical position, or under exercise, or after a full meal. If the hyperæmia be prolonged, however slight in degree, the albuminuria gradually becomes persistent owing to the permanent dilatation of the blood vessels, and thus tends to the destruction of the kidneys. He thinks, moreover, that many cases of albuminuria which have been attributed to overwork should be classed under this category, and he finds that in their treatment a dose of blue pill is far more efficacious than cessation from work.

There is much that is attractive and plausible in the line of reasoning adopted by Dr. Clement Dukes, and there is, I think, little doubt that harm may result from taking too sanguine a view of the relative unimportance of this 'albuminuria of adolescence.' I prefer to retain the term, as it conveniently applies to a large number of transient forms of albuminuria occurring during early life; but I am convinced that in all such cases it is most desirable to attempt to arrive at the underlying cause, and to correct errors, and treat the individual instead of resting satisfied with allaying anxiety with the assurance that the symptom is one of little importance, which will be outgrown. Careful inquiry of habits, careful examination of the water, and close attention to the frequency of the symptom and the time of its occurrence will often furnish useful data for advice and treatment. These cases are constantly coming under my observation in insurance work, and in the examination of young men for various appointments, and in a large proportion it is possible to refer the case of 'adolescent albuminuria' to one of the foregoing categories, and to provide for appropriate treatment of the digestive or nervous system. In some, however, I must confess that this effort fails, but I am disposed to think that the failure may be ascribed to the lack of candour on the part of the patient. Still, even in these cases, the condition should not remain untreated. Most of these patients, with their lethargy, pallor, and dark lines below the eyes, furnish, even in the absence of a history, sufficient data for a hypothetical line of treatment, which in most cases includes modification of diet, the use of purgatives, early rising, and the encouragement to indulge moderately in some form of athleticism. Many such patients are morbid and self-conscious, and require rousing from their apathy. I am by no means convinced that, if left to themselves, most of these cases of adolescent albuminuria pass on gradually to the establishment of a chronic kidney disease, but I regard the condition as essentially pathological and not physiological, and

I fear that much harm to the individual may result from leaving the condition unchecked. So far as the patient is concerned, I am sure, with Dr. Clement Dukes, that it would be safer to fear the later development of chronic kidney disease, than to lull him into a false sense of security by calling the symptom 'physiological.'

CHAPTER II

HÆMATURIA

HÆMATURIA occurs so frequently in connection with albuminuria that it merits separate attention, even though in the etiology this involves a certain degree of repetition. Thus it is to be met with in a large number of the cases of extra-renal, false, or accidental albuminuria; it occurs also in many of the consecutive class of the forms of renal albuminuria, and in the course of both acute nephritis and chronic nephritis.

Unless the quantity of blood in the urine is very small, its presence may usually be recognised by the colour. When it is derived from the kidneys it is equally diffused through the urine as it is passed, and it imparts to it a reddish or smoky tint, and, after standing, the blood subsides and forms a dark-brown cloudy deposit. If, however, the blood has been added from some part of the urinary tract, from the ureters, the bladder, or the urethra, the colour is usually more brilliant and distinct, and clots may be found in the deposit. When examined with the microscope, if the urine is acid and of average density, the corpuscles may be recognised, but they speedily disappear in alkaline urine, or in urine of low specific gravity. When the specific gravity is high, they may either retain their ordinary shape, or they may shrink and become more or less crenated. In dilute urine they absorb fluid and swell, so that they lose the normal bi-concave appearance, and appear like pale discs with sharp outlines. They may be distinguished from other cells by the delicacy of their outline and by the absence of visible cell contents, and especially by the absence of a nucleus. They may be sometimes mistaken for confervoid sporules, or for the nuclei of renal epithelium. The former are frequently oval, and may show signs of budding, while the latter have greater sharpness of outline, readily absorb colouring agents, and are frequently partially surrounded by some portions of the epithelial cells. On spectroscopic examination the presence of blood may be recognised by the two dark bands between Frauenhofer's lines D and E. Frequently, however, it is more convenient to test with tincture of guaiacum and ozonic ether, and to obtain the characteristic blue colour.

When blood is present there is always of necessity more or less albumin; hence the conditions already described as giving rise to accidental albuminuria are in many cases also causes of hæmaturia. It may be convenient, however, to group together the conditions under which hæmaturia is most likely to occur. Hæmaturia may result from either (1) local lesions, or (2) it may be symptomatic of some other disease, and (3) it may be supplementary or vicarious.

1. *Local lesions.*—By far the greatest number of cases of hæmaturia arise from local lesions, due to over-distension or rupture of blood vessels within the substance of the kidney, the pelvis of the kidney, the ureter, bladder, prostate, or urethra. When the hæmorrhage comes from the substance of the kidney it is always associated with tube casts, which commonly contain blood corpuscles, often more or less altered in nature, but still distinctly recognisable. This form of hæmaturia is most commonly seen in acute Bright's disease, or in the course of active congestion supplementary to chronic Bright's disease. The frequency with which hæmaturia occurs as part of an attack of acute nephritis, or as an indication of an acute congestion interrupting the course of a chronic nephritis, are so well recognised that it is perhaps unnecessary to give details of illustrative cases, but hæmaturia frequently trenches on the border-line separating medicine from surgery, and it is no uncommon occurrence for some hesitation to be experienced in the out-patient department as to whether the case when first seen should be considered as medical or surgical. Thus a man, J. G., aged 58, was transferred from one department to another on account of his hæmaturia. The urine passed in the out-patient department was dark-red in colour, and deposited an abundant sediment as it was left to cool. The urine was acid, its specific gravity 1016, it contained a large proportion of albumin, and it gave the characteristic reaction with tincture

of guaiacum and ozonic ether. From its appearance it was quite easy to understand that acute nephritis or acute congestion might be diagnosed; but the man's account was that this condition had only occurred at frequent intervals during the past six weeks; that the blood was not always present, although, as he expressed it, he had passed blood 'dozens of times' during that interval. He stated that sometimes the urine was white and milky, and that it generally had considerable deposit. His chief complaint was of pain across the lower part of the abdomen, pain which apparently commenced in the median line and radiated round to the lumbar region, and pain which, he stated, preceded the hæmaturia, and was relieved by the act of micturition. He brought with him a turbid sample of urine which had been passed on the day he came to the hospital, and the turbidity was found to be due to the presence of urates, a portion of the fluid in the test-tube clearing up on being heated, while the upper zone became turbid from the precipitation of albumin. In this particular case the pain was not like that associated with renal calculus, or with acute congestion of the kidney, while the frequent passage of water of normal colour was alone sufficient to indicate that the hæmorrhage was not due to an acute nephritis, and that the case was more probably surgical than medical.

Hæmaturia sometimes results from injuries. I remember one of our students many years ago having severe hæmaturia after being injured at football. The history in that case was so clearly connected with the history of injury that there was little doubt that the appearance of blood was due to some laceration of the kidney. The hæmorrhage ceased after a few days, and no permanent damage to the kidney appeared to follow. At about the same time I became interested in the case of a boy who had had profuse hæmaturia after another boy had suddenly jumped on his back at school; and although many of the later symptoms appeared to indicate that a renal calculus might have been displaced by the injury, it was found later that the hæmaturia had been really due to laceration. This patient, at intervals extending over some years, complained of considerable pain, although there was no return of hæmorrhage and no albumin. The pain, however, was so distressing that eventually an operation was undertaken to ascertain its cause, when it was found that the kidney was firmly united to the descending colon by a firm cicatrix, and it was then remembered that although he had stated that pain was readily excited by jolting movements, as in driving in cabs or omnibuses, yet he had also mentioned that it was liable to occur with fits of severe constipation or diarrhœa, when evidently the cicatrix was drawn upon by the alteration in size and position of the descending colon.

Saundby has given particulars of cases in which severe persistent hæmorrhage has resulted from displacement of the kidney. When the kidney has been dislodged from its position, or when its attachments are abnormally lax, it may occasionally be rotated upon its axis so as to cause compression of the renal vein and thus to lead to passive congestion. Hæmaturia from this cause is not very frequent, and it is difficult to prove its connection with the abnormal mobility of the kidney unless the condition improves with rest and pressure over the site of the kidney.

Dr. David Newman, of Glasgow, considers that increased vascular tension in the kidney is to be regarded as a cause of renal pain, hæmaturia, and albuminuria, and he collected five cases which he described in some detail before the Clinical Society. In one of these cases the hyperæmia from torsion of renal vessels and ureter was associated with a movable enlarged kidney, and the prominent symptoms were severe paroxysmal pain, hæmaturia, gastric disturbances, &c., simulating the symptoms of renal colic. In the second case, severe paroxysmal pain and hæmaturia, with occasional blood casts in the urine and sometimes with albumin independent of blood, were also found to be due to displacement of the kidney and rotation on its short axis. In the third the symptoms of renal colic were more marked, and the urine was normal between the attacks of colic, and although at the time of operation the kidney was found to be deeply injected, enlarged, and moderately movable, no torsion of the ureter or vessels could be made out. In the fourth case, after an accident (the patient having been thrown from his horse), a movable tumour was found in the hypochondriac region. In the fifth there was pain in both loins, and the urine contained albumin, but no casts. There was a history of small oxalate calculi and occasional hæmaturia. On operating, the kidney was found to be enlarged, tense, and of a chocolate colour; no calculi were found. All of these cases improved after operation, the albuminuria and hæmaturia ceasing and the pain being relieved, if not entirely cured.

When hæmaturia occurs in the course of Bright's disease, although the quantity of blood lost may appear to be excessive, there is really no special immediate danger. Roberts has, however, pointed out that the remote consequences may be extremely serious, since the effused blood tends to coagulate within the tubules, and unless these plugs of coagula are expelled by the pressure of the urine from behind, they may destroy the function of relatively large portions of glands. Saundby states, also, that in rare instances the hæmorrhage may be alarmingly profuse and fatal.

Hæmaturia is relatively frequent in cases of renal calculus, but it is only large in amount when the calculus has been dislodged, by sudden jolts or strains, and in such cases the symptom is usually accompanied by the pains of renal colic—in fact, the pain generally precedes the hæmaturia. The pain is generally unilateral, and shoots in the direction of the ureter towards the groin, and is associated with vomiting and retraction of the testicle. Such pain may sometimes be mistaken for the colic associated with the passage of a gallstone, especially if the pain starts in the right side of the body; but in biliary colic the pain usually passes upwards and backwards around the thorax, and may seem to be centred below the right shoulder-blade. The detection of blood in the urine is sufficiently constant to enable a certain diagnosis to be made, but the presence of albumin would not be diagnostic. Cases of greater difficulty are those in which the hæmaturia depends upon minute concretions formed within the tubuli uriniferi, since in these cases there is frequently very little pain, or only a slight sense of fatigue in the lumbar region. In such cases the presence of microscopic calculi of uric acid and crystals of oxalate of lime may considerably aid the diagnosis. As a rule, in such cases more albumin is passed than would correspond with the amount of blood detected. Transparent casts may sometimes be found, and these frequently contain the microscopic crystals of oxalate of lime.

Hæmaturia as the result of local lesion may also occur with ulceration of the kidney, and with cancer, tubercle, and syphilis. When it occurs with tubercle it is generally associated with pus, and the history mostly shows that the urine has contained pus for a long time, although blood has been present on certain occasions. Tubercle of the kidney is rather more common amongst children than adults—in fact, in cases of general tuberculosis in children, it is comparatively rare not to find small tubercles just below the capsule, but unless the tubercle has grown to large size, symptoms are usually absent. To a large extent the diagnosis of tubercle of the kidney is assisted by consideration of the family history and by the general appearance of the patient. Sometimes the diagnosis may be assisted by the evidence of tubercle affecting other organs.

When cancer of the kidney leads to hæmaturia, the hæmaturia is generally very profuse; but cancer of the kidney may attain enormous dimensions without the production of this symptom. It has been stated that only in one-fifth of the cases reported has hæmaturia been the first symptom that has been noticed before the discovery of the tumour; usually the development of an enormous new growth attracts attention long before hæmaturia arises. On the other hand, Saundby mentions a patient who suffered from hæmaturia for six years, and who died ultimately from cancer of the kidney and liver.

Dr. David Newman [1] believes that renal calculus may act as an exciting cause of malignant growth, and points out that in other organs, also, it is prolonged and comparatively slight irritation, rather than intense and transitory excitement, that predisposes to the development of cancer. The presence of a palpable swelling in the loin is an almost constant sign of malignant disease; but cases have been recorded where the patient died from general dissemination of the disease without the primary growth in the kidney being detected.

Hæmaturia is the most significant and important symptom

[1] *Glasgow Medical Journal*, March 1896.

PLATE II.

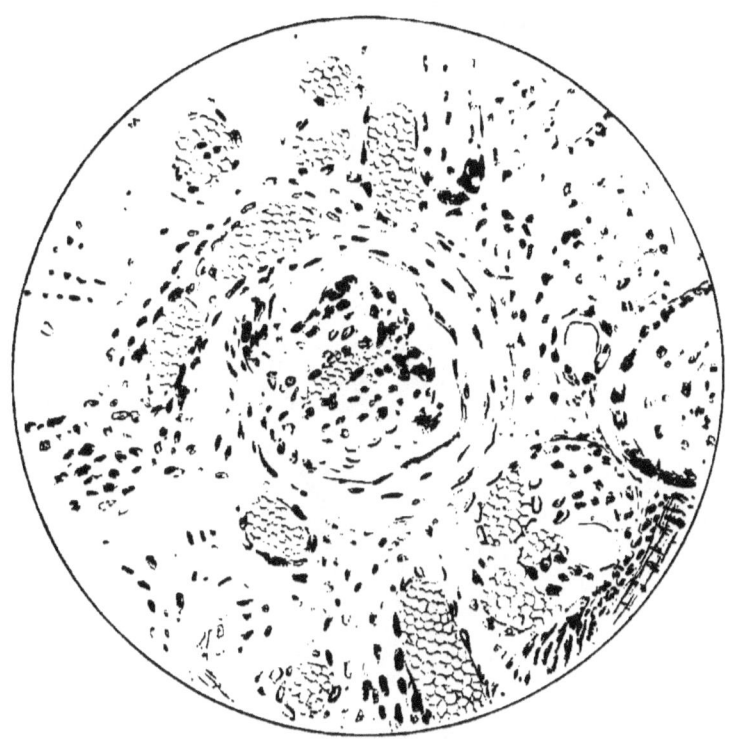

Section of Cortical portion of Kidney in Chronic Nephritis, during a Subacute Attack. Compressed blood corpuscles are seen in the Malpighian tuft of capillaries, also filling the tubules, and compressing the renal epithelium. The Malpighian capsule is much thickened and there is great increase in the corpuscles intervening between the tubes. To the right two tubes are seen in transverse section, containing casts.

(*See pp.* 61 *and* 143.)

N. Tirard, Del.   Mintern Bros., imp.

of malignant disease of the kidney, but its diagnostic value is reduced from the circumstance of its being a symptom of other renal affections associated with a swelling in the loin—for example, tubercular disease, hydatids, calculus, pyonephrosis, &c. Hæmaturia from malignant disease is generally more profuse and less transient than that from calculus, and is sometimes so copious as to cause marked anæmia. In malignant disease the bleeding may be so copious that the blood coagulates and causes obstruction of the ureter or urethra. The urine, in addition to blood, may contain tube casts, epithelium, and what have been called by some observers cancer cells. Constitutional effects are produced within a comparatively limited time, especially in cancer of the kidney; anæmia, loss of flesh, and change in the colour of the skin, may supervene even although the patient takes his food well, and the loss of blood has not been excessive.

The connection between syphilis and hæmaturia is not very definite, but cases where the hæmaturia has been associated with a syphilitic sore throat have been described, and I remember many years ago seeing one case where the hæmaturia, which came on suddenly, yielded to treatment primarily directed against syphilitic keratitis. On the other hand, it is well known that gummatous affections of the kidney may sometimes attain an enormous size without causing hæmaturia. A specimen was recently shown at the Pathological Society by Mr. Bowlby, where gummatous affection of the kidney had caused a large renal tumour. The patient, a woman aged forty, had suffered from syphilis twenty-one years previously. She complained of a tender swelling in the right lumbar region, which steadily increased in size. There were no other symptoms, and except for an occasional trace of albumin the urine was normal in amount and composition. The swelling attained such a size that it simulated a large new growth of the kidney, and when removed by lumbar nephrectomy it weighed over a pound, and was found to be a kidney so completely infiltrated with gummatous growth that it was almost impossible to find any trace of the renal tubules, and as its removal was not followed by any diminution of the quantity of urine, it is almost certain that it was not functionally active. Two years later the patient was in excellent health, and there was every reason to believe that the other kidney was sound.

The endemic hæmaturia seen in Egypt, the Cape of Good Hope, and some other hot countries appears to be due to the presence of a parasite, *bilharzia hæmatobia*. This generally attacks the bladder, but in some cases it appears to extend to the pelvis or to the substance of the kidney. The ova and embryos of characteristic appearance may be detected in the urine by microscopic examination. Many years ago I had the opportunity of studying this condition in a young Egyptian student at King's College. In this case the hæmaturia was somewhat intermittent, and was always greatest when the ova were most numerous. Hydatid cysts may occasionally develop in the kidney and lead to hæmaturia; this cause is also to be recognised with the microscope by fragments of hydatid membrane or by hooklets.

Congestion of the kidney leading to hæmaturia may ensue after extensive interference with the functions of the skin, whether by burns or by prolonged application of cold, as in bathing or exposure; and it may also occur as a complication of various acute specific diseases, such as scarlet fever, tonsillitis, diphtheria, typhoid fever, &c. In these the boundary line separating hæmaturia from acute nephritis is frequently very ill-defined.

Hæmaturia very often follows the employment of preparations containing cantharides or turpentine. The external application of preparations of cantharides has sometimes been followed by slight hæmaturia; but, as a rule, the symptom only arises when the drug has been administered internally and in fairly large doses. With regard to the production of hæmaturia by turpentine, this symptom arises occasionally when fairly large doses have been employed, doses, however, which are insufficient to produce purgation. Under these circumstances the turpentine is absorbed and eliminated by the kidney instead of being passed out of the system by the bowel; in fact, it is well known that the danger of turpentine lies in the employment of moderate doses.

Many writers maintain that garden rhubarb can cause hæmaturia in exceptional cases, and the general opinion appears to be that the symptom results from the production and elimination of oxalates.

Two very curious cases of hæmaturia resulting from over-exertion have been described by Klemperer,[1] who attributes them to hæmorrhage from the kidney rather than to hæmorrhage from any lower part of the urinary tract. They followed respectively upon excessive horse riding and cycling. Most cases of hæmaturia occurring under such conditions would be probably referred to hæmorrhage from the urethra or neck of the bladder, but Klemperer distinctly states that he regarded the hæmorrhage as being due to rupture of small renal vessels, which rapidly healed when the patients were kept at rest, and he gives the warning that when dealing with such cases other possible causes of hæmorrhage must be carefully excluded.

At the Pathological Society, Dr. Drew recorded a case of villous papilloma of the kidney, ureter, and bladder undergoing malignant change. The patient was a man aged fifty-six, who had for three and a half years suffered from renal colic and profuse hæmaturia. Nephrolithotomy revealed no calculus. The wound was subsequently opened up, and for two and a half months it discharged pus and flakes of epithelium with pus cells. After death the left kidney was hydronephrotic from the obstruction caused by the villous growths, which involved the renal pelvis, ureter, and bladder around the orifice of the urethra.

Hæmorrhage from the pelvis of the kidney and ureters generally results from the passage of calculi, and in these cases the renal colic is usually well marked; sometimes coagula have formed in the interior of the ureter, and long dark clots may be passed. When hæmaturia is the result of hæmorrhage from the bladder, the symptoms are usually sufficiently definite. There is generally pain in the hypogastrium and excessive frequency of micturition. The pain is sometimes referred to the neck of the bladder, and the intermittent nature of the hæmaturia and the appearance of the blood are usually sufficient to call for exploration of the bladder, when calculi or morbid growths may be detected. Thomas Bryant[2] described a case of fibrous polypus of the prostatic portion of the urethra, associated with profuse hæmaturia, which had lasted

[1] *Deutsch. med. Woch.*, Feb. 25 and March 4, 1897.
[2] *Medical Chirurgical Transactions*, vol. lxxvi. 1893.

for six years, and had been sufficiently severe to produce symptoms of collapse from loss of blood. The removal of the polypus was followed by somewhat tedious convalescence, but when the case was reported, a year and a half after the operation, the patient had recovered.

In the following case the hæmorrhage was in all probability due to a villous growth, but the patient refused to come into the hospital for further examination, and as she is still apparently in good health the diagnosis remains uncertain. It is quoted, however, as an instance of the difficulties occasionally to be met with.

In 1891 a patient, Miss C. F——, aged 26, told me that four years previously she had had an attack of hæmaturia, and she stated that she had then been an in-patient in King's College Hospital for three weeks. She complained at that time of some aching pain in the back, not sufficiently severe, however, to be attributed to renal calculus. Her water was high-coloured, contained lithates and a very minute trace of albumin. She had no indication of dropsy, and in all other respects appeared to be in good health. Microscopically, urates and numerous oxalates were found, but no casts. I saw her at frequent intervals until April 1892, when she had sudden profuse hæmaturia unaccompanied by pain. She had no increased frequency of micturition, no diminution in the quantity of water passed, and only complained of slight aching pain over the left ovary. This attack passed off in the course of two days, and there has been no return of the hæmaturia, if, indeed, the case was one of hæmaturia. This patient made no complaint of shivering, and she asserted that but for the appearance of the water she would not have known that she was not in perfect health. The nature of the cardio-vascular system and of the digestive system, as well as the frequent examinations of the urine, were sufficient to indicate that the case was not one of Bright's disease or of heart disease, while the absence of severe pain precluded renal calculus. The idea of a villous growth of the bladder was considered, but the absence of any clots appeared to negative this hypothesis. In another case, that of a lady of about the same age, recurrent hæmaturia with the same marked absence of general symptoms was undoubtedly due to a villous growth, and the hæmorrhage was so frequent and severe that a suprapubic operation was performed and the growth removed.

2. *Symptomatic hæmaturia.*—Symptomatic hæmaturia is sometimes seen in cases of purpura hæmorrhagica. When the hæmorrhage is in the subcutaneous tissues and in the mucous membranes, it may be associated with severe epistaxis and hæmaturia. Occasionally it is seen also in cases of scurvy. When the symptom occurs in the course of specific fevers, malarial fever, cholera and yellow fever, it is generally of fatal import. In all these maladies the diagnosis of the primary condition is sufficiently easy, while the hæmaturia, although a serious complication, can rarely be treated as a separate condition.

Hæmorrhage from the kidney occurs in some rare cases of hæmophilia. This origin of the hæmaturia is determined largely by the family history, and personal history of the patient. The comparative rarity of hæmaturia among the symptoms of this disease is certainly somewhat curious, since hæmorrhage from other parts occurs on such slight provocation. It is possible that experience has taught these patients to avoid all causes of general strain upon the circulation, and that thus, although slight injuries give rise to disproportionate hæmorrhages, the vessels of the kidneys are but rarely injured by severe and sudden increase of blood pressure. It may also be suggested that in hæmophilia, when hæmorrhages occur independently of traceable traumatic causes, they affect mucous or serous membranes and joints before the kidneys, and that hence precautions may be taken which avert the additional risk of hæmaturia. Klemperer considers that the source of the bleeding may be determined by tenderness in the region of the kidney, by blood passed, or by the negative result of examination with the cystoscope. In cases of uncertain origin Klemperer considers that exploratory operations on the kidney should only be carried out when, after treatment for several weeks, the bleeding still continues, and the anæmia endangers life; and he says further that if the kidney be then found healthy, it should not be removed, but the effect of such exploratory operation should be awaited.

3. *Supplementary or vicarious hæmaturia.*—With regard to this group, the cases which appear to warrant this classification are comparatively rare. It has been stated that hæmaturia may be vicarious of menstruation, hæmorrhoids, and asthma. Sir William Roberts mentions a single case of spasmodic asthma which disappeared suddenly on the occurrence of hæmaturia; and he also quotes from Dr. Basham the case of a shoemaker who was subject to attacks of hæmaturia, which always recurred on the occasion of his drunken wife's misconduct. Similar hæmaturia has been described as following fits of passion, and occurring spontaneously in acute mania and general paralysis.

Diagnosis.—The diagnosis of those cases in which the colour of the urine becomes so greatly altered does not generally offer very much difficulty. Mere examination of the urine, and even microscopical examination, may not help to any very great extent. If when blood-colouring matter is present, red corpuscles are absent, a strong presumption is raised in favour of paroxysmal hæmoglobinuria, and this is rendered more certain if the urine speedily regains its normal colour. On the other hand, the occurrence of casts containing red blood corpuscles will frequently leave the exact diagnosis an open question, since when the urine is acid casts are formed whenever transudation of blood occurs from the capillaries of the glomeruli. Casts, therefore, will only indicate that the blood is derived from the substance of the kidney without necessarily indicating the cause. More valuable assistance is to be obtained from the consideration of the history of the case. When sudden hæmaturia occurs after one of the acute exanthemata, there is a strong presumption in favour of the existence of acute nephritis. The co-existence of pain with the onset of hæmaturia will, if the pain is severe, favour the diagnosis of renal calculus, since with acute nephritis pain is frequently absent, or, if present, it is only of a dull, aching nature. Sharp pain, especially if it is sufficiently severe to cause collapse and vomiting, indicates spasm of the ureter and acute dilatation of the kidney. Much may be learned from the localisation and radiation of pain. When hæmaturia is dependent upon the presence of a stone in the bladder, the pain is often referred to the neck of the bladder, and is most intense during the act of micturition, especially in those cases in which this act becomes spasmodically arrested. The existence of coagulated blood in the urine indicates that the hæmorrhage has come from some part of the urinary tract below the kidney. Sometimes, in cases of renal calculus, long dark clots appear to be formed in the ureter, but in such cases the pain, which is referred to the course of the ureter, is sufficiently characteristic. When hæmorrhage occurs within the bladder as the result of malignant or villous growths, or of vesical calculus, clots are not uncommonly present, but these are then of irregular shape and size, and are frequently passed with difficulty.

Variations in the temperature in cases of hæmaturia mostly indicate the existence of an acute nephritis, but it is not uncommon to find this disease runs its course with very little alteration of temperature, unless it occurs as a complication or sequel of scarlet fever. On the other hand, with paroxysmal hæmoglobinuria the temperature is generally raised, and the patient presents the ordinary symptoms of malarial fever.

It is frequently somewhat difficult to distinguish between injuries and lacerations of the kidney and renal calculus. The accidents which might cause laceration might also be expected to dislodge a renal calculus, but the pain is not usually so severe in cases of traumatism.

Prognosis.—The prognosis in these cases necessarily depends upon the diagnosis. Traumatic cases generally recover, renal calculus tends to recur; and in the other conditions above enumerated the prognosis must necessarily be that of the disease which causes the appearance of the red colouring matter.

Treatment.—All cases of hæmaturia must be treated with rest in bed, which alone in a large majority will cause rapid diminution of urgent symptoms. Warmth is essential, more particularly in cases of acute nephritis and in paroxysmal hæmoglobinuria; while in the hæmaturia due to renal calculus, warmth will occasionally tend to relax spasm. Alterations in the diet must be adapted to the cause of the symptoms; for instance, while an exclusive milk diet is suitable for acute nephritis, it is unnecessary in the other varieties. It is impossible to lay down any general rule for the medicinal treatment of a symptom which depends upon such a variety of causes. In purpuric cases advantage is sometimes derived from the use of ergot, while other astringents, gallic acid, tannic acid, alum, and various preparations of iron are frequently employed. Obviously, in many of the cases above enumerated, medicinal treatment is wholly inapplicable, and surgical aid must be invoked.

CHAPTER III

HÆMOGLOBINURIA—CHYLURIA

UNDER the term hæmoglobinuria a curious condition has been described, in which the blood-colouring matter, hæmoglobin, is added to the urine, and gives all the appearance of blood until it is examined microscopically, when no blood discs are to be detected. Hæmoglobinuria is necessarily totally independent of any injury to the capillaries of the kidney, or of any part of the genito-urinary tract, and it is invariably accompanied by albuminuria, which sometimes appears to precede the appearance of the blood-colouring matter. The condition essentially depends upon rapid destruction of the red blood corpuscles, and in connection with this process the spleen generally becomes somewhat enlarged, while the work of both the liver and the kidney is interfered with.

The causes of hæmoglobinuria are extremely numerous. Those which are easiest to trace are connected with the action of various poisons. Vogel and others have stated that it follows the inhalation of arseniuretted hydrogen, and it has also been described with poisoning by hydrochloric acid, sulphuric acid, carbolic acid, pyrogallic acid, pyro-catechin, hydrochinon, resorcin, naphthol, nitro-benzol, iodine, and chlorate of potassium. Under the influence of these poisons the red corpuscles appear to be disintegrated with the liberation of the colouring matter in the blood serum. The influence of chlorate of potassium in the production of hæmoglobinuria is especially interesting, as this condition was at one time wrongly attributed to diphtheritic nephritis, when in reality it was produced by chlorate of potassium used medicinally. The toxic power of chlorate of potassium is now well recognised, and the albuminuria and hæmoglobinuria which occur when this drug is being used are not now likely to be misunderstood. Some authors have thought that the first influence of the drug consists in impairing or destroying the oxidising power of the red blood corpuscles, but a more recent theory is that the chief change consists in the transformation of hæmoglobin into methæmoglobin, which has no power of absorbing oxygen from the atmosphere. Chlorate of sodium has been stated to produce symptoms as serious as those resulting from chlorate of potassium, but the former substance not being so commonly employed, the symptoms have been less frequently observed. The possibility of producing urgent symptoms, with marked cyanosis and hæmoglobinuria, has to a large extent caused chlorate of potassium to be avoided as an internal remedy, and even when used as a gargle or a mouth-wash there may sometimes be danger from its absorption. Some of the recent antipyretics, more particularly the cold tar derivatives, produce destruction of red blood corpuscles and hæmoglobinuria.

Hæmoglobinuria has been described in the course of certain diseases, as, for example, typhoid, scarlet fever, small-pox and intermittent fevers—diseases which are in all probability associated with some definite toxic agent.

Dilution or alteration of the composition of the blood, resulting either from the injection of water or of salt solutions, or from the transfusion of the blood of other species, has caused destruction of red blood corpuscles with liberation of colouring matter and the production of hæmoglobinuria. According to Ponfick, experimental hæmoglobinuria produced from the latter cause results from the hæmoglobin of the transfused blood corpuscles being dissolved in the blood serum of the recipient animal.

Excessive irritation of the skin by severe burns, or as the result of lightning stroke, has led to similar destruction of red blood corpuscles in the injured parts, and the circulation of the altered blood has sometimes caused hæmoglobinuria, and at other times a genuine nephritis.

Hæmoglobinuria is frequently associated with some forms of malarial fever, and it occasionally occurs in connection with syphilis.

Baccelli[1] considers that in malaria the disintegration of the

[1] *Il Policlinico*, Jan. 15, 1897.

hæmoglobin is not due to the malarial parasite, but to its toxic products; and he further puts forward the interesting suggestion that besides hæmoglobinuria directly due to malaria, there are a certain number of cases of malaria where the administration of quinine, even in moderate doses, causes hæmoglobinuria. He considers that in order to produce this result it is not necessary that the attacks of malaria should be severe, and he thinks that the hæmoglobinuria may be due to quinine idiosyncrasy.

The influence of malaria in producing the appearance of blood or blood-colouring matter has come under my observation amongst those who have worked on the West Coast of Africa. One of our former students, who was attached to one of the stations on the West Coast, suffered from black water fever, and told me that this condition was extremely common amongst Europeans who were not acclimatised. In 1891 I saw another young medical man who had been at work in the Niger district, and who had had two attacks of malaria, with hæmoglobinuria. Although he was considerably reduced in strength both by the loss of hæmoglobin and by the weakening influence of the malaria, I found no trace of albumin in his water when I examined him a year after the last attack.

Another case under my care was that of an old soldier who had been in India and had suffered there from malarial fever, and also undoubtedly from syphilis. Blood-colouring matter appeared in the urine in large quantity without any pain, the patient merely complaining of shivering sensations and of slight rise of temperature. In this case the urine was dark brown, and no formed red corpuscles could be detected. The attacks of hæmoglobinuria recurred on three occasions while he remained under observation, and beyond the weakness caused by the destruction of red blood corpuscles, his attacks did not appear materially to affect his general health. I have occasionally seen this patient since, and there has been no return of the symptoms.

In the absence of all suspicion of malaria or syphilis, and as illustrating the production of this symptom from exposure to cold and over exertion, the following case which occurred in my private practice will probably be interesting.

A boy, aged 17, was brought to me in the winter of 1896,

with the history of having had five attacks of hæmaturia or hæmoglobinuria. The medical attendant stated that he had had hæmorrhage from the kidneys, which disappeared very readily. The account he gave of himself was that at Easter he caught a severe chill, which was not, however, followed by any definite symptoms; that he continued well until the early autumn, when he passed dark-coloured water on two occasions, the urine afterwards resuming its normal appearance. He said that he felt 'slack' the day before this occurred. On going home for his holidays he made no mention of the occurrence, until it was repeated twice after bathing when at the seaside, and it occurred twice more before I saw him. On the first occasion the urine was rather pale, specific gravity 1025, and it gave a faint line of opalescence with nitric acid and with trichloracetic acid. When examined microscopically, beautiful minute uric acid crystals were found in the deposit, but no casts. A second specimen, examined a fortnight later, had a specific gravity of 1030, and gave no reaction with either of the above tests. The pulse was normal, the heart sounds normal, and there were no retinal changes. This boy was born in India; but he had never to his knowledge suffered from any malarial affection. During the winter he had been doing a good deal of long-distance running with hare and hounds.

The minute trace of albumin on the first occasion when I examined him appeared to be referable to the albuminuria of adolescence, which is so often characterised by small traces of albumin in urine of high specific gravity and good colour. I have not yet had an opportunity of seeing this lad during one of the attacks, but the sudden appearance of dark urine, the total absence of pain, and the rapidity with which the urine regained its normal colour, leave very little doubt about the nature of the disease.

Symptoms.—The symptoms of hæmoglobinuria vary with the cause. When it is the result of toxic influences, the symptoms are primarily those produced by the specific poison, rather than those due to the altered condition of the urine. With poisonous doses of chlorate of potassium there is severe and increasing dyspnœa, together with marked cyanosis, the pulse is small and thready, and sometimes the conjunctivæ, the skin, and the urine become tinged with bile. In exceptional cases nervous symptoms develop, and coma may supervene.

On the other hand, the symptoms may be relatively slight when they result from malaria, or from exposure to cold; the patient may feel weakened or 'slack,' owing to the disorganisation of blood corpuscles, but may think little of his sensations until frightened by the appearance of the dark-coloured urine. Examination of the blood sometimes reveals marked changes in the red blood corpuscles, which are occasionally discoloured, and mixed with granular débris; the serum, in extreme cases, becoming tawny. As in hæmaturia, the degree of discoloration of the urine varies greatly; in some cases it is only light red, but frequently it may be more deeply tinged, so that it becomes dark brown, or even the colour of porter. On standing it deposits a dirty-brown sediment. Owing to the interference with the work of the kidney, especially with the excretion of urea, the specific gravity of the urine is greatly reduced, and, as already indicated, when jaundice is present, the urine, after the brown sediment has deposited, may be an olive-green colour from the presence of bile. When due to poisoning by chlorate of potassium, death may be preceded by anuria; this has been ascribed either to obstruction of the renal tubules with masses of hæmoglobin or to intense adynamia; it is interesting to compare this anuria with that sometimes seen in severe cases of diphtheria, which may similarly result from adynamia or possibly from the absorption of toxic material from the diphtheritic patch. Microscopic examination of the sediment in hæmoglobinuria shows the presence of much reddish-brown granular matter, often aggregated so as to form casts, which are sometimes numerous and of large size.

Paroxysmal hæmoglobinuria.—In 1865, in the 'Medical Chirurgical Transactions,' the late Dr. George Harley described two cases of paroxysmal hæmoglobinuria. Since that time very numerous observations of this condition have been made, and it has been called periodic, paroxysmal, or intermittent hæmoglobinuria; the names 'hæmoglobinuria à frigore' and 'winter hæmoglobinuria' have also been used to indicate the production of this condition by the influence of cold. It has been described by some authors as the result of a rheumatic tendency, or as being produced by over-exertion. Some observers consider that in the intervals of the attack the renal function is perfectly performed, while others think that the condition may lead on to definite renal changes.

Sir William Roberts has given a masterly summary of the symptoms of the cases which have been recorded. He states that the paroxysm usually commences with a feeling of cold or shivering, resembling the cold fit of ague, and terminates with the discharge of very dark bloody-looking urine. The symptoms improve after this has been passed, and the urine speedily resumes its natural healthy appearance. These paroxysms sometimes recur once a day or even oftener, but as a rule they return on alternate days or less frequently, and sometimes the length of the interval does not present any definite course. Like attacks of ague, the onset is usually sudden, and the first symptoms experienced are coldness of the extremities, general chilliness, and sometimes distinct rigors. Occasionally complaint may be made of a sense of weight or of a dull heavy pain in the loins, which may spread towards the umbilicus or pass down the thighs; there is also frequently pain or sense of stiffness or weakness in the lower extremities. Complaint of thirst, of headache and drowsiness, are sometimes made; retching is not uncommon, and vomiting has occasionally been described. These symptoms may continue for a varying period, rarely extending beyond two hours, and they are sometimes followed by a hot or sweating stage, during which a quantity of dark-coloured urine is passed, and thus the attack terminates, and the patient continues well until the next paroxysm. The appearance of the urine is generally very characteristic; its colour often resembles that of porter, though sometimes it is pervaded by a red tint. It is mostly turbid, and on standing deposits an abundant deep brown-coloured sediment. The specific gravity is generally fairly high, mostly ranging from 1020 to 1025, but it may be much lower or much higher. It contains an abundance of albumin, and when this has been coagulated by boiling and allowed to subside, the urine still retains a dark-red colour. The amount of urea may in some cases be in excess of the normal quantity, but this condition is not constant. The sediment is generally amorphous and granular, but dark granular casts are sometimes found. Crystals of hæmatin have been described as being occasionally present, while crystals of oxalate of lime are generally to be met with, and a few red blood corpuscles may at times be detected. Sir William Roberts states that the albumin and the hæmoglobin as a rule appear and disappear together, but Rosenbach, who was the first to show that hæmoglobinuria could be produced in men by the sudden cooling of the body as by a cold foot-bath, calls attention [1] to the fact that an excretion of albumin sometimes immediately precedes hæmoglobinuria as the result of cold, and he thinks the phenomenon may be explained in the following manner: The effect of cold is to destroy a certain number of red blood discs, and thus there is produced a certain amount of plasma useless for the immediate requirements of the organism; this plasma has therefore to be excreted, and this is partially accomplished by the liver, which uses the colouring matter in the preparation of bile, and partially by the kidneys, which separate the albumin only until the hæmoglobin from the destroyed corpuscles amounts to more than the liver alone can possibly use up, when the kidneys begin to separate it also.

Diagnosis.—Rosenbach suggests that the diagnosis of such cases may be aided by an examination of the fæces for increased bile secretion, which may be inferred from the conspicuously dark colour characteristic of such secretion. On the other hand, it has been stated that the albumin may sometimes persist after the disappearance of the hæmoglobin, and one case has been described in which the blood-colouring matter was present in the urine when no albumin could be detected. Coldness and cyanosis of the extremities of the nose and ears have been noted during the attack, and sometimes an eruption of urticaria occurs. The occasional increase in size of the liver and spleen during the attack may probably be explained by Rosenbach's hypothesis above mentioned. During the attack certain changes in the blood have been observed; for instance, the red corpuscles no longer tend to form rouleaux, they have also been found to be altered in shape, while Ponfick has described *phantom corpuscles*, that is, red corpuscles devoid of colouring matter. The

[1] *Berl. klin. Woch.*, Nov. 24, 1884.

temperature is generally somewhat raised during the paroxysm, but it may remain unchanged, or in some cases a slight fall may precede the rise. It has already been stated that during the intervals of the attack the patient may appear perfectly well, though the general health occasionally suffers. The patient sometimes appears sallow and slightly jaundiced, and at other times the general condition is one of anæmia. After the attacks the conjunctivæ are sometimes slightly yellowish, but this colour in all probability is due to a solution of hæmoglobin in the blood serum, rather than to a deposit of bile pigment. The disease appears to be more frequent amongst young adult males, and is probably hereditary, although its connection with tubercle, rheumatism, and gout is somewhat doubtful.

Prognosis.—The prognosis is generally favourable. Most of the cases which have been observed have completely recovered so far as could be ascertained, although it must be admitted that with a condition which may extend over months and even years it is difficult to say when restoration to health is complete. The immediate exciting cause of the disease has in some instances been traced to malarial poisoning, but in the majority the connection with exposure to wet or low temperatures has been clearly proved. The attacks may sometimes be averted by the avoidance of chills, as in the well-known case recorded by the late Sir George Johnson, in which the patient was free from paroxysms so long as he remained in bed. It is extremely doubtful whether the primary cause of this disease is due to any alteration in the blood or to some affection of the kidneys. Rosenbach and Lépine consider that the kidneys are primarily affected, but the majority of observers hold that the condition depends upon some alteration of the red blood corpuscles under the influence of cold. Ehrlich constricted the fingers of a person suffering from hæmoglobinuria with an elastic ligature, and then immersed them in cold water, and he found that the red corpuscles became disintegrated as the result. The absence of renal epithelium in the sediment appears sufficiently to indicate that the condition does not result from any form of true renal disease, and this contention is, moreover, supported by the normal character of the urine in the intervals between the attacks.

Treatment.—The treatment of paroxysmal hæmoglobinuria

is essentially unsatisfactory. Many remedies have been employed, but it may be doubted whether they have in any way materially influenced the course of the disease. From what has already been said it follows that patients with paroxysmal hæmoglobinuria must be kept in bed in a warm room; but, beyond this passive treatment, these cases tend to recover whatever measures are employed, and although cupping over the loins, vapour baths, quinine, gallic acid, and various forms of iron have been used, they do not appear to have essentially affected the hæmoglobinuria. Benefit has been claimed from the employment of mercurials and quinine, and also from fairly large doses of compound tincture of cinchona. Some improvement has also been claimed as the result of the administration night and morning of a powder containing tannic and gallic acids and burnt alum, together with a mixture containing quinine, sulphate of iron and sulphuric acid. Other drugs that have been employed are arsenic, perchloride of iron, syrup of iodide of iron, iodide of potassium, and chloride of ammonium. If there is a history of malaria or of syphilis, the effect of quinine, mercurials and iodide of potassium may well be tried. Such patients are generally advised to resort to a warm climate and to wear woollen clothing, and these hygienic measures seem to be of greater importance than the employment of drugs.

CHYLURIA.—This disease merits brief mention in this place, since it is almost invariably associated with traces of albumin in the urine, and there may also be indications of the presence of red blood corpuscles. It must not, however, be supposed, from its inclusion here, that the disease is, in any sense, dependent upon structural changes in the kidney. In the somewhat scanty records of *post-mortem* examinations the kidney is usually said to have been normal, though in one case it was the site of tubercular changes; a further argument against renal affection is to be found in the invariable absence of casts in the urine.

Two forms of Chyluria have been described:

1. Non-Parasitic.   2. Parasitic.

Of these the latter is by far the more frequent, and indeed many observers maintain that all cases of chyluria are to be regarded as of parasitic origin. This contention, however, fails to explain some well-authenticated observations by Dr. Osler, and some cases recorded by Sir William Roberts, Dr. Saundby and others, where the affection has occurred in temperate regions, and in connection with which the efforts to prove the presence of a parasite have been unsuccessful.

Etiology.—Very little is known of the etiology of the non-parasitic class. The condition has sometimes been attributed to pregnancy, and it has been assumed that pressure of the gravid uterus, combined in one case with unduly tight clothing, caused rupture of dilated lymphatics, with the escape of lymph or chyle into the urine. Another case with mitral disease was attributed to hepatic obstruction.

The parasitic cases are widely distributed in tropical and sub-tropical countries; they have been met with in India, China, the Mauritius, the West Indies, and in the Southern States of America, and they appear to be frequent in Queensland and in Samoa. They depend upon the development of the *filaria sanguinis hominis*, for the history of which we are largely indebted to the researches of J. R. Lewis, Bancroft, and Patrick Manson. The adult female worm which lives in the lymphatics is from three to three and a half inches long, and only one-hundredth of an inch broad; it looks like 'a delicate thread of catgut, animated and wriggling.' The male worm is much smaller, and has only occasionally been found. Embryos, in extraordinary number, enter the blood current through the lymphatics. They vary from $\frac{1}{75}$ to $\frac{1}{90}$ of an inch in length, and they are about the breadth of a red blood corpuscle. When prematurely discharged, the ova are very much shorter and thicker, and it has been suggested that it is to this form that the obstruction of lymph channels is due, since the full-grown embryos may be present in the body without causing any symptoms. The appearance of embryos in the blood occurs with curious periodicity; they are as a rule relatively or entirely absent during the day, and numerous at night; it has been shown, however, that when the patient sleeps during the day and takes his meals at night, the periodicity is reversed. Manson found that the further life history of the filariæ was connected with the mosquito; they were found in the stomach of mosquitoes which had gorged upon a Chinaman known to have filariæ in his blood, and after four or five days they had developed rudimentary generative organs, an alimentary canal and a mouth with three or four nipple-like papillæ. In this state, possibly, they fall into water, which may subsequently be used for drinking purposes. The duration of life of the adult worm is apparently very great; Osler mentions a case which lasted intermittently for eighteen years; living filariæ have been found in the blood of a man aged fifty, who had had lymph-scrotum from the age of eighteen, and in another case chylous urine was passed by a native of Mauritius from the age of twenty-five to that of seventy-three. It was then absent for fourteen months; after this interval it returned and continued to the age of seventy-eight.

Symptoms.—Both the non-parasitic and the parasitic forms of chyluria are marked by the same general symptoms. The patient passes opaque white urine, which may either have a slight reddish tint or may be more obviously mixed with blood; shortly after it has been passed the urine forms a firm jelly-like mass, which a little later liquefies and breaks up into flaky clots, while a cream-like material rises to the surface, and a pinkish sediment gradually falls. When shaken with ether the urine becomes clear, and on subsequent evaporation the ethereal solution leaves a large quantity of fat. Traces, or even a large amount of albumin may be found by the heat and nitric acid test. In some cases the quantity of urine may be normal, but it is generally increased. When examined microscopically, granular nucleated corpuscles, some few red blood corpuscles, and numerous minute granules are found. The granules represent the fatty matter, and in exceptional cases they may form visible oil globules. The absence of casts from a fluid which so readily coagulates sufficiently indicates that the chylous admixture does not proceed from the renal vessels.

The appearance of chylous urine is often intermittent; weeks, months, or even years, during which time the urine is normal, may intervene between the different attacks; it is sometimes more persistent, but the amount of coagulum generally varies from day to day, and is often increased after meals. Cases have been recorded in which the day urine almost completely coagulated and contained much blood, while the night urine did not form so large a coagulum and was more milky, and reference has already been made to the curious reversal of these conditions, with total change of habits.

The coagulation may occasionally occur within the bladder, so that the urine is only passed with great pain and straining. Uneasy sensations in the lumbar region have also been recorded.

Though the general health may be but little affected, especially when the disease is intermittent and when there is not much loss by hæmaturia, yet some cases are marked by great weakness and wasting, and occasionally by great increase of appetite and thirst.

The explanation of the disease is generally considered to be an obstruction in some of the lymphatic vessels or lacteals by the immature ova of the filaria; when the coagulum is opaque the lacteals coming from the intestine are probably involved. The obstruction leads to distension of lymphatics in some part of the bladder, ureter or renal pelvis, with consequent admixture of lymph or chyle with the urine.

It is unnecessary to take up space here in dealing with the diagnosis of a disease marked by such definite symptoms, though it is undoubtedly interesting to prove the parasitic origin of most cases by the examination of the blood and the recognition of the filariæ. What has already been said of the usually prolonged course of the disease leaves little room for prognostic considerations. When patients are greatly weakened they may readily fail with any intercurrent disease, but otherwise the duration may be almost indefinite.

The treatment is, as a whole, most unsatisfactory. Some benefit has been attributed to gallic acid, and to other astringents taken internally, and in one case the symptoms appeared to be arrested by injections of perchloride of iron into the bladder. Tonic modes of treatment are naturally indicated, but, apart from the improvement of the general health, they have no influence whatever upon the chyluria.

CHAPTER IV

RENAL CASTS

SINCE renal casts were first described by Henle in 1844 a large amount of attention has been devoted to them, and at one time it was hoped that their characters might form sure and certain indications of the nature of the renal disease, and even of the stage which had been reached in any individual case. Increased experience has shown that these hopes are to a large extent fallacious, and that, while the presence of casts in the urine does not necessarily prove an anatomical lesion of the kidneys, their absence is equally no proof that such lesion does not exist. In many cases of advanced renal disease the most diligent search may fail to demonstrate the existence of casts in the urine, even though the clinical picture is perfectly clear, and the nature of the case may be rendered certain by its subsequent course, and the diagnosis confirmed by *post-mortem* examination. In general, however, whenever true renal albuminuria exists, casts can be found in the urine, and although the appearance of these casts may vary considerably at different times, they may frequently afford very material help in estimating the nature of the changes in the renal epithelium, and thus may assist largely, not only in the diagnosis, but also in the prognosis.

It is as a rule customary, when examining for renal casts, to allow some five or six ounces of the urine to stand for several hours in a conical-shaped vessel, and to withdraw a small quantity of deposit by means of a pipette. This is then examined in a shallow cell, and it is never advisable, when examining unstained fluids, to use a strong light, as it may sometimes increase the difficulty of recognising the outlines of some varieties of casts. This method of examining may occasionally fail to demonstrate casts, even though a few may have been found in the same specimen of urine immediately after it was passed; for although it has long been recognised that the development of micro-organisms in the urine may speedily cause destruction of renal casts, yet they have been known to disappear when no such rapid putrefactive changes had occurred. Sehrwald [1] has suggested an interesting explanation for such cases. He considers that this diminution or disappearance of casts must depend either upon a modification of the state of the kidneys, or upon some alteration in the nature and composition of the urine. He does not believe it can be due to a modification of the state of the kidneys, since the disappearance of casts is not followed by any alteration in the quantity of the urine or of the albumin. He maintains that ferments exist in the urine, one of which has an action analogous to that of pepsine. He found, by testing the urine every hour in a case of parenchymatous nephritis, that the quantity of casts varied considerably in the course of the day, and that decrease in the amount of the pepsin-like ferment in the urine coincided with diminution in the proportion of casts. He suggests that the peptic power of urine may begin in the kidney and favour the detachment and excretion of casts, even though it may ultimately lead to their complete destruction, if the water is left to settle too long after being passed. He has noted that in the cases of disappearance of casts, the sediment shows, upon microscopic examination, a large quantity of granules collected in masses, free nuclei, and a few short, twisted, pale casts, and these, he believes, favour the theory of a digestion of the casts by the urine, either inside or outside the bladder, when the urine is kept in a warm place.

To avoid this source of error it is now usual to examine the urine as soon as possible after it has been passed, and the necessary separation of deposit may be readily effected by a centrifuge. Another method that has been recommended is the filtration of urine through very fine, smooth blotting-paper, and the subsequent examination of the residue left upon the filter.

Numerous classifications of casts have been suggested, and the following will perhaps be found useful, yet it must be remembered that the different varieties may often be

[1] *Deutsche Wochenschr.*, No 24, 1890.

met with in a single case, and that transitional forms are very common.

1. *Blood casts.*   2. *Epithelial casts.*   3. *Hyaline casts.*
4. *Metamorphosed casts*, including (*a*) *Granular and fatty casts.* (*b*) *Hard waxy, or amyloid casts.*

1. *Blood casts.*—These are composed of red blood corpuscles and fibrin, and they result from the coagulation of blood within the tubules. They are the only casts to which the term 'fibrin casts' can properly be applied, since the other varieties generally consist of albumin, together with some form of protein. The hæmorrhage which has contributed to the formation of blood casts mostly proceeds from engorged and ruptured capillaries of the Malpighian tuft. As the blood passes down the tubules it coagulates, and hence assumes the form of cylindrical casts of the tubules.

2. *Epithelial casts* are largely composed of epithelial cells derived from the tubules, and result from rapid proliferation and desquamation of the renal epithelium. In most cases they appear to have a basis of hyaline material, in which the epithelial cells are entangled. Sometimes the cells resemble leucocytes, though they are somewhat smaller. They appear as distinct, round, granular bodies with definite outlines, though sometimes, when the cells are more closely packed together, not only are their outlines lost, but the nuclei also may be rendered indistinct.

3. *Hyaline casts* are colourless, transparent, and homogeneous; they may be slightly striated, and perhaps dotted with bright, highly refractile spots, or they may be more or less opaque from fatty degeneration. From their transparency they are often very difficult to find, especially if the urine is examined under a strong light, but sometimes by reducing the size of the diaphragm they may be rendered evident. They readily take up various colouring matters, such as carmine, aniline dyes, or iodine and picric acid. They are found almost solely in acid urine; the addition of an alkali or the spontaneous development of an alkaline reaction in the urine causing them to disappear very rapidly.

4. *Metamorphosed casts*, as the term implies, are the result of changes occurring in any of the preceding. The formation of

granular and fatty casts is due to degenerative changes: the outlines of the epithelial cells, and of their nuclei, become indistinct, and as disintegration proceeds they are replaced by granular matter, which frequently assumes a dark-brown tint. Occasionally, further metamorphosis causes the granular matter to become homogeneous and hyaline; the casts then become more refractive and more compact, and are termed *hard waxy* casts. They are also said by Bartels occasionally to give the amyloid reaction, but this is very rare.

Casts vary in size from $\frac{1}{2500}$ to $\frac{1}{500}$ of an inch in diameter, the size depending partly upon the size of the tubule in which they are formed, and partly upon the degree to which desquamation of its epithelial lining has progressed. They are generally formed in the convoluted tubes, though sometimes they appear to originate within the straight tubes. However formed, or whatever their appearance, it is necessary to remember that several varieties of casts are commonly present in every case, and that their pathological significance, as Sir William Roberts observes, must be deduced from the prevailing types, rather than from the absence or presence of one or two of a particular character. In addition to the transitional forms of casts other peculiarities may be noted: crystals of oxalate of lime, of urates or of uric acid, may be entangled in the hyaline substance of the cast, or may be adherent to its surface, and micro-organisms may be densely grouped.

In general, casts are short, straight, and of the same diameter throughout, the extremities are blunt and truncated; but sometimes, if of considerable length, they may become filamentous and filiform, and they then much resemble the mucoid cylindroids. Vierordt has described a form of dichotomic or branching cast, but these I have never been able to detect: on the other hand, the curved form described by V. Jaesch is fairly common. Although hyaline casts mostly appear homogeneous, and look like little solid plugs, I have occasionally found that they gave the impression of being hollow cylinders, as when seen in optical section they have a double outline which seems inconsistent with any other formation, and under such circumstances the irregularity of the extremity of the casts further favours the idea of their hollow nature.

Origin of renal casts.—Casts may be formed in various ways. Blood casts are undoubtedly formed by coagulation of extravasated blood, though sometimes the so-called blood casts are really hyaline casts containing red blood corpuscles. Langhans[1] thinks that hyaline casts are formed from epithelial casts, and he has described a colloid metamorphosis by which epithelial cells become wholly or partly hyaline or glass-like in appearance. Although the fourth group of metamorphosed casts undoubtedly originates in this way, the theory is not universally applicable. Thus Fagge notes the very short time which sometimes passes between the commencement of a morbid change in the kidney and the appearance of casts in the urine, and he thinks this affords a strong argument in favour of the view that renal casts arise by coagulation of exuded plasma.

In some cases they appear in the urine a few hours, or even a day or two, before albumin is discoverable. In the urine of *jaundiced* patients casts of a greenish-yellow colour are often found, and Dr. Finlayson says that, as a rule, in such cases no albumin is present.

The abundance of casts in a case of Bright's disease is usually proportionate to the amount of albumin in the urine; but to this rule there are exceptions, and in the same patient the number of casts may vary from day to day.

It has been suggested that fibrin is formed by the action of the dead epithelium on the fibrinogen of the blood serum; but this is improbable, since casts are soluble in distilled water, especially when the water is warmed, and they do not increase in size on the addition of acetic acid. It is therefore far more probable that, as Fagge suggests, they are due to coagulation of albumin, though whether this coagulation is effected by acidulation of the renal epithelium (Saundby) or by the acid urine still remains doubtful. Upon this point Saundby quotes the following interesting experiment: Ribbert tied the renal artery of a rabbit for $1\frac{1}{2}$ hour, and then injected a weak $2\frac{1}{2}$ per cent. solution of acetic acid into the jugular vein. After boiling the excised kidney he found Bowman's capsules filled with a hyaline mass, and after hardening in alcohol this mass became granular. He also boiled an albuminuric kidney in acidulated water, with

[1] Virchow's *Archiv*, Bd. lxxvi.

the result that beautiful hyaline masses were formed in it; uric acid, phosphoric acid, and hydrochloric acid gave equally good results, but urea did as well, so that acidulation *per se* does not appear to be the essential condition. Ribbert also made intravenous injections of carmine; the carmine was excreted by the glomeruli, and appeared not only in the albumin of the capsules, but also in the casts, while the renal epithelium remained unchanged. This experiment goes far towards proving that casts result from the coagulation of albumin which has transuded from the glomeruli.

After ligature of the ureter in rabbits, Aufrecht found hyaline casts within the tubules, though the epithelium and the blood-vessels appeared intact. Hence it has been inferred that casts might result from an exudation or a secretion from the epithelium of the tubules. Although intermediate stages have been described and figured, in which the lumen of the tubules is filled by exuded droplets or globules together with a homogeneous plasma, yet Fürbringer states that, according to recent researches, these globular formations are also found under normal circumstances in the tubuli uriniferi. Saundby believes casts are very rarely formed by transudation, and he bases his opinion upon their rarity in so-called functional albuminuria. He holds that where there is only *congestion*, casts should be formed by *transudation*, but where *inflammatory* conditions are present, by *secretion*.

The *clinical significance* of renal casts is based partly upon their number, and partly upon the predominant type or types. *Blood casts* always indicate acute engorgement of the Malpighian tufts, and when they are associated with desquamated renal epithelium and with minute uric acid crystals, and when they occur in urine which is much reduced in quantity, they may be taken as almost certain evidences of an acute nephritis, either primary or secondary to a chronic nephritis.

Epithelial casts are generally indicative of a disease of recent origin. They are generally found in urine which is reduced in quantity, and contains in addition free renal epithelium, red blood corpuscles, and leucocytes. They indicate the proliferation and desquamation of the renal epithelium, which is the constant accompaniment of acute renal inflammation.

Hyaline casts are those which give rise to the greatest uncertainty, and at the same time they are by far the commonest. They may result from any form of Bright's disease. In rare cases they may be the precursors of blood casts, and of epithelial casts in acute nephritis; frequently they are found at a later stage mingled with blood casts and epithelial casts. They may be present in any congested condition of the kidney, as in chronic valvular disease of the heart; they may indicate the slighter forms of irritation, as in jaundice, diabetes, and pregnancy. In jaundice it is probable that the excretion of bile has injured the renal epithelium; while in diabetes casts mostly indicate the onset of structural renal change consecutive, not only to the overwork due to the large amount of water, but also to the irritation due to the sugar. They are occasionally seen in the dietetic forms of albuminuria, as well as in conjunction with lithuria and oxaluria, and they have also been described in connection with prolonged muscular exertion. Small quantities of delicate hyaline casts may sometimes be met with in the so-called physiological albuminuria, and in the albuminuria of adolescence, conditions possibly dependent upon circulatory abnormalities; as a rule, however, they are absent.

Metamorphosed casts, granular, fatty, and waxy, occur in the later stages of acute nephritis, and in all forms of chronic nephritis. The appearance of these casts in the course of an acute nephritis mostly indicates the transition from the acute to the chronic stage. If the majority are of small diameter they do not call for any special anxiety, but when a number of large sized granular and fatty casts are present, they cause much uneasiness, and point to the establishment of chronic disease, since they are formed in tubes denuded of epithelium. Still, there is no doubt that Sir George Johnson is correct in saying that the appearance of oily casts and cells excites less alarm now than formerly. It is true they indicate that in certain parts of the kidney the secreting cells and the inflammatory exudations are undergoing fatty transformation, but it is well known that all parts of the kidney are rarely simultaneously or equally affected; hence, in spite of advanced disease in some portion of the kidney, sufficient healthy tissue may be left for the maintenance of life without discomfort. Sir George Johnson has seen many cases of complete recovery after oily casts and cells in great numbers had appeared in the urine continuously for many weeks.

That it is unsound to attempt to dogmatise from the nature of casts is now the opinion of most observers; thus Dr. Lionel Beale says:[1] 'Dr. Basham thinks he can judge of the stage of Bright's disease by the character of the urinary sediment. I wish I could agree with him in this conclusion. The more carefully the matter is investigated, the more convinced am I that it is unsafe in many cases to attempt to draw inferences as to the stage of the disease from the character of the urinary sediment only. Nothing but a careful consideration of every point connected with the case will enable us to arrive at a general conclusion concerning the state of the disease. Dr. Basham says: "The most untractable and hopeless form of *morbus Brightii* is that represented by the presence of the fatty or oily cast." This statement requires some qualification, for although it is quite true that some of these cases are terribly and rapidly fatal, it must be admitted that some live for twenty years or more, and die at last of other disorders.' Sir J. Grainger Stewart says, in his work on 'Bright's Disease,' casts 'are of undoubted value in establishing the existence of Bright's disease, considered generically, but they afford comparatively little assistance in the differential diagnosis of the different forms. Any form of tube cast may occur in any form of the disease, and at almost any stage. Indeed, all the leading varieties may occur simultaneously in one case.'

In dealing with cases of suspected renal disease it must be remembered that neither the absence of casts, nor even the absence of albumin, precludes the existence of chronic affections. In the worst cases of contracted kidney renal casts are often sought in vain. The most definite symptoms of uræmia, convulsions, coma, and renal asthma may be present, in fact patients may die of Bright's disease, and yet the most careful and repeated examinations may have failed to show tube casts, although albumin may have been constantly present in the urine.

Conversely, casts may sometimes be found in urinary deposits when the tests ordinarily employed fail to detect albumin. This condition may occur during the stage of convalescence

[1] *Kidney Diseases, Urinary Deposits, and Calculous Disorders.*

after scarlatinal nephritis, and even in the course of chronic nephritis casts may occasionally be seen in the intervals when no albumin can be found. Sometimes the same unexpected occurrence is met with in cases of renal engorgement from valvular disease of the heart, from chronic bronchitis or from emphysema, conditions which are more commonly associated with a fair proportion of albumin.

Without denying the importance of renal casts, Fürbringer thinks that other deposits are often of even more significance than the casts themselves, for, to use Frerichs' expressive phrase, they are the ' forerunners of processes in the kidneys.' The significance of renal epithelium is sufficiently obvious. Numerous leucocytes denote inflammation, red corpuscles are indicative of hæmorrhage, and oil globules, especially in connection with oily casts, indicate degeneration of the renal epithelium.

In conclusion, it may be stated that, notwithstanding all the above reservations, renal casts often afford the best and clearest indications of the nature of the changes that are affecting some part of the gland tissue, even though they do not and can not give any clue to the extent to which the whole of the kidney is affected.

CHAPTER V

ACUTE NEPHRITIS

NUMEROUS names have been used for the condition at present under discussion. It has been termed acute tubal nephritis, croupous nephritis, acute desquamative nephritis, acute parenchymatous nephritis, acute infective nephritis, and acute Bright's disease. All of these terms, however, are open to objection, as they indicate a form of inflammation which spreads more or less symmetrically over the whole of the kidney. It is important to remember that, owing to the somewhat irregular supply of blood to the glomeruli, the inflammation which is characteristic of this condition consists, as Fürbringer has pointed out, of an inflammation of more or less confluent localisations, which are, however, separated from each other by intervals of healthy tissue. Many of the names above enumerated are unsatisfactory in fixing the attention too much upon a portion only of the pathological change, and it is therefore preferable to employ the term 'acute nephritis,' which is more free from objection.

Etiology.—The influence of age is somewhat marked in connection with acute inflammation of the kidneys; it occurs mostly in young adults, though it is occasionally seen in early middle age. It is more frequent amongst males than amongst females, and this is probably to be explained by the former being more liable to exposure to the various conditions under which the disease arises. It is also more common amongst the middle and labouring classes, owing to the general circumstances of their occupations, their clothing, and their habits. Amongst young adults, cold is one of the most common causes of acute nephritis, and it is the more likely to produce this disease when the individual has been exhausted with work or exercise, or when the skin has been actively perspiring. The sudden contraction of the cutaneous vessels under these circumstances is likely to be followed by internal engorgement, which starts the subsequent changes in the kidney. Amongst the labouring classes, the danger of contracting acute nephritis is greatest when the work is irregular in character, leading to great muscular activity for a short time, and involving subsequent chill while in a state of perspiration. It has also been frequently produced by cold and wet, affecting those who are heated by hunting, or by cycling; while exposure after dissipation has also resulted in this disease. Amongst children it is relatively rare to find acute nephritis attributable to cold, unless the individual has previously suffered from one of the exanthemata, notably scarlet fever. Dr. Ralfe states that he never succeeded in obtaining a history of exposure to cold and wet in a case of acute nephritis occurring in childhood; in fact it must be admitted that the disease is rare amongst children, unless as a consecutive malady. I have, nevertheless, seen three or four cases at the Evelina Hospital in which the closest inquiry failed to prove the previous occurrence of scarlet fever, while the history of chill was perfectly distinct. The influence of cold has been challenged, however, both on theoretical and experimental grounds. Theoretically, it has been urged that it is unsatisfactory, as the mode of action is so difficult to explain, while many observers maintain they have been unable to meet with a single case where the origin could clearly be attributed only to cold. From the experimental side comes the strong argument of the failure to influence the renal circulation by the application of hot or cold water to the skin of animals. Theoretical and experimental objections can have little weight when compared with clinical observation, and the balance of this experience, amongst those who have treated riverside labourers and dock hands, tells strongly in favour of the etiological importance of cold and wet in the production of acute nephritis.

Next in importance as an etiological factor stand various febrile diseases, such as small-pox, measles, erysipelas, typhoid, and pneumonia. The nephritis caused by these maladies is sometimes slight and abortive, and is limited chiefly to the time of the pyrexia. Such mild cases have already been referred to under the heading of 'Febrile Albuminuria.' Occasionally, however, acute nephritis associated with these diseases may be accompanied by the more prominent symptoms of the serious malady, such as dropsy and hæmaturia.

Henoch[1] has recorded four cases of nephritis which were apparently the result of chicken-pox. The attacks of chicken-pox were accompanied by moderate fever, and the nephritis ensued from eight to ten days after the onset, and was marked by albuminuria, pallor, and œdema of the face, hands, and feet. On the seventeenth day one of the four cases terminated fatally with œdema of the lungs, and moderate hypertrophy and dilatation of the left ventricle.

The frequent connection of these diseases with renal changes led to the employment of the term 'acute infective nephritis,' under the idea that the pathological condition was the result of an inflammation excited by bacteria. It is now known that micro-organisms are absent in most cases of nephritis, and it is generally held that the renal changes are due to the action of toxic materials resulting from the growth of the specific organisms within the body.

M. Vignerot,[2] while combating the direct etiological action of cold in the production of nephritis, makes the interesting suggestion that in infective diseases certain alterations in the kidney are produced by micro-organisms, and that these changes may sometimes pass away without leaving any trace; while in other cases they may become chronic, leading to changes in the epithelial elements and to proliferation in the interstitial tissue. He thinks that cold probably gives an impulse to a morbid condition already present, and he argues that it is difficult to conceive how a simple and momentary congestion, brought about reflexly, could produce a true nephritis without pre-existing alteration in the kidney.

Numerous drugs may cause acute nephritis, especially those which are absorbed into the blood and eliminated by the kidney. Prominent amongst these may be reckoned cantharides, turpentine, copaiba, phosphorus, and alcohol. The acute nephritis due to alcohol is sometimes of short duration, as in the case referred to by Sir George Johnson, where profuse hæmaturia resulted from a drinking bout. It is undoubted, however, that irritation

---

[1] *Berlin. klin. Woch.*, No. 2, 1883.　　　[2] *Arch. Gén. de Méd.*, Oct. 1891.

started by means of alcohol may be rendered more serious and more persistent if, at the same time, the individual is exposed to cold. Mostly, however, the influence of toxic agents is limited to the production of a temporary congestion leading to albuminuria or hæmaturia, rather than to the establishment of a true nephritis.

Extensive injury to the skin by disease, by burns, or by a lightning stroke, may sometimes excite acute nephritis. For these cases various explanations have been offered. Some hold that they are due to the direct interference with the functions of the skin, and the non-elimination and consequent retention in the blood of deleterious excretory products, while others suggest that the injury causes a general depression of the temperature of the body in consequence of the great loss of heat, and that it acts in the same way as a continued obstruction of the orifices of the sweat glands by cooling the uninjured skin.

It will be observed that in the above account very little mention has been made of scarlatinal nephritis, which is reserved for later consideration. Apart from this condition, the majority of cases of acute nephritis met with amongst young adults are to be attributed to exposure to cold.

Morbid anatomy.—The morbid anatomy of any form of Bright's disease may be most conveniently studied if we remember that the different structures of which the kidney is composed may frequently be affected independently, and that when different structures are concurrently affected, the extent to which each part is involved is liable to great variations. Thus the tubules and their epithelium, which together constitute the parenchyma of the kidney, sometimes show the most marked alterations, and this is especially seen in most of the acute forms of kidney disease. In more chronic conditions the interstitial tissue, which in the healthy kidney is only present in small quantity, may increase considerably as the result of inflammatory processes; and thirdly, the blood vessels and the glomeruli appear liable to separate affection, and indeed the epithelial cells which coat the capillaries of the glomerulus have been described as undergoing an inflammatory process which, for some authors, constitutes the primary and perhaps the most important change in the kidney when diseased.

In acute nephritis the primary changes are undoubtedly connected with the tubules and the glomeruli, and these changes are found to be fairly constant when the kidney is examined microscopically, although the size, shape, and the general appearance of the kidney are largely dependent upon the stage the disease has reached when death occurs. Sometimes the kidney is very little larger than the normal, the cortex is of a dark colour, and the glomeruli stand out as minute pale spots. Sometimes the kidney is increased considerably in size, it may indeed be swollen to almost twice its normal bulk. It then has a more rounded appearance than usual; the capsule can be separated easily, and the surface is pale. On section, the increase in size is found to be due mainly to an increase in the thickness of the cortex, which is of a greyish-red colour, while the central portion, the pyramids, are of a deeper red, owing to the congestion of their vessels. Frequently, both on the surface and on section, bright red spots are found scattered through the kidney. Sometimes these are due to minute hæmorrhages, sometimes to engorgement of the glomeruli.

In a third variety of acute nephritis the degree of congestion is very much greater, so that the colour is dark red or brown, and on section the kidneys have been described as 'dripping with blood.'

On examination microscopically, changes are found both within the tubes, in the interstitial tissue, and within the glomeruli, although the extent to which each anatomical division is affected varies considerably in different cases. The change within the tubes mostly consists in a peculiar opaque appearance of the epithelial cells; these may be swollen and granular, or they may be filled with fat granules, and they frequently tend to separate readily from the wall of the tubule. The lumen of the tubule is often obliterated by *débris* of altered epithelial cells, leucocytes and coagulated albuminous fluid; and sometimes the tubules appear to be blocked with a compact mass of blood corpuscles. Hyaline, epithelial, and blood casts are often seen within the tubes, both in the cortex and in the looped tubules of the pyramids. When the kidneys are large, it is frequently found that leucocytes have exuded from the blood-vessels, and that they have been accompanied by an inflammatory fluid; these

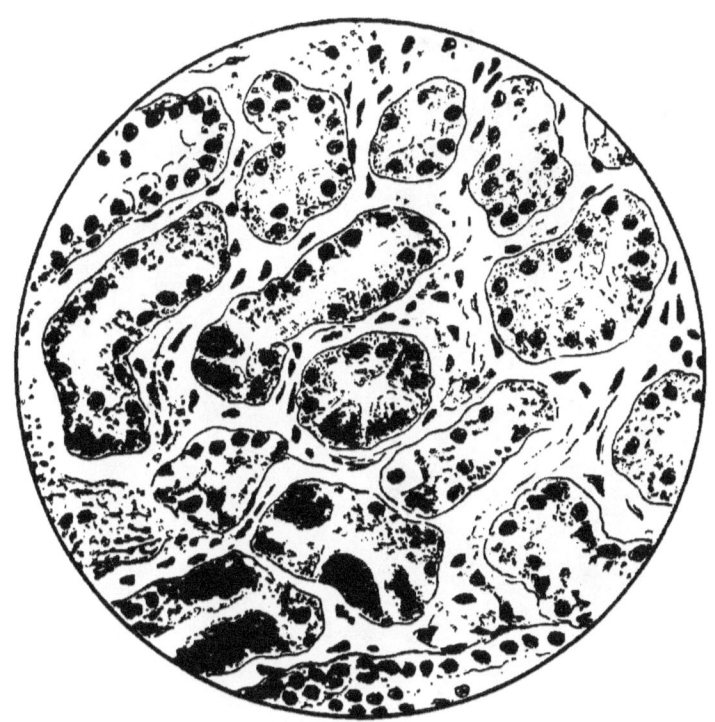

Section of Tubules in Acute Nephritis, showing Epithelial changes. The epithelial cells are granular, much swollen, and encroach upon the lumen of the tubules. The outlines of the cells are indefinite in some parts. The intertubular tissues are not materially altered.

(*See p.* 96.)

N. Tirard, Del.   Mintern Bros., imp.

inflammatory exudations are most marked in the neighbourhood of the Malpighian capsules. The glomerular changes, upon which some authors have so much insisted, have been described as a form of capsulitis. The capsule is distended by a finely granular mass, enclosing numerous small nuclei, and sometimes hæmorrhages occur within the capsule. From both of these conditions it is reasonable to assume that the glomerular tuft has been subjected to considerable pressure, which must necessarily have interfered with the circulation through the capillaries, as well as with the excretion of water. Klebs, Klein, and Greenfield consider that the nuclei of the capillary tufts in the glomerulus proliferate, and that this proliferation is accompanied by an excessive growth of nuclei within the capsule, which leads to adhesion between it and the glomerulus, and ultimately to compression and atrophy of the latter. These lesions are sometimes limited to a few of the glomeruli, but they have been also described as affecting a very large proportion of them. This condition has been termed glomerulo-nephritis, and it appears to be most common in the form of acute nephritis consecutive to scarlet fever. In such cases the lesions within the tubules have been considered to be secondary to the abolition of the work of the glomerulus. Glomerulo-nephritis is not, however, peculiar to scarlatinal cases, for Cohnheim, quoted by Fagge, has met with a typical example of it in the case of a man who died some weeks after having had his skin rubbed all over with petroleum for four consecutive days.

The transition from the morbid anatomy of acute nephritis to that of chronic nephritis is extremely ill-defined, and this doubtless is the explanation of the great variation in the appearances which have been described. To this subject, however, it will be necessary to return when dealing with the morbid anatomy of chronic nephritis.

Symptoms.—The commencement of acute nephritis after exposure to cold is indicated by chills, or even slight rigors, which are followed by a varying period of pyrexia. The temperature may be only slightly raised, or it may reach 103° or 104°. Whatever the mode of onset, the subsequent course of the pyrexia is never typical. During this preliminary modification of temperature, the pulse rate is proportionately raised, and its volume may sometimes be increased. When the nephritis originates in one of the infectious diseases (with the exception of scarlet fever) the onset is rarely marked by such unmistakable symptoms, and unless the urine is tested from day to day, the commencement of this complication may escape observation. From the beginning the tongue is commonly furred, and the bowels are somewhat constipated.

The urine.—Almost from the first there is notable diminution in the quantity of urine passed, and occasionally the excretion of urine appears to be totally arrested. When the disease is fully established, the amount generally varies from six to sixteen ounces in the twenty-four hours, and in spite of this diminution in quantity the patient is troubled by a frequent desire to micturate, only a few drops of urine being passed at a time with much straining. The specific gravity of the water is increased, and it may be found as high as 1030 or 1040, although these alterations are largely dependent upon the quantity passed. So soon as signs of improvement commence and the quantity is augmented, the specific gravity falls more nearly to the normal. Generally, during the acute stage, the reaction of the urine is acid, and quantities of albumin are present. Mahomed described a *pre-albuminuric* stage in which, although no albumin was present, the blood-colouring matter could be detected by the guaiacum test, and he attached much importance to an increase of arterial tension as indicating the onset of this condition. The colour is dark reddish-brown, turbid and smoky, indicating the presence of blood-colouring matter, and the sediment, which is abundant, is composed largely of blood casts, blood corpuscles, renal epithelium and granular urates. The relative proportion of these constituents is subject to considerable variation, according to the stage of the disease. Blood corpuscles and epithelial cells generally predominate, but casts are always present, though their prevailing type changes as the disease progresses. During the early stages, blood casts and epithelium casts are especially numerous, but when the case is becoming more chronic, granular casts and fatty casts replace them, and hence afford valuable indications of the stage of the disease. In spite of the high specific gravity of the urine, the daily elimination of solids is generally diminished, and, as has been already indicated, the specific gravity is dependent on the altered quantity of liquid, instead of being due to an increased elimination of solids. The urea is decreased in quantity from 25 per cent. to 50 per cent., and the chlorides similarly undergo great diminution. During the early stage of the disease, complaint may sometimes be made of uneasiness or discomfort in the region of the kidneys. This may occasionally amount to actual pain, extending thence along the ureters towards the bladder, but pain, when present, is mostly connected with the act of micturition, rather than with the degree of inflammation of the kidney. As a general rule, renal affections of prolonged course are not associated with pain, and this fact to a certain extent is to be explained by the comparative absence of nerves of common sensation in connection with the kidney. There is, it is true, a free supply of sensory nerves to the capsule and the pelvis of the kidney, but these are only likely to be influenced by affections causing sudden distension of the kidney, and the general characteristic of inflammatory diseases of the kidney is for the pain or discomfort, if present, to be reflected to some other site.

Dropsy.—When due to cold, this is one of the commonest and earliest indications of the disease, and it is frequently the one which first attracts attention. In mild cases it generally commences about the legs and the cheeks; the latter may be found puffy on first rising in the morning, the extent of œdema varying considerably in different cases. The œdema usually commences in the lower eyelids, and the conjunctivæ are affected at the same time, so that in the early stages the eye appears brighter than usual, and the characteristic watery appearance of the eye in renal disease is frequently present. In severe cases the œdema spreads rapidly from the face to the trunk and to the extremities; even in mild cases the feet may be swollen towards evening when the œdema has, to a great extent, disappeared from the face. When the dropsy is only slight in amount, the general appearance of the patient is much like that associated with chlorosis. It is far more common, however, to find the whole trunk infiltrated and œdematous, the œdema generally being most marked in the parts that are most dependent. Considerable swelling is often to be found at the lower part of the back, constituting the well-known lumbar pad, which is frequently seen also in chronic cases. The genitals, especially the prepuce, may be affected, and the œdema may be so excessive as to interfere with micturition.

From the first, renal dropsy is associated with a curious white appearance of the skin, due in part to the presence of fluid in the subcutaneous tissues, and in part the result of the rapid development of extreme anæmia; hence in the early stages of acute nephritis patients may not only be unrecognisable from the distortion of their features, and the smoothing out of irregularities of the face, but they are also commonly of a pale yellow waxy colour. Usually, as the subcutaneous tissue becomes infiltrated, the serous sacs are simultaneously involved. The abdominal cavity is commonly found to contain fluid, and occasionally serum may be also detected in the pleura and in the pericardium. These accumulations may cause considerable danger, as they impede the action of respiration and of circulation. Still more dangerous, but fortunately more rare, is œdema of the glottis, which develops with extreme rapidity, and in some instances has caused death from asphyxia.

Digestive system.—Interference with digestion is extremely frequent, even in mild cases of acute nephritis. The appetite is bad from the beginning, especially during the time of pyrexia; the tongue is furred, and in the early stages there is usually constipation, though later this may be replaced by diarrhœa, independently of treatment. The diarrhœa in such cases has been attributed to a natural eliminative effort to remove accumulated excretory matters. During the early stages nausea and vomiting are frequent. It is difficult to explain their occurrence at the commencement of the disease; they may possibly be reflex symptoms, but at a later stage in all probability the vomiting is of uræmic origin, and when uncontrollable it presents a serious complication.

Circulatory system.—It has generally been held that the circulatory system is not materially affected in the early stages of acute nephritis, and the changes connected with the heart and smaller arteries are commonly considered to occur with chronic renal affections, or to develop as an acute attack gradually passes onwards into the chronic stage. Dr. Dickinson, however, has suggested that quite from the beginning of acute kidney trouble there is some alteration of the wall of the capillaries, and he considers that this alteration, if permanent, contributes largely to the subsequent hypertrophy of the arterioles and of the left ventricle. Those who hold with Mahomed that there is marked increase of arterial tension in all cases of renal affection, will no doubt consider that these alterations of the capillaries are always present; but on the other hand, it must be admitted that it is by no means uncommon for cases of acute nephritis to recover completely without any permanent alteration in the nature of the pulse tracing. Sometimes acute enlargement of the left ventricle may occur, but this is also a transient feature in the majority of cases, all evidence of hypertrophy, dilatation, and increased blood pressure passing off as the albuminuria ceases.

It has already been indicated that anæmia is an early and characteristic symptom of acute nephritis; it has been suggested that this is caused by the loss of albumin through the kidneys, or else, as is more probable, by the degree of hæmaturia which is usually present. It must be admitted, however, that when the pallor is very rapidly developed in connection with dropsy, the anæmic appearance is in all probability due rather to the infiltration of the tissues with dropsical serum than to blood changes. In advanced cases of acute nephritis, the red corpuscles of the blood are always reduced in number; the albumin is diminished, and the serum contains a large proportion of water; in addition to these changes, it is common to find either urea, uric acid, or both, and perhaps other urinary derivatives, added to the blood. In some few cases, especially in those associated with fevers, pericarditis may occur, and when the effusion is purulent in character the disease nearly always terminates fatally. It is very rare in acute nephritis to meet with epistaxis or to find hæmorrhages in the retina, symptoms which are so commonly seen in chronic forms of kidney disease. For the production of these symptoms hypertrophy of the left ventricle and alteration in the structure of the walls of the small vessels appear to be necessary.

Respiratory system.—Alterations in the respiratory system are not essential features of the disease, they only occur as complications. Pleurisy has already been mentioned, but bronchitis and pneumonia may develop in severe cases. All these complications are frequently of fatal import; the pleurisy of acute nephritis is especially dangerous, since, like the pericarditis, it is frequently purulent. It is not uncommon, however, for mild cases of acute nephritis to be associated with indications of slight pulmonary engorgement; the degree of engorgement mostly varies inversely with the amount of fluid in the pleural cavity. Slight congestion of the lungs, although it may lead to troublesome cough and sleeplessness, is not necessarily a serious complication.

Nervous system.—The effects of acute nephritis upon the nervous system may develop with considerable rapidity. Even in the early stages headache is commonly present; if there is much pyrexia the significance of this headache may be overlooked, while if the digestive system is much disturbed the headache may often be attributed to disorders of digestion. As a rule, however, the association of headache, œdema, and scanty urine will be quite sufficient to indicate the true nature of the disease. The degree of headache varies greatly; it may merely be a dull sense of weight, or, if the interference with the excretion of urine is considerable, the headache may be very intense. When the amount of urine passed is very much reduced, it is not uncommon to find that uræmic convulsions may suddenly appear. The general characteristics of these convulsions are described in detail under the heading of uræmia, but it may be here remarked that in some cases they are almost of a hemiplegic type. During the convulsions the temperature may rise, but subsequently it is mostly found to be subnormal. The uræmic convulsion is often succeeded by coma, and the degree of coma generally indicates the severity of the attack. Sometimes several uræmic convulsions occur at short intervals, the patient remaining comatose between the attacks of spasm; sometimes the depth of the coma increases after each attack of convulsions, so that at last the patient can no longer be roused. Occasionally when the coma passes off, or when the convulsion has not been followed by coma, the patient may suffer from partial or complete blindness. This uræmic amaurosis is mostly a transient symptom, and in its short duration differs from the amaurosis of chronic forms of kidney disease. With acute nephritis it is rare to find any permanent interference with any of the functions of the nervous system. The uræmic convulsions are the expression of the retention of toxic materials, and unless the case terminates early in a convulsion, the nervous symptoms usually speedily pass away.

Course and duration.—The course and duration of acute nephritis are subject to very great variations. The initial rise of temperature may continue for four or five days, or at most for a week, but very often cases first come under observation when the temperature is normal or only slightly raised. The early symptoms which are then commonly noted are those of dropsy and of alteration in the nature of the urine. The extent and degree of dropsy varies with the amount of urine passed, so that in the first few days the dropsical condition is generally much more marked than at a later period; sometimes, however, when the suppression of urine is progressive instead of occurring with extreme suddenness, the dropsy may reach its highest stage towards the end of the second week. In most attacks the dropsy develops with great rapidity, but undergoes considerable improvement with the re-establishment of the work of the kidney. In many cases, if the patient is put under favourable conditions and suitably treated, there is speedy diminution in the amount of albumin, blood corpuscles and casts, and the urine, from being of a deep red or smoky tint, regains its normal characters in a few days. If, on the other hand, the quantity of urine progressively diminishes, secondary affections of the nervous system are likely to arise, and the patient may die during an attack of acute uræmia.

Occasionally the onset of acute nephritis is much more gradual, and the various symptoms are less strongly marked. There may be progressive diminution in the quantity of urine, gradual increase in the extent of dropsical effusions, and indications of secondary affections of the lungs or of the various serous membranes. The favourable progress of cases of acute nephritis is sometimes interfered with by distinct relapses, in which the symptoms resemble those of the primary attack.

Such relapses are mostly to be attributed to alterations of temperature, to exposure to cold, or to the premature use of ordinary forms of diet. In all probability, these relapses indicate an extension of inflammation to some portion of the kidney previously unaffected, and hence they constitute not only an immediate danger, but they further imperil the patient's chances of ultimate recovery.

With cases that are doing well, it is generally found that the amount of urine exceeds the normal quantity; since, when the kidneys have once more resumed their eliminative functions, they have the additional work of removing from the body a large quantity of dropsical material. Hence the colour is diminished, the specific gravity is very much reduced, and the amount of albumin decreases rapidly, the decrease affecting the total quantity of albumin passed in the day, as well as the percentage in any particular specimen. As the patient progresses towards recovery, the nature of the sediment alters, epithelial cells and free blood corpuscles become less numerous, and the epithelial and blood casts are gradually replaced by hyaline and granular casts, which in turn decrease in number, and may ultimately disappear.

Although the above is true of a large number of cases of acute nephritis, it unfortunately frequently happens that after a certain degree of rapid progress the improvement appears to come to a standstill, and although the amount of urine passed differs little from the normal quantity, yet it contains traces of albumin which may vary slightly from day to day. The casts also become more granular, and fatty casts may be found. These indications of lack of progress are sometimes accompanied by persistence of slight dropsy. These symptoms always cause anxiety about the ultimate recovery of the patient, as they indicate a tendency to a gradual transition from the acute to the chronic form.

From the above account it will be seen that it is impossible to predict the course or the duration of any case of acute nephritis. Towards the end of the first week the improvement may be rapid, and the patient may seem to be convalescing, yet it is not safe to build too much upon such rapid improvement, and the patient must be kept in bed and the diet must be regulated, even though the albumin has disappeared and convalescence appears to be established. Usually the duration of an acute attack varies from two to six weeks, but when relapses occur, recovery may be delayed for eight weeks or more. If after this time albumin is still found, while the hæmaturia has disappeared, and if casts, especially granular and fatty casts, are still present, the case must be regarded as having passed into the chronic stage. When a fatal termination occurs, it may be due to the extent of the dropsy or to the severity of other symptoms. Great accumulations of fluid in the pleura or pericardium, or, in rare cases, œdema of the larynx, may be the ultimate cause of death. Frequently death may occur in the course of acute nephritis as the result of œdema of the lungs, or from a combination of œdema and pneumonia. Sometimes acute inflammation of the pleura or of the pericardium appears to give rise to more urgent symptoms than the chronic effusion of dropsical fluid; at any rate they cause more distress and pain, and they add to the risks by interfering with the patient's rest. Many cases terminate with acute uræmia, sometimes during the first attack of convulsions, sometimes from a succession of attacks, and in rare cases death may be due to gradual failure of the heart's action, owing to dilatation of the left ventricle.

The immediate cause of death appears to depend to some extent upon the age of the patient; in children death mostly results from inflammation of the respiratory organs, while in adults it may be due to uræmic poisoning, or to one of the direct consequences of dropsy. Obstinate vomiting, the result of uræmia, may hasten the end, or in cases with severe dropsy, erysipelatous inflammation or abscesses in the cellular tissue may follow acupuncture or incisions.

Diagnosis.—The symptoms marking the onset of acute nephritis are generally so well defined that they present very little difficulty. Alterations in the appearance and in the quantity of the urine mostly attract the patient's attention at a very early stage, even when the onset is not accompanied with dropsy. The presence of blood corpuscles, epithelial cells, and casts of varying type will generally indicate the nature of the case, and assistance may frequently be afforded by consideration of the recent history of the patient. The pallor which is mostly associated with acute nephritis, even when dropsy is absent, will generally assist in rendering the diagnosis clear. It must be admitted, however, that many cases of chronic nephritis present symptoms which are at first almost indistinguishable from those of acute nephritis. In the former there is undoubtedly an acute engorgement, which is often to be regarded as an acute nephritis, superadded to the chronic kidney trouble, and it becomes important not to speak too hopefully of the ultimate recovery during the early days of the attack. Assistance may be obtained from a consideration of the previous history, from the degree of hypertrophy of the heart, from the recognition of marked accentuation of the cardiac sounds, and from the high tension of the pulse. These indications are rarely absent in chronic cases with an intercurrent acute attack. Marked alteration of the heart sounds and of the pulse should always lead to careful inquiry about the previous history, and even when in such cases the history appears vague, the recovery is often prolonged and tedious, and a trace of albumin persists long after the disappearance of urgent symptoms.

Cyanotic induration of the kidneys is occasionally accompanied by alterations in the urine, which resemble those of acute nephritis; the urine is reduced in quantity, and is of dark colour and high specific gravity, but in these cases there is generally only a small and variable amount of albumin, and the sediment exhibits only a few hyaline casts, instead of the great variety of *débris* so commonly found in acute nephritis. In cyanotic induration, moreover, if dropsy is present, it generally affects the lower extremities instead of being universal, as in acute nephritis; while an examination of the heart and the nature of the dyspnœa usually indicate the cause of the cyanotic induration and of the alteration in the appearance and nature of the urine. Reference has previously been made to the occurrence of febrile albuminuria, and to the probability of this condition warranting the term of 'abortive nephritis.' With this special form, all the symptoms dependent upon renal changes are less marked than in acute nephritis. There is not so much alteration in the quantity of the urine, there is generally but little albumin, and the occurrence of blood is rare. Although there may be some anæmia, the degree of pallor is not so marked as in acute nephritis; dropsy is absent, and the symptoms speedily pass away with diminution of the pyrexia.

Prognosis.—A large number of cases of acute nephritis terminate in complete recovery, but so long as the amount of albumin remains stationary, anxiety must always be felt about the prospects of recovery. Sir William Roberts considers that the prognosis is more favourable amongst old people, and he states that in his experience the disease is mild in persons over sixty, and always ends in recovery. The small amount of urine passed during the early stages of the disease frequently causes anxiety, as great diminution may indicate danger of the development of uræmic symptoms. The quantity of blood passed is also an important consideration, as it indicates to a certain degree the amount of acute engorgement, and therefore the extent of interference with the eliminative work of the kidney. Although convulsions are always indicative of danger, in a large number of cases of acute nephritis they do not, unless frequently repeated, lead to a fatal termination. Even uræmic amaurosis and uræmic coma may occur without the case ending fatally, and indeed it is not uncommon for cases, which have been marked by these urgent symptoms, to recover completely after suitable treatment has been adopted.

Complications connected with secondary inflammations of lung, pleura, or pericardium are of graver import. When pleurisy or pericarditis become purulent the case almost invariably terminates fatally. When, under the influence of treatment, the dropsy diminishes and the amount of urine increases, the aspect of the case is improved; and the prognosis is rendered still more hopeful if, at the same time, there is diminution in the amount of hæmaturia and in the quantity of deposit. Even when the urine no longer presents the characteristic reactions for blood, it will be necessary to note the daily percentage of albumin, since this percentage affords valuable indications of the risks of chronic changes. So long as the daily amount of albumin decreases, and other symptoms improve, there are fair grounds for a favourable prognosis; and even when, for a long time, the amount of albumin remains almost stationary from day to day, it must be remembered that under such conditions a permanent recovery has occasionally occurred. When, however, the specific gravity continues low, and the daily amount of albumin shows little variation, it is to be feared that the case has passed from the acute to the chronic stage.

Treatment.—The treatment of any case of acute Bright's disease must largely depend upon the stage that has been reached when it first comes under observation, and it must further be influenced by the severity of the prominent symptoms. Still, this is essentially one of those diseases in which it is possible to lay down general rules for guidance, with the distinct understanding that these rules are subject to modifications. Probably few cases of Bright's disease can be treated on absolutely identical lines. The leading indications in every case are to secure physiological rest for the kidney, to take measures which will diminish risks of further damage to that organ, and to obviate dangers likely to arise from the great interference with the work of elimination. Stated briefly, these indications are followed by keeping the patient in bed, by attention to diet, and by the use of diaphoretics and purgatives. In addition, it is frequently necessary to pursue symptomatic treatment for various complications, such as persistent vomiting, profound anæmia, or even long continued albuminuria, while circulatory or respiratory troubles have to be treated on general principles. Even when the state of convalescence has been reached, it is necessary to continue watchfulness and precautionary measures.

So soon as the diagnosis of acute Bright's disease has been rendered probable, the patient should be strictly confined to bed, and it is advisable to maintain warmth by woollen garments, and further, by the removal of sheets, to avoid the risk of chilling the surface.

The diet in severe cases should be rendered as non-nitrogenous as possible. There is much to be said in favour of keeping patients entirely upon milk during the early stages of acute Bright's disease, and my own practice is to continue a pure milk diet so long as there is any blood in the urine, and so long as the daily percentage of albumin passed is steadily diminishing. Some authors consider that a milk diet does harm, and would substitute for it a plain water gruel made with arrowroot or barley meal, to the total exclusion of milk and bread. Sir George Johnson laid great stress upon the importance of a pure milk diet during the acute stages of nephritis, and indeed he considered a modification of this diet was only warranted when it produced disturbances of digestion, as indicated by heartburn, diarrhœa, headache, or other symptoms of dyspepsia. He recommended that the milk should be taken cold or tepid, from half a pint to a pint at a time, and was in favour of not giving skimmed milk unless dyspeptic symptoms followed the use of pure milk. Skimmed milk is extremely liable to produce troublesome constipation, and this symptom it is most desirable to avoid. If it is found impossible to enforce pure milk diet, it may be necessary to substitute some form of liquid nourishment, such as barley water or arrowroot, together with beef-tea, or broth made with chicken, veal, or mutton, and, if these are found insufficient for the patient's needs, an egg, lightly boiled, may also be occasionally added. In a large proportion of cases these measures are speedily followed by improvement. During the early days it is well to keep the nourishment to the smallest amount possible consistent with the patient's comfort, as the diuretic influence of milk is not to be desired so long as there is any large proportion of blood in the urine. Later, as the functions of the kidney become re-established, the amount of milk may be increased. Some patients rebel against the milk diet from the idea that it is not sufficiently nourishing, but Sir George Johnson has quoted the history of one patient who was able to live on an exclusive milk diet for more than five years. During the later stages of acute Bright's disease it is advisable to use diluent drinks freely, and the one which is most readily taken is the 'imperial drink,' which is made with acid tartrate of potash and lemon juice.

It is customary to employ purgatives at an early stage in acute Bright's disease, with the object of diminishing the amount of work which is thrown upon the kidney. When there is much dropsy or troublesome constipation, the employment of purgatives is particularly necessary. Some authors recommend the use of mercurials, but these cannot be continued, and it is much better to employ salines or mild hydragogue purgatives, although these should not be given as a mere matter of routine. Apart from dropsy, the chief indications for the use of purgatives are those which result from uræmia, such as headache, delirium, convulsions, or coma. The selection of the purgative to be employed under these circumstances is purely dependent upon the urgency of the case. When convulsions or coma have occurred, croton oil is the most convenient, as its action is rapid and it may be administered to an unconscious patient in a small dose; on the other hand, if headache is persistent and severe, calomel and compound colocynth pill may be given. Sometimes the compound jalap powder may be used in place of this pill; or if a purgative of greater strength is desired, the following formula recommended by Sir George Johnson may be employed, viz.:

Scammoniæ resinæ	gr. v
Potassii tartratis acidi	gr. xx
Pulveris zingiberis	gr. iij

which may be given once or more as required. For the treatment of suppression, Ralfe employed one or two grains of calomel, followed three hours later by a full dose of compound senna mixture. For ordinary cases, a small glass of Hunyadi Janos, or from half an ounce to an ounce of Rochelle salt in half a glassful of water, may be administered. The febrile symptoms at the onset rarely require any special treatment beyond the enforced rest, the use of purgatives and the modification of diet, but aconite has however often been recommended with a view of reducing inflammation through its action as a circulatory depressant.

Many authors lay stress upon the importance of diminishing the acidity of the urine, or of rendering it alkaline as early as possible, since the coagulation of albumin or of blood within the tubules may possibly cause permanent interference with the work of the kidney, and this coagulation is most likely to arise in acid urine. It is doubtless important to prevent this occurrence if possible, but it is extremely difficult to render the urine alkaline without administering alkaline diuretics, such as the salts of potassium or sodium. These are converted into alkaline carbonates within the body, and are eliminated in this form by the kidneys. For this reason they have therefore been recommended, and Sir William Roberts urges that they should be employed freely from the commencement of the treatment, and states that he has obtained the best results from the free administration of citrate of potassium. In no instance where the urine has been rendered alkaline during the first week of the complaint has he observed the more severe uræmic symptoms or secondary inflammations. Such a statement coming from such an authority requires very careful consideration, the more so as this treatment has been advocated by other authors, who recommend that the acetate or citrate of potassium should be given every two hours or so largely diluted with water, and have asserted that under this plan of treatment anuria and uræmia are avoided.

I must confess that my own practice is scarcely in accordance with these recommendations, and that I prefer deferring the use of alkaline diuretics to the time when an increase in the amount of water indicates that the engorgement of the kidneys has largely subsided. To employ a stimulant diuretic during the earlier stages is, I believe, likely to favour uræmic symptoms by increasing the amount of engorgement of the renal vessels. When this engorgement has been relieved by the use of purgatives and diaphoretics, alkaline diuretics will undoubtedly do good, both by increasing the amount of water eliminated by the kidney and by diminishing the risks of coagulation within the tubules. These considerations naturally suggest the substitution of other methods which will diminish the renal engorgement before using alkaline diuretics, which will increase it. Prominent amongst these measures is to be placed the stimulation of the skin, either by the wet pack or by the hot-air bath; this stimulation is frequently necessary when there is much dropsy and severe headache. It is not advisable to continue the use of the hot-air bath for more than fifteen or twenty minutes, and as soon as the action of the skin has commenced, the patient should be wrapped in blankets, so as to favour the continuance of profuse perspiration. In general, the wet pack is perhaps more convenient, as it requires no special apparatus. The patient is simply enveloped in a sheet which has been wrung out of warm water, and the sheet is covered with three or four dry blankets. If it is necessary to continue the use of the wet pack for any length of time, this is most conveniently effected by covering the blanket next to the sheet with a mackintosh cloth. In this way the patient speedily becomes surrounded by an atmosphere of vapour. Sometimes this method has, however, the disadvantage of producing some discomfort and headache. After removal of the wet pack it is advisable to dry the patient quickly with soft warm cloths and to envelop him in blankets. The diaphoresis is generally continued after removal of the wet sheets, but by drying the surface chill is avoided. The action of the skin may be increased by copious draughts of simple diluent drinks; these may be given warm, unless they promote vomiting or nausea. It is only necessary to resort to these measures, however, when there is much dropsical effusion; and it is very rarely necessary to remove fluid from the subcutaneous tissue by operation. When, however, all forms of baths produce intense discomfort, when purgatives give no relief, and the limbs are greatly distended, it may occasionally be advisable to puncture the skin over the malleoli with a lancet, or to drain off the fluid with Southey's tubes. Acupuncture is sometimes preferred, but the continuous oozing of fluid over the extremities is apt to be followed by inflammatory action.

In ordinary cases baths or other measures calculated to produce profuse diaphoresis are unnecessary. It has sometimes been urged that diaphoretics should always be avoided, as they diminish the amount of water which is eliminated by the kidney, and may therefore promote the retention of materials within the uriniferous tubes. In severe cases, however, diaphoretic measures undoubtedly relieve congestion of the kidney by diverting blood to the surface of the skin; they also favour the removal of fluid from the areolar tissues and the serous cavities. Further it is a clinical fact that after profuse diaphoresis the amount of urine passed speedily increases, showing that the temporary relief of congestion has favoured the resumption of normal work. A few years ago pilocarpine was largely recommended as a diaphoretic in acute Bright's disease. Subsequent experience has shown that this drug often produces distressing symptoms of salivation and depression, which are frequently very severe; it is therefore essentially one of the drugs which would only be used when other measures fail. I have seen some good results from its administration in cases of chronic Bright's disease, particularly in uræmic asthma, but in acute Bright's disease the disadvantages appear to outweigh the benefits. With indications of uræmic poisoning, especially if associated with much lumbar pain, relief may sometimes be afforded by dry-cupping over the loins or by the local application of leeches. These measures, however, are mostly reserved for cases where the amount of urine is small and the headache severe, for to a certain extent the same result may be produced by the local application of warmth by means of hot fomentations or poultices.

The use of active diuretics should be reserved for the later stages of acute nephritis, when most of the traces of blood have disappeared from the urine. At this period various preparations of digitalis may be employed, and there is no objection to the simultaneous use of broom tops or of alkaline diuretics, which, as has been previously indicated, are not in my opinion advisable during the earlier stages. Ringer states that he finds the diuretic action of digitalis is limited by the existence of dropsy, for when dropsy disappears this remedy no longer causes an increased secretion of urine. The diuretic action of digitalis may sometimes be increased by giving a mercurial in combination; e.g. small doses of blue pill or of calomel may be conveniently made into a pill with powdered digitalis leaves.

Caffeine has been recommended in preference to digitalis, and it has been urged in its favour that it is more prompt in its action and that the effect passes off more readily. Dr. H. C. Wood, speaking of the use of caffeine, states that, if used at all, it should be employed with caution in acute Bright's disease, though it is preferable to digitalis, as it does not disagree with the stomach, and it has no cumulative tendency.

The restlessness and sleeplessness which often occur in the course of acute nephritis may be alleviated by bromides, by hyoscine, or sometimes by aconite. Cannabis indica has also been recommended, especially when there is much hæmaturia, but its action is very uncertain. Opium has been given in small doses, but if employed it must be used with great caution, from the risk of inducing symptoms of uræmia.

Persistent vomiting in acute nephritis frequently taxes the therapeutic resources of the physician; when it occurs early, relief may sometimes be afforded by the administration of dilute hydrocyanic acid and preparations of bismuth, together with the application of ice. If it continues in spite of these measures, drop doses of tincture of iodine every half hour may be given, or small doses of creosote or carbolic acid. Vomiting always requires modification of diet; nourishment should be given cold, in a liquid form and in repeated small quantities. Benefit occasionally ensues from the application of poultices to the epigastrium. When vomiting occurs at a later stage, as an indication of uræmia, similar measures may be adopted, but they often fail, and it is necessary to treat the uræmia, rather than this particular symptom, by baths, wet pack, diuretics and purgatives.

Persistent albuminuria during convalescence is, as a rule, to be treated by strict attention to diet, by the avoidance of cold, and of all muscular and mental strain. Prolonged muscular efforts or business worries are almost invariably followed by an increase of albuminuria. Many drugs have been advocated for their power of diminishing the loss of albumin. Those which are most commonly employed are the persalts of iron, especially the perchloride, which may be given in conjunction with digitalis or strophanthus. Occasionally ergot has, in my experience, appeared to be beneficial; tannic acid and gallic acid have also been recommended, while drop doses of tincture of cantharides have been used, though in the opinion of Dujardin Beaumetz this drug is always dangerous and frequently useless.

Strontium salts [1] are said to lead to a remarkable and often rapid diminution of albuminuria, and they are further useful indirectly by improving digestion. According to Constantin Paul, strontium is only useful in parenchymatous nephritis, and has no action in the interstitial forms, in renal tuberculosis or in syphilis. Gaucher and Gallois say that strontium acts rather on the symptom of albuminuria than on the actual morbid condition. When the drug is discontinued the albumin appears in as large an amount as formerly. If these statements are correct, strontium would be indicated in cases of abundant

[1] *Journal des Prac.*, Jan. 4, 1896.

albuminuria, where it is desirable to diminish the albuminous loss. Gaucher and Gallois give the following formula:

Pure lactate of strontium	50 grams
Water	375 ,,

Dose, three tablespoonfuls or six grams of lactate of strontium per day.

It must be admitted, I think, that drugs possess very little power of directly controlling the loss of albumin, and that better results follow from precautionary hygienic measures and from the use of tonics, than from the many other remedies which have been recommended.

During the later stages of acute Bright's disease advantage is frequently derived from the use of hæmatinics, such as the various preparations of iron, or arsenic; it is generally preferable to employ the non-astringent preparations of iron, so as to avoid the undesirable constipating effects of other preparations. For a certain length of time after acute nephritis it is necessary that the diet should be strictly regulated, that it should contain relatively large proportions of milk, and that the effects of other articles of diet should be carefully watched by examinations of the urine. Patients who have suffered from this disease should avoid exposure to cold, and, if their means allow, should winter in some warm southern health resort.

CHAPTER VI

SCARLATINAL NEPHRITIS

THE frequency with which acute nephritis accompanies and complicates cases of scarlet fever appears to separate this type clinically from other forms of febrile albuminuria, as well as from other forms of simple nephritis. The pathological conditions and the symptoms are somewhat different from those of ordinary cases of acute nephritis, and although it must be regarded as an acute inflammatory disease, yet from its importance it merits separate detailed consideration. From the frequency of its occurrence there can be little doubt that it depends upon the action of some poison peculiar to scarlet fever. It is well known that epidemics are often of different intensity and danger; hence, in all probability, there may be great variation in the formation of this poison, and this would account for the relative frequency of scarlatinal nephritis, in various epidemics.

With regard to the proportion of scarlet fever cases which develop nephritis, recent observers give very different results. Thus, F. M. Turner[1] gives a percentage of 31·1 out of 6,000 cases; Goodhall, out of 5,443, had a percentage of 8·4; Caiger, out of 415, found simple albuminuria or nephritis in 7·69 per cent.; Dr. Hillier and Dr. Dickinson found albuminuria in half the cases of scarlatina they investigated, and it appears probable that, although in some of these cases the albuminuria should be regarded as pyrexial, yet in a large number the albuminuria was distinctly due to renal change. Some authors maintain that albuminuria, whenever it occurs in the course of scarlet fever, indicates structural disease of the kidney, which under adverse circumstances may develop severe symptoms, and may even

[1] *Guy's Hospital Reports*, vol. 51.

pass on to the formation of chronic disease. Although the frequency both of albuminuria and of nephritis must undoubtedly be admitted, yet there is very little certain knowledge as to the exact causation of nephritis in any individual case, and in some epidemics the renal changes are undoubtedly more frequent than in others. Wagner and Leichtenstern hold that nephritis is especially likely to occur when the cervical glands become secondarily enlarged after once subsiding; in numerous instances, however, this suggestion fails to be of service, for the cervical glands are frequently considerably inflamed and enlarged without the subsequent development of nephritis. Caiger,[1] describing adenitis in 7·1 per cent., states that the large majority of these patients had no albuminuria, although, perhaps, albumin was relatively more frequent in patients suffering from adenitis.

The influence of a high degree of fever has also been suggested, and certainly in many cases the temperature is found to be high at the time when the albuminuria develops, but, beyond the ordinary influence of producing febrile albuminuria, it does not appear that a high temperature alone will afford much indication of threatening nephritis. In many cases the temperature may rise independently of nephritis in the course of scarlet fever; thus, any inflammatory affection of the lungs or other organs would be indicated by a rise of temperature, without the kidneys necessarily undergoing any degeneration. The actual severity of the original attack of fever appears to have no causal relation to the production of nephritis; in fact, my own experience would lead me rather to consider that nephritis is unusually common amongst children in whom the original febrile attack has been slight, especially amongst those in whom the attack has been entirely overlooked, and where the diagnosis of the scarlatinal origin can only be based upon the subsequent course of the disease, or upon the co-existence of an epidemic of scarlet fever in the neighbourhood. Dr. Mahomed maintained that nephritis, when the result of scarlet fever, was always preceded by an increase of arterial tension, together with constipation and the presence of blood-colouring matter in the urine, and it is certainly interesting to note that many

[1] *Lancet*, June 6, 1891.

other observers have found an apparent connection between constipation and nephritis.

Predisposing causes.—The development of nephritis as a complication of scarlet fever depends largely upon the age of the patient. It is uncommon during the first year of life, and the frequency increases rapidly up to the fifth year, after which time it gradually decreases until adult life. It is somewhat more frequent in males than in females, the proportion having been stated as three to two; and it has also been found to be more fatal to males than to females, while the mortality is greater the younger the patient. Dr. Turner finds that sometimes several brothers and sisters who have scarlet fever together will all develop nephritis, but the influence of family predisposition is not always shown in this marked way; indeed, it often happens that of two children who suffer equally severely with scarlet fever one develops nephritis and dies, while the other escapes altogether. Other observers, however, have found that nephritis occasionally complicates nearly every case of scarlet fever occurring in certain families, and, considering the frequency with which family predisposition influences the occurrence of other forms of nephritis, there appears to be little reason for questioning its influence in connection with scarlatinal nephritis.

The date at which the disease develops is generally somewhat late. Usually it occurs after the 12th or 14th day, or during the early part of the third week. Albuminuria may have been discovered earlier than this, but then in all probability it is merely febrile, and corresponds with Friedländer's initial catarrhal form. Occasionally nephritis is not discovered until the fourth, fifth, or sixth week, but there appears to be reason for thinking that in such cases it has probably existed for a greater length of time, and may have been overlooked. Fürbringer states that the disease can commence as early as the end of the first week of scarlet fever, and both he and Henoch have met with a case commencing as late as the end of the sixth week.

The immediate exciting cause of scarlatinal nephritis is generally held to be exposure to cold during the stage of active desquamation, and upon this supposition the routine treatment of the later stages of scarlet fever has been based. Dr. Caiger, from his observations at the South-Western Fever Hospital, came to the conclusion that cold weather *per se* seemed to have very little influence in producing albuminuria. There was a slightly higher rate during the months of October and November, but otherwise the albuminuria was spread nearly uniformly over the year. On the other hand, he found that there was an apparent connection with the degree of humidity of the atmosphere. Damp, cold, or muggy days were marked by the coincidence of several fresh cases, while a return of bright weather was frequently accompanied by rapid improvement amongst the slighter forms of scarlatinal nephritis. These observations have more recently been confirmed by F. M. Turner, who finds that a sudden change of temperature or a thaw in winter sometimes coincides with the appearance of several cases of hæmaturia. In opposition to the influence of exposure to cold as a cause of scarlatinal nephritis, it may also be pointed out that it is extremely rare under ordinary circumstances for exposure to cold to give rise to acute nephritis in children, although in adults, especially amongst those who are fatigued, the influence of cold is undoubtedly well marked. Purdy suggests also that if the nephritis of scarlatina is caused through exposure to cold it should occur more frequently among the poorer classes, where exposure is vastly more common than among the rich, but the statistics show, however, that this is not the case.

The view generally held at the present time is that scarlatinal nephritis depends upon the action of a specific poison which produces irritation in the kidney during its elimination, yet this subject can hardly be considered as conclusively settled. Micrococci have been described in the blood of patients with scarlatina, and micro-organisms have been found within the kidney, but these observations are scarcely sufficiently numerous, or sufficiently certain, to allow of definite statements concerning their influence. It is far more probable, as already indicated (see 'Acute Nephritis'), that the renal changes are due to the irritation of the kidney by some toxic material resulting from the growth of micro-organisms in the system. As M. Vignerot has suggested, these changes may be almost quiescent until they receive a sudden impulse from the congestion brought about in a reflex manner through exposure to cold, or through climatic conditions.

Morbid anatomy.—When death occurs in the course of scarlet fever, or during convalescence from this disease, the kidneys are almost invariably found to be greatly altered in appearance. The deviations from the normal type are in part due to the nature of the renal affection. Thus Friedländer describes three distinct forms of changes in the kidney associated with scarlet fever: (1) Initial catarrhal, the usual form; (2) the large, limp, hæmorrhagic kidney, interstitial septic form; and (3) nephritis post-scarlatinosa, the glomerular form. The first appears with the onset of the fever, and usually clears up after one or two weeks; the second form appears early, but is very severe, and is also usually connected with so-called diphtheritic affections, cervical phlegmon, &c.; the third is an affection characteristic of scarlet fever, and is often manifested by œdema, hypertrophied heart, suppression of the urine, and death.

Friedländer's initial catarrhal form in all probability coincides with the ordinary appearances of febrile albuminuria or abortive nephritis, and it is found under conditions in which the renal symptoms have not given rise to anxiety, and when death has resulted from some other grave complication of the fever. The septic form may also have attracted very little attention during life—sometimes it may be quite latent; hæmaturia is rare with this condition, and considerable albuminuria is the exception rather than the rule. The third form constitutes scarlatinal nephritis, the disease here under consideration, and the appearances of the kidney are largely dependent upon the duration of the disease. For descriptive purposes it will be convenient to separate three broadly differentiated types of scarlatinal nephritis, but it must be remembered that this arrangement is purely arbitrary—the boundaries are ill-defined, and the separate types frequently merge. Transitional stages affect not only the naked-eye appearances, but also the changes found microscopically.

When death has occurred during the first or second week, the kidneys are very little altered in size; they appear engorged, and the capsule can be readily separated. The surface may show radiating red lines of injection or small extravasations. On

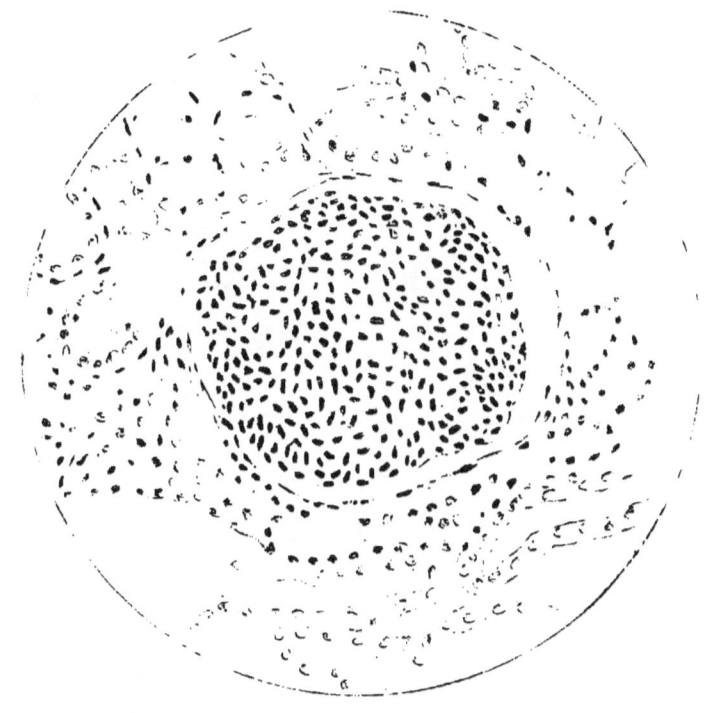

Section of Kidney in Acute Nephritis (Glomerulo-Nephritis). In this specimen the most important change is the great increase in the nuclei of the glomerular tuft. The epithelial cells are somewhat cloudy, and in some parts show swelling, with consequent irregularity of outline. The intertubular tissues are but little affected.

(*See pp.* 97 *and* 121.)

N. Tirard, Del Mintern Bros., imp.

section, the whole parenchyma may be of a chocolate hue from intense engorgement.

From the second to the sixth week the kidneys are enlarged and firm, and the surface is more pale and mottled, yellowish spots are scattered over the surface of the kidney, which is either of normal colour or more pale than usual. These appearances are seen to extend through the cortical layer, but the medullary substance is still hyperæmic, from its junction with the cortex almost to the ends of the papillæ. The hyperæmia is often associated with striæ of a deep colour passing along the pyramids.

At a later stage contraction occurs, so that the kidneys may be of normal size, or even somewhat smaller. They may still be pale in colour, but they are much more firm, and they may even be rather difficult to cut.

The microscopic changes in scarlatinal nephritis mainly affect the glomeruli and the tissues in their neighbourhood. In the early stages the vessels of these parts are found to be crowded with masses of corpuscles, which are most numerous between the vessels of the tuft of capillaries, while they are also frequently found in considerable numbers outside the tuft, but within Bowman's capsule. The vessels of the tuft sometimes rupture, and Bowman's capsule becomes filled with blood corpuscles, which are often seen extending down the tubules; compact masses of corpuscles due to hæmorrhage may also be found in lines between the tubules. The epithelial cells in the convoluted tubes are enlarged and cloudy, and they may be swollen to such an extent as to almost obliterate the lumen. Similar changes affect the epithelial cells lining Bowman's capsule. At a later stage, the round cells in the neighbourhood of the vessels and round the capsules of the glomeruli proliferate, and the epithelial cells lining Bowman's capsule undergo rapid desquamation; hence the space between the tuft and the capsule is filled with collections of exfoliated epithelium. The appearance of the capillary tufts depends upon the extent of the changes within the capsule; the tufts may be engorged so that they occupy the whole of the space within the capsule, or they may be compressed and relatively empty, owing to the pressure exerted upon them by the desquamated epithelium and the hæmorrhagic effusions. The epithelial cells in the convoluted tubes are more granular and opaque at this stage, and undergo rapid desquamation; hence the tubes are often found choked with granular *débris*, which may be entangled in the form of casts.

When the kidney is undergoing contraction in the third stage, Bowman's capsule is greatly thickened, and the whole Malpighian body is larger than usual, owing to the great increase of nucleated cells surrounding and compressing the capillary tuft. This solidification of the glomerular tuft may therefore be due to a combined growth of epithelial cells outside the capillary membrane, and of other cells, connective tissue corpuscles, and leucocytes, within it. Similar increase of connective tissue corpuscles is found round the outside of Bowman's capsule, and between the convoluted tubes, which may be compressed and distorted by the new growth. The epithelial cells of the convoluted tubes are generally flattened at this stage, and the lumen, which may be larger than in the normal condition, is often filled with *débris* and casts.

In all these stages the interlobular arteries and arterioles are thickened and prominent, the extent to which they are affected increasing with the duration of the disease.

In view of the well-marked nature of the alterations within and around the capsule in scarlatinal nephritis, both Langhans and Nauwerck have suggested that vascular alterations, limited probably to the glomeruli, might cause fatal uræmia, and hence they have described this condition as glomerular nephritis, and they consider the changes in the tubules and in the interstitial tissue to be the result of the glomerulitis. This view has been vigorously contested, and, while it must be admitted that the alterations in the tubules and in the glomeruli nearly always co-exist, there is little doubt that the glomerular changes are not invariably the first to appear.

Symptoms.—The onset of scarlatinal nephritis is generally marked by definite symptoms, although it occasionally appears to commence insidiously. During the fever, or after the attack, transient albuminuria may sometimes be noted without any other obvious interference with the general health, and without the production of any symptom beyond colour. As a rule, there is some rise of temperature. This may be very slight, but occasionally it may rise to 101° or 102°; it is quite independent of that which accompanied the onset of scarlet fever, and occurs most commonly towards the end of the second or during the third week. The pyrexia may be preceded for a few days by more or less definite symptoms, such as headache, loss of appetite, and pallor; these are sometimes associated with constipation, and unless care is exercised they may be referred entirely to this condition. When these symptoms occur with a rise of temperature, the urine must be examined, especially if the pulse is increased in frequency and in tension. These symptoms are frequently followed closely by rapid diminution in the quantity of urine passed, by alteration of its specific gravity, and by the appearance of albumin and blood in the water. The state of the urine is found to vary considerably with the stage of the nephritis. At first, when scanty and thick, it may clear on boiling, owing to the presence of quantities of lithates, but within a short time albumin is found to be present. The amount of water passed at the commencement of nephritis may be but little affected, but it is speedily greatly reduced, and sometimes the quantity is only from one to three ounces in the twenty-four hours, while occasionally it may be totally suppressed. In spite of this diminution there is, as in acute nephritis, frequent desire to micturate, and the act may be accompanied by pain. The urine in scarlatinal nephritis is always acid in reaction, and the specific gravity is mostly low, from 1010 to 1015. Fürbringer, on the other hand, maintains that the specific gravity is increased, ranging between 1020 and 1025. The colour varies a good deal with the stage of the disease. It is mostly of a dark red, brown, or blackish-brown colour, and the colour may in part be due to the presence of lithates, though it is more often dependent on the presence of blood; indeed, the colour generally affords a rough indication of the amount of blood. Later in the disease the urine clears, and may become transparent; but frequently, although rapid improvement occurs within the first few days, some slight deposit remains for weeks after the commencement of the disease. The quantity of albumin is generally considerable, and some may be found in the later stages of the disease, long after the hæmaturia has entirely ceased. As the case progresses, the amount of albumin varies greatly from day to day. It may be present in large amount on one day, while small quantities only may be found on the following day; and there may even be great variations at different times in the day. In exceptional epidemics, there appears to be little reason to doubt that scarlatinal nephritis may occur without the association of albuminuria; at all events, numerous observations have been made of cases of dropsy without albuminuria.

Henoch believes in scarlatinal nephritis in which, in spite of repeated examination of the urine, neither albumin nor microscopic indications of nephritis could be found. He doubts the possibility of scarlatinal dropsy without affection of the kidneys, however, because most of his cases which appeared at first sight to point in this direction were found either to develop albuminuria shortly before death or to exhibit unmistakable signs of acute nephritis on post-mortem examination. He points out also, in explanation of the epidemics of so-called 'simple scarlatinal dropsy,' that œdema after severe scarlet fever may often be regarded as the result of weakness and anæmia. These cases are uncommon, but they appear to occur in epidemic form. Amongst English observers they have been described by Basham, Taylor, Sir Dyce Duckworth, and Goodhart. From time to time I have seen such cases at the Evelina.

The microscopical examination of the urine in the early stages of scarlatinal nephritis reveals red blood corpuscles. Sometimes they are variously altered in shape—the margins, for instance, may be crenated; sometimes they are collected in blood casts; rarely they appear as discoloured discs. Renal epithelial cells are also frequently met with, but the amount varies greatly in different cases, and also in the different stages of the same case; these cells may be included in casts, or they may frequently be found alone, and they appear to be enlarged, granular, and cloudy. In addition, leucocytes are often met with in abundance. Many varieties of casts are commonly found in connection with acute scarlatinal nephritis; they may be hyaline, but are more frequently epithelial; there may also be blood casts in addition to hyaline casts. In the early stages of the disease the casts are generally small, but after a few days casts of all dimensions may be found. As the disease undergoes improvement, metamorphosed granular casts may be met with, while the epithelial and blood casts diminish in number. Very commonly minute uric acid crystals and crystals of oxalate of lime are found in connection with scarlatinal nephritis.

In many cases of scarlatinal nephritis, so far at least as hospital work amongst out-patients is concerned, general œdema may be the first symptom to attract notice, and it has been held that it is commoner in cases marked by total or relative suppression of urine. The degree of œdema is, however, subject to very considerable variations; sometimes the eyelids only are affected, or sometimes the feet and ankles alone may be swollen. Henoch states that in some cases the penis and scrotum may be especially involved. The œdema is usually first noted around the eyes, and it may rapidly extend, so that after a few hours the child is almost unrecognisable. In severe cases, when the dropsy is general and extreme, fissures may form, and lead to extensive excoriations. Although the œdematous condition is not generally associated with discomfort other than that due to the limitations of movement, yet tenderness may be complained of when the tension is great. Both Caiger and Turner, speaking from experience of cases treated within fever hospitals, find that dropsy is not a prominent symptom of scarlatinal nephritis in cases which develop while the patient is continually under observation in the wards. Caiger states that in his cases dropsy was not a prominent symptom—when present it showed itself in the form of surface œdema, mainly in the face and legs; while Turner states that, although there is not sufficient evidence to show whether the hospital routine prevents nephritis, yet it certainly appears to prevent the occurrence of severe œdema. Even slight œdema is said to be rare in the fever hospitals, and, curiously enough, the development of œdema is stated to have no relation whatever to the diminution or suppression of the urine. In my former experience of cases seen in the out-patient room at the Evelina Hospital, severe œdema was very frequent, and its direct connection with sudden and great diminution in the amount of urine very marked. In times of epidemics of scarlet fever, numerous pale, puffy children were brought to the hospital: there was nearly always evidence of peeling, and the water was almost invariably blood-tinged and scanty. This experience was gained in a very poor neighbourhood, before the establishment of many of the present fever hospitals, and before the system of notification was introduced; hence it is possible that such cases are now more rarely seen, since from an early stage of the fever the children are placed under more favourable conditions.

In severe cases the abdominal cavity may become affected by dropsical effusion, and occasionally similar collections of fluid may be found in the pleura and pericardium. Indications of fluid in the pleura and pericardium may cause great anxiety, as they are sometimes of inflammatory origin, and there is a marked tendency for pleuritic and pericardial effusions to become purulent, a tendency which is far greater than that already mentioned in connection with simple acute nephritis.

Digestive system.—Reference has already been made to the frequency of constipation at the commencement of scarlatinal nephritis. Its etiological importance, and the significance of diarrhœa and vomiting, do not differ materially from the conditions already described when dealing with acute nephritis (see p. 100). In fatal cases continued vomiting is a prominent symptom, but, on the other hand, diarrhœa, unless it weakens the patient by its excessive quantity, is usually beneficial rather than otherwise.

Circulatory system.—The alterations of the pulse and the initial rise of temperature have been already mentioned. As the disease progresses the pulse generally becomes more slow, and perhaps irregular, while the tension is increased. Henoch regards irregularity of the pulse as an indication of danger from uræmia, and he mentions one case of a girl aged eight, with hæmorrhagic nephritis, in whom the pulse, which had previously been quite normal, became slow and irregular when headache, nausea, vomiting, and drowsiness supervened; as these symptoms passed off, the pulse returned to its normal condition. The increased tension of the pulse, although it is generally most marked after the disease is fairly established, may be the chief of the premonitory symptoms, and it is characteristic of Mahomed's pre-albuminuric stage. With cases which tend to the establishment of chronic nephritis, the pulse undergoes but little improvement; in fact, a continued high tension may frequently be taken as an indication of permanent renal changes.

With cases of cardiac dilatation, on the other hand, the pulse sometimes undergoes rapid diminution of tension.

Cardiac hypertrophy is one of the most common forms of circulatory change in connection with scarlatinal nephritis. In a large majority of cases the apex beat of the heart is in quite an early stage displaced outwards and downwards; this alteration in the position of the apex beat occurs with great rapidity, and it is generally considered to be due to hypertrophy rather than to dilatation, inasmuch as the sounds of the heart undergo accentuation, the second sound at the base being markedly increased in intensity and frequently reduplicated. When cases of scarlatinal nephritis are undergoing improvement, the improvement affects the nature of the sounds of the heart, and the apex beat quickly returns to its original site. The rapidity with which this recovery occurs would seem somewhat to favour the idea that the displacement of the apex beat may, to a large extent, be due to dilatation rather than hypertrophy, but in cases that terminate fatally the increased thickness of the left ventricle is as a rule easily recognisable. Cardiac dilatation, however, sometimes occurs, and it adds to the dangers of scarlatinal nephritis, as it favours pulmonary changes. It is frequently followed by œdema of the lung and by urgent dyspnœa. The onset of acute cardiac dilatation may sometimes be recognised by the alteration in the character of the pulse, which becomes rapid, thready, and weak, the respirations become more rapid, and at the same time the patient complains of coldness of the extremities. These two changes in the cardiac muscle have given rise to numerous conflicting explanatory theories. Sir George Johnson thought that the hypertrophy of the ventricle was secondary to hypertrophy of the small arteries. More recently Dr. Dickinson places the early changes further back, and assumes an alteration in the structure and work of the capillaries. On the other hand, Henoch considers that the increased pressure in the aortic system may be caused by the obstruction of the glomerular loops and by the great diminution of fluid excretion. By both Sir George Johnson and Dickinson, however, the hypertrophy of the ventricle is regarded as a reflex effort to overcome resistance to the onward passage of blood. The dilatation is somewhat more difficult to explain.

No fatty changes are present, as in some cases of renal cirrhosis; the dilatation therefore does not appear to depend upon degenerative changes, but to result from the wall of the ventricle proving unequal to cope with the increased pressure within the smaller arteries or capillaries. It has been suggested that dilatation may be induced by some influence paralysing the cardiac muscle, and Henoch, who has seen rapid dilatation connected with distinct signs of uræmia, attributes the change to some disturbance in the work of the pneumogastric, owing to uræmic influence.

In all cases of scarlatinal nephritis changes in the blood appear to occur very early, but, as in cases of acute nephritis, it is necessary to indicate that the pallor of the patient may be due rather to œdema than to actual anæmia.

Respiratory system.—Little need be said of the changes in the respiratory system in connection with scarlatinal nephritis. The liability to rapid œdema of the lung is greater than in simple acute nephritis, and this appears to be largely owing to cardiac dilatation. The œdema presents a very serious obstacle to respiration, the air cells and air passages speedily becoming blocked with transuded fluid. This tendency to œdema constitutes, apart from uræmia, one of the greatest dangers of a fatal termination. Pneumonia and pleurisy are frequent complications of this disorder, and, as already noted, the tendency of pleuritic effusion to become purulent is very marked.

Uræmia.—The indications of uræmia are particularly prone to occur in connection with scarlatinal nephritis, and they are extremely difficult to differentiate from many of the symptoms referred to above. In all probability the apathy, sickness, headache, restlessness and dyspnœa of the early stages of scarlatinal nephritis are the expression of uræmic poisoning, and these symptoms are more commonly met with at later stages, where there is marked diminution in the amount of urine eliminated. Severe symptoms of uræmia, however, may occur independently of alteration in the quantity of water passed, and it is not uncommon for uræmic symptoms to arise in dropsical cases when, after temporary suppression, the excretion appears to have been fairly re-established. This has been explained by the reabsorption into the circulation of various excrementitious matters which had previously passed into the subcutaneous tissues.

The uræmic convulsions do not differ materially, if at all, from those of acute nephritis, and to a certain extent they resemble those of puerperal nephritis. They are preceded sometimes by vomiting, dimness of vision, drowsiness, and by alterations in the frequency of the pulse, which becomes more slow and irregular. Between the convulsive seizures the intervals are mostly marked by drowsiness, and in severe cases the convulsive seizures may be separated by a period of actual coma. After, or even independently of, these convulsions, the patient may suffer from severe asthmatic attacks, and there appears to be no doubt that uræmic dyspnœa may arise quite independently of any affection of heart or lung. Dimness of vision or even actual blindness occasionally follows uræmic convulsions. Von Gräfe thinks that the amaurosis is due to transient œdema of certain parts of the brain, while others speak of œdema of the retina. Hæmorrhages or other changes constituting albuminuric retinitis are not frequent with this form of kidney disease. More serious lesions may follow the uræmic seizure—hemiplegia, aphasia, tetanus, and trismus are sometimes present; and in some cases hæmorrhagic patches have been found in the brain, although undoubtedly the hemiplegia of uræmia is not always dependent upon hæmorrhagic effusions. Although uræmia necessarily adds largely to the risk in cases of scarlatinal nephritis, it does not appear to be as frequently fatal as in other forms of nephritis.

Course and duration.—Scarlatinal nephritis is generally recognised at the end of the second or during the third week, and the early symptoms are those of malaise and headache, with diminution in the quantity of water and increased frequency of micturition. Dryness of the skin was formerly thought to be characteristic of the early stages of the disease, but more recent extended observations have shown that, with the onset of an acute attack, perspiration is often profuse, and that the dry skin once thought to be characteristic does not occur until some days or weeks after the establishment of the disease, and is by no means constant. As has already been stated, albumin may early be found in the water, together with blood and casts. These alterations are speedily followed by dropsy, and although it is possible for dropsy to occur independently of change in the water, it is sometimes the first symptom to attract attention. Under appropriate treatment, improvement speedily follows in a large majority of cases, the improvement being most marked towards the end of the first week from the commencement of symptoms. The urine increases in quantity, the albumin diminishes and the blood disappears, or, at least, its colour is less evident to the naked eye, although sometimes the guaiacum test may indicate its continued presence. With these symptoms of improvement dropsy rapidly decreases, and the patient seems well, but anæmic. Albumin, however, is usually found in the water long after other symptoms have passed away. Indeed, albuminuria sometimes continues from four to six weeks; if the albumin lasts longer than this, there is much danger of chronic nephritis having become established. At the commencement of the disease, the symptoms are occasionally more urgent, diminution or suppression of urine being followed quickly by uræmic symptoms. The steady improvement is occasionally interrupted by frequent relapses; the water becomes again small in amount, high coloured and very albuminous, and more rarely the dropsy undergoes similar marked increase. In addition to the dangers of œdema of lung, œdema of the arytenoepiglottidean folds must be referred to, as this occurs with extreme rapidity, and is generally fatal. In fatal cases the chief symptoms are continued vomiting, drowsiness, which may later give place to a restless, tremulous stage, anæmia, wasting, and an erythematous rash.

The alterations of the pulse in the course of the disease have been already mentioned in detail. It may be sufficient here to indicate the need of extreme caution when the pulse becomes irregular and feeble, and when the extremities become cold.

Only a small proportion of cases pass directly into chronic nephritis. The majority recover completely in from two to three weeks. On the other hand, it must be admitted that when scarlatinal nephritis has once occurred, the liability to subsequent attacks of nephritis appears to be more marked.

Diagnosis.—There is generally very little difficulty in the diagnosis of scarlatinal nephritis. When the disease develops in a patient who has been under treatment and observation on account of scarlet fever, alterations in the temperature, or in the digestive system, probably direct fresh attention to the urine, and to microscopic examination of the sediment. When, however, the primary disease has been overlooked, although similar symptoms may cause the patient to be brought under medical notice, it is more frequent for varying degrees of dropsy, marked anæmia, or alterations in the appearance of the water and frequency of micturition, to be co-existent. All these symptoms are so characteristic that the diagnosis scarcely needs the elucidation afforded by the history of cases of fever in the family, the house or the neighbourhood, or the more common account of slight sore throat some two or three weeks previously, or even the positive evidence of peeling, so often to be found in the palms of the hands, the soles of the feet, or occasionally on the back or chest. These indications may, however, serve to differentiate the case from one of simple nephritis from cold.

When dealing with adults, it is not always easy to make sure that the case is not one of simple nephritis, or even one of chronic nephritis complicated by a recent acute extension of the area affected. Assistance may be obtained from any of the indications above mentioned; failing these, the diagnosis must be guided by the nature of the pulse and of the heart, which are so often profoundly implicated in chronic nephritis. When these are not materially affected, if there is the slightest history of sore throat a provisional diagnosis may be made, even though the occurrence of a rash may be stoutly denied.

Since it is well known that in rare cases the onset of scarlatinal nephritis may be insidious, and that indications of the disease have been found after death, although no albumin had ever been detected in the urine, it is advisable not only to test the urine daily during convalescence, but also to make microscopic examinations from time to time. It is thus occasionally possible to recognise the presence of renal epithelial cells, of blood corpuscles, leucocytes and casts, when chemical tests only give negative indications.

Prognosis.—The immediate prognosis in scarlatinal nephritis is somewhat grave, but if the patient survives the risks incurred during the first three or four weeks, the prospects of ultimate recovery are good. Dickinson says the rule of the disease is death, or recovery after a course of weeks or months. As compared with acute nephritis from other causes, the liability to the development of chronic nephritis is relatively slight. The circumstances influencing the prognosis are, in other respects, very much the same as those of acute nephritis. The dangers are those due to uræmia, to suppression, and to complications affecting the respiratory and circulatory organs, especially indications of rapid dilatation of the heart or of cardiac failure. The special risks arising from persistent vomiting or diarrhœa have already been mentioned.

To some extent the prognosis is rendered more grave with the youth of the child, but in every case it is uncertain, owing to the rapidity with which serious phases may supervene. Even when convalescence has been entered upon, progress may often be delayed owing to a return of albuminuria or hæmaturia with some error of diet or climatic change; hence it is as a rule necessary to give a guarded prognosis until the albuminuria has disappeared and ordinary habits of life have been resumed.

Treatment.—The frequency of the occurrence of scarlatinal nephritis calls for the utmost watchfulness and care during the later stages of scarlet fever. Although the reports from fever hospitals indicate the extreme frequency of albuminuria and of mild cases of nephritis in connection with this disease, they also indicate most conclusively that when the disease has been under observation and careful treatment from the commencement it is free from many of the more severe symptoms which have been described above. Thus, in Caiger's cases convulsions only occurred in two instances, one of which proved fatal; and although he draws attention to the contrast presented by his statistics compared with the ordinary view of the frequency of this condition, his results were probably largely due to his cases having been under favourable circumstances from the commencement. There can be little doubt, therefore, that by watchfulness and care the tendency to scarlatinal nephritis and its dangers may be much diminished. Undoubtedly Mahomed's suggestion of the influence of constipation is correct within reasonable limits, and it is therefore essential in the treatment of the later staegs of scarlet fever to combat this symptom, if present, by frequent administrations of some mild laxative. Small doses of grey powder may be given at bedtime when the bowels have not acted during the day, and the rapidity of action may be increased by administration of some effervescing saline on first rising on the following day, or else by the administration of an enema.

In the later stages of scarlet fever the diet should consist largely of milk. Many have called attention to the curious rarity of scarlatinal nephritis during the first year of life, and by some this has been attributed to an exclusive milk diet, which is commonly followed at this time. During the whole course of scarlet fever there appears to be a large consensus of opinion in favour of either an exclusive milk diet or of a diet in which milk predominates. Some recommend that an exclusive milk diet should be continued to the end of the fourth week; but if the child can be kept under control, and the condition of the urine is constantly watched, this treatment appears rather severe. Although the child may feel well during the period of desquamation, he should still be kept in bed, not only from the risk of spreading the disease, but also from the danger of favouring nephritis or albuminuria by exposure or by violent exertion.

Alterations in the kidney and urine may sometimes be provoked by drugs which have been administered for the treatment of some complication of the primary disease. The influence of chlorate of potassium in producing albuminuria, or even hæmaturia, has been referred to in an earlier part of this book (see p. 72). From the risk of producing or increasing such symptoms, this drug should not be given internally in cases of scarlet fever, and, notwithstanding the sedative influence of gargles of chlorate of potassium, they should only be used when patients can be trusted not to swallow them. Previous reference has also been made to the danger occasionally attaching to the administration of salicylates, and, although patients with scarlet fever may be the subjects of joint pains and high temperature, it is generally advisable to avoid the use of salicylates, from the dread of provoking nephritis.

Hygienic and curative treatment.—Cases of scarlatinal nephritis or albuminuria must be rigidly confined to bed so soon as the condition has been recognised, and if previously they have been on liberal diet, the diet must be altered in the way above indicated. Sometimes, when there is much anæmia, eggs may be added to the diet, although these should be employed with some degree of caution, and should never be administered in any indigestible form. They are prone to excite constipation and to disturb gastric digestion if given hard boiled; but, on the other hand, if administered in the form of custards, or if merely beaten up with milk, they frequently appear to be beneficial. Some observers have objected that their administration is likely to increase the amount of albuminuria, but my own experience agrees with that of Caiger, and I have found that patients will more rapidly put on flesh, lose their albumin, and gain colour, if not withheld from a light, solid diet, including lightly boiled eggs.

If the dropsy is excessive in the early stages of scarlatinal nephritis, it is generally advisable to employ frequent warm vapour baths, or the wet pack. These may be used in the way already described in dealing with acute nephritis.

The rules of medicinal treatment of scarlatinal nephritis do not differ very materially from those affecting acute nephritis.

Ringer advocates the employment of aconite at the earliest period in cases of inflammation of the kidneys in scarlatina. He lays stress on the importance of the recognition of the first onset of acute inflammation, which he considers to be indicated by a rise of temperature, and he recommends that should such a rise occur during convalescence aconite should immediately be given. He adds, 'the fever, it is true, may depend upon some cause other than inflammation of the kidneys, but even then it will probably be inflammatory in character, arising from gastric catarrh, over-feeding and the like, and in any case aconite is indicated.' Purdy and others look upon digitalis as being of the utmost importance in the early stage, and indeed in all stages of this disease, and they expect from it not merely direct diuretic influence, but also improvement in the strength of the circulation. I have rarely found it necessary to employ digitalis in this way, although I have seen benefit from its use in cases of cardiac dilatation or collapse. When hæmaturia is profuse, advantage may be derived from the administration of ergot, but it is comparatively rare for the hæmaturia to persist after the patient has been kept in bed for a few days, and after the administration of two or three warm baths.

Another drug which I am in the habit of constantly using in connection with scarlatinal nephritis is perchloride of iron. The influence of this drug appears to be exerted partly as a hæmatinic, but it also seems to reduce the amount of hæmaturia. When using perchloride of iron, however, the simultaneous administration of purgatives is essential, since this drug is very apt to cause constipation. Some authors speak highly of the value of the citrate or acetate of potassium and sodium in the early stages of scarlatinal nephritis, and, although there is much to be said in favour of rendering the urine alkaline, I am in the habit of reserving these drugs until the arrest of hæmaturia. This subject has, however, been fully dealt with in connection with acute nephritis.

Reference has already been made to the need of closely watching the condition of the intestine. Constipation must be avoided, but it is also most important to avoid arresting diarrhœa, unless great exhaustion is being produced by the profuseness of this symptom.

It is comparatively rarely that any complaint is made of pain in connection with scarlatinal nephritis, but occasionally, if there is discomfort in the lumbar region, advantage may be derived from the application of leeches over the loins, by cupping of the loins, or by the use of hot fomentations.

When cases tend to become chronic, doses of quinine, together with iron, may be useful, but some authors object to this remedy, as they consider that it may enfeeble the action of the heart and cause diminished excretion of urea and uric acid. Sometimes, when the quantity of urine passed is fully normal, and when therefore the use of digitalis might scarcely seem necessary, it may be advisable to use strophanthus for its influence on the circulation; it undoubtedly powerfully stimulates the cardiac muscle, while it has little or no influence upon the excretion of urine, other than that indirectly derived from its action on the circulation. The whole treatment of scarlatinal nephritis demands continual watchfulness and patience; the administration of drugs is of secondary importance compared with the necessity of keeping the patient in a recumbent posture, and of watching the influence of diet upon the amount of albumin and casts in the water. So long as albumin is present in quantity, and so long as epithelial casts are also found, the case must be rigidly kept under observation.

(For further details of treatment, see chapter on 'Acute Nephritis.')

CHAPTER VII

CHRONIC NEPHRITIS

THIS form of nephritis has been described under numerous names which are intended either to indicate the naked-eye appearances of the kidney, or to summarise the microscopic pathological changes. It corresponds with the following: The large white kidney, non-desquamative nephritis, chronic parenchymatous nephritis, chronic tubal nephritis, chronic catarrhal nephritis, chronic diffuse nephritis; and it differs very little, if at all, from the forms which have been termed sub-acute and chronic diffused nephritis, or speckled contracted kidney.

Nearly all the terms which are above enumerated are open to objections: the chief objections are that the restrictive terms are scarcely applicable to any single case, and that, although changes occur within the tubes and affect the parenchyma, the degree with which each tissue is affected will vary considerably. Hence it appears more reasonable to describe the condition as being a chronic form of Bright's disease, without employing any term which might seem to limit the nature and extent of the pathological changes too rigidly. In the early stages the condition here described as chronic nephritis undoubtedly corresponds with the pale, marbled, or mottled kidney, and with the large, smooth, granular kidney described by Bright, but in the later stages the pathological appearances are widely different from this type.

Etiology.—Chronic nephritis in the large majority of cases is the result of a continuance of the changes due to acute nephritis. Coming after acute nephritis, it therefore occurs somewhat later in life. Frequently there is a distinct interval between the attack of acute nephritis and the onset of symptoms resulting from chronic nephritis, though if the urine is tested daily after an attack of acute nephritis small quantities of albumin may be found, either persistently or occasionally. This presence of albumin, however, may not give rise to any symptoms which might lead the patient to recognise or fear the existence of a chronic disease. The symptoms of chronic nephritis are mostly observable between the ages of twenty-five and forty, and in this respect the condition differs essentially from the age affected by cirrhosis of the kidney (chronic interstitial nephritis), a disease occurring more commonly in persons between forty and fifty, or fifty and sixty.

Scarlet fever.—Many cases of chronic nephritis result from acute scarlatinal nephritis, and there is reason to believe that chronic nephritis may even follow this disease without the recognition of the acute stage. As in the acute attack, the connection between nephritis and scarlet fever is often a matter of inference. It is well known that cases of scarlatinal nephritis may occur when the scarlatinal origin appears doubtful —where, in fact, the attack of scarlet fever has not been suspected prior to the appearance of symptoms of nephritis. It will be readily understood, therefore, that if the symptoms of scarlatinal nephritis are slight, if dropsy is not present, the disease may be overlooked, and, in the absence of treatment, may thus be allowed to become chronic. Reference has already been made to the many cases of scarlatinal nephritis where, in spite of diet and other forms of treatment, a small amount of albumin persists, although all other symptoms have passed away. If these cases are not closely followed up, it appears to be certain that they ultimately pass gradually into the form of chronic nephritis here under consideration.

Cold.—The influence of cold in the production of acute nephritis has already been mentioned, and there is common agreement that frequent exposure to wet, and residence in damp and cold climates, also favour the onset of the chronic form. It is curious to note, however, that sailors, who are much exposed to cold and wet, are not abnormally liable to chronic nephritis, which occurs more commonly amongst riverside labourers and amongst workmen employed in excavations. It is somewhat doubtful, however, whether the cold acts as a direct cause of nephritis, or whether it merely increases predisposition to the disease. It has been suggested that the congestion due to cold might develop an old-standing nephritis—that, for instance, after various exanthemata, more particularly scarlet fever, some permanent damage is done to the kidney, which causes no symptoms until engorgement, the result of exposure, once more starts the morbid processes.

Pregnancy.—Pregnancy has been sometimes assigned as a cause of chronic nephritis. In a large number of cases, however, it is probable that the pregnancy has little determining influence in producing this disease. As a rule, the albuminuria of puerperal nephritis subsides soon after delivery, and in those cases in which the albuminuria is persistent, there appears to be little doubt that the nephritis originated previously and independently of pregnancy. In many cases of puerperal albuminuria the fact of the presence of albumin is then noted for the first time, although it may have been in existence for a long time previously, and it would therefore be wholly unfair to consider that in all such cases the renal disease is due to the pregnancy.

Chronic suppuration.—Chronic suppuration resulting from phthisis, necrosed bone, or other cause, may produce chronic affection of the kidneys. The change that results is usually a form of lardaceous disease, mainly affecting the Malpighian tufts, but this alteration is very frequently accompanied by chronic nephritis; in fact, it is relatively rare to find lardaceous disease in the kidney without some form of chronic nephritis. When the kidneys suffer as the result of chronic suppuration the lardaceous changes are as a rule more advanced in children, while the nephritic changes are more marked in adults. It must be remembered, however, that these changes frequently occur simultaneously, and that it is merely a question of degree whether the kidney is to be described as lardaceous or as an example of chronic nephritis.

Malaria.—The influence of malaria as an etiological factor for chronic nephritis is open to considerable doubt. Some authors have associated chronic nephritis with malarial districts, and German authors more particularly have stated that this factor accounts for the frequency of nephritis along the northern coasts of Europe. There is, however, very little to show that a pure form of nephritis may result from exposure to malarial influences. Dr. I. E. Atkinson [1] made some elaborate

---
[1] *American Journal of Medical Sciences*, July 1884.

investigations in this connection, and he found that transitory albuminuria was not uncommon in the course of malarial fevers, and he attributed this to the intense visceral congestion characteristic of these affections; but, apart from this form of albuminuria, he found that in a certain proportion of cases, varying with the locality and type of the prevailing epidemic, or else with individual conditions, true inflammation of the kidney occurred accompanied by dropsy and by the usual symptoms of nephritis. The usual form of this nephritis, according to Dr. Atkinson, is one in which the inflammation seems to be most intense in the neighbourhood of the glomeruli, and although the tendency of malarial inflammation of the kidney is towards recovery, yet he concluded that the frequent repetition of malarial troubles might lead to structural changes characteristic of chronic Bright's disease. It must be admitted, also, that observations made in Algiers and at Bombay show that in these places the association of chronic Bright's disease with malaria is as marked as it is in colder climates; hence the supposition that malarial nephritis is essentially due to exposure to cold scarcely seems to be tenable.

Syphilis.—The connection with syphilis is fairly close, and chronic changes within the kidney may be associated with chronic syphilis independently of the growth of renal gummata.

Toxic agents.—In some cases chronic nephritis has been attributed to the use of mercury, while lead is also said to cause a form of chronic inflammation of the kidneys of the same nature. The connection between chronic nephritis and lead-poisoning is not so strong as between gout and lead-poisoning, which are so often associated with cirrhosis of the kidney.

Alcohol.—The relation of chronic alcoholism to chronic nephritis is less open to dispute, though, as in the case of lead-poisoning, chronic alcoholism is more likely to lead to renal cirrhosis than to chronic nephritis.

Chronic nephritis secondary to other conditions.—Chronic nephritis occurs fairly commonly as the result of chronic diseases of the urinary passages. Chronic stricture of the urethra, purulent cystitis and prostatitis, and calculus pyelitis are all liable to give rise to chronic nephritis; the nephritis which arises under these conditions is frequently associated with lardaceous changes.

Theory of the causation of chronic nephritis.—Although it is commonly considered that chronic nephritis has its origin in an acute attack, and although this position is not materially shaken by the statement that it may sometimes commence as a slow, lingering process, yet it is interesting to note that the changes are not universally attributed to anatomical lesions. According to one theory the disease depends upon an alteration of the blood, and the renal lesion plays a secondary part.

Another hypothesis is that Bright's disease is part of a general nutritive disturbance which interferes with the assimilation of albumin, and the source of this interference has been attributed to some alteration of the functions of the skin, whether these functions are disturbed by cold, by interference with the freedom of perspiration, or by some form of skin disease. It must be admitted that in many forms of chronic Bright's disease the skin does not act with its customary freedom, and Semmola has compared persons with Bright's disease to animals whose skin has been varnished.

Another interesting theory is that chronic Bright's disease results from irritation by various toxic substances produced by incomplete oxidation of the tissues, as, for example, creatin, creatinin, leucin, tyrosin, xanthin, and hypoxanthin. This theory may, to a certain extent, receive support from the undoubted occurrence of chronic nephritis in connection with diabetes.

Other observers attribute chronic nephritis to some disease of the central nervous system, by means of which an alteration is produced in the flow of blood to the kidney.

These various theories have little practical bearing; perhaps the most interesting is that dealing with the frequency with which alterations in the functions of the skin are associated with chronic Bright's disease. These alterations were many years ago pointed out to me by the late Sir George Johnson, and he then indicated that the change in the functions of the skin did not affect all cases of chronic nephritis.

Pathological anatomy.—The appearances of the kidney in chronic nephritis are subject to the greatest variations, variations for which one is wholly unprepared in view of the great similarity of symptoms. Thus, cases which are practically indistinguishable so far as the symptoms are concerned, may be associated with either large white kidney, or with the smaller granular kidney, or with the speckled kidney. Sometimes, too, the naked-eye appearances indicate very little, if any, deviation from the normal type. In spite of these differences, however, the microscopic examination will generally indicate fundamental points of resemblance. If the disease terminates within a year of the first development of symptoms, the kidney is, as a rule, found to be larger than usual. Sometimes this enlargement is extreme, and the kidneys may be from twice to three times their normal size. Fagge mentions three cases in which the weight of a pair of kidneys was $28\frac{1}{2}$ to 29 ounces. The capsule is usually readily detached, and the surface of the kidney is smooth and somewhat pale; sometimes the capsule cannot be so easily stripped off, and after removal the surface is finely granular and perhaps somewhat torn. The cortical part of the kidney usually shows stellate hæmorrhages or engorgements of the stellate veins. On section, whitish or yellowish streaks and spots may be found passing through the substance of the cortex, and these may give the appearance of the kidney having been strewn with fine sand. The cortex is considerably thickened, so much so that it may nearly equal the thickness of the cones. It will be remembered that the normal relation between the cortex and the medulla is generally as 1 to 3; in chronic nephritis the cortex is so much increased that it may be from 1 to 2, or the parts may even be of equal thickness. The cones are usually of a darker red than the cortex, and form a marked contrast with the pale cortical portion of the kidney. As in cases of acute nephritis, the microscopic examination shows that the changes are not uniformly distributed through the kidney, but that they affect certain areas, while intervening tracts of tissue appear to be normal. All the structures of the kidney may, however, be involved in chronic nephritis. The condition is one in which alterations are found not merely in the tubules, but also in the Malpighian tufts, in the interstitial tissues and in the blood vessels. In the convoluted tubes the epithelium is generally swollen, cloudy, and less transparent than usual; the degree of swelling may be sufficient almost to occlude the tubule, and also to interfere

PLATE V.

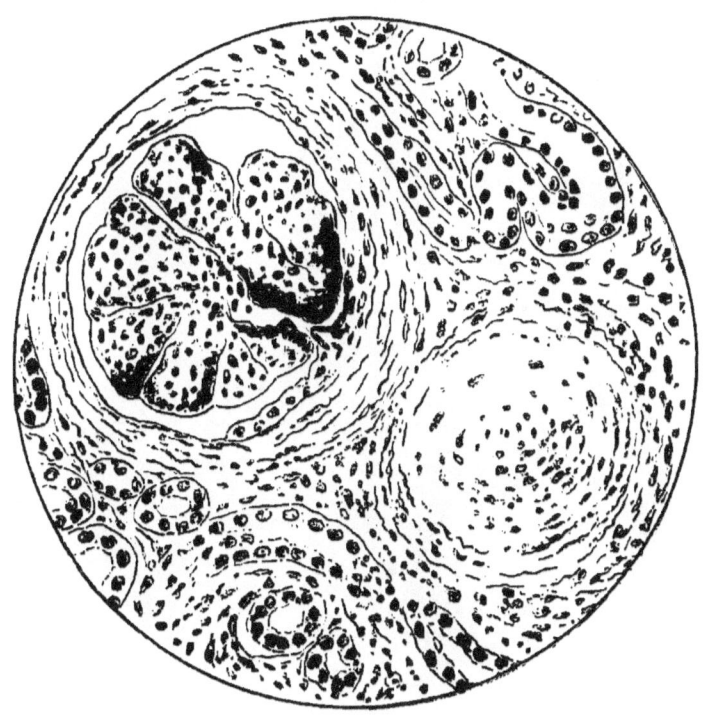

Section of Kidney in Chronic Nephritis, showing Peri-Capsulitis and Endo-Capsulitis. Much new cellular infiltration is seen outside the capsules, while the capsule itself is thickened by concentric laminæ, which are greatest in amount near the attachment of the glomerular tuft. On the right the glomerular tuft is not included in the section, which shows only the capsule.

(*See pp.* 143 *and* 122.)

N. Tirard, Del.   Mintern Bros., imp.

with the freedom of circulation. The combined result of the distension of the tubes, and of the compression of the blood vessels, is seen in the white or grey colour of the cortex Sometimes, however, the tubules are found with the epithelium desquamated or proliferating; sometimes the tubules may be entirely denuded of epithelium. Occasionally the renal epithelium is replaced by thin, flattened cells, the lumen of the tube being considerably increased in diameter. The extent to which the interstitial tissue is affected will also vary considerably. It is generally considered that there is cellular infiltration of the spaces between the tubules, which subsequently results in the formation of fibrous connective tissue, and undergoes contraction. The extent to which this development of interstitial tissue occurs, may lead ultimately to irregularities of the surface of the kidney, and may be responsible in some cases for the partial adhesion of the capsule.

Although this interpretation of the appearances is the one that is generally adopted, it must be remembered that they have received another interpretation, and that the nuclei of the interstitial inflammation have been referred to the obliterated blood vessels, while the tracts of fibrous tissue have been described as tracts in which the tubules have been similarly obliterated. Inasmuch, however, as the large white kidney undoubtedly occurs in a later contracted form, there seems to be every reason to believe that the contraction is due to the subsequent alterations in an overgrowth of fibrous tissue.

The changes affecting the Malpighian tufts are similar to those characteristic of acute nephritis. As the result of subsequent changes, however, the glomeruli appear more or less atrophied, while the capsule of Bowman is considerably thickened, and its epithelial lining has undergone degeneration. Frequently the Malpighian tuft is infiltrated with leucocytes, and the surrounding tissue also presents an excess of nuclei. Greenfield has described three changes connected with the capsule:—1. Peri-capsulitis, or cellular infiltration and tissue formation occurring chiefly outside the capsule; 2. Hyaline thickening of the capsule itself; 3. Endo-capsulitis, or the formation of concentric laminæ of cells and tissue inside the capsule, between it and the glomerular tuft. In chronic cases these concentric laminæ are due to a new formation between the capsule and the tuft, and the capillaries meanwhile undergo hyaline thickening. The capsule, in advanced cases, is striated and concentrically thickened, and blends with the sclerosed glomerular tuft.[1] These changes are not invariably present; they are most common in chronic nephritis originating in scarlatinal nephritis, but even in such cases they are occasionally absent. The branches of small arteries within the kidney are invariably found to be considerably thickened, the hypertrophy affecting the muscular coat, as described by Sir George Johnson. Some thickening, however, of the fibrous wall of the vessel must also be recognised. The vessels alone may sometimes appear to be engorged with blood, but more often some of the tubes also show the presence of red blood corpuscles closely packed together, while in other parts of the kidney the lumen of the tubes may be occupied by casts. The increase in the size of the kidney is generally due to inflammatory deposits in the parenchyma and interstitial tissues. If, however, the overgrowth of interstitial elements is associated with marked atrophy of the parenchyma, the absolute size of the kidney may not appear to have undergone any very material alteration.

On the other hand, if the new connective tissue undergoes contraction, the size, weight, and appearance of the kidney will differ greatly from the appearances above described. The kidney, however, remains more pale and mottled than in the normal condition, and, though the surface may become uneven and granular, the colour alone indicates that the case is one of contracted white kidney, instead of being one of small, red, granular, or cirrhosed kidney. When the kidney is diminished in size in this way, the chief change is one affecting the cortex, which becomes narrower than before, and on microscopic examination of the cortex, wide tracts of fibrous tissue, almost homogeneous in appearance, may be found lying either immediately below the capsule or in the course of the interlobular arteries. In this tissue, atrophied tubes, Malpighian bodies and blood vessels may be found, and in the intervening spaces between these patches of fibrous tissue, the epithelial cells of the convoluted tubes are seen to be fatty and opaque, and small cysts, similar to those so

[1] Auld, *Lancet*, 1892.

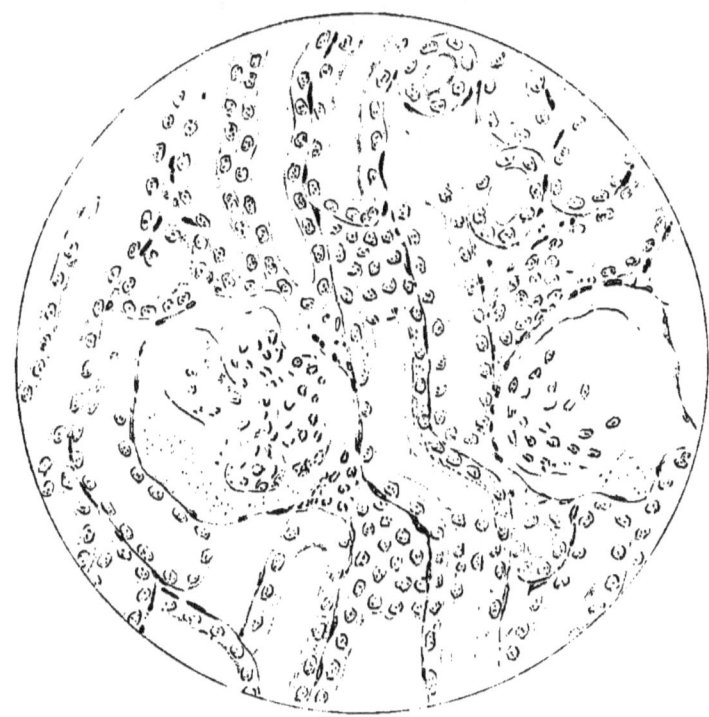

Section of Kidney in Chronic Nephritis, showing Cast in a Tube. The tubes are seen to be distended, the epithelial cells cloudy, the nuclei poorly stained. A long curved cast is to be seen in the interior of one tube, with detached nuclei lying on its surface. The space between the glomerular tuft and the capsule is occupied by granular débris.

(*See pp.* 145 *and* 121.)

N. Tirard, Del. Mintern Bros., imp.

common in renal cirrhosis, often result from blocking of the tubes. In other respects the changes of the Malpighian bodies, of Bowman's capsule, and of the smaller arteries, are similar to the changes described in connection with the large white kidney. The large white, or rather the large yellow, kidney is found more particularly in cases of scarlatinal nephritis, which have passed into a chronic stage and terminated relatively early. Otherwise, apart from cases exhibiting lardaceous changes, the large white kidney is not very frequently seen; in fact, my colleague, Dr. Dalton, Professor of Pathology at King's College, recently told me that there had of late been relatively few instances of the large white kidney, while the contracted white kidney was found more frequently than hitherto. The explanation he suggested was that possibly the cases of large white kidney were proving to be more amenable to treatment, and hence that a greater length of time had been allowed for the occurrence of contraction.

From the above description it will be seen that although the macroscopic appearances of the kidney are so very dissimilar, yet the microscopic changes are merely those which might be anticipated as the result of a chronic process; in fact, the difference in appearance depends largely upon the length of time that has elapsed between the commencement of the disease and its termination. Neither condition is essentially parenchymatous or essentially interstitial. The parenchymatous changes may be more apparent in the earlier stages of the large white kidney, while the interstitial changes predominate in the later conditions, but all the tissues are simultaneously affected, and the size of the kidney seems undoubtedly to depend upon the degree of contraction and atrophy that has succeeded the inflammatory process. Lardaceous changes may occasionally develop in connection with chronic nephritis, but they are of slight extent, and do not materially affect the size of the kidney. The tendency of chronic nephritis is undoubtedly towards atrophy and contraction, and indeed some authors consider that the later stages, when the kidney is small, pale, with a narrow cortex and granular surface, have always been preceded by an earlier stage in which it was enlarged, white, and with a thickened cortex.

Symptoms.—From what has been said of the variable character of the appearances of the kidney after death, it will be readily understood that the symptoms are subject to great variations. Sometimes the disease may follow a rapid course, but sometimes, if it has been detected in the earlier stages, the symptoms may extend over a far greater period. It is only in exceptional cases that the transition from acute nephritis to chronic nephritis can be watched so that the clinical picture is complete in all its details; far more commonly the patients come under observation when the disease has already been of long standing. Some of the earliest indications are to be found in alterations in the urine, in the occurrence of dropsy, and in the development of anæmia, which is frequently profound.

The urine.—The quantity of urine passed is to a certain extent dependent upon the degree of dropsy, and, although the daily quantity is subject to great variations, it is on the average less than the amount passed in a normal state of health. The decrease, however, in the early stages is not very considerable, and it is by no means comparable with that which occurs in the course of acute nephritis. In the early stages the colour is generally somewhat darker than usual, and to a certain extent the colour is dependent upon the amount passed. It is often noteworthy that with chronic cases the amount may be reduced to half the normal quantity or even less, but cases of complete suppression are comparatively rare, and as a rule anuria only occurs shortly before the fatal termination. Usually, as the dropsy increases the amount of urine progressively decreases. In the early stages the specific gravity is slightly lower. If the case has been followed from its commencement in an acute attack, it will have been noted that as the signs of hæmorrhage decreased the urine presented a cloudy deposit; this is generally to be considered of serious import. When examined, it is found to consist largely of casts, which in the early stages are mostly of the hyaline variety, though with any sub-acute inflammatory complication epithelial casts and blood casts may be superadded. At other times the casts present oil globules as well as evidence of granular degeneration. In chronic nephritis casts are generally present in very large quantity, and they are readily to be detected. In addition, however, numerous corpuscles may be met with. Sometimes these consist of large white corpuscles or leucocytes; more rarely red blood corpuscles may be found. The red corpuscles may occasionally become relatively numerous, although they are never present in such large quantities as in acute nephritis. Renal epithelium may sometimes be detected, and when present it is frequently somewhat opaque or cloudy, indicating the existence of degenerative changes. Occasionally also there is much granular *débris*—sometimes floating freely in the urine, more often collected around the casts.

In the early stages of chronic nephritis albumin is always present in considerable quantity. It has been stated that in cases of large white kidney there are on an average larger quantities of albumin than with the spotted or contracted kidney; but this, however, is certainly not always the case. As the disease progresses, the quantity of urine may increase to the normal, or may even be slightly above the normal amount; at the same time the urine becomes more pale, the specific gravity falls, and the amount of albumin is diminished. Throughout the disease the quantity of urea is greatly diminished, and it is owing to this diminution that the specific gravity of the urine falls below the normal. Fürbringer lays stress upon the theory that the decrease in the daily quantity of urine depends upon the decreased rapidity of the blood current, and also upon the impermeability of the glomeruli.

Within certain limits, it is possible to estimate the degree of renal change by the alterations in the urine. As the contraction proceeds the amount of urine becomes greater, while the specific gravity is diminished and the quantity of albumin is also decreased. These changes therefore tend to render the urine somewhat similar to that which is passed by patients with a contracted or cirrhotic kidney.

A curious result of chronic nephritis is that the kidney loses its normal power of eliminating various drugs. Thus the elimination of the following may be impeded: iodide of potassium, salicylic acid, quinine. The power of transforming benzoic acid into hippuric acid is also stated to be impaired.

Dropsy.—Although the changes in the urine are so characteristic, patients most commonly come under observation on account of the development of dropsy. The dropsy of chronic nephritis usually develops slowly, and in the early stages is not excessive. At the commencement it is comparable with the œdema of chlorosis, inasmuch as the puffiness of the face which attracts the patient's attention on first rising gradually subsides during the day, while the ankles increase in size towards the evening. When the disease is fully established the dropsy may become excessive, and may affect not only the lower extremities, but the whole of the subcutaneous tissue, and it may also involve the serous cavities. When patients are kept in bed, swelling of the scrotum or of the back may develop. When the œdema has once claimed attention, it is generally one of the most difficult symptoms to deal with, since, although it may appear to yield to treatment, it rarely disappears entirely, and sometimes, with little warning, it increases rapidly, so that the extremities become enormously swollen; not uncommonly the distension may result in cracking of the skin, which allows the escape of the dropsical effusion. Sometimes the degree of distension so much interferes with the nutrition of the skin that patches of the surface may slough. The amount of effusion within the abdominal cavity is occasionally considerable, but it almost invariably occurs subsequently to the swelling of the legs. The ascites occasionally impedes respiration and circulation, though these functions are more likely to be interfered with owing to the presence of fluid within the pleural cavity or within the pericardium.

One form of œdema which is particularly prone to produce a fatal result is the œdema of the glottis, which may develop with great rapidity.

In milder cases, the dropsical effusion may vary greatly in amount, the degree of swelling of the legs or scrotum showing but little variation until the supervention of some sub-acute inflammation, owing possibly to exposure or to some irregularity of diet.

Anæmia.—The degree of anæmia which is present in cases of chronic nephritis is always very noticeable. In cases that are proceeding from acute nephritis to chronic, the development of extreme anæmia will excite considerable anxiety, and even when the transition has not been medically observed there is no mistaking the pallor and puffiness of patients with chronic nephritis. Moreover, it appears probable that some of the most troublesome symptoms from which the patient may suffer are indirectly the result of anæmia. It is quite possible that in the early stages the dyspepsia, the severe headache, and the frequent shortness of breath are to be in part attributed to the intense anæmia. The poverty of blood also interferes largely with the general nutrition of the patient. With chronic nephritis patients very frequently waste very considerably, and the degree of wasting, although to a large extent masked by the dropsical swelling, may become very evident if, under treatment, the œdema is rapidly reduced. Another evidence of the interference with nutrition is to be found in the great loss of muscular power.

Circulatory system.—The degree to which the circulatory system is involved in cases of chronic nephritis is to a certain extent dependent upon the stage of the disease. There is generally dilatation and hypertrophy of the left ventricle, and some hypertrophic change affecting the smaller arteries. The extent to which these alterations proceed increases as the kidney diminishes in size, so that with advanced contraction of the kidney there will be much hypertrophy of the heart, and also of the smaller vessels. These changes, however, are not so extreme as in cases of chronic renal cirrhosis. Sometimes acute dilatation of the ventricle occurs, and is accompanied by dyspnœa and cyanosis. Far more commonly the dilatation is accompanied by hypertrophy, which is to a large extent compensatory. It must be distinctly remembered that the pulse changes are not so marked as in cases of cirrhosed kidney. The rapidity of the pulse in chronic nephritis is usually increased, and the tracings are marked by dicrotism. That the blood pressure is not markedly increased in chronic nephritis is shown by the comparative rarity of retinal hæmorrhages and cerebral hæmorrhages. When these supervene, they are indications that the kidney has already undergone contraction.

Muscular system.—Reference has already been made to the loss of strength which occurs in chronic nephritis. As the dropsical effusion increases, the patient almost invariably complains of marked loss of strength, which he is at first inclined to attribute to the weight of his limbs; he is more readily fatigued with slight exertion, and more prone to sit down after walking a short distance, more ready to keep to his chair or his bed with any slight cold or over-exertion. The degree of muscular wasting is, however, not apparent until the dropsical effusion in the lower extremities is diminished, but frequently the contrast between the thin flabby upper arms and deltoids and the enormous size of the hands and wrists sufficiently indicates the extent of loss of muscular substance.

Digestive system.—From the early stages the digestive system appears to be implicated in cases of chronic nephritis. Patients have usually very little appetite, and are apt to become somewhat fanciful with regard to the choice of their diet. They may develop a distaste for meat, and frequently they attribute their dislike to certain food to impaired digestion. This distaste for food sometimes becomes excessive, and may proceed to actual nausea and vomiting. These symptoms cause great distress to the patient, and undoubtedly increase the tendency to anæmia, even though they may be partly the result of this condition. Frequently the material which is vomited consists largely of water, and it has therefore been suggested that it may be the result of œdema of the mucous membrane of the stomach. In all probability, however, the vomiting of chronic nephritis is to be regarded as one of the indications of uræmia, but it is undoubtedly due also to some excess of local irritation, as may be inferred from the fact that it is frequently excited by some of the remedies that are employed, which in the normal condition would not produce this result. In the later stages of the disease diarrhœa is occasionally excessive, the motions not only being more frequent, but containing large quantities of liquid. All these symptoms are very exhausting to the patient, and they have the further disadvantage of being extremely difficult to treat. They frequently defy all therapeutic measures that are adopted, and contribute largely to the weakness from which the patient ultimately sinks. Occasionally ulceration of the intestine occurs, and the diarrhœa then alters in character, pus, blood, and shreds of mucus being present.

Nervous system.—Notwithstanding the diminution in the excretory work of the kidney, symptoms of acute uræmia are comparatively rare in connection with chronic nephritis, and it has been suggested that the rarity of this symptom results from the retention of urea in the dropsical fluid. As in cases of acute nephritis, uræmic symptoms have been observed when, under the influence of vapour baths, the reabsorption of the dropsical effusion has commenced, and this occurrence certainly favours the idea that this reabsorption throws into the circulation a large quantity of toxic material. In dealing with uræmia, it will be noted that the toxic material which causes uræmic convulsions in all probability does not consist of urea. Nevertheless, the rarity of acute uræmic symptoms with cases of excessive dropsical effusion is noteworthy, and, in all probability, the excessive effusion serves to protect the system from the results of the impaired excretory work of the kidney. Symptoms of chronic uræmia are, on the contrary, relatively frequent, the chief of these being severe headache, impaired mental activity, frequent vomiting, dyspepsia, and diarrhœa, and occasional attacks of an asthmatic nature which cannot be referred to alterations in the lung, the heart, or the pleura.

Reference has already been made to the occasional occurrence of retinal changes, which may perhaps be considered as indications of extreme contraction of the kidney, but, in addition to these disturbances of vision, amaurosis may be developed occasionally, independently of any retinal change.

It is somewhat doubtful under what heading the following symptoms should be classified—whether they are to be regarded as uræmic or as the result of disturbances of the nervous system ; but it is fairly frequent to find that patients with chronic nephritis suffer from numbness in the fingers, itching, pins and needles, or even burning pains in the hands and arms. These symptoms, which may be attributed either to vasomotor affections or to a neuralgic condition, are more frequently seen in connection with advanced chronic nephritis, where contraction of the kidney has probably occurred.

Secondary inflammations. — Secondary inflammations are mostly the cause of death in cases of chronic nephritis, and they may affect either the external or internal organs. Thus, the tendency to erysipelas and to gangrene is peculiarly marked in cases of this nature, and this tendency must be borne in mind whenever the skin has been broken by the excess of dropsical effusion, or by puncture with a view to relieving distension.

Notwithstanding the utmost antiseptic care, erysipelas and gangrene frequently supervene.

In connection with the digestive system, the frequency of vomiting and diarrhœa has already been mentioned. Occasionally, towards the termination of the case, severe hæmorrhages may occur, either from the stomach or from the bowel.

Of the pulmonary complications, secondary pneumonia is the most important, while the tendency to pleurisy and to the development of pus within the pleural cavity is relatively frequent. It is not uncommon to find pericarditis develop with considerable rapidity, and frequently a pericardial rub may be heard even when the patient is not complaining of pain. The pericarditis of chronic nephritis is not usually associated with much effusion, while. the fluid tends to become purulent; occasionally, however, the whole pericardium may be distended with muco-purulent fluid. The degree of engorgement of lung varies greatly, and it is usually in inverse proportion to the degree of effusion within the chest. Although changes within the spleen and liver are occasionally noted, they do not lead to symptoms which differ in any way from those due to chronic engorgement of these organs. Abortion is said to be favoured by chronic nephritis, and this has been attributed to premature detachment of the placenta, or to the development of white nodules, probably degenerative, within this organ.

Abnormal types.—Sundry abnormal types of nephritis may occasionally be met with. One of these constitutes the chronic hæmorrhagic Bright's disease without œdema which was described by Wagner; this type is marked by the frequent recurrence of periodic hæmorrhages. These attacks only last a few days at a time, but may return at intervals of a week or a month. Between the attacks the urine is in every respect similar to that which is characteristic of contracted kidney, and the general health suffers very little. In some of these cases tertiary syphilis was also present, but cases of this type are, however, so uncommon that it is impossible to state whether they have any dependence upon syphilis.

Another variety, which is not so rare, presents symptoms of acute hæmorrhagic nephritis of sudden development in the course of the chronic disease, and this type is especially prone to be mistaken for general acute nephritis. During these attacks the quantity of urine passed is increased occasionally to a great extent, and it is invariably mixed with blood. Cases marked by these intercurrent symptoms frequently run a short course. There is some reason to believe that in many cases this form of acute hæmorrhagic nephritis is a true inflammatory process constituting an extension of original disease, and, when it is remembered that in cases of chronic nephritis certain areas only of the kidney are affected, it will be readily understood that the healthy intervening spaces may become the subject of an acute attack.

Anomalous cases of chronic nephritis sometimes occur, which exhibit only some of the prominent symptoms, such as anæmia, dropsy and dyspepsia; but though the patient may be free from obvious symptoms, yet the microscopic examination of the urine indicates the presence of granular casts, renal epithelium, and granular *débris* characteristic of this disease. In these cases, in all probability, the area affected is small and circumscribed, but the changes are undoubtedly those of chronic nephritis.

Course and Duration.—From what has already been said of the varying types of chronic nephritis, it is obvious that the duration and prognosis of these cases will differ considerably. When the disease can be traced onwards from an antecedent acute nephritis, the duration may be almost indefinitely prolonged. The albumin may diminish after some weeks or months, and may even disappear entirely. In such cases, however, there is very little doubt that a certain portion of the kidney has been permanently damaged, and that the disease may recur at a later period.

With cases in which dropsy is a marked feature from the commencement, and where the initial inflammatory stage cannot be determined, the duration is still exceedingly variable. The majority terminate within a year or two, owing either to the enfeeblement produced by impaired nutrition, or to the drain upon the system from the extreme dropsical effusion; as has been already indicated, the termination may also be preceded by one or other of the secondary inflammations. Occasionally, the duration may be considerably longer; and in some cases, although without a doubt the patients are suffering from chronic nephritis, a fair amount of general health may be maintained during a period of from five to ten years. Dropsy is the symptom which is the most persistent in connection with chronic nephritis; but although this may be extreme, and may even threaten life, yet under exceptional circumstances it may entirely pass away, and the patient may resume a condition of apparent health marred only by the presence of albuminuria and anæmia. This condition of apparent health may be prolonged until exposure or some irregularity of life may once more start active inflammatory changes in the damaged kidney, when the clinical picture again assumes the urgent characteristics.

Diagnosis.—As in most diseases of the kidney, there is little difficulty of diagnosis in classic cases. The chief indications are the profound anæmia, the excessive dropsy with characteristic localisation, the copious albuminuria, and the diminished amount of water passed. In addition to these may be noted the relative quantity of casts of various forms, the great number of leucocytes, and the frequent admixture with epithelial cells which have mostly undergone fatty degeneration. These indications are usually associated with great debility and with anorexia. The diagnosis may, however, be somewhat obscured if the onset of the disease has been gradual, and if it has not been marked by dropsy or by excessive albuminuria. The forms of Bright's disease which are most likely to give trouble with the diagnosis are: (1) Cyanotic induration of the kidney; (2) lardaceous disease; (3) cirrhosis of the kidney; and (4) occasional cases of acute nephritis.

The points which may help the diagnosis of these types are the following: In cyanotic induration the dropsy is generally confined to the lower extremities, or the history indicates that it has commenced in the lower extremities; the amount of albumin is then relatively small, and varies greatly from day to day. The renal casts are usually hyaline and of small size, and although leucocytes may be present, they are not so numerous as in cases of chronic nephritis. Unless the disease has reached an advanced stage, the general condition of the patient is comparatively good, but the symptoms are often those of disease of the heart: valvular murmurs may be heard, and the patient's breathing is usually more embarrassed, although in the most advanced stages of chronic nephritis there may be urgent dyspnœa, owing to engorgement of the lung, or to accumulation within the pleura. Generally, but not always, the skin is dark and cyanosed, and contrasts markedly with the pallor of chronic nephritis.

With lardaceous disease the amount of urine is usually greatly above the normal quantity, and the history of the case points generally to some chronic disease, often associated with prolonged suppuration. Increase in size both of the liver and the spleen may mostly be detected, and the indications of gastro-intestinal trouble occur more early and are more persistent. Although diarrhœa is one of the symptoms of chronic nephritis, it occurs at a late stage, while in lardaceous disease of the kidney it is an early symptom.

To distinguish chronic nephritis from cirrhosis of the kidney it is necessary to consider the history very closely, since the symptoms of cirrhosis are very similar to those of chronic nephritis with contraction of the kidney. When the case has been one of primary cirrhosis there is generally a complete absence of dropsy. The amount of albumin passed is relatively small, and the quantity of urine is increased beyond the normal amount. In cirrhosis the alterations in the heart and in the blood vessels develop early and precede dropsy, which does not always occur in connection with this disease. On the other hand, in chronic nephritis the cardio-vascular changes only occur at a late stage, and are almost invariably preceded by dropsy. Even when cardio-vascular changes appear in connection with the contracted stage in chronic nephritis, they are not usually so marked as in cirrhosis.

Diminution in the amount of hæmoglobin in the blood occurs especially in parenchymatous nephritis, the amount of hæmoglobin lost being proportionate to the severity of the disease, while in chronic interstitial nephritis there is no diminution of the hæmoglobin. The blood pressure in the former disease tends to fall below normal at first, and only in the later course rises above normal, without, however, approaching the high blood pressure which is presented by interstitial nephritis in the advanced stage. On the contrary, in the latter condition the blood pressure is increased from the beginning, and in the course of years reaches the highest degree which can be attained in the human body.

With regard to acute nephritis, the distinction is again largely determined by the history of the patient. Previous attacks of dropsy, or a history of persistent dropsy, will help to prevent mistakes, even though the urine may contain blood and blood casts. In the absence of definite history, it is sometimes extremely difficult to differentiate a superadded sub-acute nephritis from a simple acute nephritis. The appearance of the urine may be very misleading, but in chronic nephritis it is generally not so deeply blood tinged, and after the disappearance of the hæmorrhage, the amount of albumin present is subject to less variations than in cases of acute nephritis. The cases which present the greatest difficulty are those in which there is reason to believe that the chronic nephritis has been in existence sufficiently long for considerable contraction of the kidney to have occurred. In connection with these cases the appearance of the patient may afford some help, while the history of repeated attacks of dropsy will further tend to indicate that the case is one of a contracted kidney, the result of chronic nephritis rather than of cirrhosis of the kidney.

Prognosis.—The prognosis of cases of chronic nephritis is to be based largely upon the results of treatment. As a rule, the prognosis is bad, but the danger is less imminent when the disease appears to be secondary to malaria or syphilis, as under such circumstances the treatment of the cause may materially influence the prognosis of the resulting renal disease. Even when the result of treatment is to cause rapid diminution of the dropsy, and apparent restoration to health, it is necessary to speak somewhat guardedly about the ulterior prospects of the patient. These improvements are in most cases merely an indication of partial and incomplete cure. The prognosis is rendered more grave when the amount of albumin is considerable, when the daily excretion of urine is much diminished, and when the sediment exhibits numerous leucocytes; on the other hand, the presence of casts affords very uncertain indications upon which to base a prognosis. Much hypertrophy of the heart, indicating the transition to the contracted kidney, usually forms an element of grave import, but it is never well to despair of patients, even when the symptoms appear most threatening. This is shown by the case quoted by Fürbringer, in which a patient with probably very large white kidneys was able to wander about the hospital gardens without experiencing any pain, and who, nevertheless, had a few months previously been twice moribund, who had remained weeks in uræmic coma, and from whom over fifty quarts of chylo-serous fluid were drawn by puncture. This patient, who during the winter had been enormously swollen with œdema, was, when the account was written, the subject of renal marasmus, and the urine, which had mostly contained a large quantity of albumin, then only gave slight reactions.

As a rule, the prognosis is more favourable in cases of recent onset, and the outlook becomes more gloomy if the symptoms continue to be severe some time after the original onset. The prognosis is also rendered more unfavourable when the proportion of renal solids is materially diminished, since diminution in these, especially a diminution in the daily excretion of urea, indicates extensive pathological changes within the kidney.

The prognosis of some complex forms of nephritis is very difficult. Although some cases of chronic nephritis present the typical symptoms of parenchymatous nephritis (large white kidney), and others those of genuine interstitial nephritis, Ziemssen[1] believes that the mixed form is more common. The preponderance of parenchymatous or interstitial nephritis may be diagnosed from the clinical features, and Ziemssen thinks the gradual transition of the parenchymatous form into the secondary contracted kidney may often be observed, and in such cases there may be distinct improvement in the patient's condition. Improvement may also occur in patients presenting symptoms of a parenchymatous and mixed form of chronic nephritis. Thus, in a case of marked dropsy, with scanty urine and albuminuria, the œdema may disappear without operation, and the patient may for a long period remain free from symptoms, with the exception of albuminuria, and it is possible that a true healing of the kidney affection may occur, and that regenerative processes may result.

[1] *Deutsches Archiv für klin. Medicin*, Band lv.

In cases in which albuminuria persists for many years, and in which the excretion of albumin often reaches a high degree, whilst the quantity and the specific gravity of the urine are almost normal, and general disturbance is absent or only slight, Ziemssen believes that there are circumscribed inflammatory changes in the kidney substance, from which localised patches the excretion of albumin occurs; and he considers it possible that such cases of partial nephritis may recover. When exacerbations of the disease are produced by various causes, such as infectious diseases, pregnancy, &c., the pathological process advances, and leads ultimately to a fatal termination.

Treatment.—The prophylactic treatment of chronic nephritis must always be considered when dealing with acute nephritis which is running a prolonged course. Thus, in connection with acute nephritis from scarlatina or any other cause, there is reason to believe that the supervention of chronic symptoms may occasionally be prevented by keeping the patients under observation so long as any albumin is present in the water. Certainly, so far as scarlatinal nephritis is concerned, the influence of exposure and of cold appear to be well marked, both as favouring the onset of the acute attack and also as prolonging the disease, and thus favouring the establishment of chronic changes.

Reference has previously been made to the need of care in the dietary of patients with acute nephritis, and there can be no doubt that by means of sensible hygienic measures the chronic form of the disease may frequently be prevented. The restrictions of diet which have been recommended in the treatment of acute nephritis are equally necessary in connection with sub-acute nephritis complicating chronic nephritis. The patients must be kept in bed, and, during the hæmorrhagic stages, should be kept rigidly upon a milk diet. When, however, the disease is of a slighter nature, or more obviously chronic, it is unnecessary to limit the diet so strictly as to eliminate all forms of nitrogenous diet. It is essential that the strength should be maintained, and patients frequently do well when various nutritious soups and light nourishment are given, together with an abundance of milk.

The medicinal treatment of cases of chronic nephritis is as a whole somewhat disappointing. As a general rule, it may be asserted that it is almost, if not quite, impossible to cure the disease, and the utmost that can be done is to improve the work of the kidneys and of the organs secondarily affected. There can be no doubt, however, that some rare cases tend to spontaneous recovery, in spite of treatment, rather than on account of the drugs which have been employed.

It will be most convenient, perhaps, to consider the treatment under the following headings: (1) The treatment of the cause; (2) the treatment of the disease; and (3) the treatment of the various symptoms which may develop in the course of the disease.

(1) *Treatment of cause.*—In the majority of cases it is absolutely impossible to treat the cause, since the patient comes under observation at a time when the disease is fully established, and the causation is uncertain or remote. When the disease is, however, due to malaria, or syphilis, or when it is the result of suppurative processes, the treatment can be carried out more hopefully. If due to malaria, quinine and other antiperiodics may be of value; while syphilis is to be treated upon general principles. If any cause of chronic suppuration exists, this may be treated by surgical measures, according to the special indications of the case. Attempts have been made to treat or to avert chronic nephritis by the employment of various antiseptics administered internally. Thus carbolic acid, salicylic acid, sulphocarbolates and salicylates have been administered with a view of arresting the activity of micro-organisms. It is extremely doubtful whether these drugs can be given in sufficiently large doses to arrest the action of microbes within the kidney, and it must be remembered that they frequently increase albuminuria if it is already existent, and that they may produce hæmaturia or albuminuria during their time of elimination. For the same reasons, chlorate of potassium is to be avoided. Numerous instances of toxic or uræmic symptoms have resulted from the injudicious employment of chlorate of potassium in cases of diphtheria. Even when mercury is used in connection with chronic nephritis, its employment must be carefully watched, since the results of its use may add largely to the dangers of

the case. Though it may be employed in cases of syphilis, its effect on the nature of the urine must be carefully noted. In cases of prolonged suppuration, although it is tempting to employ iodoform externally, the use of this drug requires considerable caution, since there are risks of its absorption and of its producing an increase in the quantity of albumin and a diminution in the amount of renal excretion.

(2) *The treatment of the disease* is still more unsatisfactory. It is far easier to indicate what remedies have produced symptoms of danger or of discomfort than to point out what drugs may be beneficial. The inflammatory process within the kidney is of such a low type, and so gradual in its advance, that it is almost impossible to employ any remedies with any chance of success. Various astringents have been recommended, with the view of influencing the circulation through the kidney, and although these may occasionally reduce the amount of hæmaturia, or even the excretion of albumin, there is little evidence that they possess any power of controlling the inflammatory processes. The same uncertainty attaches to the use of tartar emetic and of nitric acid; and, indeed, these remedies, although once highly vaunted, are now rarely, if ever, employed with a view of diminishing renal inflammation. It was formerly part of the routine treatment to employ counter-irritants over the lumbar region, but, although these doubtless possess some advantages in cases of acute nephritis, they appear to be absolutely useless for the chronic form. If there is much complaint of pain in the lumbar region, relief may sometimes be afforded from the application of fomentations, or from dry cupping over the loins. Generally, however, the disease is not characterised by pain of a sufficiently severe nature to need special local treatment. It is even impossible to say on general principles that a patient with chronic nephritis should be kept in bed. Although it is necessary to relieve the work of the kidney as far as possible, and thus it might seem desirable to keep the patient in repose, yet undoubtedly many patients lose appetite more early, and the disease appears to progress more rapidly, if they are kept too closely confined to bed, or even to one room. When, therefore, the strength is fairly maintained, and the dropsy is only slight, it is generally

better to encourage the patient to take outdoor exercise, under favourable circumstances, while it is only under the converse conditions that it is advisable to keep the patient in bed. The chief indications for absolute repose are the existence of pain or extreme dropsy, great loss of muscular power, and the development of any of the inflammatory complications which have been previously enumerated.

The beneficial influence of exercise, especially if the skin is acting freely, is well illustrated by a case which is quoted by Fürbringer. 'A patient with Bright's disease, who had been kept in bed for months, suffered so much from the continual inactivity that he ran away from the hospital in the middle of the summer. He went into the forest, and perspired to such an extent that his dropsy disappeared. This patient, whom we believed to be dead, returned to us a few months later cured.'

(3) *Symptomatic treatment.*—In connection with chronic nephritis, some deviation from the normal type, or some great predominance of a particular symptom, will frequently call for special treatment. The chief indications will therefore be treated *seriatim*, although it must be remembered that even when attention is mainly directed to one symptom it is difficult to produce any marked results which shall not at the same time influence other conditions. Thus, although in the following pages it is convenient to speak separately of the treatment of diminished elimination of water, of increased albuminuria, of excessive dropsy, and of various other symptoms, yet while treating any one of them individually a beneficial influence is probably being simultaneously exerted on the others.

1. *Diminution of urinary excretion.*—The decrease in the elimination of water will frequently cause anxiety, both as occasioning an increase in dropsical effusion, and as favouring the occurrence of headache and other discomforts; hence efforts are frequently made to increase the elimination. The diuretic treatment is, of course, not to be attempted in cases marked by hæmaturia—in fact, this treatment must be reserved for chronic cases, where the daily excretion has been gradually diminishing. The functions of the kidney may sometimes be restored by the administration of large quantities of liquid; thus the diuretic influence of copious draughts of water is

frequently of service. In many cases, it is better to replace the water by milk, as milk in itself is nourishing as well as diuretic, and the weakness of these patients calls for the employment of remedies which shall, if possible, increase nutrition, at the same time that they influence the kidneys beneficially. When milk disagrees, or when patients are much tormented by thirst or by dryness of the mouth, the imperial drink or home-made lemonade may be given, and sometimes patients are enabled to take larger quantities of these drinks if they are made mildly effervescent. When giving much liquid, with the idea of promoting diuresis, it is always well to estimate the daily loss of albumin. As gauged by the specific gravity, or by the degree of deposit in the test-tube, it might often be thought that the daily loss of albumin is less under the influence of the diuretic, when in reality it is greater if the increased quantity of water passed be borne in mind. Benefit may at times be derived from the use of cardiac tonics, which, by increasing the circulation through the kidney, favour the elimination of water. Strophanthus and digitalis have been thus employed, and it may be well to alternate the use of these, or to conjoin with them citrate of caffeine or theobromine. Ringer speaks very highly of the powerful diuretic action of iodide of potassium in Bright's disease: he states that during its administration he has seen every vestige of dropsy, even in most severe cases, entirely disappear in a fortnight, but that while increasing the urinary water, and removing the dropsy, this drug produced very little effect on the amount of albumin. He does not confine the beneficial action to syphilitic cases, but says that it is sometimes seen also when the nephritis has originated in scarlet fever or cold. When moderate doses (5–10 grains) fail, he advocates an increase, and states that in one case no diuretic action was obtained until 100 grains were given daily, and that even this dose had to be increased to 200 daily to maintain the effect and eliminate all the dropsy. Although I have often given this drug with good results, I have never employed such heroic doses, which are generally contra-indicated by the existing depression. Diuretin sometimes gives good results when other remedies fail, but its use should be reserved for chronic cases with no hæmaturia. It has been suggested that cases in which the elimination of water was much reduced should be treated by diminishing the amount of liquid given by the mouth, and it was thought that under such circumstances the kidney would resume its functions more readily. Even in acute nephritis, however, there is no advantage in torturing the patient by provoking the sense of thirst. In cases of chronic nephritis, it must be remembered that complete suppression of urine may sometimes occur, and it is therefore always well to percuss out the bladder before passing a catheter under the idea that the patient is suffering from retention.

2. *Albuminuria.*—It is frequently questionable whether it is necessary to attempt to reduce the loss of albumin in cases of chronic nephritis. Many patients with chronic nephritis, when living under favourable conditions, appear to suffer very little from the disease; at the same time, the course of chronic nephritis is usually more rapid than that of cirrhosis of the kidney, and there is every probability that much of the extreme weakness resulting from the former disease must be attributed to the excessive loss of albumin. Under these circumstances, it is undoubtedly desirable to endeavour to diminish the loss, or, if this is impracticable, to administer food containing sufficient albuminous matter to replace the drain from the blood. In many cases, it is, I believe, absolutely wrong to advocate a diet devoid of albumin. Both extremes of diet have been recommended. Thus, under the idea that eggs might increase the loss of albumin by the kidney, they have been completely forbidden by some practitioners; whilst others recommend that eggs, meat, and other albuminous substances should be given freely. In many cases, the solution of the difficulty can only be determined by experiment, and in this experiment the influence of diet is to be measured not so much by the amount of albumin which is lost by the kidney when taking albuminous food, as by the general well-being of the patient. Thus, if it is found that the strength and general health improve while administering nitrogenous food stuffs, it is a matter of small moment if the amount of albumin eliminated is increased. On the other hand, if it is found that the patient's discomforts are increased

when taking a somewhat liberal diet, if he finds difficulty in digesting meat, if he is more prone to suffer from dyspepsia, or if the headache increases, while at the same time the amount of albumin passed also increases, these indications for limiting the diet must not be ignored.

When speaking of the influence of diet in acute nephritis, reference was made to the advisability of a strict *régime* so long as there was any hæmaturia, and this rule holds good in cases of chronic nephritis complicated by hæmaturia: although the disease may be essentially chronic, yet for the time being it must be treated and dieted as though one were dealing purely with an acute attack. Undoubtedly in these cases nitrogenous nourishment, especially in the form of meat, will not only immediately increase the amount of albumin passed, but will increase the amount of hæmorrhage, and in all probability will, at the same time, extend the area affected by the inflammatory process. The number of casts will increase largely, and the general condition of the patient rapidly deteriorate. In chronic cases, however, the only limitation to the amount of albuminoid substances administered lies in the possible occurrence of dyspepsia, and this may be sometimes combated by encouraging the patient to take small quantities of nourishment at short intervals. Sometimes, however, the tendency to dyspepsia is so great that patients are of necessity restricted for a time to pure milk diet, but in chronic cases we more frequently find that the patients rebel against a continuance of a strict milk diet, and that they improve, certainly so far as comfort is concerned, when this rigid diet is relaxed. On the other hand, occasional cases have been recorded in which a persistence in milk diet, extending over some months, has ultimately led to a complete arrest of albuminuria. Sir George Johnson has described one striking case of this nature, in which the albumin only finally disappeared after an interval of more than six years, and other observers have had similar experience. Nevertheless, as a rule, it is wise not to persist in rigid milk diet after hæmaturia has ceased. Milk should still constitute a large proportion of the patient's dietary, but nitrogenous materials and starchy foods may be administered simultaneously, and patients often do well with small quantities of green vegetables, which may assist in counteracting the tendency to constipation produced by the milk and the amylaceous diet.

Medical men are frequently asked what forms of alcoholic stimulants may be taken, or whether it is advisable to give up the use of alcohol entirely. The answer to such enquiries should be guided partly by the general habits and partly by the condition of the individual. When dealing with patients who throughout their lives have been in the habit of taking stimulants, it is not generally desirable to enforce total abstinence. The appetite may fail, and the patients may become depressed, if their habits are totally changed. In such patients small quantities of alcohol, well diluted and given at meal times, will increase the patient's comfort, and also enable him to take more nourishment. Many physicians have advised that the various kinds of wine or beer should be discontinued, and that, if a stimulant be given at all, it should consist of either whisky or gin well diluted. Fürbringer considers that light wine or beer is preferable to concentrated remedies; and some advise the use of good old claret. These undoubtedly might disturb the digestion less than strong alcoholic liquors, but the rule which I have followed is to recommend that whatever the form of alcohol it should always be freely diluted, and should never be taken except at meal times. When patients have not been accustomed to the use of stimulants, there is no advantage in prescribing them so long as the general condition of the patient does not call for their administration. Sometimes, particularly in bedridden patients who have much cardiac weakness, stimulants are distinctly required, and, if administered with caution, the pulse is found to be more regular and to gain in force.

With regard to the administration of drugs intended to influence the amount of albumin lost, numerous substances have at various times been recommended for their power of checking the drain of albumin from the system, but it is to be feared that in many cases they may have been recommended on theoretical grounds, and that in others the decrease of albumin noted during their administration has probably arisen totally independently of the drugs employed. During the comparatively early days of chronic nephritis, the amount of albumin lost will frequently be found to undergo considerable improvement when patients are first kept in bed, and it is therefore all the more necessary to avoid drawing fallacious conclusions, which attribute the improvement to the drugs which have been given at the same time. Most of the remedies recommended are astringents, and those which have found most favour have been classified as remote astringents. These drugs are supposed to influence the size of the blood vessels during their elimination, but it must be remembered that before the drug can influence the blood vessels of the kidney so as to check the loss of albumin it must have been absorbed in fairly large quantity from the stomach.

The following considerations indicate the limitations and the dangers of the administration of astringents. If given in large quantity, or if given repeatedly, they undoubtedly tend to disturb the digestive processes and to irritate the stomach; hence these remedies may have to be discontinued, even though the amount of albumin is diminishing during their administration. Of the astringents, the one that has found most favour is acetate of lead, and although this drug possesses considerable power of controlling hæmorrhage in the lower part of the intestine, and also of arresting hæmorrhage from the kidney, it can rarely be administered for any length of time, owing to the frequency with which it causes symptoms of dyspepsia. It might perhaps be reserved for cases with profuse hæmaturia, but it has previously been noted that the hæmaturia of chronic nephritis speedily improves under conditions of rest, warmth, and diet, independently of the administration of any drug. It is only in quite exceptional cases that I have ever felt justified in using this remedy, which, even if it diminishes the amount of excretion of albumin, may, on the other hand, largely interfere with the absorption of albumin. Of other drugs, the astringent salts and preparations of iron have frequently been employed: the latter are undoubtedly often beneficial in cases of chronic nephritis, but their beneficial action seems to result from their hæmatinic effect, rather than from any direct hæmostatic properties. Though during the administration of iron the colour of the patient may frequently improve, this improvement may be unaccompanied by any diminution in the amount of albuminuria.

On some occasions the internal administration of preparations of ergot have given apparently good results. Certainly in cases of profuse hæmaturia, when the bleeding persists in spite of hygienic measures and of other forms of medicinal treatment, the administration of ergot has been followed by improvement which appeared to be referable to the use of the drug. On the other hand, this remedy has not in my hands influenced the excretion of albumin when unaccompanied by hæmaturia.

Tannic acid and gallic acid have also been recommended in cases of hæmaturia, but these remedies have rarely been successful; and the same may be said of fuchsin and benzoic acid, the results being almost purely negative. It cannot be too strongly insisted upon that any of these remedies may do considerable harm so far as the general condition of the patient is concerned, and it is therefore essential not to concentrate attention too closely upon the albuminuria without carefully watching their influence upon digestion and the general well-being of the patient.

Dropsy.—As uræmic symptoms constitute the chief dangers of cirrhotic affections of the kidney, so dropsy causes the greatest discomfort and attracts the greatest attention in cases of chronic nephritis; indeed, the influence of treatment on dropsy is often to a large extent the measure of the beneficial influence of our remedies. The mere accumulation of fluid in the lower extremities and in the abdominal cavity may cause little danger, although producing considerable discomfort, and in the early stages of chronic nephritis the extent of effusion may be greatly influenced both by hygienic treatment and by various drugs. It is only under exceptional conditions, and in advanced stages of the disease, that the dropsical effusion causes great anxiety.

There are various ways of treating this form of renal dropsy. Sometimes the rest in bed and warmth, together with alterations of diet, are sufficient to favour reabsorption of dropsical effusion. More often, however, it is necessary to adopt more energetic measures, and to relieve the system by withdrawing fluid from the blood, so as to favour the reabsorption from the subcutaneous tissues. This object may be attained in several different ways. Thus, the action of the skin may be stimulated, the elimination of water from the intestine may be favoured, and the work of the kidney may be increased; and sometimes it may be necessary to relieve cases of extreme distension by operation. Many of these measures may be combined in particular cases. Thus, it is usual to employ diaphoretics and hydragogue purgatives simultaneously, and it is only when these fail to produce further beneficial effects that recourse is had to the use of diuretics, or that surgical treatment is considered. Sometimes, however, if the case seems essentially chronic, and if the urine is scanty and albuminous without containing blood, the diuretic treatment is adopted at an earlier stage.

With regard to diaphoresis, it is most commonly favoured by external agencies. It must be distinctly understood that when employing diaphoretics, whether externally or internally, the patient must be kept in bed. The choice of the means by which diaphoretic action is favoured is largely a question of individual experience. Some practitioners are in favour of the frequent use of hot baths, assisting the continuance of the action of the skin by quickly drying the patient and then wrapping him in warm blankets. Sometimes vapour baths or hot-air baths are preferred to the hot-water bath, and the subsequent perspiration is favoured by wrapping the patient in very hot damp sheets. Occasionally, these measures appear to increase the discomfort, and preference is expressed for the use of the simple hot pack, the patient being enveloped in wet sheets covered with three or four layers of warm blankets. The amount of fluid lost by the skin is sometimes considerable, and the symptoms frequently abate under one or other of these forms of treatment. It has already been indicated, however, that in some instances the skin acts very imperfectly in chronic nephritis, and when this is the case any of these measures may increase discomfort and produce a feeling of weakness, headache, and palpitation. These sensations may sometimes be obviated by the use of stimulants and by the application of cold compresses to the head; but in spite of these measures the discomforts following the bath or the wet pack may forbid the continuance of their employment, and it is always well that the symptoms accompanying the first use of these external diaphoretic measures should be carefully noted, and that the baths should not be prolonged if they fail to produce speedy relief.

Various arrangements have been devised for applying heated air to the surface of the body, and Turkish baths have sometimes been recommended. Undoubtedly the Turkish bath is wholly inapplicable to the majority of cases, since the patients are too ill to be moved backwards and forwards to the bath establishments. Of the devices adapted to home use, there are two distinct varieties, either of which may be serviceable. The first is to be employed when the patients are sufficiently well to be able to sit up, and it consists merely of a metallic spirit lamp, provided with a wick which can be raised or lowered, placed under the centre of the chair upon which the patient sits, the patient himself being well enveloped with blankets reaching down to the ground. This description of lamp must be watched from time to time, on account of the risk of the flame increasing in size; and some contrivance should be at hand for extinguishing it at a moment's notice if necessary. This form of hot-air bath certainly has the advantage of simplicity, but it cannot be recommended for patients who are very much weakened by disease. The patients are obliged to sit up, and the posture, enveloped in blankets, is far from being one of comfort. The better plan, perhaps, is to place the lamp on a wooden plank in the centre of the bed, and to raise the clothes at the foot of the bed by a surgical cradle like that employed in the treatment of fractures. Within the confined space the lamp will burn for a time, and will favour free perspiration of the extremities.

More complicated arrangements have been suggested, intended to convey the heated air to the interior of the bed from a lamp or gas stove outside. Long pipes, similar to those in use with bronchitis kettles, have been arranged under the bed-clothes, which are kept from contact with the body of the patient by an ordinary surgical cradle. Although it is claimed for this arrangement that there is no danger of setting fire to the bed-clothes, there may be some risk of blistering the patient if the pipes are allowed to come into contact with his limbs, since sensation is considerably reduced by the dropsical distension, as well as by the apathy so frequently associated with the advanced stage of the disease. I must confess that I am in favour of using the wet pack rather than the vapour bath. I have not seen any special advantage from the use of the latter where treatment by means of the former had failed. The hot-air or vapour bath is generally difficult to manage, and if the skin is not ready to act with the wet pack the patient's discomforts may possibly be increased by the hot-air or vapour bath. I must repeat that in certain cases it is distinctly unwise to persist in the endeavour to stimulate the action of the skin by means of baths, since they often cause great discomfort and headache if they fail to produce diaphoresis.

Of the medicinal diaphoretics which have been employed in such cases, few have given rise to so much hope and to so much disappointment as pilocarpine. When this drug was first introduced, it was hoped that by its subcutaneous injection it would be possible to produce diaphoretic action in the most rebellious cases, and that by judicious use this drug might obviate all the trouble and inconvenience connected with the various forms of baths. It has fallen into such great disfavour at the present time that it may be doubted whether there is not a tendency to refrain from using it when perhaps it might be of some benefit. It must be remembered, however, that it does undoubtedly cause symptoms of weakness, and sometimes even of collapse; hence it requires to be employed with caution. Many patients complain bitterly of the sialogogue effects of the drug, and in obstetric practice general experience tends to show that it is not safe to employ pilocarpine with unconscious subjects. It has been used perhaps most largely in connection with the form of eclampsia associated with the puerperal state, and the balance of testimony indicates that in exceptional cases, when patients are unconscious, it may not only produce profuse sialogogue action, but also may cause dangerous pulmonary œdema by stimulating the secretions of the bronchi. If used at all, pilocarpine should, as a rule, be reserved for cases where other measures have failed, and should certainly not be employed when there is much weakness of the heart or with advanced pulmonary complications. I have seen a few cases in which much benefit resulted from its use, but the benefit was limited to the relief of symptoms of uræmic dyspnœa, for which the drug had been employed. Many observers have spoken of the value of stimulating the action of the skin by pilocarpine, and I see no reason against its tentative employment; but I should urge that the symptoms produced by the drug should be carefully watched, so as if necessary to check its administration as early as possible. At one time it was held that pilocarpine could cure chronic kidney disease. Such exaggerated statements, however, cannot be trusted; the benefits accruing from the use of this drug are limited to the relief of symptoms of dyspnœa, or of symptoms due to dropsy. If, however, the skin can be roused into activity by small doses of pilocarpine, the action may be further stimulated by the subsequent employment of the bath, and the drug may thus become the starting point of beneficial diaphoresis.

Proben[1] also very strongly opposes the routine treatment of the uræmia of Bright's disease by injections of pilocarpine. Under the influence of this drug, there is an increased frequency of the cardiac beats, the pulsations often increasing forty to fifty a minute, with a decided lowering of the vascular pressure, demonstrated by diminished arterial tension; and he thinks these effects are due to a relaxation of the arterioles, caused by vasomotor paralysis, and a direct depressing effect on the cardiac muscle, diminishing its energy. After the exhausting sweats of pilocarpine comes a stage of marked depression, sometimes associated with chilliness, frontal headache, dizziness, drowsiness, and disturbance of vision. Severe collapse may ensue with nausea, vomiting, and diarrhœa, together with contracted pupils, slow, sighing respiration, and rapid, feeble pulse.

Observers are much divided in opinion as to the value of this drug; thus, although Wood and Osler praise pilocarpine, Barber, Henoch, and Sawyer maintain that it is often dangerous in puerperal eclampsia and in the uræmia of chronic Bright's disease. Proben thinks the depressing effects call for the greatest caution, for though it may be beneficial in uræmia when there is a simple hypertrophy of the heart, with a strong action, in other cases the paralysing effects on the arterioles and the heart muscle favour stagnation, and thus retard rather than relieve the circulation. As this stagnation influences the pulmonary as well as the systemic circulation, it favours rapid

[1] *New York Medical Journal*, July 18, 1896.

transudation, with hyperæmia and resulting œdema of the lungs, a very frequent cause of death when pilocarpine acts unfavourably. Any dulness, therefore, at the posterior portion of the lungs, and fine crepitations, with accentuated pulmonic second sound, act as distinct contra-indications to the use of pilocarpine. General emphysema of the lungs, with dilated right ventricle, forms another decided contra-indication, and pilocarpine would also be hazardous in pleurisy with marked effusion, displacing and thus embarrassing the heart. Another interesting danger indicated by Proben is the risk of filling the bronchial tubes with saliva when pilocarpine has been used for a comatose patient, since during coma the reflexes are inhibited, and the abundant saliva formed is therefore neither swallowed nor expectorated.

Before employing pilocarpine, it is absolutely necessary to ascertain by auscultation the condition of the cardiac muscle. Progressive valvular lesions, degeneration of the cardiac walls, including fatty degeneration, dilatation and the so-called senile heart, all contra-indicate the use of this drug.

Many patients with dropsy as the result of chronic nephritis derive considerable advantage from the employment of hydragogue purgatives. These may be repeated daily, especially if it is found that during their employment the dropsy diminishes and the pulse gains in strength. The selection of the remedy to act upon the intestine demands a certain amount of caution. Simple laxatives are seldom of much use, and even the hydragogue purgatives should not be pushed to the extent of weakening the patient's strength. Jalap is the drug which gives the most satisfactory results, and it may be frequently combined with small quantities of scammony. The compound jalap powder of the Pharmacopœia, which contains acid potassium tartrate, may be given daily for weeks at a time, and many patients seem to bear the drug well in this form; in fact, the urgency of symptoms may sometimes be found to increase whenever the administration of this drug has been checked. Simple salines, such as sodium sulphate, acid potassium tartrate, and sodium potassium tartrate, are often beneficial, both in reducing dropsy and in relieving headache, sickness, and other uræmic symptoms. They are best administered in concentrated solution, as recommended by Matthew Hay, who advised that six drachms or an ounce of magnesium sulphate should be given in an ounce of water before food, and directed abstention from fluids for some time afterwards.

The weakness of the patient prohibits the employment of more drastic purgatives, even though these may act more rapidly and more copiously than the compound jalap powder; in fact, it must be remembered that the object in view is to promote the continuous elimination of small quantities of water by the bowel rather than to produce a rapid succession of watery evacuations. Whatever purgative is used, the dose must be regulated according to the strength of the patient, and according to the effects that it is desired to produce.

Many of the drugs that cause an increase in the amount of urine excreted (see p. 113) may be used to promote absorption of dropsical effusions. For this purpose alkaline diuretics are especially valuable, and foremost must be placed the carbonate and citrate of lithium; the citrates and tartrates of potassium and sodium are also frequently employed. As in acute nephritis, better results are obtained from their use when there is no hæmaturia. Ringer and Obolensky[1] speak highly of balsam of copaiba as a diuretic to hasten the reduction of dropsy in chronic nephritis; the former states, however, that it may occasionally fail, and that in some cases it may cause hæmaturia.

Uræmia.—Although uræmic symptoms do not usually occur in the early stages of chronic nephritis, they are by no means uncommon in the later stages, when the kidney is contracted; and, indeed, it has been stated that they are more common in connection with the contracted kidney of chronic nephritis than with the cirrhotic kidney associated with more purely interstitial changes.

Numerous different methods have been advocated for the treatment of uræmic symptoms, and these are sometimes extremely contradictory. Of the various methods, perhaps those which receive the greatest amount of favour are the diuretic, the purgative, and the diaphoretic. On the other hand, some practitioners do not hesitate to say that they have

[1] *British Medical Journal*, August 8, 1891.

derived much satisfaction from the use of various narcotics, and pilocarpine has received a certain amount of support in special cases. The explanation of such divergent plans of treatment may consist in the uncertainty of the precise etiology of uræmia. Chronic uræmic symptoms certainly are most prone to develop with long-continued diminution in the daily excretion of water; hence the diuretic and diaphoretic forms of treatment naturally suggest themselves as means of affording relief. For the same reason, purgatives are frequently resorted to; and all three groups above mentioned seem to give the best results in cases of chronic uræmia associated with much dropsy. Fürbringer maintains that the claims of the different modes of treatment are to be explained by the fact that in many of its forms uræmia is cured spontaneously. Still, whatever the pathology of the symptoms of chronic uræmia, there can be no doubt that they frequently improve when the daily excretion of urine is brought more nearly to the normal quantity, and there can also be no doubt that this change is most frequently induced by stimulating the skin or the intestine, and occasionally by direct stimulation of the kidney. In speaking of the treatment of uræmia, it is necessary to remember that the symptoms are sometimes acute and severe, sometimes chronic and more mild.

The chronic type of uræmia is that which is mostly met with in connection with chronic nephritis, and it is essentially the type which is best treated by diuretic and diaphoretic measures. When dealing with cases with considerable dropsical effusion, it has often been urged that there is danger of inducing symptoms of uræmia by means of the hot bath, and reference has previously been made to the possibility of uræmic disturbances resulting from the reabsorption of a copious dropsical effusion rich in excrementitious material. Still, when patients are complaining of severe headache, or when there is persistent vomiting or diarrhœa, it is always well to use the hot bath, carefully watching the effects upon the general symptoms. My own practice in such cases is to employ simultaneously hydragogue purgatives and diaphoretic measures, and I do not remember having had occasion to regret this plan of treatment, although occasionally the hydragogue purgatives have had to be discontinued, owing to the weakness of the patient. Although I have known cases in which uræmic symptoms have occurred subsequent to the use of the hot bath, I am not at all certain that they have been induced by that measure. In combating uræmic symptoms, it is always advisable to give considerable quantities of liquid—either milk or imperial drink, home-made lemonade, or weak tea. These, by increasing the volume of liquid in circulation, tend to stimulate the work of the kidney, and thus to assist the removal of excrementitious matter. When uræmic symptoms are developing, saline diuretics, such as potassium acetate, are sometimes used, but these have the disadvantage of frequently favouring symptoms of dyspepsia.

In the treatment of uræmic symptoms, as in the treatment of dropsy, pilocarpine has been recommended, and the remarks concerning its employment in renal dropsy hold good for the principles for guidance in connection with uræmia. Though its employment requires the utmost caution, yet in cases of uræmic dyspnœa pilocarpine has in my hands occasionally given good results. In acute uræmia, where convulsive seizures form the prominent feature, it is always well to attempt to relieve the symptoms by purgatives and by the use of the hot bath, and in exceptional cases to only use pilocarpine. Sometimes, when the patient is comatose, the only purgative that can be trusted to act quickly and efficiently is croton oil: the smallness of dose enables it to be administered without voluntary effort on the part of the patient. Uræmic convulsions have sometimes been treated with chloroform, and it has been asserted that this will at once arrest an attack. The same beneficial action has been claimed for nitrite of amyl administered by inhalation. For both of these remedies, however, time is necessary, and I have never been able to satisfy myself that they diminish the duration of uræmic convulsions.

There is much difference of opinion concerning the value of morphine in uræmia. Some observers claim that uræmic convulsions are rendered less frequent and less severe by the administration of morphine, either by the mouth or subcutaneously. On the other hand, some do not hesitate to say that in their experience morphine has done more harm than good in the treatment of uræmia. Sir George Johnson has quoted numerous instances in which, in his belief, the use of morphine was followed by rapidly recurring and ultimately fatal convulsions; and when it is remembered that morphine diminishes the excretory work of the kidney, and also produces constipation, it must be readily understood that it may in certain instances give rise to serious symptoms, although its calming effect upon the nervous system may at first appear to be beneficial. Guided by Sir George Johnson's experience, I have always refrained from the use of a drug which might purchase present comfort at the cost of the life of the patient. Dr. Stephen Mackenzie[1] published two cases in which uræmic symptoms were treated with morphine, and he claims that they serve to show that morphine may be given with safety and benefit in cases of renal disease, in spite of the general opinion of the danger of administering opium and its salts when the kidneys are diseased. He does not recommend its indiscriminate use, claiming for it but a palliative and not a curative influence, and 'in the light of the asserted susceptibility of patients with disease of the kidneys to the toxic effects of opium, it will be given with eyes open to its danger.' Dr. Ralfe treated a case of chronic uræmia with morphine with similar good results, and the employment of this remedy has also been advocated by Loomis. Under similar conditions, hydrate of chloral has sometimes been given, occasionally in the form of an enema. If the state of the heart permits the use of the latter drug, it certainly serves to relieve the sleeplessness from which these patients often suffer; but the same effect can often be obtained with bromide of potassium, or from the use of sulphonal, which causes less depression. In one case I obtained much satisfaction from hyoscine hydrobromide as a sedative and hypnotic in uræmic vigil.

Uræmic cases have sometimes been treated by venesection, but although occasionally applicable in the course of scarlatinal nephritis, it is less likely to give good results when dealing with uræmia from chronic nephritis, where the anæmic condition practically forbids the employment of any measure likely to increase that symptom.

It has lately been suggested that uræmia might be treated by abstracting a certain quantity of blood from the veins, and

[1] *Lancet*, August 3 and 10, 1889.

replacing the amount by the introduction of a hot sterile saline solution. It has been estimated by Beverly Robinson that thus about ten times more urinary constituents are eliminated from the body than by diaphoresis. When the danger is imminent, the patient robust, with a high-tension pulse, the abstraction of five or six hundred, or even a thousand grams of blood has been said to be followed by the most surprising results. Syncope is avoided by the introduction of one or two litres of hot saline solution, which dilutes the toxic elements and produces the most prompt and rapid diuresis known. Proben[1] believes that venesection is but rarely indicated, and that the fluid to be supplied to the vessel may be taken up by the lymphatics from high rectal enemata, or subcutaneous injection, but when a prompt action is required intravenous infusion will give the best result.

Strophanthus and digitalis are frequently used in cases of chronic uræmia, the special indications for these drugs being found in the condition of the pulse and in the sounds of the heart. Digitalis is frequently of value for its stimulant action upon the kidney, in addition to its regulating power over the contractions of the heart. The influence of digitalis must always be carefully watched, and it is generally advisable to employ only moderate doses of the tincture or the infusion, and not to persist in the use of the drug if the pulse, after being regular, becomes rapid and feeble. If the employment of this drug is not followed by diuresis, it is rarely advisable to resort to large doses. With these precautions the use of digitalis seems to be free from objection, and I confess that Fürbringer's statement, that in his hands digitalis has several times produced alarming results, such as asthma, loss of strength, and somnolence, excites some curiosity as to the dose he employed.

Reference has previously been made to the difficulty of treating vomiting and diarrhœa when they occur spontaneously in the course of chronic nephritis. Some benefit is sometimes obtained from alterations in diet, but more commonly these symptoms resist almost every form of treatment. In severe cases patients are sometimes able to take small quantities of strong beef-tea at frequent intervals; but it may be necessary to treat

[1] *New York Medical Journal*, July 18, 1896.

uræmic vomiting by nutrient rectal enemata. When the vomited material is ammoniacal, various acids may be used, but as a rule vomiting must be treated rather as uræmic than as the expression of disturbed gastric functions. The same principles underlie the treatment of the persistent diarrhœa, which so often contributes to the fatal termination in chronic nephritis. When the diarrhœa is frequent, it is generally possible to afford relief by the injection of enemata containing opium, while astringents given by the mouth usually do little good, and may sometimes disturb the digestive system.

Similar considerations govern the treatment of the uræmic dyspnœa which is so common in connection with chronic nephritis. When the uræmic dyspnœa is obviously dependent upon the state of the circulation, or upon the presence of fluid in the pleural cavity, or even upon engorgement of lung, relief may be obtained from the use of the ordinary remedies and measures calculated to influence the work of the circulatory and the respiratory systems; but, on the other hand, certain cases are met with from time to time in which the uræmic dyspnœa is undoubtedly of asthmatic nature, and the dyspnœa must then be treated on the general principles underlying the treatment of uræmia, that is, we must resort to diuretics and diaphoretics rather than to expectorants and cardiac stimulants. Such cases sometimes improve with pilocarpine, sometimes with diuretic remedies, such as digitalis, squill, acid potassium tartrate, caffeine, or diuretin. Nitrites and nitro-glycerine seem only to give relief if the asthma is of cardiac origin. The dangers of cardiac failure frequently call for treatment in the later stages of this disease. It must then be remembered that the symptomatic treatment must take precedence, that is, the urgency of the case demands the employment of cardiac stimulants, regardless of the influence they may have upon the kidney.

In the foregoing remarks attention has been concentrated mainly upon severe cases, which require to be kept in bed; but in cases of chronic nephritis which are not so severe, or in which the danger is not so immediate, much may be done to retard the progress of the disease by sheltering the patient from the risks incident to the English climate. If the means of the patient permit, he should be instructed to winter in some warm climate, either in the South of Europe, in Egypt, or in Algiers, or, if it is impossible for him to go so far, he may repair to the South of England, to Torquay, Bournemouth, or Ventnor. Benefit sometimes results from the use of one or other of the mineral waters. The alkaline springs and chalybeate waters are those which are most preferred, and there can be no doubt that this benefit is to a large extent due to the stimulation of the kidney and to the removal of nitrogenous waste. Lastly, while there can be no doubt that it is generally inadvisable to cut off all occupation from patients who are able to continue to do light work, it is equally undesirable to permit of any occupation which involves constant mental excitement or physical strain.

CHAPTER VIII

CIRRHOSIS OF THE KIDNEY

THIS form of nephritis has been described under various names, viz. chronic interstitial nephritis, red granular kidney, granular atrophy, granular degeneration, gouty kidney, chronic gouty nephritis, chronic Bright's disease, and renal cirrhosis.

The leading characteristics of this type may be briefly summarised. The course is essentially slow and chronic from its commencement. It mainly occurs towards the later part of middle life and during advanced age. As with the contracted kidney of chronic nephritis previously described, the part mainly affected is the renal cortex, which is greatly diminished in thickness, while the surface of the kidney becomes uneven and granular. During a large part of the course of the disease the urine is copious and of low specific gravity; the amount of albumin passed is very small—indeed, in many cases there may be no albumin for days or weeks at a time. Dropsy is mostly absent with this form of kidney disease, unless it is complicated by acute or chronic nephritis; but, on the other hand, the changes in the heart and in the arteries are far more developed than in other renal affections. The ending of cases of chronic interstitial nephritis may be produced by uræmia, by cerebral hæmorrhage, or by cardiac failure.

Etiology.—In a disease which is so chronic in its nature, the etiology necessarily becomes somewhat uncertain. While recognising the general value of many of the etiological factors here enumerated, it is often impossible, in any particular case, to ascribe the origin conclusively to any single exciting cause. In spite of this, however, there seems to be good ground for believing that the supervention of cirrhosis of the kidney may be influenced by the age and sex of the individual, as well as by heredity.

Age.—It is very rare to find this form of kidney disease amongst children, or even amongst young adults; as a rule, when death occurs in early life, if small kidneys are found the disease is in all probability consecutive to acute nephritis, and is therefore the result of the contraction of the kidney which has been previously much enlarged. The case is therefore to be regarded as a late stage of chronic nephritis, rather than as renal cirrhosis. Towards middle life, however, the tendency to cirrhosis is greatly increased. Below the age of thirty it is extremely rare to find typical examples of cirrhotic kidney, the majority of cases occurring between the ages of forty and sixty, while from thirty to forty the proportion is about equal to that which occurs between sixty and seventy. In spite of these general conclusions with regard to the age at which patients are affected by cirrhosis of the kidney, it must be remembered that this form of kidney trouble is the one which is most likely to escape observation; and it is therefore one from which patients may have suffered for many years previous to the actual recognition of the disease. Most of the cases of albuminuria met with in insurance work fall into two classes, both marked by the presence of traces of albumin, and by the slight character or the total absence of other symptoms. The age of the proposer is of importance in differentiating these two classes. While numerous cases of slight albuminuria during early life are to be regarded as functional or intermittent, the slight trace of albumin which is found in later middle age is generally the result of contracted kidney, and there can be no doubt that in very numerous instances the medical examination at the time of insurance has been the first occasion when the deviation from the normal condition has been noted.

Sex.—With regard to the liability of the sexes to this form of disease, it occurs far more frequently among males than females. According to Fagge, the proportion is almost exactly in the ratio of two to one. Other observers have placed the proportion more highly. Thus, Purdy considers that cirrhosis of the kidney occurs from three to four times more frequently in the male than in the female. This is undoubtedly the result of the greater exposure of the male sex to the conditions likely to give rise to this disease.

Heredity.—Although the hereditary character of renal cirrhosis has attracted the attention of numerous observers, the hereditary tendency is not so marked as in the case of phthisis or cancer; indeed, when regarded from the point of view of an insurance office, the risk to the offspring of those who have died of Bright's disease is practically ignored. This curious circumstance probably finds its explanation in the fact that the disease, if it develops, develops late in life, and the increased risk is therefore likely to be met by tabular rates. On the other hand, it is frequently interesting to note the association of cirrhosis or other forms of kidney trouble in various members of a family, and although it is customary to regard this association as pointing to the hereditary character of cirrhosis of the kidney, it may be questioned whether it does not point rather to the hereditary character of the conditions likely to produce this disease. This contention is largely supported by the frequent association of cirrhosis of the kidney with gouty tendencies. I have seen numerous instances in which the history has shown that the parents have died of gout or of Bright's disease, and that two or more of the descendants have suffered from albuminuria. In one case, where the father died of Bright's disease, one son for many years suffered from albuminuria, and ultimately from renal calculus; another son has had intermittent albuminuria, and from time to time passes large quantities of uric acid crystals, while the pulse and the sounds of the heart indicate the cardio-vascular changes so frequently associated with this disease. Dr. A. V. Meigs[1] states that he has met with five cases of Bright's disease in one family—the father, son, and three daughters; one of the daughters (the sole survivor) had had the disease for nearly nine years when the account was written. In spite of such cases, however, I must repeat the warning against laying undue stress upon the hereditary character of cirrhosis of the kidney. Cases similar to the above are the exception rather than the rule, and although doubtless the predisposition to Bright's disease of this type is somewhat greater when the parents have suffered from the affection, yet a large number of the offspring escape without showing any renal change.

[1] *Trans. Col. of Phys.*, Philad. 1883.

Gout.—The intimate connection of renal cirrhosis with gout has long been a matter of common observation, and, indeed, the connection is responsible for many of the terms which have been employed to describe this affection of the kidney. The term 'gouty kidney' is, however, inappropriate, inasmuch as the disease arises under numerous conditions independently of gout. It is generally held that gout predisposes to the development of renal cirrhosis, and on more than one occasion I have had the opportunity of watching the gradual development of albuminuria in the presence of repeated attacks of gout. It has been held, however, that in many cases gout is the consequence rather than the cause of the renal affection, and that it results from the failure of the kidney to perform its normal eliminative function. It is far more probable that renal cirrhosis follows from the constant irritation due to the deposition of uric acid in the solid form within the substance of the kidney. One of my patients certainly has had uric acid crystals in his water for the past fourteen years, and during the earlier part of this time he exhibited no symptom of cirrhosis of the kidney. In recent years, however, the tension of the pulse has gradually increased, the sounds at the base of the heart have become accentuated, and small traces of albumin are frequently to be found. Similar cases have been described by Dickinson and others; hence, although allowing that gout may occasionally be consecutive to cirrhosis of the kidney, I would hold that it is far more frequently to be regarded as the cause. It is mainly in recognition of this association of the conditions that insurance offices are in the habit of charging an extra premium in cases of repeated gout.

Dyspepsia.—Like the preceding condition, dyspepsia has been regarded both as the cause and as the result of renal cirrhosis. The late Sir George Johnson maintained that renal degeneration is brought about by the long-continued elimination by the kidneys of the products of faulty digestion. While admitting that disorders of digestion may frequently be responsible for transient forms of albuminuria, there is some doubt whether chronic renal affection is to be started in this way, or whether when prolonged dyspepsia is found to be accompanied by permanent slight albuminuria, dyspepsia is not to be looked upon as a symptom of the disease rather than as an etiological factor. I have elsewhere[1] given reasons for regarding the dyspepsia as a symptom of the disease, and indicated the frequency with which chronic dyspepsia occurring in middle life forms the first indication of renal cirrhosis; and I have shown in the paper referred to that this contention is supported by the results of treatment, that these forms of dyspepsia improve with remedies calculated to relieve uræmia rather than with those mainly directed to the relief of the dyspeptic symptoms.

Habits.—There is very little doubt that this disease frequently arises in patients who have been somewhat reckless in their mode of living, both eating and drinking to excess. Of the two forms of excess, large quantities of nitrogenous foods probably play the more important part, since they lead to an undue amount of work being thrown upon the kidney. If at the same time these patients take a relatively small proportion of liquid, the urine becomes concentrated, and therefore more irritating, and the tendency to the deposition of uric acid and of oxalates is enormously increased. Although it is impossible to prove that prolonged irritation by these crystals ultimately leads to renal cirrhosis, most observers who have watched patients carefully for any length of time agree that such irritation is likely to eventually lead to destruction of renal tissue. I have above referred to a patient in whom this sequence of events was followed. The patient in question, besides having marked hereditary tendency to Bright's disease and to gout, was a large eater, living a comparatively inactive life.

Neuroses.—A condition which is frequently regarded as influencing the occurrence of cirrhosis of the kidney is that due to emotional causes. The depression resulting from prolonged anxiety, or worry, or grief, seems to have some direct influence in promoting the occurrence of this disease, although it is extremely difficult to explain the way in which nervous influences should lead to disease of the kidney. It is possible that the nervous influence may act through deranging the digestive system, or possibly through the frequency with which it leads to intemperate habits; but there seems to be very little doubt, whatever the explanation may be, that cases of cirrhosis of the

[1] *Lancet,* August 8, 1896.

kidney frequently occur as sequels of prolonged anxiety. Sometimes, perhaps, the occurrence of mental depression may merely favour the rapid development of pre-existing disease; sometimes it may contribute to distinct gouty attacks; but whether nervous depression by itself has sufficient influence in disturbing the work of the kidney as to produce cirrhosis remains somewhat doubtful. In spite of the large number of cases where mental anxiety appears to be distinctly associated with this disease, there may be no true etiological connection, inasmuch as cirrhosis, being a disease of middle age, usually occurs at a time when people are prone to the mental disturbances arising from financial difficulties or other causes of anxiety.

Lead Poisoning.—Similar uncertainty surrounds the supposed connection between lead poisoning and the occurrence of cirrhosis of the kidney. There is no doubt about the frequent association of lead poisoning and gout, and many observers have attempted to explain the influence of lead poisoning as contributing to the occurrence of gout, which in turn leads on to chronic nephritis. Fürbringer thinks that the supervention of gout is not a necessity, since a large number of patients with contracted kidney are not gouty; but, on the other hand, the connection with lead poisoning appears to have been fairly established by the statistics compiled by Dr. Dickinson, which show that nearly two-thirds of the workers in lead suffer eventually from granular kidney. Jacob has given particulars of nine patients suffering from genuine contracted kidney, eight of whom were lead miners. Various hypotheses have been put forward for the explanation of the influence of lead upon the kidney. One theory is that lead salts exert a poisonous influence upon the vascular system by causing contraction of the vessels; another, that the influence is exerted through the deposition of lead in granular form; while many hold, as above indicated, that lead poisoning induces kidney disease by favouring recurrent attacks of gout. I have seen many cases of contracted kidney amongst painters and others whose occupation favours lead poisoning, and my general impression is that, in the majority, gouty symptoms have been present in addition to the symptoms of contracted kidney.

Climatic conditions.—Cirrhosis of the kidney appears to be more frequent in temperate climates; hence it has frequently been held that it is favoured by damp and by rapid alterations of temperature. It appears sometimes to follow exposure to malarial influences, and, indeed, a type of malarial albuminuria or malarial nephritis has been described. Although, possibly, some few cases arise in this way, a large number of those affected by malaria escape subsequent affection of the kidney. Hence the assumed connection between malaria and kidney disease is scarcely to be regarded proven, since it would be obviously incorrect to ascribe to malarial influences those cases in which other possible etiological factors cannot be traced.

Chronic irritation of the bladder or of the urethra by stricture, or of the pelvis of the kidney by means of a renal calculus, may occasionally induce cirrhosis of the kidney, but far more commonly these causes lead to a separate condition, which will be described later under the heading of 'Consecutive Nephritis.'

Morbid anatomy.—The most striking change of the morbid anatomy of cirrhosis of the kidney in advanced form consists in the size of the kidneys. These are usually very much diminished in size, but the diminution rarely affects both kidneys to the same extent. Owing to this contraction, the combined weight of the two kidneys may be even less than the weight of a single normal kidney. Corresponding with the diminution in size, an increase in the amount of fat enveloping the kidney is usually to be noticed. In the early stages of the disease, however, there may be very little alteration in the size or colour of the kidneys, and the most prominent characteristic may be the increase in the thickness of the capsule and the greater difficulty of its detachment from the surface of the kidney. Even when this last condition is met with, the cortex may be very much diminished as seen on section, especially on microscopic examination. Generally, the surface of the kidney is roughened and granular, and of a deep reddish-brown colour; the capsule can only be detached with difficulty, and portions of the kidney may perhaps tear away with the capsule as it is stripped off. Sometimes the roughened granular surface is covered with little yellow spots, and frequently small

PLATE VII.

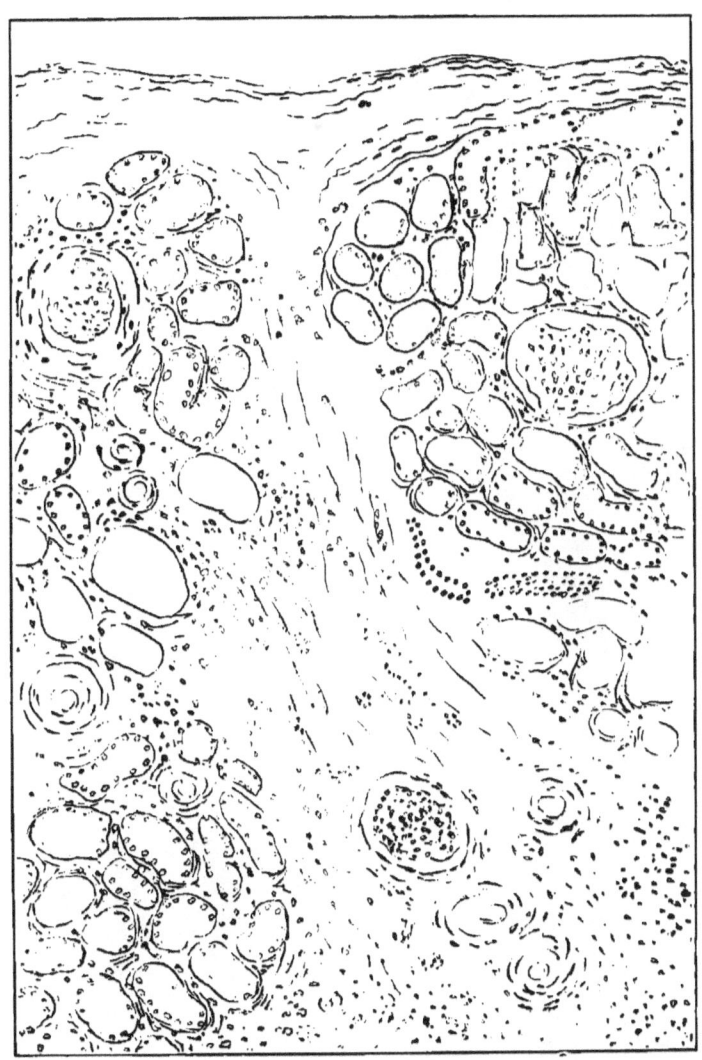

Section of Fibrous Area in Cirrhosis of the Kidney. This specimen shows, under a low power, an area in which new formations of fibrous tissue pass downwards from the thickened capsule of the kidney. In this new tissue altered glomeruli, vessels and tubules may be seen, while bands of new tissue extend into the surrounding more healthy parts.

(*See pp.* 187 *and* 188.)

N. Tirard, Del.
Mintern Bros., imp.

cysts may be found dotted about near the surface of the kidney. Though the cysts are, as a rule, extremely minute, they vary very much in size, and may even be from a quarter to half an inch in diameter. Occasionally, small white nodules may be found similarly dotted about near the surface. Notwithstanding the presence of these cysts, the kidney as a whole is firm and resistant, being at times rather difficult to cut, owing to the increased amount of fibrous tissue contained in the organ. Frequently, the degree of contraction of the kidney is somewhat masked by the dilatation of the pelvis, which is filled or even distended with an excessive amount of adipose tissue. On section, it is at once seen that the diminution in the size of the kidney is mainly due to the diminution in the thickness of the cortex, the proportion of cortex to medulla bearing the relation of from a fifth to a sixth instead of from a third to a fourth, as in the healthy kidney. The cysts and white nodules above mentioned are more evident in the cut surface, and, in addition, cicatricial tissue may often be observed spreading inwards from the cortex towards the medulla. These cysts are commonly regarded as resulting from occlusion of the renal tubules near the glomeruli, with consequent distension of Bowman's capsule. The Malpighian bodies are sometimes reduced in size, as well as in number, and microscopically they are always found to be irregular in size, and situated nearer to the trunk of the artery than usual. Another peculiarity connected with the Malpighian bodies is that they are frequently found immediately below the capsule of the kidney, instead of being separated from it by a short interval. The pyramidal portions of the kidney are generally of a dark colour, and white lines sometimes occupy the position of the straight tubes of the medulla, and indicate the presence of crystalline deposits of urates. Microscopic examination brings out the changes of the kidney in a more marked manner, since the triangular wedges of fibrous tissue, apparently devoid of true gland structure, are rendered more evident in stained specimens. The development of fibrous tissue is extremely irregular: portions of gland structure, apparently in a healthy condition, may intervene; sometimes in the triangular patches numerous nuclei are seen; at other times the nuclei are more rare, and the tissue appears more distinctly fibrillated and organised. Compressed and atrophic tubuli uriniferi are occasionally found scattered amongst the new tissue, and if these contain epithelium the cells are usually in a state of fatty degeneration. The connective tissue round the convoluted tubes is very often increased in amount, and the capsules are greatly thickened by proliferation, which tends to encroach upon the space normally occupied by the glomerular tuft, and may ultimately lead to obliteration of the glomerulus. These atrophic changes in connection with the Malpighian tufts are often regarded as the earliest features of cirrhosis of the kidney, while the atrophy of the tubules and the development of the interstitial changes are regarded as secondary results.

The tubes appear, in some cases, to be denuded of their epithelium; in others, to be somewhat distended. Occasionally in the atrophic tissue they may be plugged with colloid material, and distinct casts of considerable diameter may be found obstructing their lumen. The white nodules mentioned above are seen on microscopic examination to consist of small accumulations of epithelial cells. In the straight tubes of the pyramids the epithelium, as a rule, is normal, but crystals of urate of sodium may be found occasionally within the lumen.

The blood vessels of the kidney are often markedly altered; considerable discussion has arisen as to whether these changes affecting the smallest arteries are secondary to the alterations in the kidney above described, or whether they are primary changes which precede the alterations in the gland structure.

The small arteries may be affected in various ways, but the main change is an increase in the thickness of the walls of the vessel, together with diminution in its calibre. This increase of thickness may be due to an overgrowth of the intima, occurring without material proliferation of nuclei, and may almost entirely occlude the blood vessel. This form of affection corresponds closely with the endarteritis obliterans described by Cornil and Ranvier.

Another affection of the small arteries consists in the hyaline fibroid degeneration, which was originally described by the late Sir William Gull and the late Dr. Sutton as arterio capillary

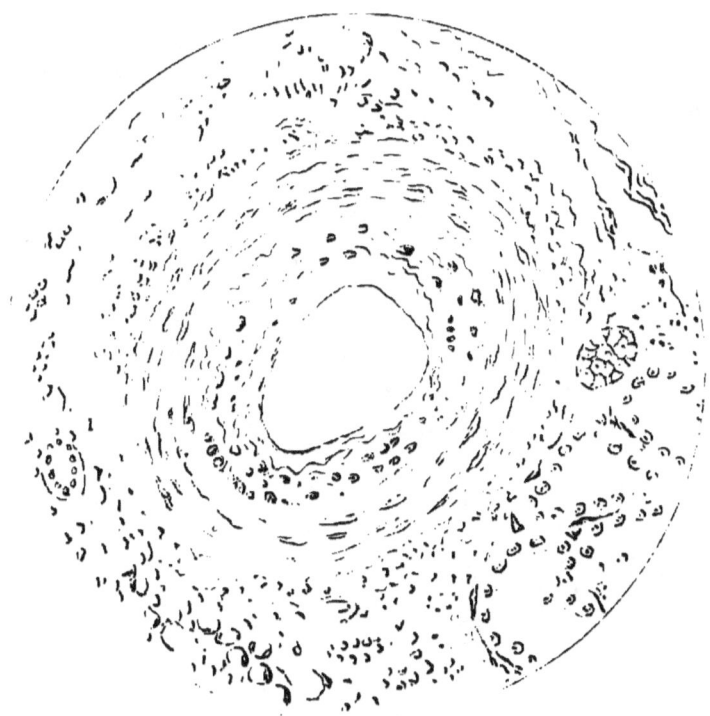

Oblique Section of a Small Artery in Cirrhosis of the Kidney. This specimen shows hypertrophy of the muscular coat, and an increase in the thickness of the intima. In the surrounding parts an increase of nucleated tissue has led to partial obliteration of several tubules.

(*See pp.* 188 *and* 189.)

N. Tirard, Del.   Mintern Bros., imp.

fibrosis. In this condition there is some increase in the amount of tissue outside the muscular tissue, and this change was, by Gull and Sutton, believed to be the form of alteration of the small arteries most characteristic of contracted kidney; in fact, they described the condition of hypertrophy of small arteries as being essentially due to this form of degeneration. The late Sir George Johnson considered that the appearances described by these authors were due to changes produced by the fluid in which the specimens had been mounted, and he certainly succeeded in demonstrating specimens closely corresponding with those described, in which the hyaline fibroid appearance was undoubtedly due to the action of the glycerine in which the vessels had been mounted. Hyaline fibroid changes, however, may frequently be observed in specimens that have not been treated with this preservative, and from examination of numerous specimens I believe that the condition described by Gull and Sutton may frequently co-exist with the true hypertrophy of muscular tissue described by Sir George Johnson. This muscular hypertrophy undoubtedly occurs at a very early stage of renal cirrhosis, and according to Dr. Dickinson it is to be ascribed to some assumed change in the structure of the capillaries rather than as a consequence of cardiac hypertrophy, as originally believed by Sir George Johnson. It is certain that increase in the thickness of the walls of the left ventricle is invariably associated with renal contraction. Sometimes this hypertrophy occurs in connection with some dilatation of the cavity, but in the early stages it is far more frequent for the amount of dilatation to be comparatively small, although the hypertrophy may be sufficiently advanced to cause alteration in the position of the apex beat of the heart. As the disease advances, and especially towards the termination, dilatation of the heart becomes more frequent; hence to a certain extent the position of the apex beat and the area of cardiac dulness may be taken as indications of the stage of the disease.

Symptoms.—The most valuable symptoms, from the diagnostic point of view, connected with renal cirrhosis may be briefly summarised. There is generally an increase in the amount of urine passed, and as a rule very little tendency to dropsical effusions. The amount of albumin is extremely variable; sometimes it may be absent for days together, but as compared with chronic nephritis the amount of albumin is always small. Corresponding with this small quantity of albumin, as a rule casts are relatively difficult to find. Dyspeptic and nervous symptoms are also early indications of cirrhosis of the kidney. As distinguished from chronic diffused nephritis, the leading symptoms of advanced cases are those indicative of uræmia.

Having thus indicated the leading characteristics, it will be convenient perhaps to consider the symptoms in greater detail under three classes, according to whether the disease is: (1) in its early stage, or (2) fully matured, or (3) the last stage, pending towards the fatal termination. The onset of the disease is so insidious that the symptoms during the early stages may frequently be misunderstood, even if they do not entirely escape observation. In a large majority of cases the disease has reached an advanced stage before the slightest suspicion of the gravity of the malady is aroused. Patients may suffer from headache, shortness of breath, or dyspepsia for many years before attaching any importance to these symptoms. Even chronic interference with the work of the lung may occasionally be endured for many years under the impression that it has no serious import, or that it is merely indicative of a tendency to chronic bronchitis. In exceptional cases, the disease may remain unrecognised until an attack of uræmic convulsions supervenes, and several cases have been recorded in which the true nature of the disease was wholly unsuspected until post-mortem examination revealed the contracted kidneys. The indication that is most likely to direct the attention of the practitioner to the gravity of the case is the increase in the quantity of urine passed; but unless patients note this fact, or lay stress upon the frequency with which they are disturbed at night, there is every probability that the early stages of the disease will escape observation. Valuable indications may often be derived from consideration of the past history of the patient, more particularly with regard to habits, and the family history may throw some light upon the nature of the case. In insurance work there are often opportunities of noting the frequency with which gouty family history is associated with small traces of albumin, indicative of cirrhosis of the kidney. Sometimes the family history may point more distinctly to the proba-

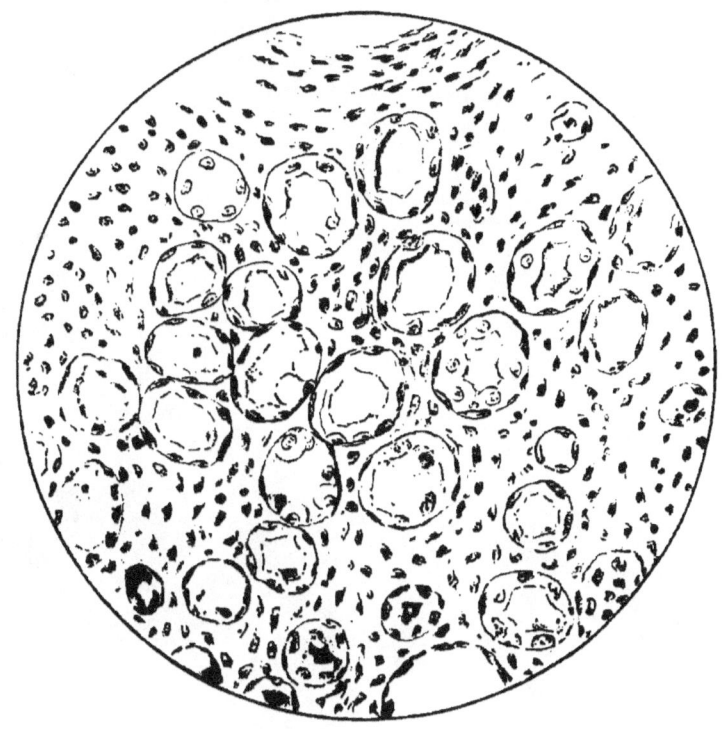

Section of Tubes in Cirrhosis of the Kidney. In this specimen the tubes are filled with colloid material, which appears to have compressed the epithelial cells. In some parts this colloid matter has apparently undergone degenerative change around large granular nuclei. The intertubular spaces contain much nucleated tissue.

(*See p.* 188.)

N. Tirard, Del.   Mintern Bros., imp.

bility of renal cirrhosis, since this form of kidney affection is somewhat more likely to occur in those with hereditary tendencies. Whenever any suspicion of cirrhosis of the kidney is aroused, the early symptoms are generally found to be those connected with the digestive system and with the nervous system. Even in the early stages of the disease the appetite is frequently diminished, and the patient complains of symptoms of impaired digestion, such as pain occurring after food, which may be associated with flatulent distension. These early dyspeptic symptoms are rarely severe; the vomiting and diarrhœa which are so often associated with cirrhosis of the kidney belong to a later stage of the disease. Stress must therefore be laid upon the importance of testing the urine carefully, and prosecuting further enquiries whenever patients of advanced middle age suffer from troublesome dyspeptic symptoms, more particularly if the general circumstances of the patient afford the slightest indications of a tendency to this disease.

Symptoms connected with the nervous system may also attract attention at an early stage. Headache and neuralgic pains are extremely common, and the neuralgia is so little differentiated from the ordinary rheumatic type, that it affords but little indication of the nature of the disease unless careful enquiries are made. Most commonly the neuralgic pains affect the occipital region, though neuralgia of other parts, as the vertex or the frontal region, may sometimes be met with. It is characteristic of this form of neuralgia that the pain, although not very severe, is more persistent than in the commoner forms of neuralgia. In a later stage of the disease sleep may be interfered with by these neuralgic pains, but as a rule the pain is generally most intense in the early part of the day, and tends to diminish towards night. Neuralgic pains of the nature of sciatica may supervene, but by far the most common type is that which imitates simple trigeminal neuralgia.

Another nervous symptom which may call attention to the case in the early stages is a form of giddiness, which may occur quite suddenly, although it is generally of short duration. The vertigo may be only momentary, and if the patient is standing or walking at the time of its occurrence, it may not cause more than a very transient feeling of giddiness, with slight staggering gait. Occasionally, the vertigo is more severe, and may cause the patient to fall to the ground; but this giddiness must be carefully differentiated from the uræmic loss of consciousness of the later stages of the disease. The vertigo of the early stage of cirrhosis of the kidney is not connected with any disturbance of auditory sensations, although it may occasionally be superadded to the unilateral headache from which these patients so often suffer. When these attacks have once occurred, they are liable to return at fairly frequent intervals.

When any of the above symptoms have led to further enquiries, it is common to find that patients will admit having to get up at night, once or more, to micturate, and they may probably realise that they are more frequently disturbed even during the day. It is by no means uncommon for this increased frequency of micturition to lead patients to seek advice under the idea that they are suffering from diabetes. The actual amount of urine that is passed is generally considerably increased, though with the earliest stage of the disease the quantity may be very little more than normal. In extreme cases, however, twice or even three times the normal quantity may be passed in the twenty-four hours.[1] The urine is light in colour, transparent, and generally, even on standing, gives only a very scanty, light, cloudy deposit. The specific gravity is distinctly lower than normal, ranging from 1005 to 1010 or 1012; it will vary according to the stage of disease, and also according to the amount of water passed. It is curious to note, however, that when the amount of water is suddenly reduced inconsequence of profuse perspiration, vomiting, or diarrhœa, the specific gravity does not vary materially; it never reaches the high specific gravity which in healthy conditions would be likely to be produced by the same causes.

Throughout the history of a case of cirrhosis of the kidney the amount of albumin is small, and in the early stages it may be entirely absent for several days at a time. The albuminuria may possibly follow a cyclical course, being found after violent exercise or after meals, while it is absent in specimens that are passed in the early morning. Occasionally the midday specimen

---

[1] Auld on 'Polyuria.'

may be free from albumin, while the morning specimen contains a trace. In cirrhosis of the kidney, however, the amount of albumin is often so small that the test by boiling is scarcely to be relied upon. I had for many years a patient under observation in whom for long periods the faintest trace of albumin could not be found, although the nature of the pulse and of the heart sounds were quite unmistakable. This patient eventually developed pericarditis, and died from undoubted cirrhosis of the kidney. In a similar case quoted by Fürbringer, the urine was entirely normal until within the last week of the patient's life, although post-mortem examination showed that the kidneys were in an advanced stage of cirrhotic contraction. In other cases quoted by the same author, transitory albuminuria occurred at the same time as violent paroxysms of headache, and both conditions were referred to contracted kidney. M. Dieulafoy [1] describes four cases, which exhibited, for many weeks or even months, some of the most marked symptoms of Bright's disease, such as vomiting, oppression, headache, œdema of the ankles, the ' bruit de galop,' itching, digiti mortui, ocular and auditory derangements, and a sensation of extreme coldness, limited to the extremities, especially the lower limbs, or to the knees. In not one of these cases was a trace of albumin found in the urine except during the last days of life.

In the scanty cloudy deposit previously mentioned, octahedral crystals of oxalates may frequently be met with, and in the early stages of the disease they may be associated with uric acid crystals. The amount of urea passed in these cases is often subject to diminution, but in exceptional cases relatively large quantities of urea may be eliminated, and to some extent the specific gravity of the urine is dependent upon the alteration of the daily excretion of urea. Renal casts are not nearly so numerous as in cases of chronic diffused nephritis; when present they are mostly small and hyaline, but larger casts may sometimes be found, occasionally containing granular *débris*, or even atrophied renal epithelial cells. In this form of kidney disease, acute inflammatory exacerbations may completely alter the character of the urine and the nature of the deposit, although this complication is less frequent than with chronic diffused nephritis. White and

[1] *Le Progrès Médical*, No. 25, 1886.

red blood corpuscles are often to be found in the deposit, and occasionally numerous leucocytes indicate the existence of catarrh of the urinary passages.

Changes in the circulatory system occur early, and afford valuable indications in connection with cirrhosis of the kidney, and wherever any suspicion as to the nature of the case has been aroused, careful attention should be paid to any alterations in the cardio-vascular system.

The pulse of cirrhosis of the kidney is fairly resistant and difficult to compress, the degree of tension being frequently easy to estimate by the amount of pressure required to arrest pulsations. The sphygmographic tracings obtained from cases of cirrhosis of the kidney are extremely characteristic, although high tension may be met with in connection with some other conditions, as with both forms of diabetes, and occasionally with hysteria, or with atheroma of the wall of the arteries.

A change which is observed with equal readiness is the alteration in the position of the apex beat of the heart. The hypertrophy of the left ventricle follows increased tension of the pulse, and the apex beat gradually travels outwards and downwards, even in the early stages of the disease. In addition to this alteration of the apex beat, accentuation of the cardiac sounds will be noted. The second sound heard over the aortic valves is especially affected, and reduplication may frequently be heard at this spot or a little below. The position of the apex beat and the area of cardiac dulness become more affected as the disease reaches the mature stage, and some dilatation of the right ventricle may cause further increase in the area of cardiac dulness. Even in the early stages of the disease, epistaxis may be a marked symptom, having been observed two or even three years before definite symptoms of cirrhosis could be detected. So far as my experience goes, however, epistaxis is more commonly met with in the later stages of the disease.

When the renal alterations are more fully established, many of the symptoms above enumerated will be more pronounced, and others may be superadded. Thus the dyspeptic symptoms are more likely to be associated with nausea and vomiting, and the vomiting may be more frequent in the early morning. This form of vomiting is extremely intractable; it frequently cannot be traced to any error of diet, and, as in cases of cerebral vomiting, no relief follows from the evacuation of the stomach. Occasionally diarrhœa ensues, and, like the vomiting, it appears to occur spontaneously and to arise without any error of diet. Both these symptoms may not only arise spontaneously, but, after having caused considerable weakness and interference with the nutrition of the patient, they may also cease spontaneously. In a late stage of the disease, however, they may contribute largely to a rapid termination, and there can be little doubt that they are the expression of a form of uræmic intoxication. As the disease progresses, the amount of urine increases, while the specific gravity becomes more persistently low. The pale yellow or almost slightly greenish colour of the urine is extremely characteristic of marked advance of the disease, and it is associated with further diminution in the elimination of urea and phosphates. Sometimes, especially before the onset of uræmic convulsions, the amount of urine passed may be considerably reduced; hence it is always important when dealing with cases of cirrhosis of the kidney to watch any alteration in the daily excretion of urine. Diminution in quantity, and the supervention of headache, must always give rise to anxiety. In other respects, the urine is not materially changed as the disease advances; the amount of albumin that is passed is still small, and the casts are few in number, though granular casts may be more frequently met with than in the earlier stages of this disease.

Respiratory system.—In the course of advanced cases of renal cirrhosis, difficulty of respiration forms a prominent symptom, and, as in chronic nephritis, it is very frequently attributable to changes affecting the lungs and the pleura. These changes can often be indirectly traced to alterations in the circulation, which will account for rapid œdema of the lung, or for great accumulations of fluid within the pleural cavity. In addition to these, however, in renal cirrhosis, and more rarely in chronic nephritis, symptoms may occur more suddenly and with greater urgency, and to these the term 'uræmic dyspnœa' has been applied. Amongst all the symptoms which have been observed in the course of chronic Bright's disease, few have given rise to greater divergence of opinion than those of uræmic dyspnœa. The cause of this may possibly be found in some uncertainty as to whether the condition is comparable to true asthma, and also as to whether it can properly be termed uræmic.

The uncertainty that has been expressed may in all probability turn largely on the pathology assigned to this condition. Some observers have described cases of uræmic dyspnœa as though the condition in almost all respects resembled spasmodic asthma, and this, no doubt, has given rise to the reservations with which some authors have spoken of the paroxysms of uræmic dyspnœa. Thus, Sir William Roberts says that paroxysms of dyspnœa belong to the least frequent forms of uræmic disturbance, if indeed such attacks have at any time a genuine claim to the designation uræmic; he quotes the details of only one case which has fallen under his observation, and he speaks of this as a somewhat doubtful example. On the other hand, Sir George Johnson regards dyspnœa as one of the most frequent and distressing symptoms associated with advanced Bright's disease. In all probability, the reservations which lead Sir William Roberts to consider the condition extremely rare are to be found in the limitations he attaches to the title uræmic. Although he disputes the claim of paroxysms of dyspnœa to the designation of uræmic, I think he would scarcely dispute the frequency of spasmodic difficulty of breathing in advanced Bright's disease.

The employment of the term 'uræmic asthma' has probably caused much confusion, since it appears to group under one heading a variety of different types of uræmic dyspnœa, and it seems to offer but a single explanation for their pathology. The forms of dyspnœa which may be met with in uræmia have been enumerated as—(1) continuous dyspnœa; (2) paroxysmal dyspnœa; (3) both types alternating; and (4) Cheyne-Stokes breathing. To these Saundby adds a form described by Lecorché as laryngeal, in which the respiration is noisy and sibilant, as in croup, attributed to spasm of the laryngeal muscles.

The pathology of uræmic asthma is not easy to follow—that is, it may be doubted whether in uræmia the spasmodic difficulty of breathing is always the result of contraction of the muscles of the smaller bronchi. Although the symptoms resemble those of spasmodic asthma, both in the suddenness of their onset and in the completeness with which the attack may pass off, yet the discomforts of the patient do not give way before the same forms of treatment, and there is every probability that another pathology must be sought. It is possible that such cases might be explained by contraction of minute arterial twigs, whether of the coronary arteries, as suggested by Sir George Johnson, or of the pulmonary vessels.

Cases of uræmic asthma do not appear to be very common, although under this name several were described by different observers in the 'British Medical Journal' of 1883. The form of dyspnœa which is more commonly met with is that associated with dropsical changes, whether these lead to œdema of the lung or to the accumulation of fluid within the pleural cavity. Certainly, the variety of uræmic dyspnœa which has most prominently come under my observation is that in which these changes have existed, and Saundby quotes numerous cases in which the paroxysmal dyspnœa has preceded the fatal ending of the case by but a short time only. Both these varieties appear to simulate the symptoms due to true spasmodic asthma. In both the difficulty of breathing commences usually at night, and the patient sits up in bed, struggling for breath for many hours. Sometimes the respirations are accompanied by sibilant *râles*, which are apparently the result of bronchial spasm. At other times, although the breathing is equally hurried and laborious, it is accompanied by loud puerile respiration over the lungs. When dyspnœa is associated with œdema of the lungs, although the attack may commence suddenly and may to a large extent pass off after a few hours of intense distress, yet the respirations continue to be more rapid than in the normal condition, indicating that there is some permanent interference with the work of respiration. Sir George Johnson considered that in some cases anæmia was the true cause of dyspnœa; but this theory, although explaining to a certain extent the shortness of breath on exertion from which so many of these patients suffer, would in no way account for spasmodic or paroxysmal attacks of dyspnœa. Another cause which has been assigned to some of these cases is the dilated and weakened state of the heart; but in this form, as in the last, the dyspnœa is excited mainly by exercise, very little distress of breathing being experienced if the patient is sufficiently ill to be kept in bed; in fact, this form of dyspnœa, although it may be associated with cases of chronic kidney disease, is more strictly to be regarded as a symptom of chronic vascular changes than as a symptom of uræmic trouble.

In the 'Practitioner' for December 1896I published the following notes of a patient who had been under my care in King's College Hospital, and who had for some months exhibited various forms of uræmic dyspnœa. A man aged sixty-three was admitted on July 7, 1896, complaining of shortness of breath and swelling of the hands and legs. There was no marked history of intemperance, although his habits appeared to have been somewhat free. He stated that he had been quite well until the latter part of December 1895, when he caught a chill, and had to take to his bed. His legs then began to swell, and from that time the swelling increased gradually; he got weaker, and lost weight considerably. He first noticed shortness of breath on exertion four weeks before his admission. At no time did he make any complaint of lumbar pain. On admission, he was found to be anæmic; there was considerable œdema of the hands, the legs, and the scrotum, and there was partial orthopnœa; the pulse was 104, and had marked high tension; the heart appeared to be displaced somewhat to the right, and the area of dulness was rather obscure; the first sound at the apex was reduplicated, the second sound at the base accentuated. At the base of the left lung there was much dulness, and the breath sounds were inaudible; vocal fremitus and vocal resonance were absent at this part; there were fine crepitations at the right base; the urine contained a large quantity of albumin and some blood, and when microscopically examined, hyaline, granular and fatty casts were seen. At 8.30 P.M., on July 9, he had a sudden attack of dyspnœa. The difficulty of respiration was so great as to cause him to lean forward and rest on his knees. The left pleura was aspirated, and thirty-four ounces of fluid removed, and breathing was immediately relieved. On July 11, at 9 P.M., he had another attack of dyspnœa, of quite sudden onset, and typically asthmatic in character, with very prolonged expiration and gasping inspiration. He became almost collapsed, with cold, clammy, profuse perspiration. Nitrite of amyl was tried, but had no effect; at twelve o'clock the attack passed off. On July 12, between nine and twelve o'clock at night, he had a similar attack, which appeared to be somewhat relieved by breath mixture containing spiritus ætheris and sal volatile. From this point the œdema of the bases and the effusion at the left base increased, and there was marked orthopnœa, apparently the result of these conditions. On the 24th he again had an asthmatic attack, lasting from 9.30 to 12.30. Nitrite of amyl again gave no relief, but the breathing became somewhat easier after twenty grains of bromide of potassium. Up to this time the quantity of urine passed averaged from twenty-four to thirty-four ounces a day. On July 25 a pint of imperial drink was given every three hours, and the following day the urine passed increased to fifty ounces; from that time to August 10 he had but one slight asthmatic attack lasting only one hour, and it is interesting to note that on this day he only passed twenty-three ounces of urine. On the 13th the dyspnœa was fairly constant, and the sounds indicated considerable pleural effusion at the left base, as well as some œdema of the right base. On August 15 the left side of the chest was aspirated again, and forty-seven ounces of fluid were removed. From that time, although the dyspnœa has continued, he has been fairly free from severe paroxysmal attacks. Frequently, as in ordinary cases of pulmonary œdema, the difficulty of breathing has been greater during the night, but it has been a question of degree rather than of a sudden temporary increased dyspnœa. The symptoms have been markedly relieved since the eliminative work of the kidney has been re-established by the use of digitalis, caffeine, and diuretin. At the time of writing, the œdema of the legs and the fluid in the thorax have both undergone considerable diminution, and although the patient still suffers from some orthopnœa, he is free from paroxysmal seizures.

Another case of uræmic asthma was described in the second volume of the King's College Hospital Reports, and although the chronic renal mischief was not so marked, yet in many other respects it will compare well with the preceding case. The patient, a woman aged forty-two, was admitted complaining of severe cough and attacks of difficulty of breathing. She had had scarlet fever when a child, and acute rheumatism eight years ago; in other respects she had always been healthy. In November 1893 she had severe paroxysmal attacks of coughing, and it was noted that she had great engorgement of the cervical veins and swelling of the face, and also that there was a trace of albumin in the urine, which was then normal in quantity. She improved, and was fairly well until five weeks before her admission in May, 1895, when she again had violent attacks of coughing, with no expectoration and no pain. Evidences of œdema of the bases were found. This soon improved, but was followed by some general bronchitis, with normal temperature. The physical signs indicated the presence of fluid on the right side of the chest; there was no œdema of the legs; the urine, which was acid, had a specific gravity of 1018, and contained a small quantity of albumin; thirty-five ounces were passed in the twenty-four hours. While in hospital she had several attacks of severe paroxysmal dyspnœa, usually lasting two hours. On some occasions these were to a certain extent relieved by free vomiting, provoked by sulphate of zinc or carbonate of ammonium. On May 12 the right pleura was aspirated, and twenty-five ounces of slightly turbid serum were withdrawn. Between the 13th and the 21st the amount of urine passed daily averaged only from twenty to thirty ounces. Under the use of brandy, digitalis, and ether, the symptoms were markedly relieved, and the urine gradually increased slightly in amount. On June 12 the paroxysmal dyspnœa was treated with nitro-glycerine, but without any relief being obtained; later in the day one minim of croton oil was given, and a third of a grain of nitrate of pilocarpine injected hypodermically. The oil produced several free evacuations, and she perspired profusely after the pilocarpine, and was sick; the cough and dyspnœa were arrested by vomiting, and she remained quiet through the evening. Several doses of pilocarpine were subsequently given, and always produced relief of the urgent symptoms. From August 17 to the date of her discharge on August 30, although she remained fairly comfortable so far as dyspnœa was concerned, she was only passing a very small quantity of urine daily, sometimes as little as fourteen ounces.

A third case which has come under my observation exhibited the Cheyne-Stokes respiration, which has been referred to as occasionally marking the closing scenes of chronic Bright's disease. This patient was a man aged forty-three, with great œdema of the lower extremities, and evidence of fluid in the abdominal cavity, associated with a well-marked mitral murmur, and with chronic kidney disease, in all probability the result of alcoholism. Although he suffered from dyspnœa for several weeks before the end, the dyspnœa was fairly continuous, and was evidently due to œdema of the lungs; but during several nights in the week before his death the breathing showed Cheyne-Stokes respirations in the typical form. He obtained some relief from the continuous dyspnœa by the removal of fluid from the extremities, but it is needless to say that the Cheyne-Stokes respiration did not improve under any form of treatment. Fürbringer thinks that uræmic asthma may be produced by the influence of uræmic blood upon the terminations of the vagus nerve, or by an irritation of the motor fibres supplied to the bronchial muscles; or, finally, by direct irritation of the respiratory centre, the last explanation agreeing with that given by Landois of cases of uræmic asthma and uræmic dyspnœa when they occur independently of local affection. Landois thinks that in some cases these symptoms may be due to the irritation of the respiratory centre of the medulla oblongata by the waste material retained in the blood, and he quotes numerous experiments in which the breathing became dyspnœic as the result of the action of chemical irritants upon the medulla. He states that experimental chemical irritation of the cortex of the brain sometimes produced severe dyspnœa, which could not be occasioned by lung affection, nor by convulsive seizures, nor by irritation of the medulla. Landois further states that, in addition to the mechanical disturbance of normal respiratory movements by the spasms, a substance is formed, perhaps an acid, which, together with the generated carbonic acid, acts as an irritant on the respiratory centre. He lays stress on the fact (and this is in accordance with my own observations) that uræmic asthma or uræmic dyspnœa is rarely continuous during chronic uræmia. The condition may come on suddenly, like any other form of uræmic seizure, and may pass off without leaving any very marked distress. Landois suggests that some cases of uræmic dyspnœa may be due to the action of accumulated material retained in the lung tissue upon the nerves of the pulmonary plexus, a form of asthma being produced which is therefore due to local toxic influence.

Cardio-vascular system.—With the advance of the disease, the evidences of interference with the action of the heart become more marked, and the patient is apt to suffer from increasing dyspnœa on exertion, which, in many cases, is due rather to weakness of the circulation than to obstruction from pulmonary changes. Frequently, however, the two conditions co-exist, and the cardiac failure leads to engorgement of lung, which in turn gives rise to dilatation of the right side of the heart. Apart from dyspnœa, the main symptoms likely to arise from cardiac hypertrophy are those of headache, ringing in the ears, giddiness, palpitation, and perhaps genuine cardiac asthma, or even angina pectoris. These symptoms are, as a rule, transitory in character, occurring during the night, or following extreme exertion or other form of excess. During the early morning hours they gradually pass off, so that the patient doses, and wakes feeling fairly comfortable. With the downward progress of the disease, however, these symptoms are liable to become more permanent, and during the last few weeks the palpitation and dyspnœa may form the most prominent symptoms, the rhythm of the heart becoming very markedly altered, and the gallop-rhythm relatively frequent. At this time the pulse may frequently lose somewhat in tension, and the sounds of the heart become less accentuated. When the heart's action is fairly regular, the sounds of the heart may, however, become louder than usual, and both the first and the second sound are frequently reduplicated. The reduplication of the second sound seems undoubtedly to be due to lack of synchronism between the closure of the aortic and pulmonary valves. The explanation of the reduplication of the first sound, however, has given rise to some difference of opinion. The theory that is commonly held is that it is due to a lack of synchronism between the two ventricular contractions, and it is perfectly conceivable that if the tension on the systemic side is greater than that on the pulmonary, the contraction of the left ventricle should be effected more slowly, and its termination complete somewhat later than the contraction of the right ventricle. Sir George Johnson, however, held that the reduplication of the first sound is due to the contraction of a dilated and especially of a hypertrophied auricle becoming sonorous, and he considered that the first division of the double first sound was the result of the auricular systole. He supported this contention by comparison with the triple friction sound so often heard in cases of cirrhosis of the kidney when a patch of lymph is formed over the surface of the auricle. This reduplication of the first sound is certainly not heard nearly as often as the reduplication of the second. One consequence of the hypertrophy of the left ventricle requires special mention, namely, the tendency to the rupture of blood vessels which may have undergone degenerative changes. Hypertrophied muscle readily degenerates, and, although during the greater part of the history of cases of cirrhosis of the kidney there can be little doubt that the hypertrophy of the arteries is an element of safety, yet as the disease advances the hypertrophied muscle is apt to undergo atheromatous changes, and so hæmorrhages may occur from rupture of minute arteries. These hæmorrhages sometimes give rise to severe and intractable epistaxis, and it is not at all uncommon in cases of cirrhosis of the kidney for the epistaxis to be so profuse and so exhausting that plugging of the nares may be required. Hæmorrhage from ruptured arteries may also give rise to apoplexy, and sometimes, but more rarely, to gastric or intestinal hæmorrhages. Still less commonly, rupture of the vessels may cause hæmaturia, but far more often hæmaturia is the result of a sub-acute inflammatory attack.

The tendency to rupture of minute arteries is also responsible for many of the retinal changes which are so often found in connection with cirrhosis of the kidney. The large flame-shaped hæmorrhages in the retina, which may occur independently of attacks of uræmic convulsions, although they are more commonly found after convulsions, are undoubtedly the result of the sudden overstrain and rupture of branches of the retinal artery. These appearances will, however, be fully described under the heading of 'Retinal Changes.'

An interesting case, exhibiting unusual symptoms of hæmorrhage, has been described by Haug.[1] The patient was a man aged thirty-nine, with alcoholic habits, who had for eighteen months suffered from cardiac weakness and irregularity of the heart's action. Nine months previously he had had profuse epistaxis, and at that time the urine was free from albumin. More recently he had a still more severe nasal hæmorrhage, which could only be stopped by plugging the nares. At this time the urine contained both albumin and casts. Subsequently there was very severe pain in both ears, accompanied by tinnitus and some deafness. Hæmorrhage was found to have taken place in the tympanic cavities and membrana tympani; an albuminuric retinitis with hæmorrhages was also noted. In the course of three weeks the blood in the ears became absorbed, without the hæmorrhagic otitis having become purulent. This case is somewhat unusual, in that the epistaxis and the cardiac symptoms together were the earliest indications of Bright's disease.

Nervous system.—Nervous symptoms are prominent in advanced cases of cirrhosis of the kidney. Reference has already been made to the frequency of unilateral headache and of vertigo. It remains, however, to mention the frequent irritability and weakness exhibited by patients in advanced stages of this disease: they often become extremely low-spirited, and lose all hope of recovery; they may even attempt to commit suicide. Sometimes, also, after attacks of convulsions, the sense of hearing may be interfered with, and a temporary deafness has been described, comparable to the temporary blindness which is far more common. Many of these patients sleep very badly, and this insomnia frequently causes anxiety, it not only tends to weaken the patient, but it resists so many of the ordinary forms of hypnotics. The more grave interferences with the functions of the nervous system are those which are ordinarily grouped as indicative of acute uræmia, namely, the convulsions and coma, which may or

[1] *Deut. Med. Woch.*, November 5, 1896.

may not be followed by uræmic amaurosis and albuminuric retinitis. The character of the uræmic convulsions has already been described : these convulsions may be anticipated when patients with insomnia suffer from persistent headache, and when the amount of urine undergoes much diminution.

Other symptoms of uræmia are frequently prominent, such as severe vomiting, digestive troubles, and urgent dyspnœa, with or without bronchial catarrh, and sometimes associated with expectoration; these symptoms may occasionally lead to errors in diagnosis if the nature of the urine is overlooked.

In renal cirrhosis, as in chronic nephritis, considerable impairment of muscular strength is relatively frequent, although the loss of muscular power is a somewhat late symptom, and does not usually occur before patients have had to keep to their beds. The amount of muscular wasting is not, however, so great, nor does it occur so rapidly, as in chronic diffused nephritis. The skin also offers a marked contrast to the appearance presented by patients with chronic nephritis. It is rarely of the blanched, anæmic tint so commonly seen in the latter disease, though it loses its healthy colour and becomes yellowish, sometimes being slightly jaundiced in late stages of the disease. This alteration in the colour of the skin is, in many cases, however, due to the simultaneous occurrence of cirrhosis of the liver. Various forms of skin eruptions have been described in connection with cirrhosis of the kidney. These may affect the skin of the face, so that acne rosacea is fairly frequent, more particularly in those cases which are due to alcoholic excess; but in addition uræmic rashes are frequently met with; patients also often complain a great deal of itching of the skin, and the irritation may give rise to the appearance of an erythematous rash.

The end is usually reached through insidious inflammation of internal organs. Many patients with contracted kidney, if they do not die in the course of uræmic convulsions, suffer from pneumonia, which may occur somewhat insidiously without the usual typical rise of temperature. They frequently also suffer from pleurisy, as well as from simple hydrothorax. The pleurisy of contracted kidney is often bilateral, and it tends to become purulent. Dry forms of pleurisy are not uncommon, inflammatory patches forming above the base of the lung without much fluid effusion.

Another form of inflammation, which may frequently reach an advanced stage without any marked symptom, is the inflammation of the pericardium. Renal pericarditis often occurs with very little complaint of pain and with little, if any, alteration of cardiac dulness; in fact, in advanced cases of disease, the stethoscope frequently furnishes indications of pericarditis which would otherwise be unsuspected. There may occasionally be some pain, but this is rarely as acute as in rheumatic pericarditis. Sometimes, when no complaint has been made, tenderness is observed over the pericardial region, and the mere examination of the patient by percussion, or the pressure of the stethoscope over the pericardium, may be sufficient to occasion a complaint of tenderness. Usually, there is very slight pain at the commencement, and this speedily departs.

Another characteristic of renal pericarditis is the rapidity with which the physical signs vary. Sounds heard in the morning may be completely altered in rhythm and character towards the evening. Variability in the character of the sounds may frequently help to differentiate pericardial from endocardial sounds, although very often at the first examination it is difficult to say whether the abnormal sounds heard are due to pericarditis or to a recently developing endocarditis.

The transition to the late symptoms of cirrhosis of the kidney is sometimes very abruptly marked, and is usually accompanied by failure in the compensatory work of the heart, failure in the eliminating power of the kidney, and increasing weakness. Three stages have, in fact, been described in the history of cirrhosis of the kidney: the first, the albuminuric stage, in which few symptoms, if any, can be detected, other than the occasional appearance of albumin and the increase in the amount of urine passed. The second, the stage when the renal trouble becomes more marked, but when the hypertrophy of arteries is associated with hypertrophy of the ventricle; in this stage, although there may be frequent complaints of dyspeptic and neuralgic troubles, yet, as a whole, the health is not very markedly impaired. In the third stage, as the eliminative work of the kidney fails and the ventricle also loses its force, the various physiological systems in turn show evidence of failing action. From what has been said, it will be gathered that, during the third stage the pulse frequently loses its high tension, and becomes small, rapid, and irregular in character. With the reduction of blood pressure the work of the kidney fails, and we find that there is generally rapid diminution in the quantity of urine eliminated, and perhaps still further lowering of specific gravity. Sometimes, however, owing to the reduction in the daily amount of liquid eliminated, the specific gravity may rise somewhat, but it rarely, if ever, reaches the normal standard.

In this late stage of renal cirrhosis dropsy may supervene, and in its character it resembles the dropsy associated with cardiac failure—that is, the swelling generally commences in the feet and extends upwards, sometimes affecting the abdominal cavity but rarely to the extent seen in cases of chronic nephritis. When dropsy occurs with renal cirrhosis it may be less permanent than that of chronic nephritis. It seems to be so largely dependent upon failure of the circulation that any improvement of the circulatory powers is almost necessarily attended by diminution of dropsical effusion. Hence, it is by no means uncommon to find that temporary improvement follows the judicious employment of drugs which increase the force of the cardiac contractions, and, although the presence of dropsical effusion necessarily presents an additional danger, the danger from this source is not so great as in cases of chronic nephritis.

Another indication of the failure of the circulation is afforded by symptoms referable to the liver. Slight jaundice may supervene, and patients may often complain of hæmorrhoids. Reference has already been made to the frequency of diarrhœa in connection with this disease. The latter symptom is apt to become more prominent and more troublesome at a late stage. The diarrhœa may sometimes be complicated by the appearance of blood, which may come from ruptured hæmorrhoids or from ulceration in the course of the intestine. The motions are not only more frequent, but they consist largely of liquid, and are extremely exhausting. It is always necessary to watch carefully for spontaneous diarrhœa, since, as many of these patients are liable to be treated, almost as a matter of routine, with hydragogue purgatives, this symptom may be overlooked. In connection with the diarrhœa of the late stage of cirrhosis of the kidney, Dr. Purdy refers to a singular circumstance, namely, that the stools are passed most often at night, and he states that he has known patients go through the whole day without any, or at most with one or two movements of the bowels, while at night from six to ten watery stools would be passed.

As the disease progresses uræmic symptoms become more marked and more constant; the headache is more persistent, the dyspnœa, on the slightest exertion, more extreme. There is also loss of flesh, as in chronic nephritis. As has already been intimated, the end may be hastened by the occurrence of some complication, such as the secondary inflammation either of the heart or of the lungs, or it may be reached through uræmic symptoms; on the other hand, a very large proportion of patients with cirrhotic kidney suffer from cerebral hæmorrhage, and it has been observed that cerebral hæmorrhage appears to occur more frequently amongst patients who have not suffered from general œdema.

Course and duration.—From the foregoing account, it is obvious that this disease follows an insidious chronic course from the commencement. Even when its existence has been recognised, it does not appear to add very greatly to the immediate risks of life so long as the circulatory system shows no signs of impairment. Cases have been recorded in which chronic albuminuria has been observed for many years. Dr. Francis Hawkins [1] narrated two such cases. In the first, a man aged 49, chronic albuminuria had been noted at intervals for 25 years, and on most of the occasions when the urine had been examined this man had been applying for assurance. The specific gravity of the urine on four separate occasions ranged from 1020 to 1024. In 1872, in 1883, and in 1892 large quantities of albumin were found, but on other occasions the amount varied from slight opalescence on boiling to a fortieth or a twelfth; and on some occasions hyaline tube casts were found. This individual always lived a country life, and hunted four or five times a week in the hunting season, and his habits with regard to food and alcohol were very abstemious. The apex beat was in the nipple line, and the sounds at the base of the heart were accentuated, but

[1] *Clinical Society's Transactions*, vol. xxvi., 1893.

there was no marked increase of tension of the pulse. Dr. Hawkins also gives brief notes of another case in which Dr. Bright found albumin, in 1849. For the last eighteen years of his life the patient was under observation, and the urine was generally of low specific gravity (1012), and there was frequent nocturnal micturition. This patient suffered occasionally from diarrhœa; his pulse was often intermittent and sometimes irregular; there was some hypertrophy of the ventricle, and the sounds at the base of the heart were accentuated. He ultimately died at the age of eighty-eight from cerebral hæmorrhage.

I have met with several cases of long duration, more particularly in connection with insurance work, and it appears to me that so long as the patient can live reasonably and take exercise, the danger may be warded off. With this disease, as with so many others, one is apt to draw an exaggerated idea of the seriousness from a consideration of hospital patients. Patients in comfortable circumstances, who are able to take care of themselves, undoubtedly live longer and with greater comfort than those whose circumstances render care and dietary precautions impossible. Cirrhosis of the kidney is the special condition which is likely to be discovered by accidental examination of the urine for life insurance. The early phases produce so little discomfort that the patient is frequently wholly unaware of the seriousness of his condition. Apart from such accidental recognition of the nature of the disease, the earliest symptom to attract attention is probably the increased frequency of nocturnal micturition, although, as has been noted above, in a certain proportion of cases dyspeptic symptoms may first bring the patient under observation. These symptoms, however, are often so slight that they are disregarded, and the first note of warning may then be afforded by impairment of vision, which generally occurs when the cirrhosis is fairly advanced. The disease may, however, remain unrecognised until the breathing power is affected, and under such circumstances it is often somewhat difficult to decide whether the albuminuria is the cause or the result of the interference with the circulation. When the disease has thus been in existence for some length of time, and hypertrophy of the ventricle and of the small arteries has occurred, the course may be interrupted by bronchitic seizures on slight exposure, and such seizures may frequently assume a pneumonic type. In the large majority of cases the hypertrophied ventricle fails sooner or later, and the patient complains of increased dyspnœa, the amount of urine passed falls below the normal quantity, and one of the complications above mentioned supervenes. The end may be heralded by attacks of diarrhœa, by vomiting, by uræmic seizures, or it may occur from cerebral hæmorrhage. It is impossible to forecast the duration of a case of cirrhosis unless the whole of the patient's circumstances are intimately known, but the greatest value attaches to the condition of the cardio-vascular system, the sounds at the apex of the heart affording valuable indications. Dr. Hawkins, in the paper already referred to, has collected records of 106 cases treated at the Middlesex Hospital. Of these 33 died between the ages of 50 and 60; 23 between the ages of 60 and 70; and of the total number 20 died with cerebral hæmorrhage.

Diagnosis.—The diagnosis of cirrhosis of the kidney is generally founded upon an examination of the urine and of the heart. Valuable indications are, however, afforded by the age of the patient, by the history of previous habits, by the nature of the occupation, and to a certain extent by the family history. If there is the slightest suspicion of cirrhosis of the kidney, the urine passed at different times of the day must be repeatedly examined before it can be safely stated that this disease is non-existent. It is necessary to note the absolute daily quantity passed, the specific gravity of the twenty-four hours' specimen, and the amount of albumin which it contains. The examination of a single specimen may frequently be misleading, since, as has been already noted, the urine at certain times of the day, and even for several days together, may contain no albumin. On the other hand, if albumin is found, if the apex beat of the heart is displaced outwards, if also the sounds at the base of the heart are markedly accentuated, and the pulse tension is increased, the elements for certain diagnosis are all present. The smallness of the amount of albumin may sometimes suggest a transitory functional albuminuria, but this condition is not associated with alterations in the cardio-vascular system, nor does it give rise to an increase in the daily excretion of urine, nor to nocturnal micturition. Persistent headache or frequent dyspepsia adds largely to the certainty of diagnosis.

The chief diseases which may be mistaken for cirrhosis of the kidney are chronic nephritis and lardaceous disease of the kidney. The three diseases arise under different conditions, and are marked by broad differences. Cirrhosis of the kidney is generally a disease of later middle age, the patients being mostly above forty; it is only in exceptional cases that this disease attacks patients at an earlier age. Chronic nephritis is generally recognised before the age of forty, and it may frequently be traced from a previous attack of acute nephritis during childhood or adolescence. Lardaceous disease, which is to such a large extent dependent upon chronic suppuration, necessarily occurs at an earlier age; it is most frequently seen in childhood.

Then, with regard to the history of these three diseases, the exciting cause in the case of cirrhosis is frequently a matter of uncertainty. The influence of lead-poisoning, gout, and of free living have already been mentioned, but in many cases the etiological factor is uncertain. Chronic nephritis can almost always be traced to an acute attack. Lardaceous disease may occur as the sequel to chronic suppuration, as in connection with diseased bone, or as the sequel to phthisis or syphilis. The occurrence of dropsy favours the presumption of chronic nephritis or of lardaceous disease. In renal cirrhosis, dropsy is generally absent, although in some few cases it may form a feature of the later stages of the disease. The character of the left ventricle will afford some help in diagnosing these three conditions. It reaches its greatest extent of hypertrophy in connection with renal cirrhosis, when the arterial tension is greatly increased. With chronic nephritis, although hypertrophy occurs, it is not so frequent nor so extensive as in renal cirrhosis. In lardaceous disease the circulation rarely exhibits indications of hypertrophy of the heart or arteries. Further, with regard to uræmic manifestations, these are most common in connection with renal cirrhosis, and they may arise at any stage, although they are most marked and most persistent in the later stages. Retinal changes, also, and amaurosis are frequent with this complaint. With chronic nephritis the chief features are those connected with dropsy and with anæmia, while uræmic symptoms are generally absent, except in the latest stages, when the kidney is undergoing contraction. With lardaceous disease uræmic symptoms are mostly absent; diarrhœa is frequent and may be persistent, occurring generally from a very early stage, and appearing to depend upon the cause of the lardaceous disease, rather than upon any alterations in the functions of the kidney.

The differences in the urine in the three conditions are usually very marked. In cirrhosis the quantity is increased, while the amount of albumin is relatively small. In chronic nephritis the albumin is usually present in large quantity, while the daily excretion of urine is either normal or rather below the average amount. In lardaceous disease the daily excretion of urine is increased, and much albumin is present. Diminution in the daily excretion of urea is characteristic of cirrhosis rather than of chronic nephritis or lardaceous disease, although in lardaceous disease the amount of urea may be diminished at a late stage.

Other diseases for which chronic nephritis may be mistaken are the two forms of diabetes, more particularly diabetes insipidus, in which the specific gravity is low, although the amount of water eliminated is increased. This disease, moreover, is not associated with any material change in the action of the heart or in the nature of the pulse. Sometimes, in connection with hysterical conditions, an increase in the daily amount of water passed, or an increase in the frequency of nocturnal micturition, may give rise to a suspicion of the existence of renal cirrhosis. Patients may complain of having frequently to get up at night, and the urine under such circumstances is found to be of low specific gravity and light colour, and generally to contain no albumin. In all these characters, therefore, it corresponds with the condition of the urine which is occasionally found in connection with renal cirrhosis. Attention to the nature of the heart and the pulse will help to prevent an erroneous diagnosis, although the excited character of the neurotic heart must be carefully distinguished from the accentuated sounds of hypertrophy due to kidney disease.

In spite of the aids to differential diagnosis above given, it must be admitted that cases are frequently met with, in which a precise diagnosis is extremely difficult. In connection with insurance work, for instance, where the previous history of the proposer is enshrouded in mystery, even if essential points are not intentionally concealed, considerable doubt may frequently be felt as to the significance of the albuminuria. Some of the most difficult cases to deal with are those in which a very faint trace of albumin is found in urine of low specific gravity, and where the conditions of examination only permit the testing of a small quantity of the urine passed on a few occasions. In these cases the diagnosis may be rendered probable by consideration of the appearance of the patient, the occupation, the age, the character of the pulse, and the nature of the sounds of the heart; but the position of the apex beat of the heart is, even in health, subject to such variations that it affords little help except in extreme instances. In insurance practice greater stress must be laid upon the accentuation of the sounds at the base of the heart and upon increased tension of the pulse, but it must be admitted that it is frequently essential to obtain a report from the medical attendant concerning the habits of the proposer, and the results of repeated examinations of the urine, before it is possible to feel any satisfaction in dealing with such a case.

Prognosis.—The prognosis in renal cirrhosis depends largely upon the cause of the disease, upon the age of the patient, his occupation, and his circumstances. When the disease has been recognised at an early stage the prognosis is far less serious than when the patient comes under observation after the hypertrophy of the heart has been in existence for a length of time. The prognosis is also rendered more favourable if the disease appears to depend upon some condition which may be altered, such as lead poisoning or gout. By the avoidance of conditions likely to provoke inflammatory affections of the kidney, the early stage of renal cirrhosis may be almost indefinitely prolonged, even though there seems to be but little prospect of effecting a cure. A certain portion of the renal tissue has been destroyed, a certain area of the kidney is undergoing contraction, and the safety of the patient depends upon the limitation of this contracting process to the portion of kidney tissue originally affected.

There is very little doubt that the area affected by renal cirrhosis is subject to rapid variations and extensions, and each time that a fresh area of renal tissue is affected the secreting tissue is diminished in quantity; hence, although the immediate urgency of a slight extension may pass off speedily, the patient is subsequently less fitted to face intercurrent diseases. On the other hand, the chief indications of danger are those dependent upon uræmic symptoms. Alterations in the regularity of the heart's action, increasing frequency of attacks of pulmonary dyspnœa, increasing frequency or more prolonged duration of attacks of diarrhœa, all indicate danger. Although uræmic convulsions are always a source of great anxiety, it is generally advisable not to give too hopeless a prognosis directly they occur.

Not long since, with Mr. Philip Birch I saw a patient who was intensely comatose, apparently as the result of uræmic convulsions. He had stertorous breathing, the pupils did not react to light, the conjunctivæ were not sensitive, and yet this patient ultimately completely regained consciousness and apparent well-being, although a small amount of albumin persisted in the urine. This case is by no means an isolated one in my experience, although it is mentioned here as the contrast between the comatose condition of the patient when first seen, and his rapid recovery, was so marked as to excite surprise. Even after uræmic convulsions and coma, it is by no means uncommon for patients to recover consciousness, and amongst hospital patients I have seen the use of tonics, such as nux vomica, strophanthus, digitalis, and iron, followed by such improvement that the patients have been enabled to leave the hospital. As a rule, however, when there is increasing weakness of the heart's action, with rapid diminution in the daily excretion of urine and uræmic symptoms, the practitioner will be wise in viewing the future with anxiety, even though he expresses some reserve as to the exact prognosis.

Treatment.—The mode of onset is so gradual and so indefinite that it is comparatively rare that it is possible to treat the cause of the disease; it is therefore necessary to devote a greater amount of attention to a consideration of symptomatic treatment. When the disease results from lead poisoning, from syphilis, or from gout, and the case comes under observation at an early stage, treatment appropriate for these several conditions should be adopted, and may exert a beneficial influence upon the urinary affection. On the other hand, when the case has come under observation at a later stage, the treatment has to be almost entirely symptomatic, although the renal nature of the disease may be recognised. In this form of Bright's disease the amount of albumin that is lost is so small that no measures need be taken with the view of its reduction. At one time astringents were recommended, such as tannic acid or ergotin, with the object either of checking the amount of loss of albumin, or of diminishing the daily excretion of urine. It is quite a mistake, however, to attempt to control the polyuria of renal cirrhosis, since diminution in the daily excretion of urine is frequently associated with diminution in the excretion of nitrogenous waste. It is far more necessary at late stages of the disease to employ remedies intended to increase rather than to diminish the amount of urine passed, since, as has been already indicated, the dangers of the later stage of renal cirrhosis are chiefly dependent upon uræmia, which is most likely to occur when the renal excretion falls below the normal limits. In ordinary cases, which come under observation at an early stage, it is desirable to curtail the amount of nitrogenous foods, so as to reduce the work to be performed by the kidney; but it is possible to do harm rather than good by too rigid a dietary, since many of these patients suffer from poor appetite, and this may be further impaired by laying down rules too severely for a plain and uninteresting dietary. Frequently benefit is derived from the employment of milk, especially in diluted form. Some physicians advise that alcohol, coffee, and tea should be avoided, but it is more generally held that, so far as alcohol is concerned, it is excess that does harm, and that these patients frequently feel benefit from moderate doses of diluted alcohol taken with their meals. The same applies to the use of tea and coffee; if these are taken hot and strong they will do harm by interfering with the digestive powers, but if taken in dilute form at a moderate temperature they often appear to be beneficial. Although milk is frequently of service in these cases, it is a mistake to attempt to restrict the patient to a pure milk diet. The dietary should always be light and nutritious, and so far as possible variation should be encouraged, with the view of stimulating appetite.

It is always advisable to see that the patient is warmly clad, since the dangers of the disease are greatly increased by sudden chills. Flannel or woollen garments should be worn next the skin, and patients should be warned of the risks of exposure to cold or damp. If it is possible, those suffering from renal cirrhosis should pass the winter in warm or temperate climates, and the benefit obtained from expatriation is frequently largely increased by the enforced separation from the ordinary cares of a busy life. Bartels advised that patients should entirely give up their ordinary occupations, but this recommendation is one which is frequently impossible to carry out; moreover, in many cases the ordinary daily routine occupation, if free from business worry, is better than enforced inactivity, which often induces great depression.

With regard to drugs, many authors recommend that iodide of potassium should be employed in fairly large doses for a lengthy period. If the disease appears to arise from syphilis, such a course of treatment may be pursued, and mercury may be given simultaneously, either in solution with the iodide or in the form of pills taken after meals. Unless the disease depends upon syphilis, it is almost hopeless to use iodide, since it possesses the disadvantage of disordering digestion, and thus promotes dyspeptic symptoms. Some observers, more particularly Americans, speak highly of the benefits to be obtained from the use of chloride of gold and sodium, administered in doses varying from a thirtieth to a tenth of a grain three times a day. It is stated that while this preparation is given the character of the urine improves, nocturnal micturition is diminished, and the patient shows other evidences of amelioration. This form of treatment, however, has not been generally adopted in this country, and even those who speak well of it state that it may cause dyspeptic symptoms. The persistent headache so commonly associated with renal cirrhosis may be treated in many different ways. The treatment which appears to be most beneficial depends upon the lowering of arterial tension by nitro-glycerine or by one of the nitrites. Nitro-glycerine sometimes gives very good results, especially when taken either in the form of the tabellæ of the Pharmacopœia, or in that of the solution. Some patients, however, complain that the headache is increased by the use of this remedy. Occasionally, nitrite of sodium gives greater relief, and is taken with greater facility. Frequently, however, the headache of renal cirrhosis can be satisfactorily treated by mild purgatives. At one time, moderate venesection was recommended for the relief of this symptom, but it is comparatively rarely that the practitioner will feel justified in employing this measure.

It is often necessary to have recourse to remedies intended to increase the force of contraction and the regularity of action of the heart. For this purpose the different preparations of digitalis are largely used, either alone or in conjunction with some other diuretic. After a prolonged course of digitalis, even when the drug has been given in moderate doses, the pulse may again become rapid and irregular, and it is then necessary to substitute strophanthus or one of the preparations of caffeine. If these measures do not suffice, the palpitations may sometimes be arrested by the employment of narcotics, although it is necessary to be very cautious in the selection of the narcotic, and in the dose to be given. Many attacks of uræmic convulsions and coma have been attributed, rightly or wrongly, to the injudicious employment of morphine or opium; but if the amount of urine eliminated is fairly large, and the specific gravity is not very greatly reduced, it is sometimes safe to employ small doses of morphine and cocaine, with a view of checking the irregularity of the heart's action.

It is very difficult, if not impossible, to lay down any general rules for the treatment of dyspepsia connected with renal cirrhosis. In some cases it may yield to ordinary simple remedies, such as preparations of bismuth or bicarbonate of soda given in conjunction with compound infusion of gentian; in others, hydrocyanic acid is of service. Mostly, it is desirable to treat dyspepsia, at first, as a simple malady, having no reference to renal trouble, since, although in a large number of cases dyspepsia is consecutive to the nephritis, yet, to a certain extent, the conditions may co-exist independently. When the dyspeptic symptoms are unusually intractable, they must always be attributed to the renal condition; in fact, the diagnosis of renal dyspepsia turns largely upon the results of treatment. When the renal origin is established, it is important not to make any sudden great change in the character of the diet. To a large extent the dietary must be dependent upon or, at least, it must be guided by the appetite and tastes of the patient, rather than by any cut-and-dried formula. Necessarily, indigestible articles must be excluded; but, as a rule, there is no harm in allowing patients to take ordinary simple forms of diet in moderation. These patients are often unable to take much nitrogenous material; even lean meat may increase dyspeptic symptoms. Mostly, they are able to thrive upon a diet consisting largely of milk, but unless fish or small quantities of lean meat promote vomiting or increase discomfort they should be administered for their nutritive value. The dyspeptic symptoms frequently appear to be markedly relieved by the administration of laxatives; and sometimes benefit is derived from treatment calculated to improve the character of the action of the heart. Small doses of digitalis and strophanthus in conjunction with vegetable bitters will occasionally give relief; at other times greater improvement results from the employment of warm baths. These various measures undoubtedly act by increasing the elimination of nitrogenous waste from the system. In advanced cases, where the dyspeptic symptoms are undoubtedly due to uræmia, vomiting frequently gives rise to considerable anxiety, and, as in chronic nephritis, often proves extremely rebellious to all forms of treatment. Occasionally, the frequency of vomiting may be reduced by keeping the patient entirely upon liquid diet given in repeated small quantities. Some authors have recommended morphine for the relief of uræmic vomiting, but this remedy must be used with caution, since, even though it may allay the reflex irritability of the stomach, it may interfere with the eliminative work of the kidney. Tincture of iodine, given in one minim doses every half hour, has been recommended for the relief of uræmic vomiting, and, though I have had no extended experience of this plan of treatment, it has been so well spoken of that it seems worthy of trial. Uræmic vomiting has also been treated with small doses of nitrate or oxide of silver, given in the form of a pill; but these remedies seem to have very little effect, and the same may be said of the administration of creosote or carbolic acid when employed for the same purpose. In fact, in the treatment of uræmic vomiting it is important to remember that the cause of the vomiting is in all probability the retention within the system of some toxic material, which is irritating the vomiting centre, and that the mucous membrane of the stomach is not primarily at fault; hence, it is of no use to employ remedies whose action is entirely confined to local sedative effects.

After dyspeptic symptoms have been present, diarrhœa is frequently superadded, and this is often as troublesome as the vomiting, and even more exhausting. Local astringents seem of very little use. The chalk mixture and preparations containing logwood or catechu have frequently been employed, but they generally fail to afford relief. Sometimes the diarrhœa can, to a certain extent, be controlled by the administration of enemata containing starch and opium, but the same result may often be obtained more conveniently by the employment of an opium suppository. The effect upon the elimination of urine must, however, be carefully watched, since it is small consolation to arrest diarrhœa if the onset of more dangerous uræmic symptoms is hastened. The frequency of action may sometimes be relieved by the use of a pure milk diet, but if this disagrees it is much better to allow a somewhat more liberal diet than to persist.

The headache, neuralgic pain, or migraine, which are so frequently characteristic of all stages of this disease, may sometimes be benefited by the administration of nitro-glycerine, nitrite of amyl, nitrite of sodium, or other nitrites. Frequently, however, the headache persists in spite of these remedies. Occasionally, antipyrine or antifebrine will diminish the neuralgic pains, but the effect of these remedies upon the pulse must be watched, and patients must be warned of the dangers of resorting to them too frequently.

It is comparatively rare for patients with cirrhosis of the kidney to suffer much from anæmia; nevertheless, hæmatinics will frequently be beneficial, either some compound of iron—the non-astringent being the most valuable—or some preparation of arsenic. Mineral waters containing compounds of iron and arsenic may frequently be given with advantage, or, if these be not available, a pill consisting of small quantities of arseniate of iron and sulphate of iron may be substituted.

The special symptoms of acute uræmia usually afford very

little scope for treatment, though that of uræmic dyspnœa, for instance, may, to a certain extent, throw light upon the pathology of the condition. Those who attempt to treat all forms of uræmic dyspnœa upon one principle will undoubtedly be doomed to disappointment. As the causes are various, so the treatment must be that naturally suggested by a consideration of the stage of the disease and of the associated symptoms. Many authors have spoken enthusiastically of the benefit to be obtained from the use of nitrite of amyl, nitro-glycerine, and other forms of vascular dilators, and it has been asserted that the nitrites will relieve cases of uræmic asthma almost magically by 'unlocking the spasm-dammed arteries;' in fact, the benefit of nitrites in uræmic asthma has been contrasted with their lack of success in so-called cardiac asthma. The limitations of the use of nitrite of amyl were fairly established by Dr. Solomon Smith in an interesting paper in the 'British Medical Journal' of June 9, 1883, in which he classified four varieties of uræmic dyspnœa, and stated that he had found nitrite of amyl most valuable where the dyspnœa was associated with degeneration of the cardiac muscle. Saundby considers that nitro-glycerine and nitrite of amyl afford some relief, but in the cases in which I have employed them the results have been somewhat disappointing. Leech has suggested the employment of ethyl nitrite, and cobaltonitrite of potassium has also been mentioned. To a certain extent these all seem to have been recommended owing to their power of producing relaxation of involuntary muscle; but in the cases in which I have employed them I have not felt that any permanent relief was afforded, and I am inclined to agree with Dr. Saundby when he says that uræmic asthma is not at all amenable to treatment. Dr. Carter, of Liverpool, recommends the use of ozonic ether, and in those forms of uræmic dyspnœa where the condition is associated with œdema or with chronic bronchitic changes, ether in some form has in my hands given satisfaction. Dr. Carter also recommends the use of inhalations of oxygen, and these again would appear to be most applicable when dyspnœa is due to consecutive lung trouble rather than to a transitory paroxysmal condition. Some cases appear to do well with the ordinary treatment of uræmia—that is, with the warm pack, with digitalis, with acid potassium tartrate, or other measures calculated either to promote the action of the skin or to exert a purgative or diuretic influence. In the case described on p. 198 much relief was obtained from the use of digitalis and caffeine, the dyspnœa passing off as the diuretic influence of these drugs became obvious; still further improvement resulted from the use of diuretin, which prompted a more copious flow of urine and produced marked diminution in the œdema both of the extremities and of the lungs. It must be remembered that the most troublesome cases of uræmic dyspnœa occur towards the termination of chronic kidney disease, and the possibility of the dyspnœa being due to paroxysmal pulmonary œdema has been advanced by Professor Bouvret. He recommends [1] the employment of alcohol in large doses, hydragogues, purges, poultices for the thorax, dry-cupping, bleeding, and in urgent cases the subcutaneous injection of caffeine and ether. In the patient above mentioned, although some relief of the continuous dyspnœa resulted from aspiration of the thorax, the paroxysmal dyspnœa was only diminished during the temporary re-establishment of the renal function. Nitro-glycerine and nitrites are also sometimes used for the treatment of uræmic convulsions, but during the acute stage greater dependence is to be placed upon remedies which increase the action of the skin. Warm baths or wet pack give greater and more speedy relief than most forms of medicinal treatment, and their diaphoretic action may sometimes be stimulated by the simultaneous injection of small quantities of nitrate of pilocarpine. In cases of uræmic coma it is frequently necessary to employ a purgative which will act quickly, and for this purpose croton oil mixed with castor oil can be given.

When there are indications of pericarditis, more particularly if the condition is associated with pain, relief may sometimes be afforded by the local abstraction of blood. Two or three leeches over the heart will frequently diminish the pain of pericarditis. It is, however, generally unnecessary to adopt any special form of treatment for this condition, since the pericarditis of renal cirrhosis so often creeps on insidiously, without giving rise to pain, and progresses in spite of the best efforts at treatment.

[1] *Year-Book of Treatment*, 1892, p. 161.

CHAPTER IX

PUERPERAL ALBUMINURIA, NEPHRITIS AND ECLAMPSIA

THE frequency with which puerperal eclampsia occurs in the practice of obstetric physicians, and the comparative rarity with which it comes under the notice of the general physician, might perhaps excuse the omission of all reference to this subject. The treatment is so essentially connected with obstetric operations, while medicinal forms of treatment appear to have such little influence on the progress of the case, that detailed considerations more properly belong to a treatise on obstetrics. On the other hand, puerperal eclampsia is almost invariably associated with albuminuria, and although the eclampsia occurs at a late stage of pregnancy, the general physician may be consulted during the earlier periods about the significance of an albuminuria which has only then been discovered. Further, a form of nephritis has been described, under the name of puerperal nephritis, which essentially differs in its clinical aspects and its course, as well as in pathological conditions, from ordinary forms of acute or chronic nephritis. Thus, for example, the amount of urine passed may be much reduced, and the specific gravity may be greatly raised, as in acute nephritis, while it is comparatively rare to find any indications of true renal engorgement; and although the urine is generally dark, it is often free from blood. Then, again, the convulsive seizures which are associated with puerperal albuminuria or puerperal nephritis are more frequent and more severe than those associated with acute nephritis; yet in spite of this severity the condition is one which comparatively rarely passes on to chronic nephritis. As will be seen later, there have been differences of opinion concerning the cause of the convulsive attacks, and by many authors the albuminuria and the convulsions are regarded as the expressions of a common cause rather than as being mutually dependent upon disease of the kidney. For these reasons it has appeared well to summarise what is now known of puerperal albuminuria, puerperal nephritis and eclampsia, although it must be remembered that the subject is one which cannot yet be said to have reached its final stage. It was only at the beginning of the present century, in 1839, that Rayer described an albuminous nephritis occurring in women who were pregnant; while, later, Cohn asserted that the albuminuria and convulsions of pregnancy depended upon nephritis. It is important to remember that albuminuria occurring during pregnancy does not necessarily indicate inflammatory affection of the kidney. Slight conditions of albuminuria are by no means uncommon during gestation, without other indications of renal change.

Knapp [1] finds that women attacked with eclampsia are for the most part young, the average age of primiparæ being twenty-four and of multiparæ $29\frac{1}{3}$ years. From a study of the statistics of other observers, he finds that in the greater number of cases the first attack comes on during parturition, and most records show a larger number of cases originating postpartum than antepartum. Many observers have held that puerperal nephritis occurs mainly during the later months of gestation, and although Purdy states that more recent statistics have shown that the disease arises usually during the middle months, yet from the investigations of Saft [2] it appears that the earliest stage of pregnancy in which albuminuria is found is from the thirtieth to the thirty-second week, and that the amount of albumin may become very considerable for several weeks before the end of pregnancy. He carefully examined the urine of 314 pregnant women, 306 women during labour, and 87 puerperæ. He found that the percentage of cases of albuminuria was somewhat lower in multiparæ than in primigravidæ, namely 4·1 per cent. as compared with 5·9 per cent. It has been assumed that primiparæ are more liable to the disease than multiparæ, but it would be perhaps more correct to consider that those who have escaped nephritis in their first pregnancy are less liable to contract the disease in subsequent pregnancies.

[1] *Monats. für Geburtshülfe und Gynäkologie*, bd. 111, May and June 1896.
[2] *Archiv für Gynäkologie*, vol. 51, Part 2.

Etiology.—Lever originally suggested that puerperal nephritis depended upon pressure exerted by the gravid uterus upon the renal veins, and this view seemed so satisfactory that it was adopted by many observers, both obstetricians and physicians. The following arguments in favour of this theory have been recently summarised by Dr. Byers.[1] In eclampsia the condition of the urine indicates some decided interference with the function of the kidneys: the urine often contains albumin, blood, renal epithelium, and casts; it is scanty, and at times there is a history of sudden suppression. One of the most constant features in these cases is the diminution in the excretion of urea during the fit. Œdema of the body has been noted, and sometimes ophthalmoscopic examination has shown changes in the fundus oculi. Post-mortem examination has mostly shown a diseased condition of the kidneys. On the other hand, the following facts would appear to disprove this theory: (1) cases of eclampsia are occasionally met with when no albumin has been present, and sometimes in fatal cases the kidneys are quite healthy; (2) patients with chronic renal disease sometimes go through the whole time of pregnancy without developing convulsions; (3) convulsive seizures do not appear to be proportionate to the intensity of the albuminuria; (4) with acute disease of the kidney, apart from pregnancy, convulsions are not common, except in cases where the renal affection is associated with some specific disease like scarlet fever; (5) in some fatal cases of eclampsia the amount of albumin present has not been more than a trace. Other arguments against the mechanical theory of puerperal nephritis are that as the uterus increases in size it is directed away from the vertebral column, and hence, as Bartels pointed out, the uterus would have to be bent backward on itself at a considerable angle, just above the inlet of the true pelvis, in order to be able to touch the anterior surface of the second lumbar vertebra (the position of the renal veins). That the nephritis is not dependent upon an increase of the general abdominal pressure is also shown by the absence of nephritis in many cases where the pressure is largely increased owing to other causes, such as the development of ovarian tumours or the accumulation of large quantities of ascitic fluid.

[1] *Lancet*, Jan. 2, 1897.

The statistics of recent examinations by Saft might, however, be quoted in partial support of the mechanical theory of puerperal nephritis, since they show that the disease is most likely to develop when the size of the uterus is greatly increasing.

Another theory is the toxæmic or blood-poisoning hypothesis. Changes in the blood are described by Frerichs. He states that the blood contains less albumin and fewer red corpuscles, while the white corpuscles are increased in number; but these alterations are insufficient to account for nephritic changes, and it is much more probable that the puerperal nephritis depends upon toxic materials circulating in the maternal blood vessels, and causing irritation of the kidneys during their elimination. This view is supported by the fact that the tendency to nephritis is increased in twin or multiple pregnancy, and in these cases there are probably larger amounts of waste products of tissue metamorphosis to be eliminated through the maternal blood. Dr. Byers [1] is in favour of the toxæmic or blood-poisoning hypothesis, and he considers that the convulsions are caused by the action on the nerve centres of a poison which has been allowed to accumulate, owing to defective work of the eliminating organs; he believes that this theory is established by the following arguments: (1) It covers all cases of eclampsia, whether albumin is present or not; (2) the clinical history of eclampsia is that of a toxæmia; (3) the post-mortem appearances support this view.

Bouchard's view as to auto-intoxication by the accumulation in the blood of the toxins of pregnancy being the cause of eclampsia has received valuable support recently from experiments conducted by Van de Velde,[2] who succeeded in producing convulsions in pregnant and non-pregnant rabbits by the injection of human urine. He found that the pregnant animals were far more prone to develop convulsions, and he suggests two possible explanations: either the presence of a greater proportion of the toxins causing convulsions in the blood of pregnant animals, or a greater susceptibility of their nerve centres to these toxins. From his experiments he concludes that pregnancy leads to the formation in the female organism of substances

[1] *Lancet*, January 2, 1897.   [2] *Wien. klin. Rundschau*, 1896, No. 50.

whose principal action is the causation of convulsions, and that these substances are only eliminated by the urine. He further finds evidence of the increased susceptibility of the nerve centres during pregnancy in that for some days after delivery the animal is more easily convulsed by these injections, even though its own urine is no longer abnormally toxic.

Morbid anatomy.—The appearances of the kidneys varies greatly in puerperal nephritis, and the history of the disease largely accounts for these differences. If puerperal albuminuria is repeated in successive pregnancies there appears to be little doubt that a form of chronic Bright's disease may be established; but, on the other hand, the rapidity with which all symptoms occasionally pass off after delivery would alone render it improbable that any permanent changes had resulted during the period of puerperal nephritis. Some authors go so far as to deny all connection between puerperal nephritis and chronic Bright's disease, and to regard the latter as an independent condition.

When death follows eclampsia it is rare to find the kidneys normal in appearance. They are somewhat enlarged, and pale yellow. They are less firm and resistant than usual. The surface is smooth, and the capsule can be readily detached. On section the cortex is brownish red, owing to engorgement, while the pyramids are hyperæmic, with dark striæ following the course of the vessels. Microscopical examination shows that the most marked changes occur in the cortex. Sometimes the glomeruli are but little affected, but mostly they are enlarged, the capillaries being distended with blood. The epithelial cells in the tubuli uriniferi are swollen, and frequently they present more or less evidence of fatty degeneration. The convoluted tubes may contain casts, or they may be filled with red blood corpuscles; sometimes they contain colloid matter, which may be mixed with fatty and epithelial *débris*. Leyden in one case found the convoluted tubes full of masses of fat globules, and Virchow, who had observed similar appearances, thought they indicated that the disease was the result of a genuine fat embolism, rather than a primary disease of the glomeruli. Hæmorrhages into the substance of the kidney are not so numerous nor so extensive as in other forms of acute nephritis, but sometimes they may occur between the convoluted tubes and around the glomeruli. The intertubular vessels and the afferent arteries are generally found to be distended.

Similar changes, in less marked form, may be present if death should occur in the earlier stages of puerperal nephritis; in fact, if the first attack should not prove fatal, and if subsequent pregnancies are associated with continuous albuminuria, the post-mortem appearances closely resemble those of the later stages of chronic nephritis, the kidney becoming smaller than usual, the surface granular, and the capsule more or less adherent.

Occasionally, changes in other organs are associated with puerperal nephritis; catarrh of the urinary organs and pyelo-nephritis have been described. Yellow atrophy of the liver has been met with, and hæmorrhages into the liver and lungs have been attributed to bacillary action. Cerebral anæmia and œdema have also been mentioned, and, according to Wiedow, the white infarcts which may be found in the placenta are to be regarded as a consequence rather than as a cause of the renal disease.

Symptoms.— During the early stages of puerperal albuminuria or puerperal nephritis the condition is extremely likely to escape observation, since it is generally devoid of urgent symptoms. Usually, it is only in the later months that symptoms develop, and even in such cases, unless the urine is examined, the cause may be overlooked. The amount of urine passed in the twenty-four hours is as a rule reduced. Sometimes its reduction is not very great, and daily measurements may be required to prove that the quantity is not the same as in health. Before the development of more urgent symptoms, the amount commonly undergoes a sudden decrease, and the degree of reduction will furnish a fair indication of the prospect of other dangers. The specific gravity is generally increased slightly, and within certain limits it varies inversely with the quantity of urine excreted. Sometimes the specific gravity rises to 1022 or 1028, but rarely beyond this, and it practically never reaches the high specific gravity so often met with in acute nephritis. An exceptionally high specific gravity, 1042, has been recorded by Dr. Deahofe:[1]

[1] *Journ. Amer. Med. Ass.*, September 27, 1890.

it occurred on one occasion in the course of a case of very marked albuminuria, which attacked a previously healthy primipara in the fourth month of pregnancy; in the fifth month she had œdema of the lungs and dropsy, together with dimness of vision, sickness, and convulsions. Labour was induced, after which she rapidly convalesced. She subsequently was delivered of another child without the recurrence of albuminuria.

With the termination of labour the amount of urine passed speedily returns to the normal quantity, while the specific gravity also tends to become more natural. The urine is generally dark, but it is rarely smoky or red, as in cases of acute nephritis. The deposit often contains various forms of casts; hyaline, granular, and fatty casts may be found, and sometimes degenerated renal epithelium is present. The amount of deposit is, however, very much less than in cases of acute nephritis. The quantity of urea is usually reduced, and sometimes it has been considerably lessened just before convulsions.

Albumin is constantly present in cases of puerperal nephritis, and although, as has been already indicated, cases of eclampsia may occur independently of the presence of albumin, it is generally present in fairly large quantities, and it is curious to note that the proportion appears to be far greater than in any other form of nephritis. During the earlier months of pregnancy the amount may be small, but it increases rapidly during the later months, and it is generally to be found in great abundance before convulsive seizures. As in other forms of nephritis, dropsy may be observed, and although in the course of pregnancy it is by no means uncommon to find swelling of the lower extremities unassociated with albuminuria, yet when the effusion affects the trunk and face, as well as the extremities, it affords fair presumptive evidence of that disease. The dropsy of puerperal nephritis is more diffuse, and it differs from the dropsy of ordinary acute nephritis in its gradual development. Very often the effusion is not considerable, although it is fairly widely spread, and when once established it mostly continues until delivery. In exceptional cases, the amount may be so great as to interfere with locomotion. The dropsy of puerperal nephritis further differs from that of acute nephritis, inasmuch as it seldom involves the serous cavities; the pleura and the pericardium are comparatively rarely affected.

Disturbances of digestion are so frequent in pregnancy that when they co-exist with albuminuria it is often difficult to decide whether there is any connection between the two conditions. It has been held that with puerperal nephritis the nausea and vomiting are more protracted, and that they occur throughout the day, whilst in simple pregnancy these symptoms are generally limited to the earlier hours. It must be remembered, however, that in many cases of pregnancy the rule of morning vomiting and nausea does not always hold good, and it would therefore be unsound to take these symptoms too seriously, if they are not supported by other evidences of nephritis.

Changes in the circulatory system have been observed in connection with puerperal nephritis. The alteration in the blood has been already referred to, but the anæmic appearance is generally not so noticeable as in other forms of acute renal diseases. Sometimes the pulse is slow and full, and the blood pressure is increased. Purdy lays stress upon the frequent occurrence of cardiac complications in nephritis of puerperal origin, although he admits that the majority of cases which have come under his observation have been those in which nephritis has either continued through succeeding gestations or reappeared in them. He describes hypertrophy of the left ventricle, which he thinks runs a more rapid course than the cardiac hypertrophy associated with genuine cirrhosis of the kidneys; he mentions one case in which nephritis was present in two consecutive gestations, and was associated with very marked dilatation of the heart, which proved fatal within eighteen months from the date of the first gestation. He considers that cardiac complications are much more frequent in the late stages of puerperal nephritis than in chronic renal inflammation from other causes, primary cirrhosis of the kidney excepted.

It is somewhat difficult to reconcile these statements with the general experience of the after-history of cases of puerperal nephritis. It is well known that during pregnancy the cardiac muscle hypertrophies independently of any pathological complication. Usually after delivery in cases of puerperal nephritis the albumin and other indications of renal affection speedily disappear, and it is very difficult to understand how the changes described by Purdy can be harmonised with the general clinical history of these cases.

Whatever view is taken of the etiology of puerperal eclampsia, there is no doubt about the frequency with which these attacks are associated with albuminuria. According to some authors, they are to be regarded as dependent upon a common cause, in all probability the presence of some poison in the blood. Saft[1] thinks the cause of 'pregnancy kidney' is probably an auto-intoxication of the organism by a product of metabolism during pregnancy, and he considers that the overloading of the organism with this virus gives rise to eclampsia. He states that the changes which occur in the kidneys and other organs in eclamptic patients are of a secondary character. On the other hand, these convulsive seizures, occurring, as they mostly do, when the quantity of urine is much reduced, when the proportion of albumin is high and the urea diminished, have been attributed to uræmia. That this theory is not always, if ever, tenable is shown by fairly numerous observations of cases of eclampsia without albuminuria, or any other alteration in the urine. In all probability Sir William Roberts is correct in thinking that we must admit the existence of several forms of convulsions associated with pregnancy. Undoubtedly some cases are entirely dependent upon confirmed and chronic Bright's disease, since there is no reason why women who are already the subjects of Bright's disease should not become pregnant.

In a large number of cases of albuminuria during pregnancy convulsive seizures occur. Rosenstein has stated that 25 per cent. may be affected in this way. The convulsions may occur at any time, but they appear to be most frequent towards the end of pregnancy. Sometimes they begin during parturition, less commonly before the commencement of labour or after delivery. The convulsions are usually preceded by wandering, and occasionally by some degree of depression; headache and gastric disturbance may indicate the approaching danger. In type the eclamptic attack strongly resembles an epileptic fit, but the duration is usually longer, and the successive fits follow

[1] *Archiv für Gynäkol.*, vol. li. part 2.

each other with great rapidity. The paroxysms are noteworthy for their violence, but sometimes the tonic element predominates, sometimes the clonic. At the commencement of the attack there is usually considerable cyanosis, with strongly pulsating carotids and turgidity of the superficial and deep-lying veins of the neck, and during the paroxysms the breathing is stertorous.

The pulse increases in rapidity, often to about 100; a quicker rate of pulse has been regarded as an unfavourable sign. Generally there is some rise of temperature during the attack, but frequently, after the seizures are over, the temperature falls to normal or below normal. As in an epileptic attack, the tongue may be bitten, and foam, frequently blood-tinged, may appear at the mouth. Consciousness is sometimes regained after the first attack, but when the attacks succeed each other with great rapidity, the intervals are sometimes marked by a comatose condition. The number of convulsive seizures varies greatly: it has been estimated that five or six occur, on an average, and the risks are increased as this average is exceeded. If the patient regains consciousness, she is frequently found to be blind, this interference with vision corresponding closely with uræmic amaurosis. As in the latter condition, the sight may be restored, but frequently the restoration is only partial.

Amaurosis sometimes occurs independently of eclamptic seizures, and it may be the first indication of the threatened danger. In cases that recover, the sight is generally speedily regained. In some few cases a condition comparable with albuminuric retinitis may supervene, when the usual retinal changes may be discovered on ophthalmoscopic examination. It has been stated that when this condition is present the nephritis is in all probability of a chronic, permanent character; but I have seen at least one case in which albuminuric retinitis was associated with other albuminuric symptoms before delivery, and remained subsequently, even when the urine was free from albumin.

It has been suggested that some form of indigestion may increase the severity and the continuance of the attacks. Zweifel[1] was unable to find any evidence in support of this supposition.

Copious diuresis during eclampsia is generally regarded as

[1] *Centralblatt für Gynäkologie,* Nos. 46, 47, and 48, 1895.

a favourable symptom, and when it occurs it is usually accompanied by rapid diminution in the quantity of albumin. Other nervous symptoms have been described in connection with puerperal nephritis. Headache has been stated to be more severe than in other forms of nephritis, and the premonitory value of this symptom as an indication of danger from eclampsia has already been referred to. Neuralgic pains in the loins are said to be frequent in such cases, and, inasmuch as these are mostly present when the urine is greatly diminished in quantity, it has been suggested that they may result from temporary compression of the ureter. Whether this explanation is correct or not, it is at least certain that the pain subsides as the quantity of urine increases. Fürbringer says that serious after-effects, such as secondary inflammation of internal organs, are always to be feared in connection with puerperal nephritis; and he also considers that the more acute the onset of the attack, the easier is the complete recovery.

Course and duration.—The course of the albuminuria in connection with pregnancy is not marked in the slighter stages by any prominent symptoms. In many cases of albuminuria the general health may remain apparently unimpaired, even when dropsy occurs during the later months of gestation. If dropsy affects the lower extremities only, it is probably to be attributed to pressure rather than to a form of nephritis. If it becomes general, and if at the same time the urine diminishes markedly in quantity, the prospects of eclamptic seizures are greatly increased. Although seizures may be deferred until after delivery, they generally occur during labour, and they frequently lead to premature delivery if they occur at an earlier stage. If dropsy and albuminuria are present in marked quantity during the seventh month of pregnancy, death of the foetus generally results, and is followed by abortion. If the patient recovers from the eclamptic attacks, and survives the risks of the later stages of labour, the indications of nephritis speedily pass away. Sometimes, however, the urine remains albuminous, and atrophic changes in the kidney ensue, accompanied by the ordinary symptoms of chronic Bright's disease. Under these circumstances, the risks in subsequent pregnancies are enormously increased; but otherwise, it is generally held that the nephritis consecutive to pregnancy runs a shorter course than any other form of chronic nephritis.

Diagnosis.—The diagnosis should not present any great difficulty. The presence of albumin alone does not necessarily stamp the case as one of puerperal nephritis. In puerperal nephritis the amount of albumin is generally considerable, and the urine contains casts—hyaline, granular and epithelial— and occasionally also some renal epithelium. The eclamptic seizures may be mistaken for genuine epilepsy or for hysterical convulsions, and the danger of this error is greater if the earlier symptoms have not been closely observed. Hysterical attacks are rarely followed by deep coma. On the other hand, a comatose condition during labour may result not only from eclampsia but also from some organic cerebral disease; but in this case, also, much help is usually derived from a consideration of the previous history of the patient. The frequent absence of blood from the urine is an important guide. If during pregnancy the urine becomes not only highly albuminous, but also deeply blood-tinged, there is fair presumption in favour of acute nephritis rather than of puerperal nephritis.

Prognosis.—The prognosis of puerperal nephritis largely turns on the occurrence of eclampsia. Cases free from eclampsia usually do well. The prognosis is also influenced by the quantity of urine passed daily: when much reduced, the prognosis is generally grave, especially if the specific gravity does not rise in proportion to the reduction of quantity. When eclamptic attacks occur, the prognosis is influenced by the time of their occurrence; they always increase the danger both to the mother and to the child, since 25 per cent. of the cases terminate fatally. Attacks occurring after delivery are more favourable than those which precede delivery, and the number of seizures, the duration of the individual convulsion, and the frequency with which the convulsions recur, are points of great importance.

Prognosis is also influenced by the pulse and the temperature. When the pulse shows little or no improvement in the intervals between the seizures, and, as Zweifel states, when a rise of temperature comes on early, the prognosis is unfavourable, while if the rise of temperature is rapid and steady the case will end fatally.

The prognosis is also largely influenced by the nature of the convulsions. If they are of short duration, and if consciousness is retained in the periods between them, the prognosis is more favourable than when the seizures are violent, frequent, and when deep coma is present in the intervals.

The death rate from eclamptic seizures is remarkably high; Rosenstein places it at at least 40 per cent. Sometimes the end occurs as the result of pulmonary œdema or apoplexy; sometimes the patient sinks exhausted owing to the frequent repetition of these severe seizures.

Treatment.—Considerations of treatment may be divided into three groups: (1) Cases of albuminuria occurring during pregnancy; (2) Cases of undoubted puerperal nephritis; and (3) Cases of eclampsia.

Cases of albuminuria may occasionally call for the adoption of special hygienic measures: the diet should be regulated and rendered as non-nitrogenous as possible. Frequently, benefit results from the adoption of an exclusive milk diet, and this diet becomes imperative if there is reason to fear that nephritis is the cause of the albuminuria. It is comparatively rarely that the milk diet disagrees, but the principles of treatment in such cases are similar to those already mentioned in connection with acute nephritis.

Ferré [1] maintains that milk treatment is most efficient from a prophylactic point of view. He states that he has never seen fits occur in any patient who has been subjected to milk diet for over a week, nor any other trouble of a toxic origin; but he is emphatic in saying that albuminuria does not necessarily cease during the employment of a milk diet. He lays great stress upon this point, since he believes that many obstetricians may give up milk diet when it is found that albuminuria and œdema persist.

Whenever albuminuria has been detected in the course of pregnancy it is advisable to keep an accurate record of the amount of urine passed daily. If the amount undergoes sudden reduction, and if other symptoms point to the occurrence of puerperal nephritis, it may be necessary to employ various diuretics. Alkaline salts, such as potassium citrate or acetate,

[1] *L'Obstétrique*, Nov. 15, 1896.

are particularly indicated in these cases, and, as in acute nephritis, it is advisable to give these in sufficient doses to render the urine alkaline. If these measures are not sufficient to raise the urine to the daily standard, no harm is likely to result from the administration of other diuretics which act on the circulatory organs as well as on the kidney. Thus the preparations of digitalis or of strophanthus may be administered, provided always that the urine is free from admixture with blood. Under these drugs the pulse may be kept both regular and full, and the quantity of urine is also generally increased. It is necessary, at the same time, to watch carefully against the natural tendency to constipation, which, as in other cases of nephritis, may favour the occurrence of severe symptoms. If general dropsy is present, some authors recommend the use of hot air baths in conjunction with hot drinks, so as to favour diaphoretic action.

Of the special forms of treatment for eclampsia, it may be said at once that these are secondary in importance when compared with obstetric questions. It is generally held that the obstetric treatment should consist in as rapid delivery as possible. One of the most anxious problems for the practitioner to deal with is the question of when it is right to hasten labour. Undoubtedly, in many cases the safety of the patient, and equally that of the child, depends largely upon premature delivery.

In cases of nephritis of pregnancy, Zweifel would never hesitate to bring on premature labour, but, while advocating the rapid emptying of the uterus, he is opposed to Cæsarean section.

On these points the reader is referred to text-books on midwifery.

Short of the adoption of measures calculated to accelerate delivery, some advantage may, however, result from various modes of treatment. Many practitioners are greatly in favour of bleeding, and in selected cases, where patients are of a plethoric type, and where their strength has not been previously reduced by prolonged albuminuria, there is no doubt that venesection has proved beneficial. This treatment, however, should not be attempted in those who are debilitated and anæmic. Some advantage has accrued from the use of various nitrites: nitrite of amyl has been recommended for inhalation, and nitro-glycerine has also been administered; but these remedies should not be essayed if the convulsions occur in the course of labour, since the relaxation of involuntary muscle due to the action of the nitrites might favour the occurrence of hæmorrhage. As in ordinary uræmia, hypodermic injections of morphine have been recommended, but, although they appear to diminish the frequency of eclamptic seizures, they undoubtedly add to the risk of the child, and the morphine treatment has therefore been given up as dangerous and mischievous.

When the eclamptic seizures are frequent, chloroform has occasionally been administered by inhalation, and hydrate of chloral has been given as an enema, and for both of these some satisfactory results have been claimed. A few years back, pilocarpine was largely recommended for puerperal eclampsia, but modern practice is decidedly against the use of this drug in these cases.

Some years ago Dr. John Phillips reported to the Obstetrical Society of London the results of some experiments bearing on the effect of pilocarpine in inducing labour pains, &c.; after a study of the literature of the subject, he concluded that pilocarpine was a dangerous drug to use, several women having died within a few days from acute bronchial or pneumonic symptoms, while in other patients it had induced excessive secretion in the bronchial tubes, a condition attended by risk in this class of cases.

Zweifel recommends the administration of vegetable acids in large quantities, but in an extremely dilute form, and he thinks these should be given even to patients who are unconscious. The object of this treatment is to prevent the formation of blood clots and minute thromboses, which imply the presence of a poison in the circulation, and are found in the blood, in the liver, in the lungs, and in the brain of the eclamptic.

CHAPTER X

RETINAL CHANGES IN BRIGHT'S DISEASE

IN many cases of advanced kidney disease complaint of altered vision may be made, and attention may thus be directed to the condition of the retina. Sometimes the complaint is merely of more or less dimness of vision, which may affect the whole field, but more usually involves only certain regions, and is perhaps more marked on one side, so that when one eye is closed some clouding of one portion of the field of vision may be experienced, although when both eyes are open there is little to attract the notice of the patient. Sometimes the whole field of vision is obscured, as though the patient were looking through a dark cloud. This condition is most commonly met with after one or more uræmic convulsions. More rarely, under similar circumstances, central vision may be lost, or complete blindness may ensue. In many cases of chronic Bright's disease, retinal changes may be discovered by the ophthalmoscope in the total absence of any apparent change of vision, or of complaint concerning the sight. Such cases come more especially under the notice of the physician, while those in which the sight is gravely affected may first be recognised by the ophthalmic surgeon. In any case, however, when there is reason to believe that chronic kidney mischief is present, it is always well to examine the fundus, both on account of the frequency of grave retinal changes without subjective symptoms, and also because of the serious prognostic indications thereby afforded. It must be remembered, however, that in some cases of uræmic poisoning, when the disturbance of vision is most marked, no obvious changes may be found in the fundi. Transitory œdema of the discs has been described by Dobrowolsky, and Litten has noticed swelling and cloudiness of the disc; but these appearances are certainly unusual, and, as a rule, so transient as to escape general observation. Before describing the retinal changes more commonly met with, it may be well to indicate that, although they are not to be found in cases of acute kidney disease, they supervene sometimes with great rapidity in cases of chronic kidney disease complicated by an acute exacerbation; hence, in cases of doubt, where the urine is scanty and blood tinged, the formation of an accurate diagnosis may often be assisted by an examination of the fundus. Marked retinal changes are essentially characteristic of cases which have already reached a chronic stage; thus they are frequently present in advanced stages of nephritis consecutive to scarlet fever or occurring during pregnancy; they are common in cases of renal cirrhosis; but they are not to be met with in cases of primary lardaceous degeneration, although occasionally they may be found when the lardaceous changes are associated with chronic atrophic changes.

The retinal changes in Bright's disease have been enumerated by Sir William Gowers as follows:—

1. Diffused opacity from œdema.
2. White patches.
3. Hæmorrhages.
4. Optic papillitis.
5. Diffused retinitis.
6. Atrophic changes consecutive to inflammation.

Of these conditions the first three are fairly common, the last three are rare. To the above list should perhaps be added the occasional occurrence of extensive retinal detachment, which seriously impairs vision. The white spots and patches are most commonly the first retinal changes to be recognised, though they are not always perhaps the first to appear. The white patches are at first due to aggregations of white corpuscles, and they are frequently accompanied by retinal hæmorrhages. Later the corpuscles undergo fatty and cholesterin degenerative changes. Mr. Marcus Gunn[1] has called attention to a hyaline condition of the arteries in some cases of renal disease, and associates this condition with the pre-albuminuric rise of tension noted by Mahomed. Mr. Marcus Gunn exhibited before the Ophthalmological Society (May 5, 1892) a patient with ophthalmoscopic evidence of arterial changes associated with chronic renal disease, and of increased

[1] *Trans. Ophthalm. Soc.*, vol. xii., 1892.

PLATE X.

ALBUMINURIC RETINITIS.

Left Eye, Erect Image.

From a man, æt. 23, who appeared to have originally contracted acute nephritis from exposure to cold and wet. Fresh exposure brought on a subacute attack, marked by severe headache and sickness, which were followed closely by three convulsive seizures. The sight failed after the first uræmic attack.

The drawing shows numerous hæmorrhages, and white patches. Some patches in the macula are small, but others round its margin are of larger size, some almost circular, others of irregular shape and size. The arteries are in several places lost behind the white patches.

From a drawing by Mr. A. Stanford Morton.

PLATE X.

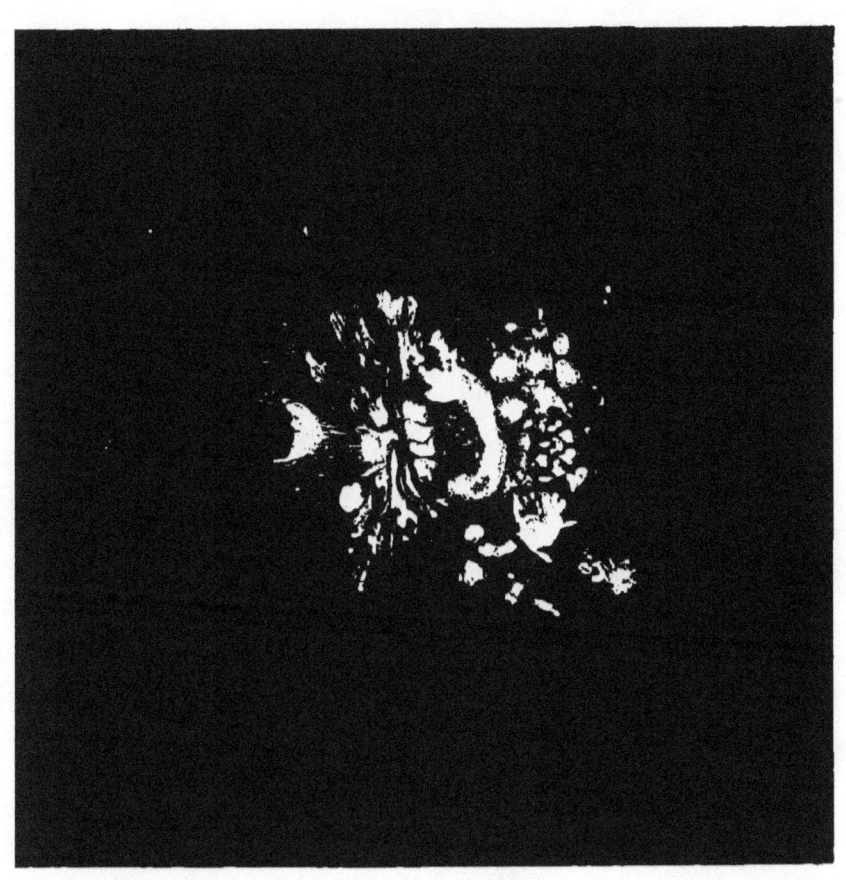

ALBUMINURIC RETINITIS.
Left Eye.   Erect Image.

A Stanford Morton del. ad nat. Mintern Bros. Chromo.

arterial tension. He described the condition as follows: 'The arteries have an exceptionally bright reflex; the central light-streak is very distinct and sharp, while the whole surface of the vessel is of a somewhat lighter colour than usual. They have, in consequence, a metallic appearance somewhat like what would be presented by bright copper wire. This condition has been observed in many cases of chronic albuminuria, and in several cases where no albumin was found, but where high arterial tension suggested the probability of changes in the arteries similar to those usually associated with chronic renal disease. The ophthalmoscopic appearance is presumably due to hyaline degeneration of the arterial walls.' Attention was also directed to the effect produced on the veins by arteries overlaying them. Where an artery, even a small twig, passes over a retinal vein, the circulation in the latter is much impeded. In some cases the vein is indistinguishable just at the spot where it is crossed, and is evidently distended for some distance peripherally from this point. There is a liability to the occurrence of hæmorrhages from a vein thus distended with blood, and the appearance must be interpreted as an evidence of high arterial tension. In a case shown to me by my friend Mr. Stanford Morton, this hyaline change in the arteries was very obvious: the arteries appeared to be much smaller than usual, and the arterial changes were accompanied by white patches and streaks of hæmorrhage, while the urine contained a considerable proportion of albumin.

The *white spots* of chronic albuminuria vary much in size; they may consist of numerous minute round dots, or they may be fused into irregular patches, as large as the disc. Sometimes they are grouped together close to the disc; but frequently they form fanlike streaks radiating round the macula. The small spots in the neighbourhood of the yellow spot are often regarded as the initial stages of degeneration, and similar changes, possibly due to a similar degeneration, are sometimes to be met with in diabetes. The larger, more irregular patches round the disc seem to be due to later changes. Associated with these white degenerative patches is the diffuse opacity which has been described as spreading more or less over the whole of the retina. This condition, although it has often been mentioned, is not easy to recognise; the fundus so frequently varies in colour that in any given case it may be difficult to be certain that the pallor is not a normal condition.

Though retinal hæmorrhages are often associated with the white spots, they may sometimes be met with alone. From their position in the nerve fibre layer of the retina they are often 'flame shaped;' they may form mere streaks, accompanying the vessels, or, if large, they may be of irregular outline, especially if they penetrate into the deeper layers of the retina.

In severe and rapidly fatal cases of Bright's disease a true neuritis or neuro-retinitis may supervene, with complete obscuration of the disc : in such cases there are usually many hæmorrhages and many white spots, the latter being, as a rule, according to Sir William Gowers, large, rounded, and soft edged. The arteries are small, and, indeed, difficult to find, while the veins are distended and tortuous. Sometimes an artery may be detected crossing a vein, and the latter may then be distended at the distal side, and collapsed at the proximal. In milder cases, when the hæmorrhages occur singly, they may in time reabsorb to a large extent, but the contracted and empty appearance of the arteries may persist.

Although the retinal changes in albuminuria commonly affect both eyes, they are generally more advanced on one side than the other. Cases, however, occasionally occur in which one eye appears normal, while the other shows advanced changes. Mr. Henry Eales, of Birmingham,[1] describes a case occurring in a man, aged twenty-five, who complained of loss of sight in the left eye, which presented all the typical appearances of albuminuric retinitis, while the right eye was normal. The dimness of vision, described like 'a cloud over the upper part of his sight,' was noticed the day after a fall in which he had twisted his left side. The urine contained albumin in small quantity : there was no history of scarlet fever, syphilis, or other illness, but the man had been a heavy beer drinker for seven years previously. The retinitis is described as typical, the retina being covered with large milky opaque effusions, with a few hæmorrhages, the yellow spot and disc being chiefly affected. Four months after treatment the disc was white and atrophied,

[1] *Med. Times and Gazette*, December 20, 1884

PLATE XI.

ALBUMINURIC RETINITIS.

Left Eye, Erect Image.

From the same patient as Plate X. This drawing was made four months later, shortly before the death of the patient. In the interval he had suffered much from headache and sickness. The urine was pale, with persistent froth, sp. gr. 1010, and a very large amount of albumin was present. Numerous leucocytes were found together with many large hyaline and granular casts.

This drawing shows the great change which may occur within a few months. Many arteries are now seen as fine white lines, while the veins are relatively larger. The changes at the macula are more evident. Some of the white patches previously present have undergone fatty degeneration and present a more glistening appearance.

From a drawing by Mr. A. Stanford Morton.

PLATE XI.

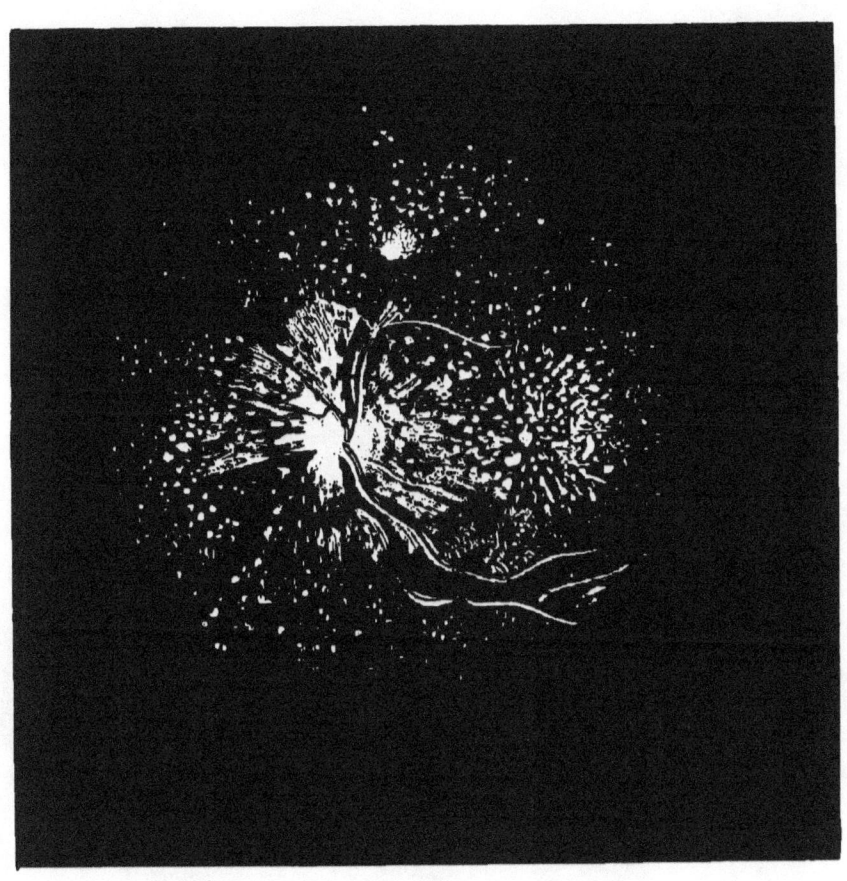

ALBUMINURIC RETINITIS.
Left Eye.   Erect Image.

A.Stanford Morton del.ad nat.

Mintern Bros Chromo

and the margin blurred; the retinal arteries were reduced to threads, and several glistening dots existed all round the macula. The urine showed merely a trace of albumin after breakfast, but at no other time during the day.

In this case, the nature of the part played by the albuminuria seems somewhat open to question; no casts were found at any time, and the history suggested a traumatic cause, rather than chronic nephritis. Mr. Nettleship, commenting on the choroidal patches in this case, observed that they were abrupt, very white and rather large, and unlike those due to severe retinitis, and he considered that the disc was suggestive of a rather slow arterial thrombosis. Yvert[1] reports an interesting case of unilateral albuminuric retinitis. It occurred in a man forty-three years of age, who, during life, presented profound cachexia, with general anæmia; the urine contained a considerable quantity of muco-pus and albumin. On ophthalmoscopic examination, the right eye appeared perfect, but the left eye exhibited well marked and advanced nephritic alterations. At the autopsy the right kidney, the right renal artery, vein and ureter were absent, although the supra-renal capsule was in its usual place. The left kidney was enlarged, and weighed eleven and a half ounces. It presented the usual appearances of parenchymatous nephritis. Yvert also refers to some cases in which contusion of one kidney was followed by anæmia, which was always much more marked on the injured side, and he suggests that possibly any irritation proceeding from one kidney is capable of acting, through the sympathetic, on the whole capillary system of the corresponding side, bringing about circulatory disturbances in the retina, as well as elsewhere.

The more general rule, however, in cases of retinitis due to nephritis is for both eyes to be implicated, although unequally so.

Regarding the causation of the various retinal changes in chronic kidney disease, many theories have been put forward, but the most scientific seems to lead to the conclusion that the high arterial tension of Bright's disease is probably the prime factor. The high tension is certainly responsible for the hæmorrhages, while the degenerative white patches may probably

[1] *Recueil d'Ophthal.*, 1884.

be ascribed to the same cause. It is reasonable to assume that high arterial tension may result in deficient circulation through the capillaries, and that this may in turn lead to impaired nutritive force. This hypothesis is supported by the fact that the white patches are most common in those parts of the retina which are comparatively poorly supplied with vessels. The theory, however, is imperfect, unless it be kept in mind that kidney disease is associated with a general dyscrasia, which doubtless exerts an influence upon the nutrition of the retina. It would otherwise be extremely difficult to account for the well-known frequency of retinal changes in the albuminuria of pregnancy.

The diagnostic value of these various changes is relatively small. Taken alone, they suggest an immediate examination of the water, and may thus help in calling attention to the serious underlying cause, but the number of cases in which attention is thus first directed to the urine is relatively few. The condition has mostly been realised long before an examination of the retina is made. On the other hand, although the retinal appearances are so well marked, they are not in themselves characteristic of Bright's disease alone. The neuritis and neuro-retinitis are frequently observed in cases of cerebral tumour and of anæmia, as well as in many other conditions. The hæmorrhages may be met with in various blood diseases, such as purpura, leucocythæmia, pernicious anæmia, and septicæmia, and also in malaria and scurvy; while, as previously noted, white patches similar to those found in chronic Bright's disease have also been met with in some cases of diabetes.

The prognostic value when the co-existence of albuminuria has been established is less open to question. It is important, however, not to lay too much stress upon the presence of the small white spots of degeneration; these are commonly the only retinal change in the albuminuria of pregnancy, and this condition (unless grave structural renal changes co-exist) generally disappears shortly after delivery. Saundby states that white specks were found in five out of fourteen of his cases of so-called functional albuminuria, but he does not give the data upon which these cases were regarded as functional rather than organic. In an important paper on the prognosis of neuro-

PLATE XII.

ALBUMINURIC AND DIABETIC NEURO-RETINITIS.

From a man, æt. 58, who stated that sugar had been found in his urine about eight years before he came under our observation. The urine was pale, frothy, sp. gr. 1020, and it contained much sugar and much albumin. In this case the renal changes are probably secondary to the diabetes.

In addition to white patches and hæmorrhages, this drawing shows great reduction in the size of the arteries and curious moniliform dilatations upon the veins together with a large number of new vessels, greatly obscuring the disc.

From a drawing by Mr. A. Stanford Morton.

PLATE XII.

ALBUMINURIC AND DIABETIC NEURO-RETINITIS.

retinitis in Bright's disease [1] Dr. Miles Miley gives the result of an enquiry into the duration of life in cases of albuminuric retinitis seen at the London Hospital. It is possible that his figures are rather too high, as the patients were all sufficiently ill to necessitate admission as in-patients rather than treatment as out-patients, but his results are none the less striking in their confirmation of the grave prognosis to be assigned to similar cases. He found that the eyes had been examined in 156 cases of chronic renal disease; in 105 cases the eyes were normal, in the remaining 51 they were affected. Of the 105, only 28 (*i.e.* 26 per cent.) died in hospital; but of the 51, 25 (*i.e.* 52 per cent.) died in hospital. He followed up the subsequent history of the remaining 26, and he found that, with the exception of six who could not be traced, all were dead at the time his paper was written. One had lived eighteen months, two fourteen months, and the rest had all died under twelve months from the time they left the hospital. All these cases were, doubtless, severe at the time they came under observation in the wards, but they confirm the bad prognosis which is generally assigned to a case of renal disease with marked retinal changes.

As has been previously remarked, however, an exception must be made in favour of the diffuse retinitis which is occasionally met with in the albuminuria of pregnancy. Unless the condition is due to antecedent kidney disease, the state of the retina and the nature of the urine commonly improve rapidly after delivery.

Dr. Lomer [2] records the case of a multipara who, in the eighth month of pregnancy, complained of intense headache and defective sight. There was no œdema, but the urine was loaded with albumin and full of finely granular and hyaline casts. In spite of milk diet and rest in bed, the headache and impairment of sight increased. Premature labour was induced, and directly after delivery the headache diminished. The albuminuria disappeared on the fifth day after delivery, but the defective vision remained longer.

These cases are by far the most hopeful, so far as recovery

[1] *Brit. Med. Journ.*, 1888, i. p. 248.
[2] *Centralbl. f. Gynäk.*, No. 43, 1890.

from the retinal affection is concerned; but in true albuminuric retinitis, although the appearances may change considerably, the retinitis commonly persists to the time of death. The hæmorrhages may vary in degree and in number, the white spots may become smaller, but indications of retinal changes, once present, appear always to remain to the end of life, which is generally not far distant. The gravity of the prognosis, when the case is really one of albuminuric retinitis, should lead to the utmost caution in dealing with retinal changes. The appearances are often fallacious, since they may result from other causes; but when any of the retinal changes above described co-exist with albuminuria and with vascular lesions the diagnosis is almost a matter of certainty, and the prognosis is grave. Hence the recognition of these retinal changes should entail further careful examination before any prognosis is given.

PLATE XIII.

RETINAL CHANGES.
Three Years after Acute Albuminuric Retinitis.

Drawing from the retina of a woman, æt. 41, in whom premature labour had been induced on two occasions owing to albuminuria. When first seen three years ago the appearance of the fundus was much like that shown in Plate X. After the first delivery she rapidly improved, but on the second occasion labour was followed by insanity which lasted three months. When this drawing was made her general health appeared good, but the urine was very pale, its sp. gr. was only 1010, and it contained a very small amount of albumin, together with granular casts. There are numerous minute white degenerative spots in and round the macula, and some few of larger size irregularly scattered. The arteries are very small, and some branches appear to be occluded. The margins of the disc, which is pale, are sharply differentiated.

From a drawing by Mr. A. Stanford Morton.

PLATE XIII.

RETINAL CHANGES.
Three years after Acute Albuminuric Retinitis.

A Stanford Morton del. ad nat.
Mintern Bros. Chromo.

CHAPTER XI

LARDACEOUS DISEASE OF THE KIDNEY

ALTHOUGH it is convenient in a book like the present to consider lardaceous disease of the kidney as a separate disease, its position is not comparable to that of the diseases already described, since it occurs as a sequel to other well-known conditions, and not as a primary renal affection. Its occurrence may produce fresh features, but the patient has been already suffering from well marked symptoms belonging to the primary disease. It presents another distinctive characteristic in being frequently allied with similar changes in other organs, such as the liver and the spleen, and the clinical aspect of the case is thus liable to be very complicated, since we have to consider the features of the original disease, as well as those which are produced by the renal affection, and possibly those resulting from the alteration in other organs.

It is convenient to describe lardaceous disease of the kidney in this place, partly because the symptoms merit attention and partly because the lardaceous change is very frequently accompanied by one or other of the forms of chronic nephritis which have been already mentioned. By itself, lardaceous disease of the kidney does not truly represent a form of Bright's disease, but both anatomically and clinically the occurrence of lardaceous degeneration frequently accompanies the changes due to chronic nephritis. The primary change of lardaceous disease is one affecting the renal vessels; the other constituents of the kidney may sometimes be intact—more commonly they show signs of chronic inflammation.

The disease has been described under numerous different names, as, for example, waxy, colloid, amyloid, albuminous, or scrofulous enlargement, the selection of the name being frequently due to ideas respecting the chemical changes produced in the vessels of the kidney. Of the names above mentioned, *amyloid* is open to the objection that the degeneration produced is not starch-like in character; *scrofulous enlargement* is misleading, since frequently the kidneys may be normal in size, or occasionally somewhat reduced, moreover the disease does not always depend upon scrofula; the terms *lardaceous* and *waxy* are those which are least open to objection, since they express nothing more than the appearance presented by the kidney.

The leading features may be briefly summarised. The disease commonly results either from protracted suppuration or from syphilis. Tubercular changes are sometimes credited with being able to induce lardaceous disease of the kidney, but it is doubtful whether this is possible unless the tuberculosis is associated with profuse suppuration. The cut surface of the kidney gives a characteristic reaction with an aqueous solution of iodine. With regard to size, the organs are sometimes unaltered, though sometimes they are very large and pale, owing to the development of parenchymatous nephritis. At a later stage, if the disease lasts long enough, the kidneys become smaller and the surface becomes granular. The amount of urine is, as a rule, greatly in excess of the normal quantity. It is pale in colour, like diabetic urine, and it contains a large quantity of albumin. The character of the urine is, however, dependent upon the degree of nephritis associated with the lardaceous change; hence, occasionally the quantity of urine may be reduced below the normal standard, and its colour may be darker. Frequently, as in chronic nephritis, there is general dropsy, but the marked symptoms of renal cirrhosis are mostly absent; there is little alteration in the pulse, or in the character of the sounds of the heart or in the position of the apex beat, and albuminuric retinitis and uræmia are very uncommon.

With regard to frequency, Fürbringer considers that it is as frequent as genuine chronic nephritis and contracted kidney together, and he thinks that the older view, according to which the disease was to be regarded as uncommon, was due to insufficient attention having been paid to lardaceous changes in the kidney.

In speaking of the large white kidney which is so frequently found with chronic nephritis, reference has already been made to the frequent association of lardaceous changes, and it is probable, or at least possible, that in many of these cases the lardaceous change has preceded the nephritic alteration.

Etiology.—Primary lardaceous change in the kidney has been described, but its occurrence is very rare. In every case that has come under my observation it has been possible to associate the disease with some other constitutional affection producing marked cachexia. Lardaceous disease is said to be most frequent in patients from twenty to fifty years of age, but I have seen it at an earlier period in children who have been subject to chronic suppuration. The occurrence of lardaceous disease has frequently been traced to the influence of tuberculosis, even of intestinal ulceration. The late Sir Andrew Clark [1] considered that in a small proportion of cases of advanced phthisis, albumin appeared in the urine, and he recognised three clinical types of different degrees of severity:—

1. 'Tubercular' cases, with a small percentage of albumin.
2. 'Pneumonic or caseous' cases, with a larger amount.
3. 'Fibroid' cases, when the quantity of albumin was largest of all.

He stated that, in his experience, in every case of extensive fibroid induration or fibroid disease of the lung, albuminuria sooner or later appeared, and it 'shaped the course of the disease and settled its issues.'

Bartels assumes that suppuration is insufficient to cause lardaceous change unless the suppurating surface is enabled to come into contact with the atmosphere, and he found that, so far as pulmonary tuberculosis was concerned, degeneration of the kidney was more prone to occur after the formation of a cavity in the lung. To this rule there are many exceptions, and cavities in the lungs are frequently found without any lardaceous change in the kidney. One curious feature in connection with the association of pulmonary tuberculosis with lardaceous disease is that the lung symptoms frequently undergo improvement with the development of the renal affection.

Chronic disease of bones leading to necrosis and profuse suppuration, such as disease of the hip joints, injury of bone from gunshot wounds, and scrofulous caries, are very often

[1] *Lancet*, vol. i., January 5, 1889.

associated with lardaceous degeneration of the kidney. The influence of syphilis, although it is well marked, stands somewhat by itself, inasmuch as with confirmed syphilis and with hereditary syphilis lardaceous changes may be found when there has been no ulceration or suppuration, and when the cachectic symptoms have not been well marked.

Other varieties of suppuration predispose to, or induce, this disease. Thus it occurs with empyema, with chronic peritonitis, with abscesses in the kidneys, with malarial cachexia, and with puerperal or other forms of suppuration connected with the female generative organs. When resulting from suppuration of one kidney, the disease is commonly bilateral. Thus, profuse suppuration dependent upon pyelitis in the pelvis of one kidney may cause lardaceous changes in the vessels of both kidneys, and may lead to chronic nephritis. In such cases it is important to remember that probably the nephritis is invariably consecutive to the lardaceous change.

The extent to which other organs are simultaneously affected varies considerably. The liver is generally found to be enlarged, pale in colour, and the edge of the cut surface appears translucent. The arteries, when tested with iodine, indicate degenerative changes similar to those found in the kidney. The spleen is commonly affected to a greater extent, and here also the lardaceous change affects primarily the smaller arteries and the Malpighian corpuscles.

Similar alterations have been described in connection with the supra-renal capsule, also in the small arteries of the intestine, and in the vessels of the pancreas and lymphatic glands; while lardaceous changes have even been described in connection with the vessels of the heart, of the placenta, and of the lungs and brain. It has been stated that lardaceous changes commonly affect the vessels of the liver, spleen, and supra-renal capsule before attacking those of the kidney.

Morbid anatomy.—The appearances of the kidney depend upon the duration of the disease. Sometimes, when death has occurred in the early stages, the kidney appears normal to the naked eye; the size is unaltered, but the capsule detaches rather more readily than usual, and the surface is as a rule somewhat paler and anæmic, though it may be apparently normal; in

PLATE XIV.

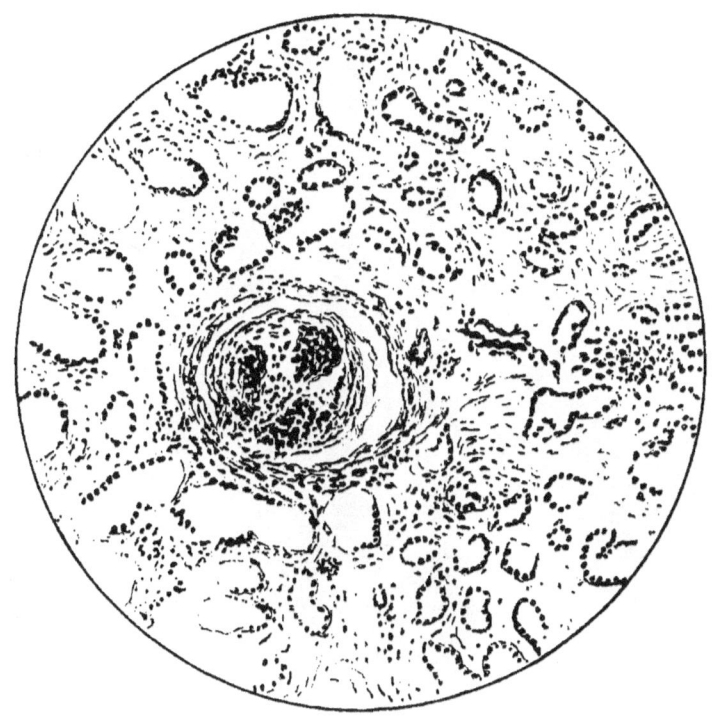

Section of Lardaceous Kidney in an Early Stage. In this specimen, which was stained with methyl violet, the dark parts indicate the affected areas, and show the unequal extent to which the capillary loops are changed. To the right of the Malpighian tuft portions of a small artery are seen to have undergone lardaceous changes. The abundance of intertubular nuclei, the changes in the renal epithelial cells, and the increased thickness of the Malpighian capsule indicate chronic nephritic changes.

(*See pp.* 248, 249, *and* 250.)

N. Tirard, Del.   Mintern Bros., imp.

fact, the change may escape observation unless the cut surface is tested with iodine, or unless the changes in the vessels are demonstrated from microscopic specimens. More often the kidney is greatly increased in size; it may even be as much as twice its normal size. On removal of the capsule, the organ is found to be perfectly smooth and anæmic, and the same appearance of anæmia is found to extend throughout the cortex, the section looking shiny, polished and pale. Spots of a yellowish red colour may be observed on its surface; and on section of the kidney, similar spots of a greyish white, semi-translucent appearance, are found in the position of the Malpighian bodies. The pyramids are generally of a dark red colour, offering a marked contrast to the yellow, pale appearance of the cortex. When the cut surface is washed and treated with an aqueous solution of iodine, the previously translucent spots assume a dark mahogany colour. The dark colour also appears sometimes in the form of streaks corresponding in position with the vasa recta. A further test consists in the addition of sulphuric acid, when the reddish brown colour should change to a deep indigo blue; this test, however, frequently fails. Specimens of great beauty may be made with methyl violet, which stains deeply all tissues undergoing lardaceous changes. When the disease has lasted longer, the appearance of the kidney is very similar to that of the contracted stage of chronic nephritis, though it may be distinguished from the latter by the surface being rather paler and by the presence of small sparkling spots. It is stated that this form of kidney is peculiar to chronic syphilis, but the appearances seem to be dependent upon the contraction of the kidney after the long duration of chronic nephritis. In all probability, both the last mentioned forms of lardaceous kidney owe their size to associated types of chronic nephritis rather than to the lardaceous changes, which in themselves cause little or no alteration in the size of the organ.

Although these three types have been described, it must be understood that transitional forms are commonly met with, and that the appearance to be found in any case is to a large extent dependent upon the duration of the disease. The microscopic appearances present alterations which differ considerably according to the stage of the disease and according to the degree of association with changes characteristic of chronic nephritis. So far as the purely lardaceous changes are concerned, these affect by preference the glomeruli and the afferent vessels, but there is considerable variation in the extent to which the Malpighian tufts are affected and the distribution of the lardaceous degeneration. Sometimes the majority of the glomeruli throughout the kidney show degenerative changes, sometimes only those in a limited portion are affected. Even in a single Malpighian tuft some of the capillary loops may have escaped degeneration, while in other parts of the kidney the whole tuft appears to be swollen and partially opaque. The efferent vessels and the vasa recta are less commonly attacked, but, as already mentioned, the vasa recta may sometimes present histological changes, which usually involve the tunica intima and tunica media. It was at one time supposed that lardaceous degeneration obliterated the calibre of the blood vessels, but it appears that, although the circulation through these vessels may be impaired, it is not arrested, since it is possible to inject the Malpighian loops. Professor Greenfield states that the various parts of the kidney are involved in the following order: (1) Afferent arterioles; (2) Groups of glomerular capillaries, especially those of the superficial cortex; (3) The arteriolæ rectæ; (4) The efferent arterioles and the capillaries into which they break up; (5) The capsule of the Malpighian body; (6) The capillaries which run between the bundles of straight tubes; (7) The basement membrane of the convoluted tubules; (8) The large interlobular arteries; (9) The walls of the straight tubules, especially near the papillæ; (10) The large branches of arteries and veins in the boundary area; (11) The connective tissue around the collecting tubules at the tips of the papillæ; and (12) In rare cases the epithelial cells.

Symptoms.—In lardaceous disease renal symptoms mostly play a very subordinate part in the early stages, since the patient has already been suffering for a long time from the disease in which the kidney changes originate. The symptoms, therefore, peculiar to this affection are superadded to those of the original malady. The existence of kidney changes may be sometimes suspected when the cachexia of the original disease is associated with much pallor, but in a large number of cases the renal changes are demonstrated rather by chemical examination of the urine than by symptoms. The appearance of the patient is very frequently somewhat misleading, since the original disease is associated with conditions which alter the colour of the skin, and produce profound cachexia. Some stress has been laid by Grainger Stewart upon the fact that patients suffering from waxy degeneration of the kidney have, in addition to the peculiar pallor of chronic kidney disease, a muddy complexion, which is especially noticeable from the deposit of pigment about the eyelids, and the distension of small blood vessels upon the cheeks.

Another feature, which is seen in exaggerated form with the supervention of chronic kidney trouble, is the degree of muscular weakness and lassitude exhibited by those patients who are still able to be up and about. This indication is, however, frequently missing, since a large number of these patients have for a long time been bedridden.

When there is any suspicion of lardaceous disease, attention will naturally be directed first to the nature of the urine; this varies according to the stage of the disease, and according to the extent to which chronic nephritis has been superadded to the lardaceous changes of the vessels. In the early stages, before there is much renal affection beyond the change in the Malpighian tufts, the amount of urine that is passed daily is increased, sometimes even to a considerable extent, so that in some instances the increase has been noticed by the patient, and has led to a suspicion of diabetes. As the disease progresses, the daily excretion of urine may be greatly reduced, especially should severe intractable diarrhœa supervene; while if there are advanced interstitial changes in the kidney the urine ceases to be characteristic of lardaceous disease, and resembles that eliminated in chronic nephritis or in renal cirrhosis. To a certain extent, therefore, the estimation of the daily quantity eliminated becomes of importance, as it furnishes an indication of the extent to which consecutive renal disease has advanced. Sir J. Grainger Stewart lays great stress upon the increased quantity of urine that is passed during the early stages of lardaceous disease; and there can be little doubt that when lardaceous disease has been diagnosed, and the daily excretion of urine is below the normal quantity, the early stages have been overlooked, and the disease, so far as the kidneys are concerned, is in a complex form. The specific gravity of the urine bears an intimate relation to the amount passed. It is, however, generally much reduced, sometimes ranging between 1005 and 1010. Where nephritis has developed, the specific gravity may rise to about the normal level, but such change is always associated with diminution in the daily quantity. As in many other pathological affections of the kidney, the urine remains acid, and it is mostly clear and of a pale colour. One great peculiarity of uncomplicated lardaceous disease is that the daily excretion of solids shows very little alteration, though they may be greatly reduced with the development of nephritis. On the other hand, the percentage of solids necessarily varies with the daily quantity of water passed, even though the actual eliminative work of the kidney is not affected. Reference has already been made to the clear appearance of the urine, and it must be added that, as a general rule, there is very little visible deposit, though specimens taken from the lower stratum, after standing, may, when examined under the microscope, show the presence of casts and other formed elements. If casts are found, they are generally few in number and of the clear hyaline variety. Sometimes, however, casts with more highly refractile walls may be detected, and these occasionally give the characteristic brown colour with solution of iodine. In addition to casts, leucocytes and epithelial cells derived from the convoluted tubes may be found. The epithelial cells generally contain granules of fat, but sometimes they may stain with iodine, and for this reason it has been assumed that they have undergone lardaceous changes comparable to those affecting the capillaries. It is comparatively rare for red blood corpuscles to be met with in these cases, but the nature of the deposit and its microscopic characters may be completely revolutionised by the occurrence of nephritis. The amount of albumin which is found in the urine is usually large, though variable: it may even be as much as from 2 to 3 per cent. This large quantity of albumin is stated to result from the combined action of two distinct diseases, the lardaceous degeneration and the changes of nephritis. It is somewhat difficult, however, to account for the large amount of albumin often found with lardaceous disease, but it is, in all probability, to be attributed mainly to the structural alterations in the walls of the blood vessels. It is very tempting, when examining specimens, to assume from the appearance that there must be an obstructed flow of blood through the Malpighian tuft, but, unless chronic nephritis has been superadded, there is no clinical evidence of obstruction, such as hypertrophy of the left ventricle or increased tension of the pulse. Sir J. Grainger Stewart thinks that the albuminuria must be attributed to an increased permeability of the blood vessels of the kidney, in spite of their increased thickness, and he compares the condition with the analogous diarrhœa which is associated with lardaceous disease of the vessels of the intestine. It must not be forgotten, however, that Lecorché maintains that there is no albuminuria so long as there is no nephritis. This view is not generally held: Bartels, for instance, thinks it is erroneous; but it must be admitted that the amount is extremely variable, and that it may sometimes disappear entirely for a short time. Wagner describes three distinct groups with which lardaceous changes may be found after death: in the first, there is no change in the amount of urine and no albuminuria; in the second, the quantity of urine is greatly increased, and there is more or less albuminuria; in the third, it is diminished and albuminuria is very evident. It has been stated by some observers that in cases of lardaceous disease the urine frequently contains fairly large quantities of paraglobuline, and that this may occasionally exceed the quantity of serum albumin.

In advanced stages of the disease dropsy may form a marked symptom, but it is extremely variable in its occurrence. Sometimes it is absent throughout; at others it is present in an extreme degree, affecting the whole body, as in ordinary cases of large white kidney. Frequently it is confined to the abdomen and the lower extremities, and under such circumstances it seems to arise more from weakness of the circulation than from definite disease of the kidney. Another factor which will influence the extent of dropsy is the frequency with which diarrhœa arises in the course of lardaceous disease, and the more profuse the diarrhœa the greater the tendency to the reabsorption of fluid from the subcutaneous tissues.

It is very difficult to differentiate the remaining symptoms from those of the original disease. Thus, the interference with the work of the digestive system may sometimes be referred to lardaceous disease, or sometimes to the underlying cause. One of the earliest features is great diminution of appetite; this anorexia may precede the albuminuria for a length of time. As the disease progresses, other symptoms develop, and may tend to add considerably to the danger of the case. Nausea and vomiting occur, as in many cases of renal cirrhosis, though it may be questioned whether these symptoms are indicative of uræmic trouble, or of alterations within the vessels in the digestive system. Both the nausea and vomiting may be very persistent, in spite of treatment. These symptoms are stated to be less commonly met with in cases of syphilitic origin. Still more common and more dangerous is the diarrhœa which supervenes at a later stage: it undoubtedly depends upon lardaceous degeneration of the vessels of the intestine, and may frequently prove so exhausting as to lead to a fatal termination.

The changes in the circulatory system are not as characteristic as those which occur in other renal affections. The patients are generally anæmic, but the anæmia is the result, in all probability, of suppuration, and it develops more gradually than the extreme degree of pallor which is met with in acute forms of nephritis.

The cardio-vascular system does not undergo changes comparable to those of renal cirrhosis unless the latter disease becomes superadded. The nature of the pulse presents but little change from that produced by the wasting disease, and the position of the apex beat and the sounds of the heart undergo no variation until renal cirrhosis develops. On the other hand, it is rare for the lardaceous changes to be limited to the vessels in the kidney; the vessels in the liver and in the spleen undergo similar degeneration, and these organs increase considerably in size. Hæmorrhages from various surfaces frequently occur, whether as symptoms of lardaceous disease, or as part of the cachexia, and the veins are sometimes prone to a low type of inflammation, leading to thrombosis, which most commonly affects the femoral vein. This condition ensued with extreme suddenness in a girl of sixteen lately under my charge in the Sambrooke ward at King's College Hospital. She was dying with rapid consumption; there were physical signs of extensive cavities in both lungs, and she had profuse frequent diarrhœa and variable albuminuria. Without much complaint of pain, in the course of one night the left leg became very œdematous, and the femoral vein could be felt as a thin cord, which was slightly tender. Of necessity, her movements in bed became restricted: bed sores threatened, and she died, exhausted, after some four days of great suffering, which could only be partially relieved by morphine. This doubtless is comparable to the phlebitis and thrombosis, which are occasionally seen in connection with other wasting diseases, such as typhoid fever.

It is unnecessary to describe in detail the enormous increase in size both of the liver, and of the spleen, which is commonly met with when lardaceous changes affect the kidney. These glandular tumours mostly develop somewhat rapidly, and without producing any evident symptom apart from discomfort and weight.

The type of symptoms described in connection with the nervous systems, under the heading of 'Renal Cirrhosis,' is markedly absent from cases of lardaceous disease of the kidney, and the absence of uræmic symptoms, in all probability, is to be explained by the small part which is played by the consecutive renal alterations. It has already been noted that in uncomplicated cases the glandular structure of the kidney is unaltered, the lardaceous change affecting only the Malpighian tufts; and though, at a later stage, the glandular substance may undergo degeneration, few survive long enough for these later changes to give rise to other usual indications of danger: the patients die exhausted by the original disease, rather than as a result of uræmic troubles.

Similar immunity from definite symptoms may be noted in connection with the respiratory system. It is rare for any form of uræmic dyspnœa to develop in connection with lardaceous disease, though when renal cirrhosis becomes superadded the lungs are prone to take on low forms of inflammation, as in those cases in which the changes characteristic of renal cirrhosis predominate. It has already been noted that when lardaceous disease arises from pulmonary tuberculosis the affection of the lung appears to be arrested or retarded during the development of the changes in the kidney.

It is unnecessary here to dwell upon the symptoms of the primary disease, which necessarily continue during the development of lardaceous changes. The extent of cachexia is naturally dependent on the degree of suppuration, and the clinical features are further complicated by the extent to which lardaceous degeneration affects other organs. In short, although lardaceous change in the kidney must necessarily be mentioned in such a work as the present, it must be remembered that the disease is a constitutional one, affecting a large number of organs, rather than one in which the main pathological changes are limited to the kidneys.

Course and duration.—The course and duration of lardaceous renal changes are necessarily dependent upon the nature of the disease from which they arise; indeed, it may be questioned whether the lardaceous disease does much more than contribute a further element of danger to a condition which is already sufficiently serious. There can be no doubt that it increases the weakness and cachexia of the patient, but none the less the condition is essentially chronic, and the dangers are chiefly those, either of gradually increasing weakness or of the development of some special complication. The chronic character is most marked in cases of syphilis, and in these, even after albuminuria has lasted for many years, recovery is still possible. On the other hand, the course is more rapid where the disease results from chronic suppuration, especially if the suppuration resists surgical treatment, or affects some organ or part of the body where surgical treatment is impracticable.

In the early stages there are very few, if any, symptoms which are distinctly to be referred to the lardaceous disease, but as the disease progresses the amount of urine will increase considerably, and the anorexia, vomiting and diarrhœa become more marked; these symptoms may continue for some time before dropsical symptoms arise. The indications of increasing danger are the persistency of vomiting, the great increase of dropsy, and the supervention of secondary inflammations. When lardaceous disease has been recognised the actual duration varies considerably. The patient may live but a few months; but as a rule death does not occur for one or two years, and in exceptional cases not until eight or ten years from the commencement.

Diagnosis.—The diagnostic features rarely present much difficulty if attention is paid to the previous history of the case. The nature of the urine, the appearance of the patient, and the history of some cause of chronic suppuration, or the history of syphilis, mostly give a clear picture of lardaceous disease. It is more difficult to estimate the extent to which other forms of kidney trouble have been developed subsequently to the lardaceous changes, but these points have been already referred to when dealing with renal cirrhosis.

Prognosis.—The prognosis is necessarily bad in all cases of lardaceous disease, since it is as a rule an indication that some local cause of weakness has become sufficiently advanced to lead to general constitutional effects. If the case has been detected at a comparatively early stage, if the patient is fairly young, and if the cause is one which can be relieved, the prognosis becomes less gloomy. As a rule, it is possible to be more hopeful when dealing with children than with adults. When there is evidence of much affection of liver and spleen, or when there is reason to believe that other renal changes are occurring, the prognosis becomes more unfavourable. Still, exceptional cases have occurred in which recovery has taken place, even after some increase in the size of liver and spleen.

If the albuminuria has only been of short duration, it appears to be possible that such recovery may be due to a return to the normal condition, but in most cases it is far more likely that the parts of the kidney affected by lardaceous changes have undergone atrophy, and that the whole renal excretory function is performed by healthy tracts of tissue, which may have hypertrophied. Similar hypertrophy of the whole of one kidney is not uncommon when the other has atrophied as the result of the presence of a renal calculus.

The advisability of operating for the relief of chronic suppuration, even in face of albuminuria, and the possibility of thus arresting a secondary albuminuria, which in all probability depends upon lardaceous changes, are well illustrated by the following case described by Dr. J. J. Holt.[1] The patient was a man aged fifty-two, who had had a deformed knee since childhood. The knee joint was injured when he was eleven years old, and had been discharging thin, serous-like pus since he was twelve years of age. The family history gave evidence of a tubercular tendency, two of his sisters having died of consumption. In May, 1896, he complained of obscure lumbar pains and restlessness at night; he was then passing a considerable amount of urine, which was acid, light in colour, specific gravity about 1012, and distinctly albuminous; under the microscope some finely granular casts were found. There were no indications of enlargement of the liver or spleen, and the heart and lungs were normal. The limb having been amputated between the middle and upper third of the thigh, convalescence progressed satisfactorily, and the albuminuria steadily diminished, until at the time the report was written it had entirely disappeared.

Treatment.—In all probability every case of lardaceous disease of the kidney is already being treated for the cause which has contributed to its production. Cases of spinal disease, of disease of the hip joint, or other conditions leading to profuse suppuration, must necessarily remain in the hands of the surgeon, and it is impossible to lay down any general rule for such cases apart from the surgical treatment appropriate to the special condition. If necrosed or carious bone is present, the antiseptic treatment offers some slight hope; or, on the other hand, when the disease arises from syphilis, iodide of potassium may be used with a liberal hand: from ten to thirty grains should be given three times daily. The administration of mercury must be decided by the stage of syphilis. Lardaceous disease rarely arises during primary or secondary syphilis, hence the majority of these cases have already been treated with mercury, and the further administration is undesirable, since it may promote the cachexia from which the patient is already suffering. Sir Andrew Clark, in the paper above referred to, when speaking of the connection between phthisis and renal changes, maintained that patients with consumption, who go to winter in Alpine altitudes, when suffering from

[1] *Brit. Med. Journ.*, Feb. 20, 1897.

albuminuria, seldom do well, and that those who, whilst dwelling there, become albuminuric, always do badly; he therefore laid down two important rules for the avoidance of danger: first, that no phthisical person with albuminous urine should be recommended to winter at any Alpine height; and secondly, that everyone developing albuminous urine when dwelling there should immediately be sent away.

With regard to symptomatic treatment, it is at all times necessary to administer as nutritious a form of dietary as possible, although care must be taken not to give large quantities of food at any time, and thus to increase the anorexia and nausea which it is so desirable to abate. Dyspeptic symptoms must be treated upon general principles, that is, by the administration of alkalies, or of salts of bismuth, and occasionally small proportions of opium can be taken with advantage, although at a later stage, when the quantity of water is diminishing in amount, and nephritic changes are advancing, opium becomes a dangerous remedy.

When diarrhœa is troublesome, various astringents may be administered tentatively, although the rebellious nature of this symptom must be borne in mind, and the dose of the astringent must never be recklessly increased, owing to the danger of increasing the gastric discomfort. Of the different astringents, acetate of lead or sulphate of copper may be given in small doses in pill form, and it is sometimes desirable to coat the pill with keratin, so as so enable it to pass through the stomach unchanged. Numerous other astringents, such as tannaform, tannigen, and tannalbumin, have been recently introduced, and deserve careful trial in such cases; all of these are stated to pass through the stomach unchanged, and to be slightly soluble in the intestine. When it is remembered, however, that in many of these cases the diarrhœa is dependent upon pathological changes affecting the structure of the small vessels of the intestine, it will be apparent that there is little to be hoped from the administration of drugs which are naturally unable to influence structural changes. In every case it is necessary to administer some form of tonic to counteract the tendency to anæmia. Iodide of iron has been largely used for this purpose, and may be given either in the form of the pill or of the syrup of the British Pharmacopœia. As in other forms of anæmia, benefit frequently results from the administration of small doses of arseniate of iron, especially if given in conjunction with one of the non-astringent salts of iron. I have often seen the anæmia markedly reduced by the frequent administration of one-twelfth of a grain of arseniate of iron in conjunction with five grains of the pilula ferri of the British Pharmacopœia. It is necessary to repeat the warning to watch carefully the effects produced by these remedies, and not to increase the amount of arseniate which is given, if there is the least indication of an increased anorexia. When given in large doses, or when taken upon an empty stomach, such a pill might do more harm than good.

In any given case the treatment must to a large extent depend upon the estimate that has been formed of the amount of nephritis which co-exists. These directions about treatment apply mainly to simple cases of lardaceous disease in which the nephritis occupies a subordinate position, but cases occasionally arise in which the symptoms of renal cirrhosis predominate, and then necessarily the case must be treated as though it were one of simple cirrhosis of the kidney.

CHAPTER XII

CONGESTION OF THE KIDNEY. RENAL EMBOLISM

THE term congestion of the kidney is applied to numerous conditions which may give rise to the presence of albumin in the water, and nevertheless may not produce permanent structural change of the kidney. Congestion of the kidney may be either active or passive.

Active congestion.—When active, it is generally produced by irritants, such as cantharides or turpentine. It may occur in connection with death from suffocation; thus, acute congestion of the kidney is generally found in individuals who have been hanged or drowned. It is, in all probability, the form which is present in most cases of febrile albuminuria; thus, it occurs in pneumonia, and also occasionally in pericarditis. It may be produced by the action of poisons which interfere with respiration, such as prussic acid, and it may be found in one kidney when the functions of the opposite kidney have been abruptly interfered with, as, for example, by the presence of a calculus blocking the ureter, or by any sudden pressure upon the ureter.

The transition from active congestion of the kidney to acute nephritis is frequently one of degree. It has been already pointed out, in connection with febrile nephritis, that in some conditions the nephritic changes become permanent, instead of passing off rapidly as the fever declines. Generally, in active congestion there is some albuminuria, although the amount is usually slight. If casts are present, they are mostly hyaline and of the small type. Occasionally, however, the casts may be accompanied by renal epithelium and by a few scattered red blood corpuscles.

The pathology of active congestion is marked by comparatively slight changes. The kidney is usually somewhat enlarged and engorged, and on the surface, which is, as a rule, darker than the normal colour, the stellate veins are engorged, and form the so-called Verheyn's stars. The amount of blood which flows from the cut surface of the kidney is subject to great variation; a large quantity sometimes follows incision, and on being wiped away, the glomeruli stand out as red granular spots. When examined microscopically, the capillaries of the glomeruli and the inter-tubular capillaries are found to be dilated and engorged with blood corpuscles. Frequently blood corpuscles are present in the interior of the tubules, and hæmorrhage may have occurred between the glomerular tuft and its capsule. Changes in the epithelium also vary considerably; mostly the renal epithelium is swollen, semi-opaque, and in advanced cases it may show fine granules indicative of fatty degeneration.

It will be seen that this description corresponds closely with that already given of the early stages of acute nephritis, and there appears very little doubt that cases of acute congestion often readily pass on into acute nephritis. In spite of this, however, the two conditions are, as a rule, extremely different in their early symptoms. Thus, dropsy is practically almost always absent in cases of acute congestion, and the albumin is usually present in relatively small proportion. Occasionally there may be slight tenderness in the loins. If the condition is the result of fever, the symptoms speedily ameliorate as the temperature declines, so that in a few days it is quite possible for no trace of congestion to be found in the water. On the other hand, when active congestion is the result of some toxic irritant, such as carbolic acid, cubebs, cantharides or turpentine, the symptoms are probably at their worst within a few hours after the administration of the poison. Thus, in a case described by Sir George Johnson, where half an ounce of turpentine had been taken, the urine became bloody within a few hours, and blood casts with a few small inflammatory cells were soon discovered. Six days later the urine still contained some blood and albumin, but the quantity of these was not so great, and by the sixteenth day the urine was free from both albumin and blood.

Active congestion may sometimes be excited by the absorption of drugs applied externally. Thus, Sir William Roberts mentions cases resulting from the external application of tincture of iodine, of styrax and of petroleum; and it is well known that cantharides may, in exceptional cases, cause albuminuria and hæmaturia when applied to large surfaces of the skin.

Reference has already been made, when describing renal casts, to the comparative frequency with which albuminuria is associated with cases of diabetes, and this disease specially serves as an illustration of a form of albuminuria which, though usually transitory, may become permanent. Most physicians have noted that, with judicious treatment, directed solely to diminishing the amount of sugar and the amount of water eliminated, the albumin, which may be found in the later stages of diabetes, may speedily undergo diminution, and occasionally may disappear entirely. It has been suggested that in these cases the kidney becomes actively congested, owing to the large amount of work it is called upon to perform, and this congestion, which is in the early stages curable, may nevertheless lead on to degeneration and destruction of the renal epithelium, to an overgrowth of interstitial tissue, and to other indications of chronic Bright's disease. The connection between congestive albuminuria and diabetes is of further interest on account of the frequency of retinal changes in connection with diabetes and with chronic Bright's disease.

Passive congestion.—Passive congestion of the kidney is, as a rule, more permanent than active congestion. It is produced by conditions which are less subject to variations in intensity, and it is therefore rather more prone to give rise to a chronic form of albuminuria, although less likely to lead to chronic renal changes. It generally occurs as the result of interference with the venous circulation through the kidney, and it leads to a condition which has been termed cyanotic induration. Sometimes this form of passive engorgement may be due to contraction or obstruction of the renal veins, or occasionally of the inferior vena cava. The circulation through these vessels may be interfered with by the pressure due to the growth of tumours, or the flow of fluid may be diminished by thrombosis within the vessels. In several cases of severe cachexia, especially in severe diarrhœa in children, engorgement of the kidney has been described. Far more commonly engorged kidney is due to interference with the general venous circulation, either through failure of the heart's action, or through interference with the pulmonary circulation.

Most cases of advanced mitral disease exhibit some indications of passive congestion of the kidney, and this consequence appears to follow most frequently when the mitral valve is not closing efficiently, and when the resulting regurgitation is not sufficiently compensated by dilatation and hypertrophy of the auricle. Cyanotic induration occurs with aortic disease, as well as with mitral, but it rarely shows itself, however, before there are indications of consecutive failure of the mitral valve. When there is much chronic obstruction to the circulation of the blood through the lung, owing to some forms of lung disease, cyanotic induration may also follow. This is far more likely to occur in connection with emphysema, chronic bronchitis, chronic pneumonia, or extensive pleurisy, than with any form of consumption. In the former group of pulmonary diseases there is far greater interference with the circulation, and further, the general nutrition is not so much impaired as in cases of phthisis, where the exhausting night sweats and the profuse expectoration, and perhaps hæmoptysis, deplete the vessels and so render passive engorgement an unlikely event. In consumption the interference with the circulation through the lung is mostly accompanied by anæmia, and the pulmonary vessels which remain intact are quite sufficient for the amount of blood which is in the circulation. Of all the conditions above mentioned, the one which is most likely to lead to cyanotic induration of the kidney is disease of the mitral orifice, resulting in general venous obstruction and engorgement; and it is most probable that the renal symptoms will arise when compensation is rendered imperfect by degeneration of the cardiac muscle, which is generally attended by dilatation of the different cavities of the heart. Engorged kidney, indeed, is usually a late symptom of heart disease, and it has mostly been preceded by the dyspnœa and distress attendant on pulmonary engorgement, as well as by the discomfort resulting from engorgement of the liver.

Pathological anatomy.—The *post-mortem* appearances depend, to a certain extent, upon the duration of the engorgement. When the engorgement is fairly recent, the kidneys are generally somewhat larger than usual. If patients die after a relatively short period of suffering, from heart disease and engorgement of lung, the kidney is only moderately enlarged, the surface is congested and purple, the cortex is slightly thickened, and the organ is hard and somewhat elastic. With more chronic conditions the kidney may be slightly smaller than usual, and of a deep purple colour. The surface may be granular in appearance, and the cortex may be found to be somewhat atrophied. Frequently, in cases of cyanotic induration, the capsule can only be detached with difficulty, and portions of renal tissue tear away with it. The microscopic appearances vary: mostly the capsules of the Malpighian tufts are thickened, and the tuft of capillaries is diminished in size, while the epithelial cells are undergoing granular and fatty degeneration. The inter-lobular veins are usually prominent and distended, and there may occasionally be much cellular infiltration of the kidney. There is, as a rule, very little space left between the Malpighian tuft and the capsule, but frequently this space is partially filled with extravasated blood corpuscles, which may also pass down the convoluted tubes. In chronic cases there may mostly be found extending from the capsule of the kidney, small wedge-shaped patches of dense tissue, with the apex directed towards the pelvis of the kidney, thus following the course of the inter-lobular arteries. In these patches the Malpighian bodies and tubules are somewhat atrophied, and the patch appears to depend upon renal embolism affecting a branch of the inter-lobular artery (*vide* ' Renal Embolism,' p. 273).

Although the cases in which cyanotic induration leads to chronic Bright's disease are exceptional, there seems to be no doubt that genuine Bright's disease and engorged kidney may occur simultaneously, and this in all probability accounts for the difficulty so often experienced in connection with chronic Bright's disease. The symptoms produced, as well as the *post-mortem* appearances, may lead to much hesitation in connection with these cases, and the possibility of the simultaneous occurrence of both conditions should therefore be always borne in mind, otherwise the prognosis is apt to be too hopeful if all the indications are attributed to engorgement.

Symptoms.—The late occurrence of cyanotic induration in connection with heart disease and other conditions, which disturb the venous circulation of the kidney, must explain the relatively slight importance of the symptoms so far as the affection of the kidney is concerned. It has already been indicated that passive congestion of the kidney occurs at a late stage, when the general circulation is failing; hence the early symptoms in any particular case are those of the disease which causes the engorgement of the kidney, while the nature of the urine may be noted as a clinical fact, although it gives rise to few symptoms of its own. So far as the circulation is concerned, the symptoms are those of failing mitral valve; the pulse is small, rapid, and irregular; owing to the over-filling of the veins, the appearance is usually somewhat cyanosed, and occasionally the veins are more prominent than usual, those of the lower extremities being most affected. The murmurs in connection with the cardiac changes present very little variation, and the failure of compensation is mainly to be inferred from the general condition and from the increased area of cardiac dulness.

In connection with the respiratory system, the symptoms are also essentially those of the primary disease, and not of renal engorgement or of interference with the eliminative work of the kidney. These patients are always short of breath, and indeed the shortness of breath and the frequency of what are termed mild bronchitic attacks will, in all probability, be the first symptoms to call attention to the serious condition of the patient, a condition, however, which depends upon the failure of the heart, and not upon passive engorgement of the kidney. It is unnecessary to enter into detail here concerning the general symptoms connected with the dyspnœa of heart failure. It may be enough to indicate that this dyspnœa may become extreme as the disease progresses, and it may be associated, not only with frequent cough and mucous expectoration, but also with orthopnœa. It is comparatively rare, in such cases, for dropsy to be absent, but when present it generally commences in the feet or ankles, and extends upwards—that is, the dropsy is of that form which we know so well in connection with chronic heart disease, dropsy in which the parts affected are largely under the influence of gravity, as opposed to the general dropsy affecting the whole of the body— the upper extremities as well as the lower, the face, as well as the abdominal cavity—which we associate more commonly with acute nephritis. The dropsy met with in connection with cyanotic induration is usually the result of the same cause, and is not directly dependent upon any interference in the work of the kidney.

The urine.—In a fairly large number of cases, although patients may, for a long time, have complained of shortness of breath, and even of frequency of cough, the symptom which attracts the greatest amount of attention and causes the most alarm is connected with alterations in the nature of the urine, occurring simultaneously with the dropsical swelling of the feet. Frequently the patient notes that the amount passed daily is far below the normal quantity, and the decrease is associated with a deepening of tint. Sometimes the colour is dark brownish red, and, as a rule, the urine is highly acid, and the deposit consists of large quantities of urates and of uric acid. The daily amount of urates and of uric acid excreted is frequently increased, while there is little alteration in the daily excretion of urea so long as the renal epithelium remains intact. At a later stage, however, owing to the development of chronic nephritis, the amount of urea may, in many cases, be diminished. During the early stages of engorgement, the specific gravity is invariably increased, sometimes ranging to 1030, occasionally reaching 1035. During this time there is mostly some albumin in the urine, although the proportion is generally small, rarely amounting to ·02 per cent.

When the urine is examined microscopically, the numerous amorphous or crystalline urates attract attention; sometimes many small lozenge-shaped uric acid crystals may also be present. In addition to these, however, some small hyaline casts may be found, and red blood corpuscles are occasionally seen floating freely in the liquid; sometimes they are adherent to the casts, and appear to be included within them. In spite of the albuminuria, however, it is not uncommon to find that no casts can be detected. Much divergence of opinion has been expressed as to the origin of the albuminuria in these cases, and the exact causation of the diminution of urine. The diminution has been ascribed to a decrease of blood pressure in the glomeruli, but this has been combated by the assertion that venous obstruction in the course of the renal vein would of necessity extend to the glomeruli, and cause an increase of blood pressure. Another theory is that this diminution may result from difference of pressure within the glomeruli and the renal tubules, but, in all probability, both albuminuria and the reduction in the daily amount of urine must be ascribed to retardation of the blood current in the Malpighian capillaries.

The evidence appears to indicate that diminution may be the result of disturbance of the secretory function of the kidney, since this alteration in the daily quantity of urine follows experimental ligature of the vena cava, while diuretics at once produce an abundant secretion of urine. Fürbringer concludes that the diminution is closely connected with injury of the renal epithelium, and that the albuminuria is due to a transudation through the walls of the tubules. That the albumin is not derived from the Malpighian bodies is also the opinion of Grainger Stewart, who says that 'clinical observation affords a beautiful piece of evidence that the albumin does not escape from the glomeruli in patients suffering from cardiac disease. When we administer digitalis to such a patient, the quantity of urine rises, and the albumin at the same time frequently diminishes, not only relatively, but absolutely. Now the diuresis is explained by increase of pressure within the Malpighian tufts; this increase would necessarily be associated with increase of albumin if the capillary loops of the Malpighian tufts were to blame.' This evidence he regards as conclusive proof that increased pressure in the vessels surrounding the tubules is the main cause of this form of albuminuria.

Notwithstanding the diminution in the daily quantity of urine, uræmic complications are not found until the supervention of chronic nephritis. This immunity is doubtless the result of the absence of change in the renal epithelium in the large majority of cases of chronic engorgement; and so long as the renal epithelium is intact, the solids of the urine remain either normal or at least sufficient for the necessary daily excretion.

It must not be forgotten, however, that patients with chronic engorgement of the kidney are peculiarly prone to chronic and sub-acute attacks of nephritis, and that the character of the urine is therefore liable to considerable alteration when the secreting substance of the kidney is thus secondarily affected.

Course and duration.—With a condition which essentially depends upon some pre-existing disease, it is obviously impossible for the symptoms to pursue a definite type, since they must be very largely due to the original disease, and only to a slight extent to interference with the functions of the kidney. Usually, however, the patients complain of dyspnœa on exertion, and this dyspnœa may be associated with an intermittent pulse, and frequently with a rapid pulse.

Reference has already been made to the tendency to repeated attacks of engorgement of the lungs, and in many cases, if the urine be examined during one of these attacks, it will be found to be diminished in quantity, of high specific gravity, and also to contain a small proportion of albumin. These changes in the water, however, are not of necessity serious, although they are indications of failure of compensation which, sooner or later, will probably be followed by more urgent symptoms. When dropsy supervenes, the aspect of the case becomes more immediately serious. Sometimes, however, even severe dropsy may disappear rapidly, and the urgency of the symptoms may pass away, while the daily quantity of urine is increased and the proportion of albumin is diminished. More commonly, however, the dropsy continues to a varying extent until death ensues. Even with those patients who show signs of improvement, the possibility of relapses must be borne in mind. When dropsy has once made its appearance, the probability is that the hypertrophied ventricle is already undergoing fatty degeneration as well as dilatation. The scene gradually closes in with increasing dyspnœa, dropsy and exhaustion, and at length the end may be due to pulmonary engorgement, to failure of the heart's action, or merely to extreme exhaustion.

It is impossible to assign any limit to the duration of a case in which the symptoms of chronic renal engorgement are marked. Sometimes the fatal termination may be delayed a few months, and cases have been known to survive for two or three years. The prospects of such a prolonged course are, however, entirely dependent upon the condition of the ventricle. When, under the influence of cardiac tonics or diuretics, the amount of urine increases speedily, while the feeble, rapid pulse becomes firmer and slower, there is a better prospect of prolonged life.

Diagnosis.—Although, in many respects, the condition above described appears fairly differentiated from other forms of kidney disease, it is not uncommon, in certain cases, to find that some difficulty arises. The small amount of albumin which is passed is by no means a certain indication of engorged kidney, since in many cases of chronic nephritis the proportion of albumin may be very small. If, however, without dwelling too much upon the nature of the urine, careful attention is paid to the other symptoms, there is generally little difficulty in distinguishing between chronic engorgement and chronic nephritis. In a large number of cases the primary symptoms are those connected with the condition of the heart, and the patient is somewhat cyanosed, the dusky tint of the complexion contrasting markedly with the general pallor so frequently found in chronic nephritis. The most characteristic indication of chronic renal engorgement is the high specific gravity of the urine, with the simultaneous diminution in quantity. It is not so easy, however, to recognise at all times when the engorged kidney exists side by side with true nephritis. If the nephritis is sub-acute, the urine is more highly charged with blood, and a certain number of epithelial and blood casts may be seen mixed with the hyaline casts. In cases with chronic nephritis the alteration in the specific gravity is the most marked feature. Although, as the result of engorgement, the amount of urine may be considerably reduced in quantity, the specific gravity is likely to be low, 1010 to 1012, and the colour will probably be pale, or at least less deep in tint than is generally considered characteristic of renal engorgement.

Prognosis.—The prognosis of renal engorgement is essentially bad, not on account of the change within the kidney, but on account of the original disease of which the renal engorgement is the outcome. In any case, however, the prognosis must be largely influenced by the results of treatment. Although cases with much dropsy and much interference with the function of the kidney must be regarded with anxiety, yet a certain proportion improve considerably under treatment; hence, although the ultimate prognosis is necessarily unfavourable, the immediate prognosis may be fairly good, so long as signs of improvement can be obtained.

Treatment.—The treatment of renal engorgement is entirely dependent upon that of the original disease, and one of the first indications is that the patient should be kept rigidly in bed, so as to diminish the amount of work which the heart is called upon to perform. Even without other treatment, many cases of dropsy and renal engorgement will speedily improve from being kept at rest for a few weeks. Attention must as a rule be paid to the position of the patient. From the frequency with which the lungs are simultaneously engorged, such patients find that it is impossible to lie flat in their beds, but require to be propped up with pillows; nevertheless, it is always desirable that the foot of the bed should be somewhat raised, so as to facilitate the return of blood through the veins, and thus to favour a diminution of dropsy.

There is very little advantage in materially altering the patient's diet, except to insist upon a supply of nutritious and readily digestible materials. Frequently, some advantage will follow the use of milk, but an exclusive milk diet is as undesirable as it is uncalled for.

The selection of a drug to increase the force of the circulation usually presents few difficulties. Digitalis gives the best results, both so far as the heart and the dropsy are concerned, and it should be administered in fairly large doses, provided that it does not cause sickness or diarrhœa. Fifteen minims of the tincture may be given three or four times a day, or an equivalent dose of the infusion may be employed. The improvement which sometimes follows the use of digitalis affects the dyspnœa and cyanosis, and at the same time the quantity of urine may be markedly increased. Sometimes, when patients have been too much accustomed to the use of digitalis, or, on the other hand, when digitalis causes disturbance of the digestive system, it may be replaced by strophanthus. With the former drug it is necessary to check the administration or to reduce the dose when the diuretic action fails, and the urine again becomes scanty, while the pulse, which was fairly regular, becomes rapid and weak. It is not only inadvisable, but it might be dangerous, to continue to employ digitalis under such conditions. In general, however, in cases of engorged kidney strophanthus does not give such good results as digitalis. It is true that the pulse may improve rapidly, and that the dyspnœa and cyanosis may diminish, but the degree of alteration in the work of the kidney is not so great; digitalis appears to act as a distinct diuretic, while strophanthus, if it causes diuresis at all, does so indirectly through its influence on the circulatory system. As a rule, therefore, it is advisable to combine the use of some other diuretic with the above treatment. Potassium acetate may be given in this way, or it may be advisable to employ caffeine, theobromine, or diuretin for their influence on the work of the kidney; these drugs may be given alone, or together with strophanthus. Their influence, however, appears to be largely exerted upon the work of the kidney, although caffeine, to some extent, seems to act through the circulatory system. In certain cases it is impossible to augment the quantity of urine excreted daily by the use of any of these drugs, and the prognosis is then extremely bad, since the dropsy which resists these remedies is frequently associated either with engorgement of lung or with collections of fluid within the pleural cavity. Many practitioners are in favour of calomel under such circumstances, and although it is undoubtedly desirable to limit the use of calomel to cases where there is reason to believe that no form of chronic nephritis is present, yet small doses given repeatedly may occasionally cause a great increase in the amount of urine passed. It is necessary, however, to use this drug with the greatest caution, as, if nephritic changes are present, salivation is readily produced, without any diuretic effect. In cases of engorged kidney the free use of purgatives is very rarely desirable. Sometimes the administration of salines may cause rapid diminution of dropsical effusion, but as a rule there is the risk of increasing the weakness of the circulation, as well as of producing digestive disturbance. In exceptional cases hot-air baths may be used to produce diaphoresis, and thus to reduce the renal engorgement as well as the dropsical effusion. It must not be forgotten, however, that the dropsical effusion is the result of failure of the heart's action, and not of failure of renal excretion; hence it is necessary to guard carefully against any tendency to faintness, and if the pulse becomes weak and irregular stimulants must at once be given, and the baths must be discontinued. Stimulants should, as a rule, be given almost throughout the treatment of a case of engorged kidney, the pulse frequently gaining in strength under the influence of moderate doses of brandy and other diffusible stimulants. It is very rare that advantage results from surgical interference. If there is much ascites, however, it may be necessary to remove the fluid by means of an aspirator.

Renal Embolism

Cases of albuminuria, and even of hæmaturia, are sometimes met with in connection with vascular disease of the heart and similar conditions, where the alteration in the urine is due to a purely local affection of a small portion of the kidney rather than to a general diffuse congestive or inflammatory process. More often the changes in the kidney and its work are so slight that alterations in the urine may be either overlooked, or else wrongly ascribed to simple passive congestion, while attention is centred on the primary affection of the heart, which is causing more marked and more urgent symptoms. The appearances of renal embolism are, however, fairly frequently seen, and the possibility of its occurrence should not be lost sight of when albuminuria is found suddenly in the course of acute rheumatic endocarditis.

The condition depends upon the obstruction of a branch of the renal artery by an embolus, which may have proceeded from the aorta, or from the mitral, or the aortic valves. Fibrinous vegetations may be deposited upon an atheromatous rough patch in the aorta, or upon the surface of a valve roughened either by endocarditis or by senile degenerative changes. As they have no organic union with the underlying tissues they may readily be detached by the blood current, and whirled onwards till finally arrested in a small artery in the brain, spleen, kidney, or elsewhere. Similar plugs or emboli may sometimes originate in the lining of an aneurism, and be passed into the blood stream, with the same result.

This result is seen mainly in the production of a wedge-shaped white infarct, with the apex directed towards the pelvis of the kidney. This white appearance was formerly wrongly attributed to the discoloration of a hæmorrhagic deposit, and the condition was described as 'hæmorrhagic renal infarct.' Although a form of true hæmorrhagic deposit may sometimes occur, it is, in the opinion of Fürbringer, uncommon. The patch is from the first pale, owing to the arrest of the blood supply through the branch of the renal artery obstructed by the embolus, and the shape depends entirely upon the mode of distribution of the smaller branches of this vessel. The outline of the wedge is sharply marked by a deep red line, which separates the renal infarct from the surrounding tissue. Although the infarct is whiter or paler than the rest of the kidney, its colour may vary—it may be white, yellow, or greyish; but, although these changes are indications of necrotic changes, it is very rare for pus to be formed. Sir William Roberts, however, states that sometimes the larger infarcts go on to suppuration, and, still more rarely, to gangrene. One result of the mode of production of a renal infarct is that, on section, its surface appears more dry than the surrounding renal tissue. Microscopical examination shows that in the affected area the renal epithelium has undergone partial degenerative changes, the granulations and the nuclei being less evident, and staining agents less readily absorbed. Usually, the patch is opaque, from the presence of fibrinous coagulum and oil globules. The inter-tubular capillaries contain fibrinous coagula, and sometimes oil globules, while similar coagula and oil globules may be seen in the Malpighian capillaries and the afferent arteries. These changes may be rendered more apparent by acting upon the section with dilute acetic acid.

The red line of demarcation is partly the result of intense hyperæmia of the parts surrounding the infarct, and partly the result of rupture of the over-distended capillaries, and the consequent effusion of blood into the surrounding tissues. It has been suggested that this effusion may be consecutive to disorganisation of the walls of the capillaries, or even to a retrograde venous current, but it is far more probable that it proceeds from the collateral vessels, which also cause the appearance of albumin and blood in the urine. Another theory ascribed the red line of demarcation to the irritation produced by the presence of the necrotic tissues; but it is well known that the sudden occlusion of an artery in other parts is always associated with hyperæmia of collateral vessels, and this is mostly regarded as being partly due to over-strain and partly to an attempt to establish collateral circulation. When death does not occur shortly after the formation of a renal infarct, the area of necrotic tissue undergoes further regeneration and absorption, owing to the formation of fresh vascular loops, and a cicatrix may result, consisting of a firm, fibrous band passing inwards from a depression in the cortex. At the same time, inflammatory changes may occur in the vicinity of the cicatrix, both in the Malpighian tufts and in the tubules, and these lead to further localised contraction.

Symptoms.—It is comparatively rare for renal embolism to produce symptoms which are recognisable. The condition may be suspected when the course of endocarditis or of disease of the aorta is interrupted by a rigor and rise of temperature, and the suspicion is strengthened if, in addition, there is complaint of sudden lumbar pain. Frequently, however, pain is absent or indefinite, and the other symptoms may be attributed to other changes. Even an examination of the urine affords but little assistance, for it may be either entirely normal, or, when albumin and blood are detected, they may previously have been present as the result of renal engorgement due to the weakened circulation: it is also well known that under such circumstances, independently of renal embolism, there are frequent variations in the amount of urine.

Treatment.—With a condition which is marked by such indefinite symptoms it is almost impossible to adopt any particular form of treatment, directed specially against a suspected renal embolism. Further, the only possible means of alleviation are, in all probability, already being used for the primary cause, and the treatment of embolism is of necessity a matter of minor importance. It is, therefore, unnecessary to say more than that, when a renal embolism is suspected, the patient must be kept in bed, and that anodynes must as a rule be administered.

CHAPTER XIII

RENAL CALCULUS

HYDRO-NEPHROSIS, consecutive renal cirrhosis, pyelitis and suppurative nephritis, which are dealt with in the next chapter, may frequently owe their origin to the irritation produced by one or more renal calculi, which, in addition, very commonly cause hæmaturia; hence, a brief account of the leading features of renal calculi may not be out of place.

The morbid conditions due to the presence of gravel or calculi in the kidney have, for descriptive purposes, been grouped under the name Nephrolithiasis, but inasmuch as this includes numerous symptoms and pathological conditions which may be due to other causes, there seems to be little advantage in retaining this term. Renal calculi may be composed of uric acid, or of uric acid with a covering of oxalate of lime, or of phosphates, the size and appearance of the calculus varying with its chemical composition. Sometimes calculi have the well-known mulberry form, or a calculus which originally had this shape may become more or less smooth on the surface, owing to the deposition of other materials. Sometimes the shape of the calculi appears to depend upon the site of their formation, so that they may be of irregular shape, with projections which have passed between the pyramids. In addition to the above constituents, calculi may more rarely be met with composed of cystine. These are of a light colour, and possess a certain lustre. Calculi composed of xanthin, of fatty matters, of carbonate of lime, and of fibrin, have also been described.

Renal calculi are more common in men than in women, and they occur at all ages. Their development appears to be favoured by sedentary habits, by gout, and by other conditions which produce increased formation and excretion of uric acid, of oxalate of lime, or of other constituents of calculi. Some degree of inflammation, or of injury to the pelvis of the kidney, has often been credited with playing a formidable part in the formation of renal calculi. In some instances the nucleus of the calculus has appeared to be formed of a blood clot resulting from injury, which, by its retention within the pelvis of the kidney, has acted as a foreign body, upon which the crystalline constituents of the urine have been deposited.

Symptoms.—When the calculi are small, they may occasionally be passed without giving rise to any symptoms, and even when of large size they may be retained within the pelvis of the kidney in a similar quiescent condition. Small calculi, or at least small potentials—that is, collections of spiculæ, of crystals visible to the naked eye—may often be passed by the patient, and cause irritation about the neck of the bladder or along the course of the urethra. I have frequently seen such collections of crystals distinctly visible to the naked eye passed with the urine, and these constitute the condition commonly known by the name of 'sand.' One of my patients for many years passed beautiful rosettes of uric acid, which were distinctly visible to the naked eye, and his chief complaint was of much discomfort about the meatus. Such concretions are, perhaps, scarcely to be regarded as calculi, but they might undoubtedly, if retained within the pelvis of the kidney, or if lodged between the pyramids, form the nuclei of masses of larger size. Such masses, while within the pelvis of the kidney, will frequently give rise to no symptoms, though possibly some cases of lumbar pain, which are so often met with in gouty patients, are to be ascribed to the presence of such concretions. When, however, these masses are dislodged from the site of their formation, and when they either fall into or are washed into the ureter they commonly cause renal colic, which, in severe cases, is of an agonising character, and accompanied by vomiting and retching.

Renal colic commonly commences with startling suddenness, and the pain is primarily referred to the region of the kidney, and to the course of the ureter on the affected side, shooting downwards later to the groin, and sometimes to the testicle, which may be swollen and retracted. Sometimes the pain can scarcely be localised. It appears to radiate through the abdominal cavity, and, in exceptional cases, it may even be referred to the umbilical region. The duration of renal colic is extremely variable. It may last only for a few hours, or it may continue, with periods of partial relief, and with exacerbations, for several days. A well-marked attack of renal colic generally forms the precursor of others, but sometimes, under judicious treatment, the tendency to the formation of renal calculi may be arrested. The liability of recurrence, however, is so well recognised that patients who have had one severe attack of colic are mostly regarded with suspicion at insurance offices. With the onset of the pain, there is frequent desire to micturate, and the act is commonly accompanied by much straining and discomfort. The urine is generally passed in small quantity, and it is commonly intimately mixed with blood. In some cases, however, in spite of the severe pain, the urine may remain clear, though reduced in quantity. These symptoms, following in rotation, cause a complete blockage of the ureter, so that the urine is totally derived from the healthy kidney, the fluid formed from the affected side being retained within the pelvis of the kidney, and tending to dilate the pelvis, and to cause pressure upon the pyramids. Under such circumstances, a complete blockage of one ureter—hydro-nephrosis—is liable to result, and the conditions described under the name consecutive renal cirrhosis, pyelitis, and suppurative nephritis, may originate in the injury thus done to the kidney. Attacks of renal colic usually follow after some violent exercise, or some jolting movement of the body, perhaps as the result of accident, during which the calculus is dislodged from the nidus in which it has been formed. The sudden jars resulting from horse exercise, or from the irregular, unexpected jerks in railway carriages, may be sufficient to produce renal colic by suddenly altering the position of the calculus. It must not, however, be considered that all cases of renal calculus are necessarily associated with renal colic. *Post-mortem* examinations frequently disclose the presence of calculi which have been wholly unsuspected during life. In such cases, the kidney may sometimes be found practically unchanged, but, more commonly, it has undergone a certain degree of atrophy, owing to the irritation due to the presence of the calculus.

Sometimes the termination of an attack of renal colic occurs suddenly after a fit of vomiting, during which there may be momentary increase of pain, followed by sudden relief, the explanation being that extra pressure has caused the stone to be dislodged from the ureter and to pass onwards to the bladder. More often the relief is more gradual, and results from the employment of some measures calculated to relieve muscular spasm of the ureter, which undoubtedly offers opposition to the onward movement of the calculus. Such relief may be afforded by the use of hot baths, or hot fomentations, or by the use of preparations containing opium or morphine. In all probability, the pain of renal colic is referable rather to muscular spasm than to local injury. Undoubtedly, the muscular spasm is the result of the irritation of the mucous membrane by the calculus; but the nature of the pain is often demonstrated by the relief which ensues with measures calculated to relieve spasm.

The existence of renal calculus may sometimes cause pyelitis for a great length of time before there is any complaint of renal colic, and in such cases the dislodgment of the calculus, notwithstanding the pain which ensues, may lead to a cure of the pyelitis.

Treatment.—The treatment of renal calculus and of renal colic has undergone a considerable modification during the last few years. Formerly, treatment was almost limited to the periods of pain, and consisted in the employment of hot baths, hot fomentations, and perhaps venesection to relieve spasm and diminish engorgement. Notwithstanding the hæmaturia, preparations of opium were employed, and, indeed, are still employed, to give relief from pain; and in many cases it is still advisable to use hypodermic injections of morphine, since, when the pain was at its worst, most remedies given by the mouth provoked vomiting. These measures are still largely relied upon in cases of renal colic, but when pain recurs frequently, and when there is reason to believe that the stone has not passed from the pelvis of the kidney to the bladder, or that more than one calculus may be present, the modern tendency is to resort to surgical interference; and it is undoubtedly an advantage, in such cases, to remove the calculus, which may otherwise lead to the total disorganisation of renal tissue. The method of operating, and the question of the removal of the affected kidney, can scarcely be properly dealt with in this book, since the removal of the kidney must depend upon the extent to which it has already been damaged by the presence of the calculus. If there is any true secreting structure still in existence, it is generally safer not to remove it, since there is always the possibility of the opposite kidney being already damaged by the presence of calculi.

As a temporary measure, chloroform may sometimes be administered by inhalation. This occasionally succeeds in relieving spasm and in favouring the onward passage of the calculus; more often, however, the pain returns as the patient recovers consciousness.

CHAPTER XIV

HYDRO-NEPHROSIS—CONSECUTIVE CIRRHOSIS— SUPPURATIVE NEPHRITIS

THREE affections of the kidney deserve consideration here, although, strictly speaking, they are not forms of Bright's disease; they are, however, in many cases, associated with alterations in the urine, which may be accompanied by hæmaturia or albuminuria. Although they have been incidentally mentioned in the earlier pages, there is, I think, some advantage in referring to them at greater length, since, although frequently of surgical origin, and to be treated by surgical methods, they not uncommonly, in the first place, come under the notice of the physician for diagnosis.

The three conditions in question are: (1) Hydro-nephrosis; (2) Consecutive renal cirrhosis; and (3) Suppurative nephritis. The first may occur independently of the others, but is often linked to the second, and this, in turn, may give rise to suppurative nephritis, although the last may also develop without association with the others.

1. HYDRO-NEPHROSIS.—Hydro-nephrosis is the term employed to indicate an over-distension of the renal pelvis with urine: it is a condition which sometimes results in the formation of a fluid tumour of considerable size, which is not to be confounded with cysts forming within the substance of the kidney, in connection with various forms of Bright's disease. This fluid tumour is dependent upon some mechanical obstacle to the flow of the urine after its formation, instead of being due to an obstruction in the course of one or more of the renal tubules.

Etiology.—Hydro-nephrosis is often a congenital condition, which results from the ureter of one or both sides being impervious, either from pressure or from being congenitally imperforate. Numerous examples of congenital malformations leading to hydro-nephrosis have been collected by Mr. Henry Morris, and he lays stress upon the fact that the congenital causes do not always give rise to hydro-nephrosis in infancy or in very early life.

More interesting, perhaps, since more within reach of treatment, are the acquired causes of hydro-nephrosis. These may sometimes be of such a nature that they affect both kidneys simultaneously, as, for example, stricture of the urethra, enlargement of the prostate, cancer of the pelvic organs, of the uterus, vagina, bladder, or rectum, ovarian cysts, vesical calculus, or cystitis. In the majority of cases, where the condition is unilateral, it results from the impaction of a calculus in the ureter; it may, however, be due to pressure exerted by pelvic tumours or by peritoneal inflammatory bands, and in some cases it has followed inflammation or ulceration within the ureter, traceable, perhaps, to the irritation produced by a renal calculus. Tumour or abscess of the bladder may involve the orifice of one ureter; cases due to papilloma and to fibroma of the bladder have been recorded. Henry Morris makes the interesting suggestion that frequency of micturition may be an etiological factor when hydro-nephrosis accompanies phymosis, stricture of the urethra, prostatic enlargement, or vesical calculus. He considers that frequent closure of the orifices of the ureters during micturition involves frequent resistance to the outflow of urine. He thinks this may materially aid in the production of the hydro-nephritic tumour, when there is partial obstruction of one or both ureters from any other cause.

Morbid anatomy.—The changes with hydro-nephrosis affect not only the pelvis of the kidney, but also the renal tissues, and they are primarily the direct results of pressure. The earliest indication is a diminution in the size of the apices of the pyramids, so that they appear flattened or even hollowed out, and separated by broad intervals. As the accumulation continues, the calyces and the pelvis undergo dilatation, the latter forming a spheroidal sac connected with egg-like pouches due to the distension of the calyces, the walls of which have become tough and thick. In extreme cases, the septa between these pouches may break down, so that a single cystic tumour results, in place of a lobulated tumour. The ureter, above the point of obstruction, may also be dilated and thickened. As the tension is increased, the kidney may undergo changes of consecutive renal cirrhosis, or, more commonly, further atrophy may affect the whole of the pyramids, and perhaps, also, the cortex, so that only small traces of renal tissue are found in the fibrous walls of the resulting cyst.

The size of the cyst may vary considerably: it may be smaller than a normal kidney, or only slightly larger, or it may, in exceptional cases, form a tumour which distends the abdomen and simulates an ovarian cyst.

The fluid in the sac sometimes consists of more or less dilute urine of low specific gravity and clear, pale colour. At other times, the fluid contains albumin, pus, or blood, and may accordingly be opaque and red. Urea and uric acid may be absent or deficient in amount, while chloride of sodium may be present in excess. The term 'pyonephrosis' has been used for cases in which the fluid has indicated the presence of pus.

Symptoms.—When due to congenital conditions, hydronephrosis may declare itself at any age; but when resulting from some other disease, it may proceed for a length of time without attracting attention, until the formation of an abdominal tumour. It has been aptly termed 'a silent complication,' on account of its insidious onset. When it reaches an advanced stage without any obvious tumour, complaint has been made of pain in the back, frequent micturition, thirst, and perhaps anuria, partial or complete. If both kidneys are affected, the interference with excretion may lead to the ordinary symptoms of uræmia, but the constipation which sometimes occurs may be referable to pressure on the colon.

If a tumour is formed, the symptoms and physical signs are largely dependent upon its size. It is frequently lobulated or irregular in outline, dull on percussion, and fluctuation may sometimes be detected. It may interfere with the work of the lungs and the heart: it often gives rise to constipation, and although, when small it may not cause pain, as it increases in size it may produce discomfort and sense of weight, or even pain of an agonising character, owing to distension. In somewhat exceptional cases the tumour may undergo sudden diminution in size, and this is mostly associated with an increased flow of urine of low specific gravity, and perhaps containing blood or pus.

If the disease is unilateral, and if this intermittent discharge does not occur, the urine presents no marked characteristics, hypertrophy of the opposite kidney sufficing for the eliminative needs.

Diagnosis.—When the hydro-nephritic distension is small and unilateral, it is frequently impossible to detect its existence, and one kidney may be completely destroyed without the production of any definite symptoms. When a tumour of palpable size has been recognised, if due to hydro-nephrosis, it must be diagnosed from one due to abscess forming in or round the kidney, from hydatid cyst, connected with the kidney or adjacent organs, and, when the accumulation is excessive, it may be mistaken for ascites or for an ovarian cyst. The conclusive diagnostic sign, the rapid diminution in the size of the tumour, with an increased flow of urine, does not often occur; hence, attention has to be directed to other diagnostic indications. With renal abscess the onset is more sudden, and it is attended with great pain, with some rise of temperature, and perhaps with rigors. With peri-nephritic abscess the tumour is not so definite nor so circumscribed, and there is usually some redness and œdema of the skin in the loin. Hydatid cysts of the kidney are not so common as hydro-nephrosis, and the history will often be of material assistance, since both conditions are, as a rule, secondary to pre-existing affections—hydatid of the kidney occurs after hydatid of the liver, hydro-nephrosis after some cause leading to obstruction to the outflow of urine from the bladder or from the ureter.

Abdominal surgery has made such strides, owing to the work of Sir Spencer Wells, Lord Lister, and others, that operations for the relief of abdominal tumours are probably undertaken at a much earlier stage than formerly, and it is now comparatively rare for ovarian tumours or hydro-nephritic tumours to be allowed to increase in size until the diagnosis is difficult. It must be remembered that it is only when such tumours are of great size that they may cause hesitation or confusion. Increased confidence in the safety and beneficial results of operation leads patients to come under observation at an earlier date, when there is but little question about the diagnosis. Still, it is an interesting fact that many cases have been recorded where the surgical treatment of ovarian tumour has been employed for cases which proved to be hydro-nephritic or renal cysts. Ordinarily the distinction may be made by attention to the history of symptoms referable to the urinary organs, to the direction of growth, to the position of the colon, and to the results of vaginal and rectal examination.

A hydro-nephritic cyst is more fixed, and the colon commonly passes in front of it, and may be detected by a resonant note on percussion; it may also sometimes be felt between the cyst and the abdominal wall. From vaginal and bimanual examination, the absence of fixation of the uterus or of ovarian or tubal changes may be recognised, and, in addition, this examination, or examination from the rectum, may serve to detect the existence of some cause of obstruction at the lower end of the ureter. When the walls of a hydro-nephritic cyst are very thin, and when much fluid is present, it may be difficult to diagnose from ascites until a small quantity of fluid has been withdrawn for examination.

Prognosis.—The prognosis is, of necessity, very uncertain, since, although in many cases, where the disease is supposed to be unilateral, the opposite kidney performs the full eliminative work, while the affected kidney undergoes increasing destruction of renal tissue, yet, unfortunately, many cases have been recorded in which the opposite kidney has been completely atrophied, owing to the presence of a calculus, and in one such case death from anuria followed the removal of the hydro-nephritic tumour.

The prognosis may, in some cases, depend upon the nature of the obstruction and the possibility of its removal. When, in spite of the pressure of a hydro-nephritic tumour of moderate size, there is no apparent diminution in the nitrogenous excretion, and when the tumour does not materially vary, and does not interfere with the work of other organs, life may be almost indefinitely prolonged, for it is essentially in these three ways that the tumour endangers life. Diminution of urea and uric acid generally indicates that, although one tumour only may be perceptible, both kidneys are seriously affected. Great increase in size may lead to spontaneous rupture into the peritoneum, and, in addition, it may embarrass the freedom of respiration and circulation, or may cause troublesome constipation. When dependent upon stricture, enlarged prostate, or other conditions involving operative measures, additional risks are incurred from the tendency to suppurative nephritis.

When the size of the tumour is subject to sudden reductions the outlook is somewhat more favourable, since the fluid may possibly disappear and never re-accumulate.

Treatment.—Apart from the adoption of surgical measures, these cases offer very little scope for treatment. Gentle massage of the abdomen, with a lubricating ointment, has, in some few instances, led to a subsidence of the tumour. Such treatment may, however, be impracticable, owing to the degree of distension, or to the increase of pain which it induces. Under such circumstances, although anodynes may give temporary relief, they must be used with caution, from the dread of interference with the nitrogenous elimination, and, at best, they are only palliatives. The adoption of surgical interference must be discussed, and paracentesis is generally performed. The fluid frequently re-accumulates, and the operation has to be repeated at intervals. It is sometimes considered advisable to make a permanent opening in the loin, through which the fluid may drain. If the fluid thus passed contains very little nitrogenous waste, while the urine continues to be excreted in normal quantity and of normal composition, the question of removal of the affected kidney may be discussed, but, in the absence of proof that the opposite kidney is functionally active, there is considerable risk in the removal of a hydro-nephritic tumour. On such procedures, however, the reader is referred to surgical text-books, in which the matter is treated in detail.

2. CONSECUTIVE RENAL CIRRHOSIS.—This condition is essentially due to obstruction to the free outflow of urine, and therefore, to some extent, the clinical features resemble those of hydro-nephrosis and of suppurative nephritis. It has been

described under the name of 'Consecutive Bright's Disease' and 'Consecutive Nephritis,' and in some surgical manuals descriptions of 'acute and sub-acute interstitial nephritis' to a great extent correspond with the symptoms, the etiology and pathology which are generally ascribed to consecutive renal cirrhosis. Since, in the main, this disease depends upon the same etiological factors as hydro-nephrosis, and since its progress may be suddenly interrupted by suppurative nephritis, the three conditions may be found together in varying degrees, though consecutive renal cirrhosis is perhaps somewhat more frequently connected with hydro-nephrosis than with suppurative forms of nephritis. Yet, in spite of the frequency with which this condition follows hydro-nephrosis, it may occasionally be found when the pelvis of the kidney does not appear to have suffered from any urinary obstruction.

Etiology.—Consecutive renal cirrhosis may originate in any of the diseases which cause hydro-nephrosis, but it is, perhaps, more prone to occur when the cause leads to chronic partial obstruction, rather than to sudden and complete arrest of the flow of urine. Independently, at any rate, of the formation of a tumour by distension of the renal pelvis, it is certainly likely to occur with such chronic partial obstruction as may result from stricture, from enlargement of the prostate, from vesical calculus, or from tumours within the bladder, and even in the latter case when only one ureter may be obstructed. It is also an occasional consequence of pyelitis and of obstruction of the ureter by the gradual development of tubercular growths, as in a case I recorded in the *Path. Soc. Trans.*, vol. xliii. p. 91, 1892.

Morbid anatomy.—When the onset of consecutive renal cirrhosis is relatively sudden, the kidneys may be somewhat larger than usual, of a soft consistence, and mottled with red and white patches. When it is the result of more gradual changes, one or both kidneys may be smaller than normal; or, when the obstruction has affected one ureter only, one kidney may be much enlarged, while the other is much reduced in size; and even when the condition results from affections of the urethra it is rare to find that both organs show the same degree of change. The surface of the kidney may be smooth or granular, and it is sometimes marked by deep puckered cicatrices. The capsule is thickened, and adherent not only to the underlying renal, but also to the surrounding adipose, tissue. The kidneys are tough and hard, and of a dull white or yellow colour; the thickness of the cortex is much reduced, but in some parts it may be of almost normal thickness. In fact, the general characters correspond closely with those of ordinary renal cirrhosis, and the same resemblance is also found upon microscopic examination. Numerous leucocytes are accumulated in different parts of the cortex, particularly round the Malpighian capsules and between the tubes. The renal epithelium is swollen and granular, and extravasation of blood may be found both within the tubes and in the inter-tubular tissue. The development of nuclei in the glomeruli, the gradual atrophy of the capillary loops, the abnormal thickness of the capsules, with increased formation of fibrous tissue—all these changes agree, in the main, with those of renal cirrhosis.

When associated with hydro-nephrosis, an early change is seen in the tubes of the flattened pyramids, these tubes being contorted by wave-like curves. At later stages, the renal tissue undergoes considerable atrophy, until it may only be represented by a sac or shell of firm fibrous tissue devoid of glandular structure.

Symptoms.—The development of this disease is as a rule extremely slow, and it is not marked by characteristic symptoms. The changes in the urine are often accompanied by pyelitis or cystitis. When free from such association, the urine does not always contain either albumin or casts, though sometimes a variable amount of albumin may be found, together with a few hyaline casts. The quantity is generally rather excessive, and the specific gravity low. The excretion of urea may be slightly reduced, but this diminution often appears to correspond with diminished appetite and digestive power.

In acute or sub-acute cases there is slight hectic temperature, an evening rise to 100°, or even 102°, with a normal or subnormal morning temperature: when resulting from the passage of a catheter, or from other surgical operation, the onset may be marked by a distinct rigor or by a succession of chills. With chronic cases of obstruction, these initial symptoms are absent, or they are so slight as to escape observation, and the first symptoms to attract attention are an increasing languor, weakness, and loss of flesh. The sense of weakness may be greater towards the evening, when there is a slight rise of temperature, and it is then associated with a marked distaste for food, great thirst, and some nausea, or even vomiting. The tongue may be but little altered, though more commonly it is covered with a thick white fur, and sometimes it may even be dry and brown. Although constipation may be present, more particularly with some forms of hydro-nephrosis, there is usually, in this respect, but little departure from the normal habit of the individual. The skin is frequently moist and clammy, but with a rise of temperature it may become dry and pungent, or, on the contrary, profuse diaphoresis may occur. In addition to the sense of languor and weakness above mentioned, there is generally little mental change; patients may be placid and satisfied with their progress, or, on the other hand, the languor may be accompanied by much drowsiness.

The end sometimes results from increasing weakness and exhaustion; sometimes from suppuration of the kidney, with more or less delirium and coma; sometimes from an intercurrent acute disease, or from gradually increasing stupor and uræmia. Under surgical treatment for the relief of obstruction it is by no means uncommon for great improvement in the general condition to result, even when the symptoms have been of an alarming nature; but, although this improvement may be of long duration, and the patients may, in all respects, appear to be well, the renal affection is permanent, and, at a later date, it is to be feared that all the previous symptoms may be repeated, either from an aggravation of the original cause of obstruction, or from fresh need for instrumental interference.

Diagnosis.—The diagnosis, which, in cases of chronic obstruction, is exceedingly uncertain, is largely based upon the previous history. The condition may be suspected when, after long-standing obstruction, there is progressive emaciation, together with anorexia, slight hectic fever, drowsiness, and thirst. When, with these symptoms, the amount of urine is rather excessive, of low specific gravity, and with little or no albumin, the diagnosis is rendered more certain.

With more acute cases, greater difficulty is experienced, since the symptoms are, to a great extent, obscured by those of the original malady. When an operation upon some part of the urinary passages has been performed recently, or when the patient is suffering from cystitis, an accurate diagnosis may be almost impossible, since many of the symptoms so strongly resemble those of acute or chronic pyæmia, septicæmia or septic peritonitis.

Prognosis.—In spite of the occasional marked improvement after surgical treatment, the ultimate prognosis is almost invariably bad. The immediate danger is estimated by the severity of the symptoms and by the extent to which the cause of obstruction is within the scope of treatment. It is necessarily more grave when the consecutive renal cirrhosis is superadded to an existing cystitis or pyelitis, since it then frequently undergoes suppurative changes.

Treatment.—Apart from the surgical relief of any cause of obstruction, cases of consecutive renal cirrhosis afford, as a rule, little scope for treatment, and even if any operative measures are employed they entail much anxiety, especially when the temperature is oscillating. Benefit may sometimes be obtained from the use of fairly large doses of quinine, and, if there is much pain, morphine or opium may be tentatively employed. In many cases, however, the treatment is almost limited to hygienic measures. The diet has to be regulated, and given in a form which is both nutritious and easily digested; stimulants are forbidden, or, in those cases where there is great weakness and anorexia, small quantities may be administered if they appear to improve appetite and digestion; muscular exertion and mental worry should be avoided; patients should be protected from the risks of sudden changes of temperature; and, if the disease is in an advanced stage, they must be kept in bed.

Consecutive renal cirrhosis is, however, one of the diseases which it is possible to prevent. The causes are so well recognised, and frequently so well within reach of gentle treatment, that prophylactic measures should be adopted before there is any reason to believe that the kidney has become the subject of consecutive renal cirrhosis.

3. SUPPURATIVE NEPHRITIS.—Under the term suppurative nephritis many affections of the kidney may be grouped which are secondary to disease in other parts of the body. Suppurative nephritis is far more commonly under the observation of the surgeon than of the physician, since the conditions which give rise to it are, in the majority of cases, of a surgical nature, and, moreover, the symptoms attributable to suppurative nephritis are very frequently vague in their indications, or at least occupy a subordinate position, the greater share of attention and of treatment being claimed by the primary affection. This form of nephritis is that to which the name 'surgical kidney' has been applied, and it is described in detail in most surgical works. Other terms which have been applied to this condition are those of 'ascending nephritis' and 'renal abscess.'

Etiology.—In many cases the starting point of suppurative nephritis lies in some obstruction in the urinary passages, and this obstruction may frequently be associated with a local inflammatory process, the result of surgical interference and subsequent purulent infection. Sometimes purulent nephritis results from the irritation produced by a calculus, sometimes it is due to stricture of the urethra, or to prostatic enlargement which has required the use of catheters. Sometimes it appears to be consecutive to injuries of the spine or diseases of the spinal cord, which have given rise to cystitis. It may occasionally follow from infection due to purulent accumulations in the neighbourhood of the kidney, as, for example, abscess in the liver or spleen, or caries. It may also occur as a sequel to pyosalpinx, to inflammatory diseases of the uterus or ovaries, or to tubercular affection either of the bladder, or ureters, or even of the kidney itself. When the tuberculosis affects the ureter, undoubtedly the suppurative nephritis is due largely to the obstruction to the outflow of urine.

Suppurative nephritis may also occur as part of a general infective process, as in connection with ulcerative endocarditis, or with pyæmic and septic conditions. In these cases the purulent collections in the kidney may attain vast proportions, though frequently they may be small and multiple.

From a consideration of the above causes of suppurative nephritis, it will be readily understood that this affection is more commonly seen amongst males than females, and also that it is of relatively greater frequency after middle age.

Morbid anatomy.—The size of the kidney varies considerably, both according to the size and the number of purulent deposits. Usually the kidney is larger than normal; the capsule is somewhat more adherent, especially if the purulent collections are numerous and situated near the surface of the kidney, and under these conditions the capsule is also thickened. The surface is, as a rule, granular and of a dull red or purple tint, though occasionally it may be more pale than usual. Sometimes, on section, the affected areas are indicated only by numerous small grey or red patches of minute size, these patches being frequently surrounded by a zone of hyperæmia. They are most numerous in the cortical portion of the kidney, though occasionally they may extend to the medulla. In the cortical area these spots may be somewhat wedge-formed, with the apex pointing towards the pelvis of the kidney, but more commonly they are rounded. In the medullary area linear hæmorrhages may often be seen. Sometimes the process may be limited to one kidney, while the other appears to be normal; but, as a rule, the disease is more extensive on the one side, though the other kidney also shows signs of infection. Frequently, the pelvis of the kidney is dilated, and its mucous membrane congested. On microscopical examination the minute spots are found to contain colonies of micrococci, which are usually grouped in the neighbourhood of the Malpighian corpuscles. The condition of the glomeruli varies in different parts of the kidney, and also according to the stage of the disease. Mostly, the nuclei in the glomeruli are increased in number; sometimes the tufts show signs of lardaceous degeneration, but, as in other forms of lardaceous disease, some of the glomeruli appear to escape infection altogether. The space between the glomeruli and the capsule is sometimes entirely obliterated by extravasated blood, and blood may also be occasionally found in the lumen of the tubules. Frequently, the arteries are obstructed by minute emboli, and the capillaries may be also distended with blood, especially those in the neighbourhood of the small purulent deposits. When the disease is of long duration, the arteries may undergo degenerative changes, the muscular coats being hypertrophied, while the inner coat indicates the presence of endarteritis obliterans. The changes in the tubules are by no means constant in their nature: sometimes the epithelium in the convoluted tubules may show signs of proliferation, and the lumen of the tubule may be filled with white corpuscles. Similar collections of leucocytes may be found in the straight tubules, and these occasionally lead to detachment of the epithelial cells. Frequently, the whole of the kidney is hyperæmic, and the distinction between the cortex and the medulla is obscured. As the abscesses enlarge great destruction of renal tissue may occur; adjacent purulent collections appear sometimes to have fused, sometimes the suppuration is so great that very little true renal tissue can be found. The purulent collection may even extend to adjacent organs, and may lead to the formation of peri-nephritic abscesses, or indeed of fistulæ, which may point in the lumbar region or in the front of the abdomen. Cases have often been mentioned of extension to the liver, or of perforation of the colon, the small intestine, or even of the lung. Reference has already been made to the lardaceous changes which affect the blood vessels; Fürbringer states that he has seen bilateral lardaceous degeneration, even when suppurative nephritis had only attacked one side.

Symptoms, course, and diagnosis.—So far as these cases come under medical observation, it must be admitted that while the development of numerous minute abscesses may be sometimes suspected, it is frequently extremely difficult, if not impossible, to be certain of their existence. In pyæmic cases, or in ulcerative endocarditis, the formation of minute abscesses may be sometimes suggested by indefinite symptoms pointing to renal trouble; far more commonly these minute purulent collections are found as revelations of the *post-mortem* examination. The pyæmic abscesses are mostly of greater size, but, unless they cause alteration in the nature of the urine, their presence may be unsuspected. They appear to form fairly rapidly, without definite local symptoms; very often, even when symptoms are present, they may be obscured by the primary affection, or may be attributed to the primary affection rather than to any change in the structure of the kidney.

The points to which attention should be directed are those

which are commonly associated with the formation of pus in other parts, but it must be distinctly understood that these indications are frequently but of a slight nature as regards suppurative nephritis. Alterations in temperature may occur suddenly, and may even be associated with attacks of rigors, but these changes are so frequently met with in connection with traumatic conditions that it is impossible to lay very much stress upon them as indications of suppurative nephritis. In the early stages the patients may vomit frequently. Pain is very variable in its occurrence; indeed many patients never make any complaint referable to the kidney. When pain occurs, it is mostly severe, and resembles that ordinarily attributed to the passage of a renal calculus. It starts in the lumbar region, and radiates thence towards the testicles or towards the thigh, and the pain is frequently relieved by absolute rest, while it is excited and rendered more severe by movement, or by examination of the abdominal wall. The pain may be so great that it will frequently disturb the sleep, and it may induce the patient to keep the thigh flexed upon the body, very much in the position of the limb in mild cases of hip disease. Since the pain is so often absent, it cannot be held to be of any very great diagnostic value, although, when other symptoms point towards suppurative nephritis, its presence will afford valuable aid to diagnosis.

The nature of the urine depends largely upon the cause which is giving rise to the suppurative nephritis. When it is the sequel to cystitis or to lesions in the ureter, the urine usually shows shreds of pus and flocculent débris, and in all respects its characters point to the primary disease rather than to changes affecting the kidney. Even when albumin is present, it is extremely difficult to decide whether the albumin is more than can be accounted for by the pus in the urine. When suppurative nephritis occurs independently of catarrh of the urinary passages, small amounts of albumin may be detected even before the admixture of the pus coming from the kidney. This albuminuria is sometimes to be regarded as febrile; sometimes it appears to be the result of secondary nephritis, which so commonly is associated with suppurative nephritis. Unless the secondary nephritis reaches an advanced stage, the urine does not ordinarily undergo much alteration in volume or in specific gravity. Cases of suppression have, however, been described, but it appears probable that these cases only arise when suppurative changes are proceeding in one kidney, while the other has been already destroyed by previous disease. Sometimes, without any particular warning, large quantities of pus make their appearance in the urine, and this occurrence is generally indicative of the discharge of an abscess into the pelvis of the kidney. The sudden appearance of pus in any quantity is frequently the earliest certain sign of suppurative nephritis, and the diagnosis is rendered more probable by the rapidity with which, as far as appearances go, the urine may regain its normal condition. Even when the urine looks normal, however, small amounts of pus may frequently be found by chemical tests, or leucocytes may be discovered by microscopic examination. The microscope may also reveal the presence of casts and of renal epithelium, indicative of degenerative changes in addition to suppurative nephritis. Fragments of renal tissue have sometimes been found in the débris of deposit in such cases; these fragments may consist of loops of capillaries from the glomeruli, or occasionally, though rarely, of portions of the renal tubules. The transition of these cases to the more advanced stages, in which the kidney becomes so much increased in size as to form a renal tumour, is one which is mainly dependent upon obstruction to the outflow of pus from the substance of the kidney. The renal tumour may then develop to an enormous extent, and the kidney may become sacculated by the accumulation of pus within the pelvis of the kidney, and by its pressure upon the pyramids.

Paralytic affections have been described in connection with suppurative nephritis. The forms of paralysis which are most likely to occur are those affecting the lower extremities and involving both the motor and sensory tract. Paraplegic affections in many cases stand in the position of cause rather than of result. It is scarcely necessary to mention here the frequency with which affections of the spinal cord lead to loss of control over the bladder, to cystitis, and then to suppurative nephritis; on the other hand, however, there appears to be good reason for believing that the nerve affection sometimes follows the renal affection, and in such cases the trouble seems to have started from the bladder, and to have given rise to an ascending neuritis.

The subsequent course of any case depends largely upon the direction in which the purulent discharge occurs. The prognosis is somewhat more hopeful when the abscess opens into the pelvis of the kidney; this may lead to an ammoniacal condition of the urine, but as the flow of pus gradually ceases the urine returns to its normal reaction. Sometimes the abscess burrows in new directions, and it may discharge itself through the intestine, through the liver into the bile ducts, or through the pleura into the lung. When the discharge occurs through the lung substance, the pus expectorated is peculiarly fœtid, and the patient rapidly becomes exhausted by the nausea and discomfort induced. Many cases of suppurative nephritis pass on by gradual stages to the development of lardaceous disease, and to a condition of extreme cachexia, which is associated with hectic rises of temperature. Sometimes the termination of the case is marked by typhoid symptoms, the tongue becoming dry and coated, the patient suffering from frequent diarrhœa, and, in addition, from low muttering delirium, alternating with headache and other symptoms of depression. These symptoms are sometimes referred to uræmia, and undoubtedly to a large extent they may imitate the symptoms commonly associated with chronic uræmia. From the frequency with which suppuration in the kidney is associated with ammoniacal decomposition in the urine, these typhoid symptoms have been referred to a form of ammoniacal poisoning. There is no doubt, however, that the typhoid condition above described may occur without any evidence of alkalinity of the urine, and it is therefore more probable that, like the symptoms of puerperal eclampsia, typhoid symptoms are to be referred to auto-intoxication, from the development and absorption of some toxic agent in the course of the suppuration.

Prognosis.—The prognosis of suppurative nephritis is to a large extent dependent upon its cause. When it is the result of pyæmia or septicæmia it adds largely to the risks of the primary disease; at the same time, when the collection of pus is freely discharged into the pelvis of the kidney, the prognosis, as already stated, becomes more favourable. The prognosis is also largely influenced by the degree of pyrexia which is associated with the suppurative process, and it is rendered more grave with attacks of diarrhœa, or with the development of typhoid symptoms.

Treatment.—The treatment of suppurative nephritis resolves itself into the treatment of the cause. When the abscess is consecutive to pyæmia or septicæmia, there is but little to be done in the way of affording relief. When it is due to some affection of the bladder or urethra, it is sometimes possible to allay irritation starting from these regions, and so to diminish the further extension of the disease in the kidney. This, however, can rarely be effected.

From what has already been said, it will be evident that the existence of suppurative nephritis can frequently only be suspected until the abscess has attained a fairly large size, and is already taking its own course of cure. When there are good grounds for thinking that the kidney is becoming involved, benefit sometimes results from measures calculated to reduce temperature or pain. The application of ice over the region of the kidney may give relief, and the same result may occasionally follow from the application of leeches over the loins, or from free cupping in the neighbourhood of the loin. When pus has been found in the water, and its origin from the kidney appears to be indubitable, it is necessary to maintain the strength of the patient by diet and by tonic forms of treatment. Occasionally, some improvement appears to follow the administration of sulphocarbolate of zinc or of sodium; more commonly, medicinal treatment appears to have no influence on the formation of pus. When pain is excessive, various anodynes may be employed, and the most valuable of these are the various salts of morphine. These must be administered frequently, in increasing doses. Occasionally relief is afforded by the local injection of morphine, even when the administration of this drug by the mouth gives but little relief to pain unless the dose is relatively large. The administration of opium in the form of suppositories, or its application in fomentations or poultices, may also give relief from pain. It is scarcely necessary to say that chloral, sulphonal, and other hypnotics are of very little value in these cases. As a whole, the treatment is largely confined to the treatment of symptoms as they arise, and to the administration of antipyretics and tonics, especially quinine, which, to a certain extent, reduces the hectic fever, and seems also to influence the formation of pus.

CHAPTER XV

URÆMIA

URÆMIA is a collective name used to describe various functional disorders of the central nervous system, also of the respiratory and digestive organs. It is met with in numerous kidney diseases (especially in nephritis connected with scarlet fever, the puerperal state, cholera, and also in chronic contracted disease of the kidney), in affections of the urinary organs with obstruction, and also in cases of liver complaint. The frequency of uræmia varies considerably under the influence of climate. Thus, in England, according to the observations made by Bright, Christison, and Gregory, about half the number of patients suffering from Bright's disease become uræmic, while in Germany and Holland, though the average barely reaches 25 per cent., yet Fürbringer states that in the medical wards of the Berlin Public Hospital about 100 nephritic patients are admitted per annum, and that about 50 show uræmic symptoms.

It is customary and convenient, to divide uræmic symptoms into two classes—acute and chronic.

Acute uræmia appears both in acute and chronic diseases of the kidney, and its most prominent features are convulsive seizures. These paroxysms may commence quite suddenly, with no warning indications, or more rarely they may be preceded for a few hours or days by various premonitory symptoms, the most marked of which are constant headache, mental apathy, drowsiness and vertigo; nausea, or even vomiting, may sometimes occur, while in some few cases there may be severe dyspnœa. Other less frequent premonitory signs are mentioned by Fagge, such as a strange, fixed expression of the face, dragging pains in the extremities, or a transient rigidity of the face, of the lower jaw, or of a limb. Amongst occasional premonitory symptoms Charcot includes tremors, similar to those of paralysis agitans.

The attack itself, whether it occurs as sequel to such symptoms, or suddenly and unexpectedly, in the midst of the habitual occupations, generally takes the form of convulsions of an epileptiform type. The patient becomes unconscious, and is seized with convulsions; sensibility and reflex actions are lessened, and frequently abolished. The spasms, which in slight cases usually confine themselves to passing contractions of the muscles of the face or of the extremities, become in serious cases more violent and general. In the very worst cases the whole body is shaken with violent convulsions, respiration falters and becomes stertorous, the pulse is small and very rapid, the face puffy and cyanotic; patients foam at the mouth and grind their teeth, while the fæces and the urine, if the latter is excreted at all, are passed involuntarily. Considerable retardation and irregularity of the pulse often set in previous to the attack, but during the paroxysms this characteristic is seldom observed. Rosenstein states that an abnormal hardness and tension of the pulse commonly precede the attacks.

During the uræmic attacks the temperature is generally low, and even sub-normal: it is only in exceptional cases that great rises of temperature have been noted. Sir William Roberts has recorded a case in which the temperature fell to 94·4°, and other observers have seen temperatures as low as 93·1°, 89·6°, and even 86·1°. These low temperatures are most often met with in nephritis consecutive to diseases of the urinary passages. They have also been said to be frequent when uræmia affects persons advanced in years, when it occurs in conjunction with exhausting conditions, such as vomiting, diarrhœa or hæmorrhages, or in connection with cancerous cachexia and marasmus.

In some cases of uræmia the temperature has been found to rise as high as 105·8° and 107·4°, but this sudden elevation has always been followed by a rapid fall. The reason of the increased temperature is not very obvious; it has been suggested that it may bear some relation to the intensity of the muscular spasms and jactitations.

Even during the convulsion the pupils usually retain their sensitiveness to light, but authorities are not agreed about their size. Fagge says they are more often contracted or normal, while Wagner states that they are generally dilated, seldom small: in my own experience they have not presented any material change with sufficient frequency to justify a general statement of any characteristic alteration.

The clonic spasms only last some minutes. When but one fit occurs the convulsions cease gradually, and the patient passes into a drowsy or comatose condition, from which he may sometimes be partially roused. It is probable that this state is due to the pernicious effect produced on the cortex cerebri by the deprivation of oxygen. After a time, varying sometimes from a quarter of an hour to several hours, the patient awakes as out of profound sleep. As a general rule, however, the attacks return after a few hours or days, with renewed vigour, the intervening stupor becomes more profound, and at last passes on to permanent coma, out of which it is impossible to rouse the patient. Death sometimes occurs during the comatose state, sometimes at the height of the paroxysm. Fagge mentions one case in which death ensued within seven minutes from the first uræmic symptoms.

The clonic convulsions may be unilateral, and may be preceded or replaced by tonic spasms, followed by contractions of long duration, 'tetanic uræmia,' and even by trismus and tetanus. Sometimes there may be no spasms, the acute uræmia appearing solely as coma, or as delirium, when the patient may scream and try to jump out of bed, &c.; on the other hand, uræmia may be observed without the slightest mental impairment. In very severe cases, the uræmic attack is sometimes accompanied or followed by some form of motor paralysis, especially hemiplegia, and this is usually unattended with any obvious cerebral lesion. The hemiplegia is frequently transient, and passes off within twenty-four hours. Generally it is incomplete: the reflexes are abolished or diminished, and the condition may be followed by contractures. Even when the face is affected, ptosis is exceptional, but conjugate deviation of the eyes has been observed. With right hemiplegia aphasia has been noted, usually hemianæsthesia is present, and the anæsthesia may affect the organs of special sense.

The occurrence of *bilateral amaurosis* is more frequent than the last mentioned disturbances, the ophthalmoscopic indications are generally negative, and the pupillary reflex is intact; the retina and the whole optic tract are therefore not affected. This attack of uræmic amaurosis, which may occur without any other symptoms, usually comes so suddenly that a patient whose vision was unimpaired before the uræmic attack may awake from the coma with total blindness. The loss of sight may sometimes be only partial, and it is usually transient, lasting only from twenty-four to thirty-six hours; recovery has, however, been known to occur even after seventeen days. Uræmia attacks the ear much less frequently, and the derangements, such as difficulty in hearing, complete deafness, singing in the ears, &c., generally come and go quickly. Uræmic deafness has been attributed to minute hæmorrhages in the cochlea, but it is far more probable that it depends upon some toxic influence upon the auditory centre.

Finally, acute uræmia may be unaccompanied by any cerebral symptom, and be manifested only by serious derangement of the respiratory or of the digestive system.

Before leaving acute uræmia, it may be indicated briefly that the symptoms produced by the toxic agent naturally fall into two classes—those due to paralytic affection of the brain and of some of the sensory centres, and those referable to irritation of the motor tract, leading to tonic and clonic convulsions and spasms.

Chronic uræmia.—Although some cerebral symptoms are generally present in chronic uræmia, they are mostly of a subordinate character as compared with the apparent disturbances of the respiratory and digestive organs. There are, however, good grounds for believing that, in all cases, the toxic influence is mainly, if not entirely, exerted on the central nervous system, even though the urgent symptoms may appear to be referable to some other part of the body. It will be convenient, therefore, to describe first those symptoms of chronic uræmia which are more obviously connected with the brain.

Chronic uræmia, so far as it affects the central nervous system, is often unrecognised in slight cases: it steals upon the patient generally in a most insidious manner, and does not usually leave him. There is frequent complaint of dull headache, which may affect the frontal region, or, more commonly, the occipital region ; the pain is sometimes more acute, and may be of a paroxysmal nature, resembling violent migraine. This symptom may be accompanied or replaced by giddiness and drowsiness, and by a marked condition of languor and inertia, affecting both mental and muscular work. In chronic uræmia these discomforts are peculiarly persistent ; there may be brief intermissions, but more commonly they continue, with but little variation, for weeks or even months. The appearance and the temperament meanwhile become profoundly affected ; the face is dull and expressionless, and the patient becomes self-centred and abstracted, taking but little notice of, or seeming indifferent to all that is occurring around him. As the lethargy increases, it may eventually lead to complete stupor, or even to deep coma, which is occasionally interrupted by attacks of delirium, or by severe convulsive seizures, analogous to those of acute uræmia. When coma intervenes, without the onset of convulsions, it may lead to symptoms which might be mistaken for those of an advanced stage of typhoid fever; the tongue becomes dry and brown, and sordes collect upon the teeth.

This description of uræmic cerebral symptoms would be incomplete without further reference to the psychical disturbances. The occurrence of mental derangements in the course of acute and chronic renal disease has been observed by various authors, and they are probably to be explained by the influence of the same toxic agencies concerned in the causation of other uræmic symptoms. Apart from the loss of consciousness, the prominent symptoms consist of hallucinations, terror, delusions of excessive persecution, and excessive motor irritability. The type of delirium is generally quiet, but exceptionally it may be furious. These attacks of mental disturbance, which only last a short time, are comparatively little known, since, in consequence of their transient character, they do not often come under the notice of the physician. Binswanger thinks that, in these cases, it must be admitted that renal disease exercises a decided influence on the formation of psychical symptoms ; and he considers this fact is proved by cases in which the mental disturbances began at the same time as the development of renal disease, and disappeared with the decrease of the same ; and he also thinks that this contention derives further support from those cases where, in the course of protracted renal disease, all exacerbations and remissions of the original disease keep pace with an increase or entire cessation of the symptoms of mental derangement. He gives the following details of a case which he observed during a period of several months. About a month after kidney disease manifested itself, the patient, fifty years of age, was seized with attacks of terror, headache, buzzing and vacuity in the head. Then insomnia, confusion, impossibility to concentrate thought, self-accusations, and fictitious ideas of crime set in. The albumin decreased when he was treated with opium and calomel, and the patient became quiet and mentally bright. Three months later, violent attacks of terror, with stupor, reappeared. Later on, the old complaint was made that the head was 'splitting,' &c. The same treatment was used, and again the patient became brighter and quieter. In the following months the condition varied, but the appearance and disappearance of albumin always coincided with the psychical symptoms. The patient subsequently recovered entirely.

Binswanger considers that the occurrence of decided mental disturbance in the course of renal disease is undoubtedly connected with the existence of an individual neuropathic predisposition.

Amongst other nervous symptoms, severe itching of the skin is very frequent, and often very severe. In old people it often takes the form of intense pruritus, which defies all local treatment. Even when patients are so far unconscious that it is impossible to rouse them, they may continue to rub or scratch themselves. Saundby mentions hyperæsthesia of the skin, with burning sensations. Skin eruptions of various kinds have been described in connection with advanced cases. Dr. Le Cronier Lancaster,[1] of Swansea, gave notes of eight cases, which, having had under observation, he considered to be of uræmic origin. The eruption, which occurred chiefly in cases of chronic interstitial nephritis, first appeared as maculæ or papulæ of a bright red colour upon the extensor surfaces of the hands, forearms and legs, and then rapidly spread over the whole body. In a few days one of three changes occurred in the rash.

[1] *Lancet*, November 21, 1891, p. 1169.

1. It gradually subsided with extreme desquamation, leaving the underlying skin brawny and thickened.

2. It became eczematous, with free exudation of a gummy fluid which dried and formed scabs and crusts.

3. In the severer cases, pustulation or even the formation of small abscesses followed the eczematous stage.

Severe itching usually accompanied all stages of the rash.

The eruption was generally of grave prognostic significance. In seven of the eight cases it was followed by death within five weeks of the first outbreak.

It must be observed, however, that rashes similar to those above described have been seen in cases of interstitial nephritis in which there were no other symptoms of uræmia, and that the uræmic nature has therefore been challenged. Rashes resembling those due to measles, erysipelas, and simple erythema have been described, as well as a form of moist dermatitis affecting the neck, arms, and legs, and an exfoliative dermatitis of general distribution. In advanced cases I have often seen numerous cutaneous hæmorrhages, resembling a purpuric rash, mainly confined to the legs and feet.

The forms and varieties of dyspnœa connected with chronic kidney affections have been already described in detail, under Renal Cirrhosis (see p. 195). It may therefore be sufficient to mention here that the only form to which the term uræmic dyspnœa can properly be applied, is that in which the attacks of dyspnœa come on in a paroxysmal form, like those due to spasmodic asthma. These attacks usually occur at night, the breathing becomes extremely rapid, and the dyspnœa is often mainly expiratory, though occasionally there may be much inspiratory difficulty. Leichtenstern considers uræmic dyspnœa to be most common in the uræmia of scarlet fever; when it occurs in chronic cases it arises usually when the primary disease is the result of alcoholism. It must be remembered that similar attacks of dyspnœa may result from gradual failure of the circulation, or from interference with the work of the lung owing to engorgement or to effusion into the pleural cavity; conditions not necessarily associated with uræmia.

Persistent hiccough is not uncommon in severe cases tending to a fatal termination. I have observed it for some days before death from renal cirrhosis, and I have also met with it in cases of extravasation of urine. Although, in my experience, this symptom generally occurs late, Wagner has mentioned one instance of chronic Bright's disease in which hiccough and slight œdema of the legs were the only obvious symptoms.

Full reference has already been made to the clinical aspect of the digestive symptoms due to chronic uræmia (see Cirrhosis of Kidney). Apart from the milder indications of dyspepsia, the vomiting of uræmia, which often ensues, is marked by its frequent occurrence in the early morning, before food has been taken. The vomited material often consists of mucous or serous fluid, which may either be acid or may have an alkaline reaction, and an ammoniacal odour. Urea has been discovered in the matters rejected, while the reaction has been attributed to the transformation of urea into carbonate of ammonium. This form of vomiting has been regarded as due to irritation of the stomach by urea or by carbonate of ammonium during the vicarious elimination of the urinary constituents, but in all probability the vomiting is of central origin, since when urea has been administered to animals with food, a distinct interval elapses before vomiting results, an interval sufficiently long to allow of the absorption of a toxic substance into the blood, and of its action upon the central nervous system. Although the vomiting must frequently be of uræmic origin, it is important to remember that genuine gastritis often accompanies chronic forms of kidney disease, and may produce symptoms closely resembling those of uræmia.

The connection of diarrhœa with uræmic vomiting is well recognised, but it is generally associated with more definite anatomical lesions; the mucous membrane may show the ordinary appearances of inflammation, while the condition sometimes resembles that of dysentery. Extensive ulcerations, or large leathery patches may at times be found, more particularly when the motions have contained much blood, mucus, or pus. In view of these definite pathological changes, it may be doubted whether the symptoms are strictly of uræmic origin.

The natural prophylaxis of acute uræmia.—In chronic forms of kidney disease, uræmic symptoms may be averted by various compensatory processes. There can be little doubt that the hypertrophy of the heart, which so largely influences the renal excretion, is to a great extent conservative, as we see by the frequent occurrence of uræmic symptoms with cardiac failure. Elimination is also favoured by an increased action of the skin; this is shown by the beneficial results of active diaphoretic measures, and by the detection of urea on the skin of uræmic patients. Fagge says that urea can only be detected on the skin shortly before death, and when the urine is almost completely suppressed. In describing the appearance of the skin under these circumstances, three similes have been employed: the face is said to have looked as though flour had been sprinkled over it, as though a lather of soap had been allowed to dry on the surface, or as though the beard were frosted. The stomach and intestine form additional channels of elimination; copious vomiting and profuse diarrhœa not only compensate for the diminished excretion of water by the kidney, but also supply an additional outlet for toxic materials which might otherwise produce more dangerous symptoms through their action on the central nervous system. There is also some reason for believing that similar excretion may be effected by means of the salivary glands and the bronchial glands.

Theories of uræmia.—From the foregoing account of the diversity of symptoms attributable to uræmia, it will be readily understood that the condition has been ascribed to an almost infinite variety of causes; of necessity these causes, in almost every case, turn upon some interference with the eliminative work of the kidney, by which one or more of the urinary constituents is retained within the system, and either exerts its toxic influence directly, or after undergoing some chemical change. The difficulty, that has been experienced in this connection, lies in the attempt to recognise one single theory as an explanation for all cases, an attempt which, in view of the great complexity of resulting symptoms, seems to be doomed to failure. Nevertheless, much good work has been performed with a view to the elucidation of uræmia, and although hitherto every theory has been found lacking in conviction and imperfect when applied to all cases, it is interesting to summarise the present position, and to give the various arguments which have been adduced for and against each particular theory.

As the most definite symptoms of acute and chronic uræmia are those connected with the nervous system, attention has largely been centred upon the various ways in which such symptoms might be explained upon theoretical grounds, or induced by experimental methods.

The theories may be broadly divided into two classes :—

1. Mechanical. 2. Chemical.

According to the first, some definite change affects the nerve centres, such as œdema, or minute hæmorrhages; on the other hand, the second group seeks to explain the symptoms upon the theory of the toxic influence produced by some constituent of the urine, or resulting from the action of some material which is formed by decomposition within the system. 1. *Mechanical.*— Traube thinks that the basis of uræmic symptoms is to be found in œdema of the brain, which, from its increased volume, induces anæmia. Two conditions predispose to œdema, the marked hydræmia and the increased arterial pressure. When there is also great hypertrophy of the ventricle, any slight cause may lead to an augmentation of blood pressure and thus favour serous transudation. Traube considers that the type of the uræmic attack is dependent upon the degree and localisation of the œdema in the brain; convulsions occur when the middle lobes are affected, coma when the œdema extends to the whole cerebrum. The following facts are in favour of Traube's theory :— (1) The frequency of cardiac hypertrophy and blood dilution in cases of uræmia. (2) The production of coma and spasms in dogs, by the injection of water into the carotid after ligature of the ureter and of one of the jugular veins. Against the theory it has been urged that the symptoms are only produced experimentally when enormous quantities of water have been injected, and that, even under such circumstances, the brain may present no indication of œdema. From the clinical side hypertrophy of the heart and hydræmia are not always accompaniments of uræmia, and *post-mortem* examination frequently fails to demonstrate œdema. It has further been argued that in those cases in which cerebral œdema has been met with, it may be the consequence of the convulsions, rather than their cause. In spite of these objections, Traube's theory of œdema in a modified form has found several adherents; thus Leichtenstern holds that in scarlet fever inflammatory œdematous conditions of the brain and its meninges co-operate with the action of some result of infection, and Rühle believes the attacks depend upon the admixture of a toxic substance formed in the blood with the dropsical fluid. It will be seen that these views link together the mechanical and the chemical theories. Numerous minute hæmorrhages have been found in various parts of the brain, but these are so rare and so uncertain, that they must be regarded as the result rather than the cause of the convulsive seizures.

2. *Chemical.*—The term 'uræmia' was first introduced with the idea that all the symptoms depended upon the non-elimination of urea, its circulation in the blood and its deposition in various parts of the body. It becomes important, therefore, to consider here the formation of urea in the body and the variations in the amount, both in health and in disease.

The amount of urea in the urine varies with the amount of proteid food which has been taken, the daily average being about 33 grams (500 grains). The percentage present varies, although generally it amounts to 2 per cent. The percentage is usually greatest some three hours after food has been taken, especially if the meal has been rich in proteids; but the percentage present does not necessarily indicate the percentage formed. When urea is excreted in quantity for any length of time, it is an indication of increased tissue metabolism. Conversely, diminished excretion of urea may result either from diminished metabolism, or from retention of urea within the body. An increase in the amount of urea formed may result from the administration of any of the following drugs : dilute sulphuric acid, potassium chloride, ammonium salts ; small doses of phosphorus, arsenic, antimony, codeine, or large doses of quinine. It may also follow from poisoning by phosphorus or arsenic. In the healthy condition it may also ensue after the application of cold to the skin, the use of hot baths, or it may be the result of excessive muscular work. An increase is also commonly noted with the onset of acute febrile diseases, also during the paroxysms of intermittent fever, and, as a general rule, with diabetes. A decrease in the quantity of urea formed may be associated with the administration of small doses of quinine, and it may occur during the decline of the fever in febrile diseases. A diminished quantity of urea is also noted in most chronic wasting diseases (anæmia, syphilis, phthisis, and dropsical affections); and towards the fatal termination of most diseases the quantity of urea may be reduced very considerably. In uræmia the excretion of urea may almost entirely be arrested; a decrease in the quantity of urea formed is also associated with diabetic coma and with all degenerative changes of the liver, especially with acute yellow atrophy. With regard to the formation and source of urea, it is clearly not formed in the kidneys, for it has been found in the blood and in the tissues after the kidneys have been extirpated; nor is it elaborated in the muscles, although possibly some intermediate change may be here effected. The liver is now regarded as the chief site of its formation; but perhaps the spleen, and the lymphatic and secreting glands, may contribute some share of the work. The hepatic origin of urea is supported by the changes which occur with diabetes, when there is active metabolism of the hepatic cells, and the formation of sugar is accompanied by a simultaneous increase of urea. This theory receives further support from the diminished formation of urea when the liver undergoes degenerative changes. It has been shown by Noel Paton that bile formation and urea formation bear a direct relationship to one another. It may further be mentioned that when there is excessive degeneration of the liver, as in acute yellow atrophy, the urine may contain little or no urea, its place being taken by leucin and tyrosin.

Although it must be admitted that urea is derived from the proteid constituents of the body, there is much uncertainty about the intermediate stages. Urea can be obtained artificially from creatin, and this has accordingly been thought by some to be an important intermediate product. Uric acid has also been regarded in the same light, but although urea can be obtained from uric acid, this view has not found general acceptance with physiologists. It is, perhaps, more probable that glycocin, leucin, and perhaps tyrosin are intermediate stages. It has been mentioned above that in acute yellow atrophy these substances are found in the urine when the amount of urea is much reduced. It is further known that when glycocin and leucin have been introduced into the bowel or into the circulation, the amount of urea is increased. It is, however, somewhat curious that when tyrosin is similarly introduced into the system there is no increased elimination of urea.

Leaving these physiological considerations and reverting to the theory that uræmia is caused by retention of urea, it has been urged in favour of this view that (1) the symptoms were most marked when the secretion of urine and elimination of urea were much reduced; (2) under such circumstances urea had been found in the blood; (3) when the excretion had been experimentally arrested by ligature of the renal arteries or the ureters by extirpation of the kidney, many of the ordinary symptoms, such as drowsiness, convulsions, vomiting and diarrhœa, were produced. Against this theory it must be admitted: (1) That all symptoms of uræmia may be absent in some cases of complete suppression which have lasted for many hours or even days, without being accompanied by vomiting or diarrhœa, through which vicarious elimination might have been effected. (2) That uræmic symptoms in their frequency and severity do not, clinically, exhibit any necessary relation to the quantity of urea excreted. (3) That occasionally no symptoms of uræmia may be present, even though large quantities of urea may be detected in the blood. (4) That when urea is given to animals with their food, no symptoms are produced so long as it can be freely excreted. (5) That frequently in dogs uræmic symptoms are not produced even by the injection of large quantities of urea into the circulation; by the extirpation of the kidneys, it has been possible to estimate the amount of urea retained within the system from the time of the operation until the time of death from uræmic symptoms, and it has been found that far larger quantities may sometimes be introduced directly into the blood without any resulting uræmia.

From calculation of the amount of sugar required to cause convulsions in animals, it would seem that for a man of eleven stones it would be equivalent to $1\frac{1}{2}$ lb. of urea, or rather more than twenty times the average daily excretion of urea from the body.[1] The amount of urea in the blood of the animals poisoned

[1] MM. Gréhaut and Quinquand, *Yearbook of Treatment*, 1885.

was as high as 0·6 per cent., whereas the amount found in the blood of patients dying from acute uræmia has rarely been noted above 0·28 per cent., while the general average may be put at 0·18 to 0·21 per cent. It is thus clear that the amount of urea [1] required experimentally to induce death by uræmic convulsions is far more than can possibly obtain under pathological conditions. Some observers maintain that if, in animals, the rapid elimination of urea is prevented by ligature of the ureters, death with uræmic symptoms occurs much more quickly than when the kidneys have been extirpated. These observations appear to show that the presence of urea is not the sole factor, but that some other deleterious material or substance is elaborated by the kidney; these experiments, however, have not been accepted universally.

As the result of much experimental work, Frerichs put forward the theory that the toxic agent is carbonate of ammonium, resulting from the decomposition of urea in the blood, owing to the presence of some ferment. It is well known that during the growth of an organised ferment, namely the torula or micrococcus ureæ, which readily occurs in stale urine, urea takes up water and is converted into ammonium carbonate, $CO\ N_2\ H_4 + 2\ H_2\ O = (N\ H_4)_2\ CO_3$. Frerichs' theory suggests that a similar chemical change occurs within the blood. The arguments in support of this theory are: (1) The comparative ease with which urea can be transformed into carbonate of ammonium; (2) the ammoniacal odour of the breath in cases of uræmia; (3) the detection of small quantities of carbonate of ammonium in the blood in some cases of puerperal eclampsia; (4) the symptoms similar to those of uræmia which are produced by the experimental injection of carbonate of ammonium; (5) the possible absorption of carbonate of ammonium resulting from decomposition of urea within the intestine or urinary passages. The objections to the theory are: (1) that the ammoniacal odour of the breath depends upon decomposition within the mouth; (2) that it occurs both in health and in sickness, and is not limited to disease of the kidneys; (3) that in uræmic persons this transformation of urea in the blood does not occur; (4) that the injection of urine which has undergone spontaneous

---

[1] MM. Gréhaut and Quinquand, *Yearbook of Treatment*, 1885.

decomposition is not followed by uræmic symptoms, which only result with the injection of urine made septic by infection.

The difficulties in the way of the full acceptance of either of the chemical theories above mentioned have led to other experiments with a view of determining whether the symptoms might not be due to some other constituent. Feltz and Ritter tested the effects produced by the intravenous injection of the various constituents of the urine, and concluded that the convulsions, coma, and death which ensued after the injection of fresh urine were attributable neither to increased pressure nor to the organic constituents, and that, of the inorganic constituents, the most powerfully toxic were the potassium salts. They found, in fact, that similar symptoms of uræmia were excited by injecting either fresh urine or salts of potassium dissolved in distilled water in the same proportions. An increase of salts of potassium has been found in the blood of uræmic animals, and also in the blood of patients with uræmia from scarlatinal nephritis. One observer is disposed to regard the retention of salts of potassium as one of the chief causes of the symptoms due to respiratory troubles, while another believes chlorate of potassium to be the principal cause of vomiting.

It has been observed clinically that there is often a marked diminution in the output of chlorides in cases of acute and chronic nephritis. Bohne[1] has found experimentally that the injection of concentrated solution of sodium chloride under the skin of the abdomen produced, even in small doses, more or less violent clonic and tonic spasms, alternating with a semicomatose condition as in uræmia. In one case in which uræmia had preceded death, the possibility of the influence of retention of chlorides in the causation of uræmic symptoms was further supported by the analysis of the liver, in which a marked excess of chlorides was found to be present. The possibility is thus suggested that the diminution of chlorides in the urine during life might be due to their retention in the liver. On the other hand, it has been asserted that, after temporary compression of the renal artery in animals, the chlorides were rather increased than diminished, while there

[1] *Fortschr. der Medicin*, February 1897.

was notable diminution of some of the other solids, affecting mainly phosphates and potassium compounds. In partial opposition to the theory of auto-intoxication by the potassium salts, it has been stated that, in two cases of puerperal eclampsia, the proportion found in the blood fell below the normal amount; it must be remembered, however, that in very many clinical features eclampsia differs from uræmia.

Symptoms resembling those of uræmia have been produced by irritation of the cortex cerebri by creatin, creatinin, leucin, and tyrosin, and Sir William Roberts regards uræmia as the result of the accumulation of these or similar substances in the blood—that is to say, of products intermediate between urea (or uric acid) and the albuminous substances from which it originates. Bouchard at one time thought that some of the toxic properties of the urine resided in the colouring matters, since urine filtered through animal charcoal was found to be less toxic than unfiltered urine. Subsequently he developed his well-known theory of auto-intoxication, according to which the human body manufactures poisons which are only prevented from destroying life by their rapid elimination; the kidneys excrete toxic substances such as urea, potassium carbonate, &c., while the intestine removes compounds of potassium and ammonium. If these substances are retained in the body, they are said to produce symptoms of uræmia as soon as the 'urotoxic co-efficient' is attained (Fürbringer).

In connection both with Frerichs' theory of the production of uræmia by decomposition of urea into carbonate of ammonium, and also with that of Treilz and Jaksch that the carbonate of ammonium was not formed in the blood, but was absorbed from the stomach or intestine, where urea had first been vicariously excreted, and subsequently decomposed, it is extremely interesting to compare the clinical frequency of uræmic symptoms in cases marked by constipation, and the readiness with which they may often be alleviated by the administration of hydragogue purgatives. The use of these drugs is often justified on the plea of favouring vicarious elimination of nitrogenous waste through the intestine, but it is an interesting question whether, in addition, if not in greater part, the improvement may not result from the removal of urea, which has already been accumulating and undergoing decomposition within the intestine. It has been supposed that in renal dropsy certain toxic alkaloids, or ptomaines, become stored up in the dropsical fluid in the serous cavities and cellular tissues of the body, and that they may, under certain conditions, especially when attempts are made to reduce the dropsy rapidly, be suddenly thrown into the circulation and thus induce convulsions and coma. Such symptoms are usually attributable to reabsorption of nitrogenous materials with the dropsical fluids; but Dr. William Carter, in his Bradshaw Lectures,[1] considers it highly improbable that dropsical fluids are toxic, since the quantity of urea and salts found in them is very small, even when the vomited matter contains much urea. He suggests that a factor, which may influence, if it does not cause some of the symptoms of uræmia, is to be found in the progressively diminished alkalinity, or perhaps actual acidity of the blood, which occurs in some cases, and in support of this contention he states that, although, under ordinary circumstances, subcutaneous effusions are alkaline or neutral, in Bright's disease they are frequently acid. He suggests that the slow, weak pulse, the low temperature and dilated pupils of uræmia may be due to the diminished alkalinity of the blood, combined with other causes.

From the above account, it will be seen that it is absolutely impossible to accept any single theory of explanation for all cases of uræmia. It is most probable that there are numerous causes that contribute to the result, and that individually they do not always bear the same relative importance; it is difficult to believe, for instance, that the symptoms of acute uræmia, which must depend upon a sudden intoxication, are due to the same causes which produce the indications of chronic uræmia. Doubtless, the definition of uræmia suggested by Dr. W. Carter may be accepted in its entirety: 'an altered condition of health caused by the accumulation within the body of poisonous products that should be eliminated by the kidneys.' This definition does not, however, limit the 'poisonous products' to any one substance, nor does it exclude the probability that in disease the 'poisonous products' may be formed in greater quantity, owing to some

[1] *British Medical Journal*, vol. ii., p. 468, 1888.

disturbance of the balance of the bodily functions. Cohnheim and Leyden make the interesting suggestion that sometimes, perhaps, the immediate cause of uræmic symptoms is the sudden failure of the heart to keep up an active circulation through the renal vessels; this is quite in accordance with clinical observations of cases of chronic contracted kidney, and it is further supported by the therapeutic results of the employment of cardiac tonics in conjunction with other measures. Still it is difficult to assume sudden cardiac failure for all cases, as, for example, in the acute uræmia of scarlatinal nephritis. In this connection, however, it is interesting to recall the remarks of Sir William Broadbent on the prognostic significance of a pulse of low tension (see p. 335).

Diagnosis.—There is no great difficulty in correctly estimating the nature of the symptoms of the acute form, and sometimes, also, of the chronic forms of uræmia, provided that the existence of kidney disease is recognised, either in consequence of alterations in the urine, or by the consecutive changes in the heart and pulse, or from the presence of general dropsy. The nature of the disease may, however, be more uncertain when, in the absence of any history, a patient is found in a comatose condition. Alteration in the position of the apex beat, accentuation of the sounds of the heart, and high tension of the pulse will afford valuable indications, and if urine, withdrawn by the catheter, is found to be albuminous, and to contain casts, there is fair presumption in favour of uræmia. An ammoniacal odour of the breath may occasionally be recognised, but this sign is frequently masked by the odour of alcohol, administered by some well-meaning bystander. In the absence of more certain indications it is, however, injudicious to assign such a case definitely to uræmia. Convulsions and coma are not uncommon amongst patients with nephritis, but they may result from cerebral lesions, cerebral hæmorrhage, or some form of meningitis, causes which are only indirectly connected with changes in the work of the kidney. The difficulties which may sometimes be encountered are well shown by a case mentioned by Fürbringer, in which the *post-mortem* examination disclosed tubercular meningitis together with genuine contracted kidney; as no vascular symptoms had been observed during life, it was impossible to decide upon the relative share of the two diseases in producing the fatal termination.

The recognition of any distinctly paralytic symptoms generally tells against a diagnosis of uræmia, even though uræmic convulsions may occasionally be more marked upon one side of the body than the other. Fürbringer states that, in his experience, with one exception, when patients with renal disease have had unilateral or central symptoms, the *post-mortem* has shown organic cerebral lesions, such as hæmorrhage, embolism, or softening of the brain. Alterations in the temperature of the body afford very little help to the diagnosis; in uræmia an increase of temperature is exceptional, while in apoplexy the temperature may be normal or sub-normal, though in cases of basal hæmorrhage it may be high.

The convulsive seizures of uræmia may at first be mistaken for hysterical or epileptic convulsions, but an examination of the urine and a consideration of the previous history (if obtainable) will remove all doubts in this connection. Uræmic coma also resembles the insensibility due to alcoholism, to opium poisoning, and to the more rare condition of diabetic coma; attention to the nature of the urine, to the pulse and the heart, mostly serves to indicate the true cause in such cases.

The diagnosis of the symptoms of chronic uræmia is often more uncertain, and it has frequently to be based upon the results of treatment. This is more particularly the case with the uræmic disturbances of circulation and respiration. The shortness of breath on exertion, the tendency to repeated recurrence of cough, and the occasional attacks of spasmodic dyspnœa can only be attributed to uræmia in the absence of physical signs of more definite cardiac or pulmonary affections; the frequency or persistent character of the attacks as well as their resistance to ordinary measures afford, however, some grounds for a provisional diagnosis. Similarly the dyspeptic symptoms, vomiting and diarrhœa, may be mistaken for the results of local lesions of the stomach or intestines; the absence of physical signs of tumours connected with the stomach, the sigmoid flexure, or the rectum, helps to differentiate uræmia from malignant diseases of these organs, although the general symptoms, especially the wasting, pallor, and weakness, somewhat resemble those which result from malignant growths. The headache of uræmia is to be recognised by its persistent character, and by frequently affecting the occipital region. The blindness and the occasional deafness are so commonly associated with convulsive seizures, and they develop so suddenly, that there is usually little room for doubt, especially when the urine is found to contain albumin; both of these symptoms, when due to uræmia, are also characterised by the rapidity with which improvement usually ensues. It need scarcely be said that in every case of doubt it is necessary not only to examine the water, which may or may not contain albumin, but to pay careful attention to the position of the apex beat, to the sounds of the heart, especially to those heard over the pulmonary valves, and to notice any alteration in the character of the pulse, as estimated from the sense of resistance and from a sphygmographic tracing. I have often been able, by means of the sphygmograph, to clear up the diagnosis of doubtful cases. It must be admitted, however, that frequently in chronic uræmia the symptoms so much resemble those due to other causes, that, in spite of the utmost care, it is necessary to await the results of treatment before expressing a definite opinion as to the nature of the case.

Prognosis.—As the symptoms of uræmia differ very widely, so their prognostic significance is very uncertain. Even convulsive seizures afford very doubtful grounds for a prognosis, since their importance varies so much in the different forms of kidney disease. Symptoms of acute uræmia always cause great anxiety; in rare cases patients may die owing to the severity of the first attack, or more often they may sink from exhaustion when the attacks are repeated at short intervals. In scarlatinal nephritis the prognosis is generally somewhat more hopeful than in acute nephritis, since the condition more frequently yields to treatment; in both the danger from uræmia is immediate rather than remote, and the prognosis depends upon the rapidity with which consciousness is regained and the extent to which the urine returns more nearly to the normal state. When convulsions occur in the course of chronic nephritis or of renal cirrhosis, they may either prove fatal in the first attack, or they indicate danger of a fatal termination within a few weeks or perhaps months; though in exceptional cases the end may be yet more remote. As in acute nephritis, a single attack affords no proof that the eliminative work of the kidney is irreparably impaired. Indications of greater danger are to be found in the prolonged stupor or coma which intervenes between the convulsions in chronic cases; when these symptoms supervene they almost invariably form the prelude to a fatal termination.

Symptoms of chronic uræmia, especially those connected with the respiratory and digestive symptoms, will always justify an unfavourable prognosis. The dangers of uræmic dyspnœa are sufficiently obvious, and vomiting and diarrhœa, as they tend to reduce the strength greatly, add very largely to the immediate risks. Other symptoms of chronic uræmia, such as giddiness, headache, and amaurosis, are of importance as indicating progressive stages of a chronic affection, but, unless they are associated with a rapid diminution of the amount of urine, they may persist for a great length of time, and even to a large extent improve under treatment; when, however, they are accompanied by a great reduction in the urine, it is to be feared that uræmic convulsions of a serious type may ensue.

Treatment.—The treatment of the various forms of uræmia has already been dealt with fully in connection with the different conditions under which they arise, hence it is unnecessary to devote further space to its consideration here. In any case, the treatment adopted must depend upon the form of uræmia, and it must be influenced by the associated symptoms.

CHAPTER XVI

GENERAL DIAGNOSIS OF ALBUMINURIA

In some acute cases of Bright's disease, and sometimes in some of the chronic forms, there is but little difficulty with the diagnosis, but cases frequently arise, both in private practice and in connection with insurance work, in which the correct estimation of the significance of albumin may cause considerable trouble and anxiety. Sometimes the circumstances of the case make the appearance of albumin a surprise to the patient and to the medical man, while at others the albuminuria may serve to explain symptoms of an otherwise indefinite type.

The mere presence of albumin in the urine can be determined readily enough in most cases, and many of the tests ordinarily employed furnish a rough idea of the amount or percentage of albumin being passed by the patient at the time of examination. It is unnecessary here to repeat directions for detecting the presence of albumin; but it may be helpful to point out that the test which gives the most satisfactory results is the contact method, in which a layer of urine is floated above a layer of nitric acid in the test tube. This test is so readily performed, and it detects such very minute proportions of albumin, that I prefer it to all other tests that have been suggested. Traces of albumin which are only deposited after a length of time, if the specimen has been acidified and then boiled, can frequently be easily recognised by the contact method. When the contact test is performed with caution, there should be no fear either of dissolving the ring of albumin through excess of acid, or of not precipitating albumin when the urine is alkaline. It sometimes happens that, when dealing with alkaline urine, the addition of even from three to seven drops of nitric acid after boiling may fail to cause immediate coagulation of the albumin, when, in the same case, addition of still more acid will cause precipitation, and testing by the contact method will at once give a satisfactory line of opacity. I venture to lay some stress upon these points, because the test of boiling, with the addition of acid, is frequently recommended as being all-sufficient, especially for insurance purposes, and I am convinced that in urine of low specific gravity small traces of albumin may be entirely overlooked by employing this test only; while, in some forms of chronic kidney disease, if the urine is highly alkaline, even large quantities of albumin may not be precipitated without the addition of a very much larger proportion of nitric acid than is ordinarily recommended. For example, I have recently tested a specimen in which, after boiling, fully ten drops of strong nitric acid were required to produce a satisfactory cloud of albumin, while boiling after the addition of two or three drops caused practically no increase of opacity.

When attempting to estimate the diagnostic importance of albumin a large number of factors have to be taken into consideration. Most important of all, perhaps, is the condition under which the albuminuria has been detected—whether it has been found as an accident in the course of an examination for life insurance, when the proposer may have had no idea that there was anything whatever the matter with him, or whether, on the other hand, the albuminuria has been found in connection with other symptoms of ill-health which have led to the examination of the urine. In the first case, the presence of albumin may probably surprise the examiner as well as the proposer, and, under such circumstances, it is occasionally extremely difficult to persuade the proposer that there is anything amiss with him, and that he should take further advice. In the second case, the task of the physician is not so difficult, since, as the patient is already troubled about his condition, it is to a certain extent a satisfaction, if even a gloomy one, to have the cause definitely decided. In dealing with the first class of cases, those presenting themselves for life assurance, the diagnosis is often to a certain extent obscure. The physician is practically wholly in the dark as to exact information respecting the proposer's habits, his occupation, and his previous history. It is true that questions upon all these points are asked, and that information is sought from many different sources, but it is almost too much to expect such questions to be answered with the same degree of fulness and accuracy that attends the account given by a patient to a physician from whom he wishes for advice on a question of health. Still, much may be gained by examining the urine at varying intervals, and, if possible, at different hours of the day. My large experience in connection with insurance work indicates that there are a great number of cases in which the presence of small traces of albumin has been determined by chemical tests in the total absence of any history pointing specially to kidney disease, and also in the relative absence of other symptoms indicative of chronic renal affection. This, I take it, is an important fact, since the tendency of those who consider albuminuria mainly from the point of view of the consulting room is to lay perhaps too much stress upon the importance of this symptom, and to take too gloomy a view of the diagnosis and prognosis.

There are numerous physical signs which are ordinarily described as being associated with chronic albuminuria, such as alterations affecting the pulse and the position of the apex beat of the heart; but I am convinced that these physical signs are wanting in a large majority of cases of albuminuria, such as those met with among young men from eighteen to twenty-five years of age. Perhaps some slight increase of tension may be noted after the albuminuria has been discovered, where, in the absence of albuminuria, the pulse might probably have been regarded as normal. Whenever it is possible, I make it a rule, in cases of slight albuminuria occurring in young men, to get into communication with the medical attendant, and to endeavour to enlist his sympathetic co-operation in clearing up the causation of the albuminuria. The medical attendant can frequently ascertain the relation which the albuminuria bears to varying conditions of diet, of rest, and of work, and he may thus afford very material assistance in proving whether the albuminuria is persistent or intermittent. The first question that naturally arises in any case is whether this drain from the system is constant or occasional, whether it occurs at all hours of the day or only at certain times, or whether it is dependent in any way upon the habits or mode of life of the proposer. I have, on more than one occasion, been able to draw the attention of a medical attendant to an intermittent albuminuria which had previously been overlooked. In one case, where there seemed to be some slight conflict of opinion as to the existence of albumin in the water, I was able, by asking the medical attendant to examine the water at midday, to convince him that albumin was then present, although it had been absent in the specimens that he had previously examined in the early morning and in the late afternoon. Whenever any conflict of opinion arises, I have always found it best to state in detail the tests I have employed with the results that have been obtained, and to endeavour to get the medical attendant to examine under precisely similar conditions; and I give this word of warning advisedly, as differences of opinion are by no means uncommon. If it is possible, with the aid of the medical attendant, to form a diagnosis, cases of slight albuminuria occurring amongst young men may be dealt with, a small extra premium being charged on account of this abnormality, even though the case must be attributed to one or other of the functional forms of albuminuria.

When dealing with proposers of greater age, it is necessary to be very much more cautious before expressing an opinion that the case is one of functional or intermittent albuminuria, and as the precautions which have to be adopted are practically the same, whether the case is one which is being examined for life insurance, or whether it is a patient who requires advice, it will be advisable to discuss the diagnostic indications more fully. In the following pages I have considered the importance of each of the diagnostic features separately, but it must be understood that in practice all these diagnostic features must be estimated collectively, and due weight assigned to the indications derived from each.

With regard to the persistency of the albuminuria, it is necessary to test the water from day to day, and at different hours of the day, and if albumin is found to be present, there is a strong presumption in favour of the existence of some form of Bright's disease amongst patients of middle age, though the possibility of a functional albuminuria must be kept in mind when dealing with younger patients. Reference has already been made to the relatively high specific gravity in most cases of functional albuminuria. Those which are commonly met with amongst young men, candidates for appointments, or for life assurance, usually have a specific gravity of 1025 or upwards; while on the other hand, in a large number of cases where the amount of albumin is the same, there is fair presumptive evidence of chronic renal affection if the specific gravity is low, unless the low specific gravity is found to be an exceptional occurrence. Small traces of albumin may sometimes be due to congestion of the kidney from heart disease, or from some other cause leading to venous engorgement, such as advanced chronic bronchitis or emphysema; sometimes a faint cloud may be found in connection with febrile conditions such as pneumonia. The albuminuria of heart disease or of some other form of engorgement generally varies considerably from day to day, and the urine is mostly scanty, of high colour and high specific gravity. It is always necessary not only to ascertain that the albumin is permanent, but also that the amount is fairly constant; it must be remembered, however, that in many cases of renal cirrhosis the amount of albumin varies from day to day, and that the urine may sometimes be entirely free from albumin. In such patients, however, the pale straw colour is characteristic, while the specific gravity will also furnish material assistance. In broad terms it may be stated that in most cases of transient, temporary, or functional albuminuria the quantity of albumin is relatively small, while the colour and the specific gravity may be normal or above normal. If the albumin is found to be intermittent instead of persistent, no certainty of diagnosis can be founded upon this fact alone, since in some cases of chronic interstitial nephritis the urine that is passed on first rising, before food has been taken, may be found wholly free from albumin. In the same way, as indications for diagnosis, little reliance can be placed upon variations in the appearance of albumin with alterations of external temperature. In many cases of functional albuminuria it is true that this symptom occurs only with sudden changes of temperature, either with a sudden access of warm weather or with sudden exposure to cold; yet in the early stages of some cases of mild nephritis the same holds good. The influence of cold and damp in increasing the amount of albumin in cases of scarlatinal nephritis has been already referred to. It is occasionally necessary to ascertain whether recumbency in bed has any influence on the presence of albumin in the water. This question has been repeatedly dealt with by Dr. Clement Dukes of Rugby, and he seems to have satisfactorily proved that there is good reason for believing that mere alterations of posture may, by altering the strain upon the capillaries of the Malpighian tufts, cause albuminuria in otherwise healthy individuals. Sir J. Grainger Stewart holds that when albumin is found to occur distinctly, and only after meals, with changes of attitude, with more or less severe muscular exertion, under mental excitement, or after cold bathing, it may be concluded with certainty that the process is functional. Although this generalisation will hold good for a large number of cases, it must be admitted that numerous other factors require to be considered before adopting such a sanguine view.

In any case of doubt, it is always advisable to determine accurately the total quantity of water passed in the twenty-four hours. In cases of functional albuminuria there is mostly no alteration in the quantity, while in those chronic forms of kidney disease which are most likely to cause hesitation in forming a diagnosis the quantity is usually somewhat greater or even considerably in excess of the normal amount, and the patient is disturbed by nocturnal micturition. Patients with lardaceous disease mostly pass a large quantity of pale urine; and the amount and the appearance vary according to the stage of the complaint. In the early stages of renal cirrhosis the amount may be but little in excess of the normal quantity, while the colour is almost invariably lighter than usual; in the later stages, when attacks of acute engorgement may occur, the alterations in quantity and in appearance usually leave no doubt about the nature of the case.

It is very rare for febrile albuminuria to cause any difficulty of diagnosis. The existence of high temperature, and the co-existence of scanty, high-coloured water depositing urates, usually afford fair presumptive evidence for considering that the albuminuria is merely symptomatic of the febrile state. This presumption is further strengthened if the amount of albumin appears to bear any relation to the height of fever. Sometimes it increases as the temperature rises, and diminishes with defervescence of the temperature. If after complete defervescence albumin is still found to be present, it may cause further anxiety, unless the case is one of diphtheria. I have elsewhere (*Diphtheria and Antoxin*, p. 54) stated that small traces of albumin occurring in the course of diphtheria seem to result from the diphtheritic poison rather than from organic renal changes, or from the febrile state. The microscopic examination of the sediment sometimes affords valuable assistance to the diagnosis, the detection of crystals of oxalates, or of knife-rest crystals of phosphates, will often favour a diagnosis of accidental or functional albuminuria; while, on the other hand, the presence of casts requires very careful consideration, since they may be found in some cases of functional albuminuria, while they are frequently absent in cases of chronic cirrhosis. Hyaline casts of small size are those which are of least diagnostic importance, while granular and oily casts, especially if fairly numerous and of large size, may indicate chronic nephritis or cirrhosis. In every case, it is necessary to consider associated symptoms and physical signs affecting the circulatory system, the respiratory, the digestive, and the nervous system. Chronic forms of nephritis and of cirrhosis are, as a rule, attended by changes in the sounds of the heart and in the position of the apex beat. The area of cardiac dulness is generally increased, the apex beat displaced outwards, the extent of displacement frequently bearing distinct relation to the duration of the albuminuria. Both sounds of the heart are modified; the first sound, though it may be somewhat faint and indistinct, is mostly booming, exaggerated, and somewhat prolonged in character. The second sound at the base is accentuated and sometimes reduplicated, but both the sounds and the hypertrophy are essentially indicative of chronic nephritis and of cirrhosis. When met with in connection with lardaceous disease of the kidney, these changes in the position of the apex beat and in the sounds of the heart are indicative of an associated nephritis.

It is unnecessary, here, to enter into theoretical considerations regarding the changes occurring in the arteries; it will be sufficient to indicate that the pulse of chronic nephritis and of renal cirrhosis shows an increase of arterial tension, being wiry

FIG. 1. From a lad, aet. 16, with history of paroxysmal haemoglobinuria, probably of malarial origin. Sp. gr. varied from 1025 to 1030, small amount of albumin present. The cardiac sounds were normal.

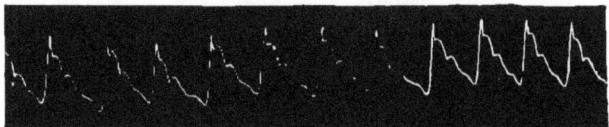

FIG. 2. From a woman, aet. 63, with congestive albuminuria, the result of ascites. Sp. gr. varied from 1008 to 1012, the amount of albumin was small and variable. The cardiac sounds were not reduplicated nor accentuated.

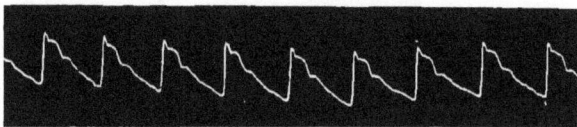

FIG. 3. From a man, aet. 54, with congestive albuminuria, due to organic disease of aortic and mitral valves. Sp. gr. was 1007; sugar was present in addition to a small amount of albumin.

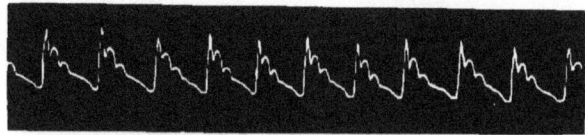

FIG. 4. From a man, aet. 55, with renal cirrhosis associated with chronic dyspepsia, headache and retinal changes. Sp. gr. 1020, amount of albumin small. Well marked pericardial frictions were present when this tracing was taken.

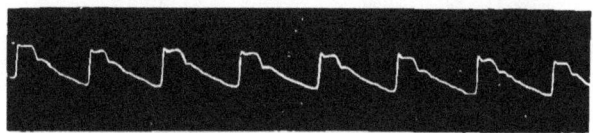

FIG. 5. From a woman, aet. 50, with renal cirrhosis, and chronic dyspepsia, much headache and vertigo. Amount of albumin small. No retinal changes. Cardiac sounds accentuated and apex beat displaced. This tracing exhibits the broad apex of renal cirrhosis, masked in Fig. 4 by co-existing pericarditis.

N. Tirard, Del.   Mintern Bros., imp.

or resisting, while the pulse tracing is generally characterised by the breadth of the tidal wave and the distance of the dicrotic notch from the up-stroke.

Information of any value is very rarely to be obtained from consideration of changes in the respiratory system. If the patient is the subject of chronic bronchitis or of chronic emphysema, very little value may attach to the discovery of small traces of albumin in the water, especially if these traces are found to vary with the condition of the lung; but it is sometimes difficult in asthmatic conditions to determine whether the albuminuria exists as a consequence or as a cause. When it occurs as the cause, the urine is mostly of low specific gravity and of a pale colour, and the quantity of albumin is generally small. On the other hand, if the albuminuria is the result of lung engorgement, the urine is more commonly reduced in quantity and its colour is deepened.

In every case of albuminuria the condition of the alimentary system deserves attention. This naturally follows from what has been said of the dietetic forms of albuminuria, and the inability of some patients to take certain articles of diet without the production of albumin in the water. On the other hand, digestive disturbances may arise in connection with chronic kidney disease, either as a sequel to the disease, or as a determining cause of chronic nephritis. The chronic dyspepsia of advanced cirrhosis is well recognised, and is marked by its intractable character, by occasional tendency to vomiting, and sometimes by sudden and severe diarrhœa.

Valuable assistance may sometimes be obtained from consideration of the nature of the skin either in respect of colour or of structure. The anæmia of chronic nephritis contrasts markedly with the reddish brown tinge which is so often seen in cases of renal cirrhosis. The anæmia of nephritis is often associated with dropsical effusions, and although these may rarely affect the face, it is by no means unusual to find slight conditions of œdema about the eyelids, and to notice that the features appear larger than usual. The frequency with which this anæmia is associated with the watery appearance of the conjunctiva in cases of chronic nephritis, must be familiar to every practitioner; on the other hand, the reddish discoloration of renal cirrhosis may depend upon the causation of the cirrhosis, especially in alcoholic individuals, in whom the engorgement of capillaries over the cheeks will frequently furnish grounds for further inquiries. Subcutaneous hæmorrhages may sometimes be found over the lower extremities, but these are comparatively rare except in advanced stages of the disease, in which there is no question of the diagnosis. Thus, also, with the conditions of extreme œdema affecting the lower extremities; when occurring in the chronic form, these are more frequently to be met with in connection with chronic nephritis than with renal cirrhosis. In some cases of doubt, the appearance of syphilitic eruptions or cicatrices or of syphilitic discolorations of the skin may indicate the probability of lardaceous disease; the diagnosis of lardaceous disease is, however, more frequently to be founded upon other and more certain signs.

In connection with renal cirrhosis the skin is sometimes abnormally dry, and it may be extremely difficult to provoke diaphoresis. This difficulty, which may arise in the course of treatment of uræmic symptoms, frequently serves to render the diagnosis of cirrhotic changes more certain. A similar condition is occasionally met with in those cases of slight albuminuria, which are so frequently associated with advanced diabetes. The dryness of the skin in such cases is dependent, however, upon the diabetic changes and upon the drain of water from the system by the kidney, rather than due to any primary renal change. This dry, parchment-like feeling of the skin is, however, noteworthy, although in such cases it is rare for the albuminuria to need special treatment, and certainly it is not necessary to attempt to provoke diaphoresis as in chronic uræmia.

From consideration of the changes in connection with the nervous system, many indications may be obtained. Reference has already been made to the frequency of persistent headache with chronic nephritis and with renal cirrhosis. These headaches are not always very severe, though usually they are of a violent neuralgic type. The headaches of chronic uræmia must be carefully differentiated from those which so often occur with functional albuminuria, as, for example, in the albuminuria of adolescence. In the latter condition, the headache is of a dull nature and associated with intense lassitude and disinclination to work. With functional albuminuria, also, it may be noted that the headache is not nearly so persistent, that it is more marked in the early part of the day, and that it often passes off with exercise or with food. Sometimes in cases of paroxysmal hæmaturia or hæmoglobinuria complaint of lassitude is made, and this occasionally precedes as well as follows the paroxysmal attack.

Renal disease may frequently be first inferred from affections of vision. A gradual development of dimness of vision may lead to an ophthalmoscopic examination and to the recognition of albuminuric retinitis, or of distinct hæmorrhages into the substance of the retina. Sometimes, however, the dimness of vision may occur almost suddenly after a fit, which may be called by the patient a 'fainting fit,' or a 'convulsive seizure,' and in such cases it is uncommon to find much evidence of retinal change. The uræmic seizures which lead to such disturbances of vision may be so slight as to escape treatment. Thus, at the present time, I have under my care a lady, aged forty-nine, who eleven months ago, after feeling giddy and sleepy for some days, lost consciousness for half an hour or so. She thought very little of this occurrence, merely noting that she was free from headache after the first fit. Five months later she again lost consciousness, and then noted that on recovery her tongue was very sore. At this time her sight failed in a marked way, and she sought advice on account of her vision, rather than on account of the fits from which she had suffered. When the eyes were examined, they were found in an advanced stage of albuminuric retinitis, and the water was extremely pale and contained a fair amount of albumin; the accentuation of the second sound of the heart over the aortic valves, and the nature of the pulse, left no doubt that she was the subject of chronic nephritis. In this case, further investigation appeared to indicate that the nephritis had its origin in repeated attacks of indigestion from which she had suffered for many years. In any case in which 'fainting fits' occur, the possibility of uræmic origin should be considered and the water should be examined. These fits of nerve disturbance are more prone to ensue in connection with renal cirrhosis than with any other form of renal change, with the exception perhaps of acute nephritis, especially when a sequel to scarlet fever. In the latter case, however, the diagnosis has probably been made long before the uræmic seizures have occurred.

Paralytic affections are also more frequently met with in the course of renal cirrhosis, as in this disease the pulse tension is greatest and the degeneration of arteries more likely to be advanced. The nature of the paralysis and the mode of the onset must, however, be considered rather closely; it is probably the result of renal cirrhosis when occurring somewhat gradually; if there is a history of syphilis it may be indicative of lardaceous disease with consecutive changes in the cerebral vessels. The diagnosis of lardaceous disease may also be favoured by the existence of any cause of chronic suppuration, such as necrosis or caries, or by a marked history of chronic syphilis.

Although it is fairly easy, by a consideration of all the surrounding circumstances and by careful and repeated examination of the water, to determine the probable cause of the albuminuria and the probable nature of the renal change, if any, it must be admitted that it is frequently difficult to determine accurately the stage of the disease, and more particularly in connection with chronic nephritis. Sometimes intercurrent attacks of hæmaturia may cause an unguarded diagnosis to be made, and this has necessarily to be altered when the subacute attack passes off, and the urine is found to remain albuminous and pale. It is still more difficult, in cases of chronic nephritis, to decide whether the kidney is in the enlarged condition, or whether it has undergone secondary contraction. These refinements, however, are of relatively little importance, compared with the question of determining the extent to which the kidney is still capable of performing eliminative work. So long as the kidney retains the power of removing sufficient nitrogenous waste from the system, and so long as it is able to remove sufficient water, the absolute anatomical change is of minor importance. These indications show that, although some parts of the kidney may be in an advanced stage of disease, other parts still retain the power of doing good work.

CHAPTER XVII

GENERAL PROGNOSIS OF ALBUMINURIA

THE concluding words of the last chapter form a certain indication of the prognosis in most forms of chronic kidney disease; it is necessary, however, in forming a prognosis to consider other questions besides the mere elimination of nitrogenous waste. One point of importance is the extent of the loss of albumin. The amount of loss in very many cases of Bright's disease, notably in cases of renal cirrhosis, is so small that it is almost a negligeable quantity—in fact, the drain of albumin is so readily repaired by the consumption of food, that the patient, in many cases, appears to suffer very little from this cause. In all probability this is the explanation of the prolonged vitality in some well-recognised cases of chronic nephritis. The prognosis becomes more grave as the loss of albumin increases. Sir J. Grainger Stewart, in considering this question, mentions one patient in whom he estimated that one-twelfth part of the elaborated albumin of the blood passed away daily, and he naturally concludes that a loss to this extent must considerably affect the prognosis. Such a large drain of albumin sometimes occurs in connection with chronic nephritis, and it is always associated with great reduction of weight and loss of strength—in fact, the weakness from which these patients suffer is undoubtedly due largely to the drain of formed albumin from the blood. In endeavouring to shape a prognosis from the amount of albuminous loss, careful attention must be paid to the frequency with which the amount of albumin will vary from day to day; hence it is naturally unwise to form an opinion on the examination of a single specimen of water; on the other hand, when the water is repeatedly examined and the percentage of albumin is always found to be very great, the prognosis becomes the more gloomy.

In speaking of the prognosis of cases of Bright's disease, it is important to divide them into two classes according to the early or late termination of the case. Thus many patients with acute Bright's disease may have a favourable early prognosis and a doubtful late prognosis—that is to say, that the immediate prognosis so far as danger is concerned may be favourable, while there may be great danger of the establishment of chronic nephritis, in which case the remote prognosis would necessarily be more hopeless. A very large number of patients with simple acute nephritis recover provided that the disease is uncomplicated—in fact, the prognosis of a case of acute nephritis depends very largely upon the complications and sequelæ. It is rarely possible, however, to speak very definitely about the prognosis in any particular case, since severe symptoms may occur and yet, in spite of these, the patient may recover. Notwithstanding the dangers of uræmia, of convulsive seizures, of diminution or even suppression of urine, there may be complete recovery, but, on the other hand, some cases which have apparently been doing well may occasionally take a bad turn and prove rapidly fatal, either from uræmia or from some secondary inflammatory change affecting the pericardium, the pleura, or the lung. On the whole, however, apart from accidents of this nature, the prognosis of acute nephritis, although full of anxiety, is comparatively hopeful, but it must be remembered that very many cases starting in an acute attack pass on gradually to chronic nephritis; hence the daily loss of albumin must be watched with anxiety, particularly when the improvement appears to have become stationary.

Puerperal nephritis stands somewhat by itself so far as prognosis is concerned. The prognosis, as a whole, is generally favourable, and the estimation of danger is to be formed from the severity and the frequency of the eclamptic seizures. The marked improvement which so often occurs after delivery has already been described in treating this condition, and reference has been made to the danger which arises from the severity of repeated convulsions. Should the patient recover from the albuminuria of pregnancy, there is very little risk of ultimate nephritis, and there is fair ground for believing that in many cases in which the albuminuria persists after delivery the patient has been previously the subject of chronic nephritis.

Independently of puerperal nephritis, the prognosis, in cases of chronic nephritis, is largely dependent upon the extent to which the drain of albumin interferes with the general health, and also upon the extent to which dropsical changes have progressed. So long as the nutrition of the patient can be kept up, so that the albuminous loss from the kidney is less than the daily gain of albumin from food, these patients may continue in a fair state of vitality for many years. They are, however, subject to dangers from exposure and from secondary complications affecting either the heart or the lung. Frequently, after exposure, the prognosis may suddenly be rendered more grave by the occurrence of a sub-acute attack of nephritis which may lead on to considerable dropsical effusion of a relatively intractable nature. These patients sometimes incur greater risks through the failure of the circulatory system, which consequently induces a rapid increase of dropsical effusion and of fluid in the pleura or peritoneum. When these effusions have occurred the prognosis necessarily becomes extremely grave, and the time limit is to be estimated by the nature of the pulse, by the quantity of urine eliminated, and by the extent to which breathing is interfered with. There appears to be fair reason, however, for believing that many cases which are generally considered to be chronic nephritis may undergo gradual improvement provided that the patients can be kept under favourable conditions, and some authors even consider that a cure is possible.

Similar uncertainty attends the prognosis of chronic cirrhosis, the danger of which is to be estimated by the extent to which the different physiological systems are involved. Very frequently cases of cirrhosis, if recognised at an early stage, may be put under favourable conditions as to climate, food, and work, and the termination may be almost indefinitely postponed. In forming a prognosis it therefore becomes important to consider the extent to which the circumstances of the individual permit of needful alterations of work or of climate, by means of which fair prospect of the postponement of danger may be afforded. The prognosis is, however, not so favourable as with chronic nephritis, inasmuch as, although it is possible to diminish the risks, it is not possible to cure the disease. In spite of all that can be done, patients with cirrhosis of the kidney pursue a downward course, and, sooner or later, suffer from cardiac failure or from uræmic symptoms. As in cases of chronic nephritis, sub-acute attacks are relatively frequent, and the danger to the patient is increased during each such attack, since for the time there is, as a rule, great diminution in the eliminative work of the kidney.

In speaking of lardaceous disease, the hopelessness of the condition, in the large majority of cases, has already been mentioned. The prognosis naturally depends upon the extent to which it is possible to remove the condition which favours lardaceous changes. Many cases have been reported in which, by satisfactory surgical treatment, the loss of albumin became ultimately arrested. It must be remembered, however, that the prognosis depends far more upon the primary disease than upon the kidney affection, and that the loss of albumin is of importance mainly as indicating that lardaceous changes are probably occurring in other organs as well as in the kidney. In these cases there is relatively little risk of danger due to interference with the eliminative work of the kidney.

In the same way febrile albuminuria is, in itself, of relatively little importance; it is not likely to produce symptoms directly referable to interference with the work of the kidney, but it is a frequent and important indication of the extent to which the febrile condition has modified the nutrition and the circulation of the individual. With some febrile conditions, as, for example, with diphtheria, the albuminuria may be taken to indicate the degree of gravity of the case, since in its most extreme forms it occurs more commonly in cases of a severe type, and in such the prognosis may be rendered more grave as the albuminuria is greater in amount; but, on the other hand, in the large majority of cases of diphtheria, small traces of albumin will be found without any additional risk being involved from this cause. In some febrile conditions the occurrence of albuminuria undoubtedly adds to the gravity of the case, since it is a source of loss, as well as an indication of the severity of the attack.

The prognosis in any particular case is largely influenced by the nature of the pulse and of the heart's action. It is less serious when the pulse is of good quality and regular than when the pulse is feeble and irregular, or intermittent. It is interesting in this connection to note that Sir William Broadbent [1] a few years ago drew attention to the prognostic significance of a low blood pressure in acute kidney disease. He had previously seen two cases where low tension was associated with symptoms indicating cirrhosis of the kidney, and in both the disease proved fatal with unusual rapidity. In dealing with cases of acute renal dropsy, Sir William Broadbent looks upon the supervention of a certain degree of high tension as an indication of favourable prognosis. He considers that the imperfect development of blood pressure is not to be regarded as the cause of slow recovery or of the complications observed in the course of the disease, but that it reveals the constitutional weakness to which these complications are to be attributed, and it probably shows that the patient 'is made of poor stuff.' From his observations, Sir William Broadbent concludes that in the treatment of acute renal disease it is desirable to raise the tone of the circulation as a help towards recovery. Further, it is of interest, in connection with these remarks, to recall the frequency with which irregularity of the heart's action and weakness of the pulse form indications of danger in chronic nephritis and renal cirrhosis.

The forms of febrile albuminuria which are of the greatest importance are those in which the febrile condition is due to some septic process. The slighter forms of febrile albuminuria which are met with so commonly in connection with pneumonia, or with typhoid fever, appear in themselves to furnish little or no indication of prognostic value. When albuminuria occurs with advanced forms of heart disease, it is indicative of failure of compensation and of backward engorgement and capillary stasis. In such cases the prognosis necessarily depends far more upon other conditions than upon the interference with the circulation in the kidney, although frequently the extent to which the treatment has succeeded may be gauged by the gradual improvement in the nature of the urine. Under appropriate measures, the amount of albuminuria diminishes in many cases concurrently with the diminution of œdema, and with the re-absorption of effusions from the various serous

[1] *Brit. Med. Journ.*, April 21, 1888.

cavities. When in spite of treatment the albumin continues in fairly large proportion, the aspect of the case becomes extremely grave, since it is an indication that the various organs are unable to cope with the work thrown upon them. In these cases, however, as in those of febrile albuminuria and lardaceous disease, the gravity of the prognosis depends upon the cause of the albuminuria rather than upon the extent of albuminous loss or of interference with eliminative work.

With regard to the various functional forms of albuminuria the prognosis is almost invariably good, provided that there is no doubt about the diagnosis. Although the forms of albuminuria described under the terms 'paroxysmal,' 'dietetic,' 'functional,' and so on, are certainly indications that the circulation through the kidney is to some extent faulty, it is very rarely that they give rise to permanent kidney trouble. In a large number of the cases of functional albuminuria, rest, treatment, and modification of habits are sufficient to remove the abnormality and to free the patient from the anxieties attendant upon albuminuria. In connection with dietetic albuminuria, in particular, the prognosis is undoubtedly favourable, if it can be proved that the rectification of some error of diet is accompanied by diminution in the amount of albuminuria. On this point it is possible to speak with considerable certainty, since I have had numerous cases, under prolonged observation, where careful attention to the digestive system and to the selection of dietary has led to the total disappearance of albumin.

The prognosis is good, also, in cases of albuminuria of adolescence. I have observed numbers of these cases where the alteration of habit and the cultivation of some form of athleticism have been followed by marked improvement and ultimately by disappearance of the albuminuria; but, on the other hand, it must be remembered that forms of dietetic albuminuria may, if neglected, lead to prolonged irritation of the kidney, and there is little doubt that in some cases renal cirrhosis has been set up by repeated attacks of indigestion. I am sure that it is a mistake to consider that the indigestion is the sequel in all attacks of indigestion associated with albuminuria; in many of them, I believe, it is to be regarded as the cause. Amongst other similar cases I have recently seen a lady in whom no other origin for renal cirrhosis could be traced. In her younger days she had bad bilious attacks; when between twenty-nine and thirty she had severe hæmatemesis, and from that time until middle age she complained every winter of bad attacks of indigestion, which sometimes extended over two or three months.

There is little that need be said of the prognostic indications of forms of albuminuria due to accidental causes—that is, to the addition of albumin or blood to the urine after it has left the kidney. In all such cases the prognosis must depend entirely upon the cause of the albuminuria or hæmaturia, as it is necessarily grave when the hæmaturia is the result of malignant disease in connection with the bladder, and more hopeful when it is due to some irritating cause, such as calculus, which can be removed. The prognostic indications being so extremely various, and dealing so largely with surgical questions, it is impossible to consider them in any detail in this work.

INDEX OF AUTHORS

ATKINS, 41
Atkinson, I. E., 139, 140
Aufrecht, 88
Auld, 144

BACELLI, 72
Bancroft, 80
Barber, 171
Bartels, 31, 34, 86, 216, 224, 247
Basham, 68, 90, 124
Beale, Lionel, 90
Berlioz, 7
Bernard, Claude, 37, 44, 47
Binswanger, 303, 304
Blackall, 2
Bohne, 313
Bouchard, 34, 225, 314
Boulby, 63
Bouvret, 221
Bowman, 5
Bright, R. D., 1, 2, 299
Broadbent, Sir W., 316, 335
Brunton, Lauder, 13
Bryant, 65
Byers, 224, 225

CAIGER, 116, 117, 119, 125, 132, 134
Carter, W., 220, 315
Charcot, 300
Christison, 2, 299
Clark, Sir A., 16, 47, 247, 258
Cohn, 223
Cohnheim, 34, 97, 315
Cornil, 188
Cotugno, 2

DALTON, 145
Danjoy, 35
Deahofe, 227

Dickinson, 101, 116, 127, 132, 183, 189
Dieulafoy, 193
Dobrowolsky, 237
Duckworth, Sir D., 124
Dujardin Beaumetz, 114
Dukes, Clement, 53, 55, 56, 325

EALES, Henry, 240
Eckstein, 42
Edlefsen, 32
Ehrhardt, 44
Ehrlich, 78
Esbach, 23

FAGGE, 34, 87, 97, 142, 181, 299, 301, 307
Falkenheim, 31
Favre, 44
Feltz, 313
Ferré, 234
Ferrier, 34
Finlayson, 87
Frauenhofer, 58
Frerichs, 91, 225, 312, 314
Friedländer, 118, 120
Fürbringer, 38, 39, 41, 43, 88, 91, 92, 118, 123, 147, 157, 161, 165, 174, 177, 185, 193, 201, 232, 246, 274, 293, 299, 314, 316, 317

GALLOIS, 114, 115
Gaucher, 114, 115
Gerhardt, 42
Goodhall, 42
Goodhart, 124
Gowers, Sir W., 238, 240
Gräfe, von, 129
Grainger Stewart, Sir T., 32, 37, 41, 46, 51, 90, 251, 325, 331

z 2

Greenfield, 97, 143, 250
Gregory, 299
Griswold, 32
Gull, Sir W., 33, 189
Gunn, Marcus, 238

HALLIBURTON, 10, 24
Harley, G., 75
Haug, 204
Hawkins, F., 208, 209, 210
Hay, Matthew, 172
Heidenhain, 5
Henle, 83
Henoch, 38, 94, 118, 124, 125, 126, 127, 128, 171
Hermann, 37
Heywood, C. F., 22
Hillier, 116
Holt, J. J., 257
Hoppe-Seyler, 6
Hufner, 5

JACOB, 185
Jaksch, von, 86, 185, 314
Johnson, Sir G., 1, 2, 50, 78, 89, 94, 108, 109, 110, 127, 141, 144, 164, 175, 183, 189, 196, 197, 203, 262

KANNENBERG, 40
Keen, 32
Klebs, 97
Klein, 97
Klemperer, 67
Knapp, 223

LANCASTER, le Cronier, 304
Lancereaux, 35
Landois, 201, 202
Langhans, 87, 122
Laschkewitsch, 37
Lecorché, 49, 196
Leech, 220
Leichtenstern, 117, 305, 309
Lepine, 78
Leube, 32, 53
Lewis, J. R., 80
Leyden, 42, 225, 315
Lister, Lord, 284
Litten, 237
Lomer, 243
Loomis, 176
Ludwig, 32, 37

MAC MUNN, 10, 24
Mackenzie, Stephen, 176

Mahomed, 98, 101, 117, 126, 132, 238
Manson, Patrick, 80
Meigs, 182
Miley, Miles, 242
Morris, Henry, 282, 291
Morton, Stanford, 239
Moxon, 52
Murchison, 39, 46

NAUWERCK, 122
Nettleship, 241
Newman, David, 60, 62
Nussbaum, 5

OBOLENSKY, 173
Oliver, 23
Ollivier, 35
Osler, 80, 81, 171

PARKES, 7
Patin, 34
Paton, Noel, 310
Paul, Constantin, 114
Pavy, 23, 51
Petersen, Oscar, 45, 46
Phillips, John, 236
Ponfick, 72, 77
Proben, 171, 172, 177
Purdy, 119, 134, 181, 208, 223, 229

RALFE, 93, 176
Ranvier, 188
Rayer, 2, 44, 223
Reese, D. M., 21
Rendall, Stanley, 46
Ribbert, 5, 46, 87, 88
Ringer, 113, 134, 162, 173
Ritter, 313
Roberts, Sir W., 16, 20, 21, 24, 52, 61, 68, 76, 77, 80, 86, 107, 110, 196, 230, 263, 274, 300, 314
Robinson, Beverley, 177
Rooke, Morley, 53
Rosenbach, 77, 78
Rosenstein, 230, 233, 300
Roy, 43
Rühle, 309

SAFT, 223, 225, 230
Saundby, 60, 62, 80, 87, 88, 196, 197, 220, 242, 304
Sawyer, 171

Schiff, 9
See, Germain, 35
Sehrwald, 84
Semmola, 141
Smith, Solomon, 220
Sutton, 189

TAYLOR, 124
Traube, 308
Treilz, 314
Turner, 116, 118, 119, 125

VAN DE VELDE, 225
Vierordt, 86
Vignerot, 94, 119

Virchow, 49
Vogel, 11

WAGNER, 117, 152, 301, 306
Wells, Sir Spencer, 284
Wells, W. C., 2
Wiedow, 227
Wittich, von, 5, 37
Wood, H. C., 113, 171

YVERT, 241
Yvon, 7

ZIEMSSEN, 157
Zweifel, 231, 233, 236

INDEX

The figures in heavy type indicate the pages where most detailed information is to be found.

ACIDITY OF URINE, 17, 110, 252
Acne rosacea, 205
Acupuncture, 112
Adolescent albuminuria, 50, 55, 328, 336
Age, influence of, in lardaceous disease, 247
    renal cirrhosis, 181, 210, 211
    scarlatinal nephritis, 118
Albumin, estimate of amount, 23
  tests for, 18
  various forms of, 23
Albuminuria, 25 ff
  associated with acute nephritis, 332
    acute rheumatism, 41
    acute tonsillitis, 40
    chicken pox, 40
    chronic bronchitis, 324, 326
    chronic nephritis, 154, 157, 158, 163, 165, 333
    concussion of the brain, 37
    congestion of the kidney, 267, 268, 269
    croupous pneumonia, 41
    delirium tremens, 37
    diabetes, 263, 328
    diphtheria, 38, 39, 326, 334
    eclampsia, 224, 230
    emphysema, 324, 326
    epilepsy, 37
    erysipelas, 41
    exposure to cold, 324, 333
    hæmatogenous causes, 33
    heart disease, 31, 324, 335
    lardaceous disease, 252, 253, 255, 258, 325
    malaria, 40, 41
    measles, 39
    mechanical causes, 30
    menstruation, 30
    muscular exercise, 32
    nerve lesion, 37
    pneumonia, 41, 324, 335
    pregnancy, 44
    purpura, 33
    purulent catarrh of the bladder, 29
    pus, 28, 29
    pyelitis, 29

344 ALBUMINURIA AND BRIGHT'S DISEASE

Albuminuria, associated with renal cirrhosis, 180, 181, 182, 183, 190, 192, 193, 206, 208, 210, 212, 214, 324, 325, 331, 333
    renal cirrhosis, consecutive, 288
    renal embolism, 33, 273
    scarlatinal nephritis, 38, 116, 130, 132, 324
    scurvy, 33
    small-pox, 39
    syphilis, 45
    tetanus, 37
    typhoid fever, 39, 335
    typhus fever, 39
    uræmia, 304, 316, 318
    whooping cough, 40
  classification of renal forms of, 26
  cyclic, 50, 51, 54, 192
  definition of, 25
  diagnosis, general, of, 320 ff
  diagnostic importance of, in life assurance, 321
  dietetic and digestive, 46, 89, 336
  diet influencing, 47, 49, 53, 234
  diphtheritic, 334
  drugs producing, 34, 35
  febrile, 37, 38, 42, 93, 106, 117, 120, 261, 294, 325, 334, 335
    symptoms of, 41
    theory of, 42
  functional, 50, 181, 210, 242, 323, 324, 325, 326, 328, 336
    prognosis of, 336
  gouty or lithæmic, 48 f
  influence of bathing on, 325
    cold on, 324
    food on, 325
    muscular exercise on, 325
    position on, 52, 325
  intermittent, 31, 36, 50, 181, 182, 183, 241, 322, 323, 324
  neurotic, 35–37
  of adolescence, 50, 55, 328, 336
  oxaluric, 47, 48, 52
  persistent, 52, 114, 322, 323
  physiological, 52, 55
  prognosis, general, of, 331 ff
  prostatic and spermatic, 29
  puerperal, 222 ff
  renal or true, 25, 30, 57
  renal, extra-, false or accidental, 25, 27, 57
  treatment of, 234
Albuminuric retinitis, 129, 231, 237 ff
    diagnostic importance of, 329
    statistics of, 243
    unilateral, 241
    with anæmia, 242
  chronic nephritis, 149, 151
  cirrhosis of the kidney, 203, 204
  diabetes, 263
  lardaceous disease, 211, 238
  puerperal nephritis, 231, 238, 243
  scarlatinal nephritis, 238
Alcohol, cause of chronic nephritis, 140
  renal cirrhosis, 328
  use of, 95, 165, 215, 221, 278, 290

INDEX

Alkaline tide, 16
Alkalinity of urine, 17, 110, 234, 296, 320
Amaurosis, uræmic, 103, 107, 129, 151, 171, 204, 211, 231, 301, 319
Ammonium sulphate test, 22
Anæmia, cause of retinitis, 242
    excretion of urea in, 310
    in chronic nephritis, 148, 153, 212, 327
        lardaceous disease, 254
        renal cirrhosis, 205, 219
Angina pectoris, 202
Aphasia, 129
Asthma. *See* Uræmic dyspnœa
Astringents, use of, 166, 215, 219, 259

BATHING, influence on albuminuria, 325
Baths, use of, 111, 112, 114, 134, 151, 168 ff, 174, 221, 235, 272, 279, 309
Bilharzia hæmatobia, 64
Biuret reaction, 23
Bladder, catarrh of, 29
    villous growth of, 66
Blood casts, 85, 88, 96, 124, 146, 156
Brain, experiments on, 37
Bright's disease, definition of, 1, 2
Brine, acidulated, test, 21
Bronchitis, chronic, cause of albuminuria, 324, 326
                          cyanotic induration, 264
    in puerperal nephritis, 236
    in renal cirrhosis, 190, 210

CALCULUS, renal, 276 ff.
    cause of congestion of the kidney, 261
                hæmaturia, 27, 61, 65, 68, 69, 276, 337
                hydro-nephrosis, 276, 278
                other renal complications, 276-278, 291
                pyelitis, 276, 278, 279
                renal cirrhosis, consecutive, 276
    description of, 276
    symptoms of, 277
    treatment of, 279
Cancer cells, 63
Cancer, cause of hæmaturia, 62, 63, 65
Cardiac dilatation and hypertrophy in acute nephritis, 181
                                        chronic nephritis, 149, 156
                                          scarlatinal nephritis, 127
Casts, 85 ff
    blood, 85, 88, 96, 124, 146, 156
    classification of, 85
    clinical significance of, 88, 90, 326
    epithelial, 85, 88, 96, 124, 146, 153, 233, 252, 261, 295
    granular and fatty, 86, 89, 90, 124, 146, 153, 228, 233, 326
    hard, waxy, 86, 89
    hyaline, 85, 88, 96, 106, 124, 146, 154, 193, 228, 233, 252, 261, 267, 288, 326
    metamorphosed, 85, 89
    origin of, 87
    size of, 86

Catarrh of bladder, 29
Cerebral anæmia and œdema, with puerperal nephritis, 227
    hæmorrhage, 180, 208, 209, 210
    tumour, cause of retinitis, 242
Cheyne-Stokes' respiration in renal cirrhosis, 196, 201
Chicken-pox, cause of acute nephritis, 94
    albuminuria, 40
Chlorate of potassium, toxic effect of, 71, 72, 133, 159
Chlorides, tests for, 8
Chloroform, use of, 236, 280
Cholera, cause of hæmaturia, 67
Chronic suppuration, cause of lardaceous disease, 211
Chyluria, 14, 79
    diagnosis of, 82
    drugs influencing, 82
    etiology of, 80, 82
    parasitic and non-parasitic, 79, 82
    symptoms of, 81
    treatment of, 82
Circulatory system in acute nephritis, 100
    chronic nephritis, 149, 333
    cyanotic induration, 266
    diagnostic importance of condition of, 326
    lardaceous disease, 254
    prognostic importance of condition of, 334
    puerperal nephritis, 229
    renal cirrhosis, 194
    scarlatinal nephritis, 126
Cirrhosis of the kidney, 180 ff
    associated with chronic bronchitis, 190, 210
        gout, 183, 211, 214
        hydrothorax, 205
        jaundice, 205
        lardaceous disease, 246, 260
        malaria, 186
        neuroses, 184
        pericarditis, 193, 206, 221
        pleurisy, 205
        pneumonia, 205, 210
    characteristics of, 180
    condition of the circulatory system in, 194, 202
        heart in, 189, 194, 202, 203, 206, 209, 210, 211, 326
        pulse in, 330, 335
        respiratory system in, 195
        skin in, 327, 328
        urine in, 180, 193, 195, 206
    course and duration of, 208
    diagnosis of, 154, 155, 210
    diet in, 215
    due to alcoholism, 328
        dyspepsia, 336
        habits, 184, 210, 211
        heredity, 180, 182, 210
        lead poisoning, 185, 211, 214
        syphilis, 214, 216
    etiology of, 180
    influence of age upon, 181, 210, 211
        climate upon, 185 f, 216

INDEX 347

Cirrhosis of the kidney, influence of drugs upon, 207, 214, 215, 216, 218, 219
    morbid anatomy of, 186 ff
    prognosis of, 213, 333
    retinal changes in, 203, 204
    symptoms of, **189** ff
        acne rosacea, 205
        albuminuria, 180, 181, 182, 183, 190, 192, 193, 206, 208, 210, 214, 324
        anæmia, 205, 219
        dyspepsia, 183, 190, 191, 194, 205, 206, 209, 210, 217, 327
        diarrhœa, 191, 192, 195, 207, 209, 219, 327
        dropsy, 180, 193, 198, 207, 328
        hæmorrhages, 203, 204, 208, 328
        headache, 190, 193, 195, 202, 204, 208, 210, 216, 219, 328
        impairment of muscular strength, 205
        insomnia, 204
        micturition, frequency of, 192, 209
        neuralgia, 191, 206, 219
        paralysis, 330
        uræmia, 195, 196, 197, 205, 208, 214, 217
        vertigo, 191, 192, 204
        vomiting, 191, 192, 194, 205, 210, 218, 327
    treatment of, 214
    consecutive, **286** ff
        associated with hydro-nephrosis, 288
        condition of urine in, 288, 289
        diagnosis of, 290
        due to pyelitis, 287, 288, 290
            renal calculus, 276, 277
        etiology of, 287
        morbid anatomy of, 287
        prognosis of, 290
        symptoms of, 288
            constipation, 289
            vomiting, 289
        treatment of, 290
Climate, change of, 179, 216, 258
    influencing renal cirrhosis, 185 f, 333
        uræmia, 299
Clothing, flannel, 216
Cloudiness of urine, causes of, 13, 27
Cold, cause of acute nephritis, 92
    albuminuria, 324
    chronic nephritis, 138
    hæmoglobinuria, 73, 75, 78
  influencing scarlatinal nephritis, 93, 118, 119
Colic, renal, 277, 278, 279
Concussion of the brain producing albuminuria, 37
Congestion of the kidney, **261** ff
    active, 261
    albuminuria in, 267, 268, 269
    causes of, 261, 263, 264
    condition of circulatory system in, 266, 269
        respiratory system in, 266, 269
        urine in, 267, 268, 269, 270

Congestion of the kidney, course and duration of, 269
　　　　　　　　diagnosis of, 270
　　　　　　　　diet in, 271
　　　　　　　　drugs influencing, 271
　　　　　　　　morbid anatomy of, 261, 265
　　　　　　　　passive, 263, 264
　　　　　　　　prognosis of, 270
　　　　　　　　symptoms of, 266
　　　　　　　　　　　　diarrhœa, 264
　　　　　　　　　　　　dropsy, 262, 266, 267, 269, 271, 272
　　　　　　　　treatment of, 271
Constipation in consecutive renal cirrhosis, 289
　　　　　uræmia, 314
Convulsions, due to hysteria, 233
　　　　　　　meningitis, 316
　　　　　　　uræmia, 300, 301, 303, 315, 318
Croton oil, use of, 175, 200, 221
Croupous pneumonia producing albuminuria, 41
Cyanotic induration. (*See* Congestion of the kidney)
Cyclic albuminuria, 50, 51, 54, 192
Cystitis associated with consecutive renal cirrhosis, 288, 290
　　　　cause of suppurative nephritis, 291, 295

DELIRIUM TREMENS, cause of albuminuria, 37
Diabetes, 212, 246, 251, 263, 309, 310, 328
Diagnosis of albuminuria, 320 ff
　　　　　　　febrile, 325
　　　　　　　functional, 323
　　　　cirrhosis of the kidney, 154, 155, 210
　　　　　　　consecutive, of the kidney, 290
　　　　congestion of the kidney, 270
　　　　hæmaturia, 68, 330
　　　　hæmoglobinuria, 77, 78
　　　　lardaceous disease, 257, 326
　　　　nephritis, acute, 105, 154
　　　　　　　chronic, 154
　　　　　　　puerperal, 233
　　　　　　　scarlatinal, 130, 330
　　　　uræmia, 316
Diagnostic importance of casts, 88, 90, 326
　　　　　　　　　condition of circulatory system, 326
　　　　　　　　　　　　digestive system, 327
　　　　　　　　　　　　nervous system, 328
　　　　　　　　　　　　respiratory system, 327
　　　　　　　　　　　　retinal changes, 329
　　　　　　　　　　　　skin, 327
　　　　　　　　　　　　sounds of the heart, 326
Diaphoretics, use of, 111, 168, 170, 174
Diarrhœa in acute nephritis, 100
　　　　chronic nephritis, 150, 151, 152, 171, 174, 177, 178
　　　　cirrhosis of the kidney, 191, 192, 195, 207, 209, 219, 327
　　　　congestion of the kidney, 264
　　　　lardaceous disease, 155, 212, 253, 254, 255, 256, 258
　　　　scarlatinal nephritis, 126, 132, 155
　　　　suppurative nephritis, 296, 297
　　　　uræmic, 300, 306
Diet in acute nephritis, 108, 114, 158
　　　　chronic nephritis, 158, 162, 164

INDEX 349

Diet in cirrhosis of the kidney, 215, 333
    consecutive, of the kidney, 290
  congestion of the kidney, 271
  hæmaturia, 69
  lardaceous disease, 259
  puerperal nephritis, 234
  scarlatinal nephritis, 133, 136
  suppurative nephritis, 297
 influencing albuminuria, 47, 49, 53, 234
Dietetic and digestive albuminuria, 46, 89, 336
Digitalis, use of, 113, 134, 135, 162, 177, 178, 200, 214, 217, 218, 220, 221, 235, 268, 271, 272
Diphtheritic nephritis, 38, 39, 64, 71
Diuretics, use of, 113, 114, 161, 174, 175, 178, 199, 221, 235, 270
Diuretin, use of, 162, 272
Dropsy in acute nephritis, 99, 103, 107, 156, 157
  chronic nephritis, 147 f, 153, 155, 157, 162, 167, 211, 212, 327, 328
  cirrhosis of the kidney, 180, 193, 198, 207, 328
  congestion of the kidney, 262, 266, 267, 269, 271, 272
  lardaceous disease, 211, 246, 253, 256
  puerperal nephritis, 224, 228, 232
  scarlatinal nephritis, 124, 125, 128, 129, 134, 155
Drugs, influencing amount of urea excreted, 309
    colour of urine, 11
    odour of urine, 18
    reaction of urine, 17
 not eliminated in chronic nephritis, 147
 producing acute nephritis, 94, 133
    albuminuria, 34, 35
    chronic nephritis, 140, 159
    congestion of the kidney, 261, 262
    hæmaturia, 64
Dyspepsia, cause of albuminuria, 336
    chronic nephritis, 329
    renal cirrhosis, 336
 in acute nephritis, 100
  chronic nephritis, 150, 151, 153, 164
  cirrhosis of the kidney, 183, 190, 191, 194, 205, 206, 209, 210, 217, 327
  eclampsia, 231
  lardaceous disease, 259
  puerperal nephritis, 229
  scarlatinal nephritis, 126

ECLAMPSIA, puerperal, 222 ff
  albuminuria in, 44, 224
  albuminuric retinitis in, 231
  convulsions in, 230
  diuresis in, 231
  dropsy in, 224
  dyspepsia in, 231
  etiology of, 225
  experiments to elucidate cause of, 225, 311
  influence of age in, 223
  pulse condition in, 231
  treatment of, 235
Embolism, renal, 273 ff

Embolism, renal, cause of albuminuria, 33
    due to heart disease, 275
    etiology of, 273
    morbid anatomy of, 274
    symptoms of, 275
    treatment of, 275
Emphysema, cause of albuminuria, 324, 326
    congestion of the kidney, 264
Epithelial casts, 85, 88, 96, 124, 146, 153, 233, 252, 261, 295
    cells, work of, 4
Epilepsy, cause of albuminuria, 37
Erysipelas, cause of acute nephritis, 93
    albuminuria, 41
    in chronic nephritis, 151
Esbach's method, 23
Experiments on brain, 37
    kidney, 5, 34, 35, 37, 44, 47, 87, 88, 93
    spinal cord, 37
    to elucidate cause of uræmia, 225, 311

FATTY and granular casts, 86, 89, 90, 124, 146, 153, 228, 233, 326
Febrile albuminuria, 37, 38, 42, 93, 106, 117, 120, 261, 294, 325, 334, 335
    symptoms of, 41
    theory of, 42
Fehling's solution test, 10, 23
Ferro-cyanide of potassium test, 22
Filaria sanguinis hominis, 80, 82
Food, influence on albuminuria, 325
    cirrhosis of the kidney, 333
Functional albuminuria, 50, 181, 210, 242, 323–6, 328, 336

GANGRENE in chronic nephritis, 151
Gastritis associated with renal disease, 306
Gout associated with hæmoglobinuria, 78
    renal cirrhosis, 183, 211, 214
Gouty albuminuria, 48 f
Granular and fatty casts, 86, 89, 90, 124, 146, 153, 228, 233, 326
Guaiacum test, 58, 59

HABITS, cause of renal cirrhosis, 184, 210, 211
    albuminuric retinitis, 240
Hard waxy casts, 86, 89
Hæmatinics, use of, 135, 166, 214, 219, 259
Hæmatogenous causes of albuminuria, 33
Hæmaturia, 57 ff
    associated with acute nephritis, 98
        specific diseases, 64, 68
        bilharzia hæmotobia, 64
        cancer, 27, 62, 63, 65, 69
        chronic nephritis, 146, 152, 161, 162, 163, 167
        congestion of the kidney, 64
        fibrous polypus, 65
        hæmophylia, 67
        hydatid cysts, 64
        hydro-nephrosis, 284

INDEX 351

Hæmaturia, associated with malaria, 67
        purpura hæmorrhagica, 33, 67, 70
        renal embolism, 273
        scarlatinal nephritis, 119, 123, 132, 134
        scurvy, 33, 67
        specific fevers, 67, 68
        syphilis, 62, 63
        tonsillitis, 64
        tuberculosis, 62
        ulceration of the kidney, 62
        villous papilloma, 27, 65, 66, 69
        yellow fever, 167
    diagnosis of, 68, 330
    diet for, 69
    due to calculus of the kidney, 27, 61, 276, 337
        drugs, 64
        hydatid cysts, 64
        injuries, 58, 59, 62, 69
        malignant disease, 27, 337
        muscular exertion, 65
    etiology of, 58
    prognosis of, 69
    supplementary or vicarious, 68
    symptomatic, 67
    test for, 58, 59
    treatment of, 69
Hæmoglobinuria, 69, 71
    associated with gout, 78
        malaria, 72, 73, 75, 78, 79
        rheumatism, 78
        small-pox, 72
        specific fevers, 72, 73
        syphilis, 72, 73, 79
        tuberculosis, 78
    drugs influencing, 71, 74, 79
    diagnosis of, 77, 78
    due to cold, 73, 75, 78
    etiology of, 71, 72
    paroxysmal, periodic or intermittent, 75
    prognosis of, 78
    symptoms of, 74–77
    treatment of, 79
Hæmophilia with hæmaturia, 67
Hæmorrhage, cerebral, cause of convulsions, 316
    in chronic nephritis, 180
        cirrhosis of the kidney, 203, 204, 208, 209, 210
    into liver and lung in puerperal nephritis, 227
    retinal, 238 ff
    subcutaneous in renal cirrhosis, 328
    uræmic, 300, 308, 309
Hæmorrhoids in renal cirrhosis, 207
Headache in acute nephritis, 102
    adolescent albuminuria, 328
    chronic nephritis, 149, 151, 163, 171, 174, 328
    cirrhosis of the kidney, 190, 193, 195, 202, 204, 208, 210, 216, 219, 328
    functional albuminuria, 329
    puerperal nephritis, 232
    suppurative nephritis, 296
    uræmia, 128, 303, 317, 319, 328

Heart disease, cause of albuminuria, 31, 324, 335
          renal congestion, 264, 269
          embolism, 275
Heart, hypertrophy and dilatation in cirrhosis of the kidney, 189, 194, 206, 209, 210, 211
          congestion of the kidney, 264, 269
          lardaceous disease, 211, 253
          puerperal nephritis, 229
          uræmia, 308
Heart sounds, diagnostic importance of, 326
Hemiplegia, uræmic, 129, 301, 317
Heredity, influence of, in renal cirrhosis, 180, 210
Hiccough, uræmic, 305, 306
Hyaline casts, 85, 88, 96, 106, 124, 146, 154, 193, 228, 233, 252, 261, 267, 288, 326
Hydatid cysts, cause of hæmaturia, 64
          due to hydro-nephrosis, 284
Hydro-nephrosis, 281 ff
          associated with consecutive renal cirrhosis, 288
          condition of urine in, 284
          diagnosis of, 284
          due to renal calculus, 276, 278
          etiology of, 281
          morbid anatomy of, 282
          prognosis of, 285
          symptoms of, 283
          treatment of, 286
Hydrothorax, 205
Hygienic treatment of consecutive cirrhosis of the kidney, 290
          chronic nephritis, 161
          scarlatinal nephritis, 133
Hypnotics, use of, 176, 298
Hysteria, frequency of micturition in, 212
Hysterical convulsions, 233

INFARCTS, white, 227, 274
Insomnia, in renal cirrhosis, 204
    uræmic, 304
Intermittent albuminuria, 31, 36, 50, 181, 182, 183, 241, 322, 323, 324
    hæmoglobinuria, 75

JAUNDICE, 89, 205, 207

KIDNEY, abscess of, 284 ff, 291 ff
    calculus of, 27, 61, 65, 68, 69, 261, 276-280, 291, 337
    cancer of, 62, 63, 65
    cirrhosis of, 154, 155, 180 ff
        consecutive of, 286 ff
    congestion of, 64, 96, 106, 154, 261 ff
    embolism of, 273 ff
    experiments on, 5, 34, 35, 37, 44, 47, 87, 88, 93
    hydatid cysts in, 64
    influence of drugs on, 34, 35
        nerves on the secretion of, 5
    morbid anatomy of, in acute nephritis, 95, 97
        chronic nephritis 141

INDEX

Kidney, morbid anatomy of, in cirrhosis, 186 ff
    consecutive, 287 f
    congestion of, 261, 265
    embolism of, 274
    febrile albuminuria, 43
    hydro-nephrosis, 282 f
    lardaceous disease, 248
    puerperal nephritis, 226
    retinitis, 241
    scarlatinal nephritis, 120
    suppurative nephritis, 292
  tumour of, 295
  ulceration of, 62
  villous papilloma of, 65, 66
  work, general, of, 3
    of epithelial cells, 4
    malpighian tufts, 3-5
    tubules, 3, 4

LARDACEOUS disease, 145, 154, 155, 211, 245 ff
  albuminuria in, 252 f
  associated with renal cirrhosis, 246, 260
  condition of circulatory system in, 246, 248, 253, 254
    heart in, 211, 253
    liver and spleen in, 248, 255
    pulse in, 246, 253, 254
    respiratory system in, 255
    urine in, 246, 251, 256
  course and duration of, 256
  diagnosis of, 257, 326
  diet in, 259
  drugs influencing, 258
  due to chronic nephritis, 245
    chronic suppuration, 211, 246, 247, 248, 256, 330
    phthisis, 211, 246, 247
    syphilis, 211, 246, 248, 256, 328, 330
    suppurative nephritis, 296
  etiology of, 246
  influence of age upon, 247
  morbid anatomy of, 248
  prognosis of, 257, 334
  retinal changes in, 288
  symptoms of, 250
    anæmia, 254
    diarrhœa, 155, 212, 253, 254, 255, 256, 258
    dropsy, 211, 246, 253, 256
    paralysis, 330
    vomiting, 254, 256
    uræmia, 212
  treatment of, 258
Lead-poisoning, cause of renal cirrhosis, 185, 211, 214
Leucocythæmia, cause of retinitis, 242
Life assurance, diagnostic importance of albuminuria in, 321
Lithæmic albuminuria, 48 f
Liver, atrophy of, in puerperal nephritis, 227
  condition of, in lardaceous disease, 255
  hydatid of, 284
  source of urea, 310

MALARIA, cause of albuminuria, 40, 41
    chronic nephritis, 139, 159
    cirrhosis of the kidney, 186
    hæmaturia, 67
    hæmoglobinuria, 72, 73, 75, 78, 79
    retinitis, 242
Malignant disease, cause of hæmaturia, 27, 337
Malpighian tufts, work of, 3, 4, 5
Marasmus, renal, 157, 300
Measles, cause of acute nephritis, 93
    albuminuria, 39
Mechanical causes of albuminuria, 30
Meningitis, cause of convulsions, 316
Menstruation, hæmaturia vicarious of, 68
    cause of albuminuria, 30
Mental derangements, uræmic, 303
Metamorphosed casts, 85, 89
Metaphosphoric acid test, 22
Micturition, frequent desire for, in acute nephritis, 98
    diagnostic importance of, 325
    in cirrhosis of the kidney, 190, 192, 209
    hysteria, 212
    lardaceous disease, 251
Morphine, use of, 175, 217, 236, 290, 297
Murexide test, 9
Muscular exertion, cause of acute nephritis, 93
    albuminuria, 32, 325
    hæmaturia, 65
    hæmoglobinuria, 73, 76
Muscular strength, loss of, in chronic nephritis, 149
    renal cirrhosis, 205

NECROSIS, cause of lardaceous disease, 247
Nephritis, acute, 92 ff
    condition of circulatory system in, 100
    digestive system in, 100
    nervous system in, 102
    respiratory system in, 102
    urine in, 98
    course and duration of, 103
    definition of, 92
    diagnosis of, 105, 154
    diet in, 108, 114, 158
    due to chicken pox, 94
    cold, 92
    drugs, 94
    erysipelas, 93
    local injuries, 95
    measles, 93
    pneumonia, 93
    small-pox, 93
    typhoid, 93
    etiology of, 92
    prognosis of, 107, 332
    symptoms of, 97-103
    diarrhœa, 100
    dropsy, 99, 103, 107, 156, 157
    headache, 102

INDEX 355

Nephritis, acute, symptoms of uræmia, 100, 102, 105, 107, 110
    vomiting, 100, 105, 114
  treatment of, 108–115
chronic, 137 ff
  albuminuria in, 154, 165
  cause of lardaceous disease, 245
    ulceration of the intestine, 150
  condition of circulatory system in, 149
    digestive system in, 150
    heart in, 326
    muscular system in, 149
    nervous system in, 150
    pulse in, 335
    urine in, 146, 165
  course and duration of, 153
  diagnosis of, 154
  diet in, 158, 162, 164
  drugs not eliminated in, 147
  due to alcohol, 140
    chronic suppuration, 139, 159
    cold, 138
    indigestion, 329
    malaria, 139, 159
    pregnancy, 139
    scarlet fever, 138, 158
    syphilis, 140, 152, 159
    toxic agents, 140
  etiology of, 137 f
  hæmaturia in, 146, 152, 167
  morbid anatomy of, 141
  prognosis of, 156, 333
  retinal changes in, 149, 151
  secondary inflammations in, 151
    to other conditions, 140
  symptoms of, 146 ff
    anæmia, 148, 153, 212, 327
    diarrhœa, 150, 151, 152, 171, 174, 177, 178
    dropsy, 147 f, 153, 155, 157, 162, 167, 211, 212, 327, 328
    headache, 149, 151, 163, 171, 174, 328
    uræmia in, 150, 151, 171, 173, 174, 175
    vomiting, 150, 151, 152, 171, 174, 177, 178
  theories of causation, 141
  treatment of, 158–179
  types, abnormal, of, 152
    various of, 137
diphtheritic, 38, 39
hæmorrhagic, 40
puerperal, 222 ff
  associated with changes in other organs, 227
    chronic bronchitis, 236
  condition of circulatory system in, 229
    nervous system in, 230
    pulse in, 231, 233
    urine in, 222, 227, 228, 232, 233
  convulsions in, 225, 230
  course and duration of, 232
  diagnosis of, 233
  diet in, 234

A A 2

Nephritis, puerperal, drugs influencing, 235
    eclampsia in, 226, 228, 230, 235, 236
    etiology of, 224
    morbid anatomy of, 226
    prognosis of, 233, 332
    retinal changes in, 231, 238, 243
    symptoms of, 227
        dropsy, 224, 228, 232
        headache, 232
        indigestion, 229
        neuralgia, 232
        vomiting, 229
    theories of, mechanical, 224
        toxæmic, 225
    treatment of, 234–236
  scarlatinal, 116 ff
    albuminuria in, 38, 116, 117, 118, 123 f, 130, 132, 134, 324
    associated with pleurisy, 128
        pneumonia, 128
    cause of chronic nephritis, 138, 158
    condition of circulatory system in, 126
        digestive system in, 126
        respiratory system in, 128
        urine in, 123, 124
    course and duration of, 129
    diagnosis of, 130, 330
    diet in, 133, 136
    etiology of, 118
    hæmaturia in, 119, 123, 132, 134
    influence of age, 118
        cold, 93, 118, 119
    morbid anatomy of, 97, 120
    prognosis of, 131
    symptoms of, 122
        diarrhœa, 126, 132, 155
        dropsy, 124, 125, 128, 129, 134, 155
        uræmia, 122, 128, 305, 316, 318
        vomiting, 126, 128, 130, 132
    treatment of, 132, 176
  suppurative, 290 ff
    cause of lardaceous disease, 296
    condition of urine in, 294
    course and duration of, 293
    diet in, 297
    drugs influencing, 297, 298
    due to pyosalpinx, 291
        renal calculus, 276, 278, 286
        tuberculosis, 291
    etiology of, 291
    morbid anatomy of, 292
    prognosis of, 296
    symptoms of, 293 ff
        diarrhœa, 296, 297
        headache, 296
        paralysis, 295
    treatment of, 297
Nephrolithiasis, 276
Nerve lesions, cause of albuminuria, 37
Nervous system, condition of, in acute nephritis, 102

Nervous system, condition of, in chronic nephritis, 150
puerperal nephritis, 230
diagnostic importance of condition of, 326, 328
Neuralgia in cirrhosis of the kidney, 191, 206, 219
puerperal nephritis, 232
Neuroses, cause of renal cirrhosis, 184
Neurotic albuminuria, 35-37
Nitric acid test, 19, 320

ODOUR of urine, 18
due to blood, 18
diabetes, 18
drugs, 18
Oxaluric albuminuria, 47, 48, 52
Ozonic ether test, 58, 59

PAPILLOMA, villous, of kidney, 65, 66
Paralysis, diagnostic importance of, 330
in cirrhosis of the kidney, 330
suppurative nephritis, 295
syphilitic lardaceous disease, 330
Parasitic chyluria, 79, 82
Pericarditis, cause of renal congestion, 261
in acute nephritis, 105, 107
chronic nephritis, 152
renal cirrhosis, 193, 206, 221
Peritonitis, septic, 290
Persistent albuminuria, 52, 114, 322, 323
Phthisis, cause of congestion of the kidney, 264
hæmaturia, 62
hæmoglobinuria, 78
lardaceous disease, 211, 246, 247
suppurative nephritis, 291
excretion of urea in, 310
Phosphates, tests for, 8
Physiological albuminuria, 52, 55
Picric acid test, 21
Pilocarpine, use of, 112, 170, 171, 172, 175, 178, 200, 236
Pleurisy, cause of congestion of the kidney, 264
in acute nephritis, 105, 107
chronic nephritis, 152
cirrhosis of the kidney, 205
scarlatinal nephritis, 128
Pneumonia, cause of albuminuria, 41, 324, 335
acute nephritis, 93
congestion of the kidney, 261, 264
in chronic nephritis, 152
cirrhosis of the kidney, 205, 210
puerperal nephritis, 236
scarlatinal nephritis, 128
Polypus, fibrous, cause of hæmaturia, 65
Polyuria, 37
Position, influence of, on albuminuria, 52, 325
Potassio-mercuric iodide test, 22
Pregnancy, cause of albuminuria, 44
chronic nephritis, 139
chyluria, 80

Pregnancy, cause of eclampsia, 223 ff
    puerperal nephritis, 222 ff
    retinal changes, 238, 242
Prognosis of albuminuria, 331 ff
    accidental, 337
    adolescent, 336
    dietetic, 336
    febrile, 334
    functional, 336
  cirrhosis of the kidney, 213, 333
    consecutive, of the kidney, 290
  congestion of the kidney, 270
  hæmaturia, 69
  hæmoglobinuria, 78
  lardaceous disease, 257, 334
  nephritis, acute, 107, 332
    chronic, 156, 333
    puerperal, 233, 332
    scarlatinal, 131
  uræmia, 318
Prognostic importance of condition of circulatory system, 334
    extent of loss of albumin, 331
Prostatic albuminuria, 29
Pruritus, uræmic, 304
Puerperal albuminuria without nephritis, 223, 232, 233
  nephritis (*See* Nephritis, puerperal)
Pulse, condition of, in chronic nephritis, 335
    lardaceous disease, 246, 253, 254
    puerperal nephritis, 229 f
    renal cirrhosis, 194, 330, 335
Purgatives, use of, 109, 111, 114, 135, 172, 173, 174, 175, 208, 221, 272, 314
Purpura, cause of albuminuria, 33
  hæmaturia, 33, 67, 70
  retinitis, 242
Pus in the urine, 28, 62, 241, 284, 294, 295, 297
Pyæmia, 290, 296, 297
Pyelitis, 29
  cause of consecutive renal cirrhosis, 287, 288, 290
  due to renal calculus, 276, 278, 279
Pyelonephritis, 227
Pyosalpinx, cause of suppurative nephritis, 291

REACTION of urine, 16, 98
Respiratory system, condition of, in acute nephritis, 102
    cirrhosis of the kidney, 195
    congestion of the kidney, 266, 269
    lardaceous disease, 255
    scarlatinal nephritis, 128
  diagnostic importance of, 326, 327
Retinal changes, 237 ff
  consecutive to other conditions, 238, 242
  diagnosis of, 242
  diagnostic importance of, 329
  enumeration of, 238
  prognosis of, 242
  statistics of, 243
  with cerebral tumour, 242
    chronic nephritis, 149, 151

Retinal changes, with cirrhosis of the kidney, 203, 204
    diabetes, 263
    lardaceous disease, 211, 238
    leucocythæmia, 242
    malaria, 242
    puerperal nephritis, 231, 238, 243
    purpura, 242
    scarlatinal nephritis, 238
    scurvy, 242
    septicæmia, 242
Retinitis, albuminuric (*See* Albuminuric retinitis)
Rheumatism, acute, cause of albuminuria, 41
    associated with hæmoglobinuria, 78

SALICYL sulphonic acid test, 22
Scarlatinal nephritis (*See* Nephritis, scarlatinal)
Scarlet fever, cause of hæmaturia, 64
    hæmoglobinuria, 72
Schiff's test, 9
Scurvy, cause of albuminuria, 33
    hæmaturia, 33, 67
    retinal changes, 242
Septicæmia, 242, 290, 296, 297
Sex, influence of, in renal cirrhosis, 181
Skin, diagnostic importance of condition of, 327, 328
    eruptions, uræmic, 304, 305
Small-pox, cause of acute nephritis, 93
    albuminuria, 39
    hæmoglobinuria, 72
Spermatic albuminuria, 29
Spinal cord, experiments on, 37
Spleen, condition of, in lardaceous disease, 248, 255
Strophanthus, use of, 135, 162, 177, 214, 217, 218, 235, 271, 272
Sulphates, tests for, 8
Suppuration, chronic, cause of chronic nephritis, 139, 159
    lardaceous disease, 211, 246, 247, 248, 256, 330
Syphilis, cause of albuminuria, 45
    chronic nephritis, 140, 152, 159
    cirrhosis of the kidney, 214, 216
    hæmaturia, 62, 63
    hæmoglobinuria, 72, 73, 79
    lardaceous disease, 211, 246, 248, 256, 328, 330
    excretion of urea in, 310

TEST, acidulated brine, 21
    ammonium sulphate, 22
    Fehling's solution, 10, 23
    ferro-cyanide of potassium, 22
    guaiacum tincture, 58, 59
    heat, 19
    metaphosphoric acid, 22
    murexide, 9
    nitric acid, 19, 320
    ozonic ether, 58, 59
    papers, 23
    pellets, 23
    picric acid, 21

Test, potassio-mercuric iodide, 22
    salicyl sulphonic acid, 22
    Schiff's, 9
    trichloracetic acid, 21
    tungstate of soda, 22
Tests for albumin, 18
    chlorides, 8
    normal constituents of urine, 8
    phosphates, 8
    sulphates, 8
    urea, 8
    uric acid, 9
Tetanus, cause of albuminuria, 37
    uræmic, 129, 301
Tonsillitis, acute, cause of albuminuria, 40
    hæmaturia, 64
Traumatic causes of acute nephritis, 95
Trichloracetic acid test, 21
Trismus, 129
Tuberculosis, cause of congestion of the kidney, 264
    hæmaturia, 62
    hæmoglobinuria, 78
    lardaceous disease, 211, 246, 247
    suppurative nephritis, 291
Tubules of kidney, work of, 3, 4
Tumours, renal, 295
Tungstate of soda test, 22
Turbidity of urine, causes of, 13, 27
Typhoid fever, cause of albuminuria, 39, 335
    acute nephritis, 93
    hæmaturia, 64
    hæmoglobinuria, 72
Typhus fever, cause of albuminuria, 39

ULCERATION of intestine with chronic nephritis, 150
    kidney, cause of hæmaturia, 62
Urea, diminution of excretion in chronic nephritis, 147
    phthisis, 310
    puerperal nephritis, 224, 228, 230
    syphilis, 310
    uræmia, 309, 310
    wasting diseases, 310
    drugs influencing excretion of, 309
    tests for, 8
    variations of amount in the urine, 309
Uræmia, 299 ff
    acute, 299
        prophylaxis of, 306
    chronic, 302
    condition of the urine in, 316, 318, 319
    diagnosis of, 316
    drugs influencing, 314
    excretion of urea in, 309, 310
    prognosis of, 318
    retention of urea in, 311
    symptoms of, 299, 302
        amaurosis, 103, 107, 129, 151, 171, 204, 211, 231, 301, 319

INDEX 361

Uræmia, symptoms of, in constipation, 314
  convulsions, 300 f, 303, 315-318
  diarrhœa, 300, 306
  headache, 128, 303, 317, 319, 328
  mental derangement, 303
  paralysis, 102, 129, 301, 317
  vertigo, 319
  vomiting, 300, 306, 317, 319
 theories of, 307
  chemical, 309
  mechanical, 308
 treatment of, 175, 178, 319
 with acute nephritis, 100, 102, 105, 107, 110
  chronic nephritis, 150, 151, 171, 173-178
  lardaceous disease, 212, 246
  puerperal nephritis, 222 ff
  renal cirrhosis, 190, 195, 196, 197, 205, 208, 210, 214, 217
   consecutive cirrhosis, 289
  scarlatinal nephritis, 122, 128, 305, 316, 318
  suppurative nephritis, 129, 151, 155, 178, 296
Uræmic dyspnœa, 195, 196, 197, 200, 205, 210, 220, 305, 317, 319
  pathology of, 196
 tetanus, 129, 301
Uric acid, tests for, 9
Urine, acidity of, 17, 110, 252
 alkalinity of, 17, 110, 234, 296, 320
 cancer cells in, 63
 casts in, 68, 83 ff, 98, 124, 130, 131, 146, 193, 195, 228, 252, 261, 267, 288, 295, 316
 colour of, 11
 condition of, in acute nephritis, 98, 106
  chronic nephritis, 146, 153, 156, 157, 326
  cirrhosis of the kidney, 180, 193, 195, 206, 326
   consecutive, of the kidney, 288, 289
  congestion, active, of the kidney, 261
   passive, of the kidney, 267, 270
  eclampsia, 224, 230
  hydro-nephrosis, 284
  puerperal nephritis, 222 f, 227, 228, 232, 233
  scarlatinal nephritis, 123, 124, 130, 131
  suppurative nephritis, 295
  uræmia, 316, 318, 319
 constituents, abnormal of, 7
  classification of, 6, 7
  sources of, 4
  tests for normal, 8-10
 gases of, 7
 odour of, 18
 persistent froth of, 13
 physical characters of, 10
 pus in, 28, 62, 241, 284, 294, 295, 297
 reaction of, 16, 98
 turbity or cloudiness of, 13, 27
 variations in colour, 11, 98, 192, 195, 212, 246, 267, 270, 324, 325, 326
  quantity, 10, 30, 98, 128, 180, 190, 192, 195, 199, 206, 207, 212, 222, 224, 227, 230, 232, 233, 240, 246, 251, 256, 267, 270, 284, 288, 289, 295, 319, 324, 325, 326

Urine, variations in specific gravity, 14, 30, 98, 180, 192, 207, 212, 227, 246, 252, 258, 267, 270, 284, 288, 289, 295, 323, 324, 326
Urticaria, 77, 130

VENESECTION, use of, 176, 235, 279
Vertigo in renal cirrhosis, 191, 192, 204
    uræmic, 319
Villous papilloma of kidney, 65, 66
Vogel's scale of colour, 11
Vomiting, due to renal colic, 279
    in acute nephritis, 100, 105, 114
        chronic nephritis, 150, 151, 152, 171, 174, 177, 178
        cirrhosis of the kidney, 191, 192, 194, 205, 210, 218, 327
            consecutive, of the kidney, 289
        lardaceous disease, 254, 256
        puerperal nephritis, 229
        scarlatinal nephritis, 126, 128, 130, 132
    uræmic, 300, 306, 317, 319

WETPACK, use of, 111, 112, 114, 134, 168, 220, 221
Whooping cough, cause of albuminuria, 40

YELLOW fever, cause of hæmaturia, 167

SMITH, ELDER, & CO.'S PUBLICATIONS.

A TREATISE on SURGERY: its PRINCIPLES and PRACTICE. By T. HOLMES, M.A. Cantab., F.R.C.S., Consulting Surgeon to St. George's Hospital; Memb. Associé de la Soc. de Chir. de Paris. FIFTH EDITION, Edited by T. PICKERING PICK, Surgeon to, and Lecturer on Surgery at, St. George's Hospital; Senior Surgeon, Victoria Hospital for Children; Member of the Court of Examiners, Royal College of Surgeons of England. With 428 Illustrations. Royal 8vo. 30s.

'Mr. Pick has revised the whole book most thoroughly, has carefully brought it up to date, and has incorporated a great deal of the modern teaching in pathology and practical surgery. ... We are sure that this edition will largely add to the great reputation which this text-book has for a long time had.'—LANCET.

'This edition may fairly claim to have been brought thoroughly up to the level of the most recent knowledge, and no doubt will retain the place which this favourite handbook has gained as one of the standard treatises on surgery.'
BRITISH MEDICAL JOURNAL.

A DICTIONARY of PRACTICAL SURGERY. By VARIOUS BRITISH HOSPITAL SURGEONS. Edited by CHRISTOPHER HEATH, F.R.C.S., Hulme Professor of Clinical Surgery in University College, London; Surgeon to University College Hospital; Member of the Council and Court of Examiners of the Royal College of Surgeons of England. In 2 vols. comprising 1,864 pages. THIRD EDITION. Royal 8vo. 32s. bound in cloth; or, in half-morocco, marbled edges, 42s.

'Altogether the work is a credit to the energy of authors, editor, and publisher, and will rank highly wherever British surgery is consulted, and wherever the English language is understood. All its contributors are to be congratulated upon its appearance.'—BRITISH MEDICAL JOURNAL.

'The Dictionary will stand undoubtedly as one of the most trustworthy works of reference published in modern times upon practical surgery, and will form a valuable and almost essential occupant of the practitioners' library.'
LONDON MEDICAL RECORD.

An INDEX of SURGERY: being a Concise Classification of the Main Facts and Theories of Surgery for the Use of Senior Students and others. By C. B. KEETLEY, F.R.C.S., Surgeon to the West London Hospital, and to the Surgical-Aid Society. FOURTH EDITION. Crown 8vo. 10s. 6d.

'Will, we trust, for many years be kept up to the imperious demands of surgical progress. The system of arrangement is just what the system in such a publication should ever be, purely alpha-

betical, and the text is written in as elegant and intelligible English as can be expected in condensations and abridgments.'
BRITISH MEDICAL JOURNAL.

The SURGERY of DEFORMITIES. A Manual for Students and Practitioners. By NOBLE SMITH, F.R.C.S. Edin., L.R.C.P. Lond., Surgeon to the City Orthopædic Hospital, and Surgeon to the All Saints' Children's Hospital. With 118 Illustrations. Crown 8vo. 10s. 6d.

'The woodcuts show very practically the points which they are intended to illustrate, and materially help the reader. We can recommend

this as one of the most practical, useful, and able handbooks of Orthopædic Surgery.'
BRITISH MEDICAL JOURNAL.

ANTISEPTIC SURGERY: its PRINCIPLES, PRACTICE, HISTORY, and RESULTS. By W. WATSON CHEYNE, M.B., F.R.C.S., Assistant-Surgeon to King's College Hospital, and Demonstrator of Surgical Pathology in King's College. With 145 Illustrations. 8vo. 21s.

'In the volume before us Mr. Cheyne has made a very valuable addition to surgical literature. The intimate professional relations of Mr. Cheyne with Professor Lister give a special importance and value to this work; for while Mr. Lister's

results and views have hitherto been published only fragmentarily in journals and transactions of learned societies, Mr. Cheyne's book affords a trustworthy and complete statement of them.'
LANCET.

MANUAL of the ANTISEPTIC TREATMENT of WOUNDS. For Students and Practitioners. By W. WATSON CHEYNE, M.B., F.R.C.S., Assistant-Surgeon to King's College Hospital, Surgeon to the Paddington Green Children's Hospital, &c. With Illustrations. Crown 8vo. 4s. 6d.

DISEASES of the BONES: their PATHOLOGY, DIAGNOSIS, and TREATMENT. By THOMAS JONES, F.R.C.S. Eng., B.S. Lond., Surgeon to the Manchester Royal Infirmary; Lecturer on Practical Surgery in the Owens College, Victoria University; Consulting Surgeon to the Children's Hospital, Pendlebury, Manchester. With 7 Chromo-lithographic Plates, 9 Etchings, and 77 Woodcuts. 8vo. 12s. 6d.

London: SMITH, ELDER, & CO., 15 Waterloo Place.

SMITH, ELDER, & CO.'S PUBLICATIONS.

NEW EDITION OF PLAYFAIR'S 'SCIENCE AND PRACTICE OF MIDWIFERY.'
NINTH EDITION. With over 200 Illustrations and 8 Plates. 2 vols. Demy 8vo. 28s.

A TREATISE on the SCIENCE and PRACTICE of MIDWIFERY. By W. S. PLAYFAIR. M.D., LL.D., F.R.C.P., Physician-Accoucheur to H.I. and R.H. the Duchess of Saxe-Coburg and Gotha (Duchess of Edinburgh); Emeritus Professor of Obstetric Medicine in King's College; Consulting Physician for the Diseases of Women and Children to King's College Hospital, to the General Lying-in Hospital, the Evelina Hospital for Children, &c.; late President of the Obstetrical Society of London; Examiner in Midwifery to the Universities of Cambridge and London, and to the Royal College of Physicians.

A SYSTEM of OBSTETRIC MEDICINE and SURGERY: THEO- RETICAL and CLINICAL. For the Student and Practitioner. By ROBERT BARNES, M.D., Consulting Obstetric Physician to the St. George's Hospital, &c.; and FANCOURT BARNES, M.D., Consulting Physician to the British Lying-in Hospital. The Section on Embryology contributed by the late Professor MILNES MARSHALL. Complete in 2 vols., with numerous Illustrations, 8vo. Vol. I. 18s. Vol. II. 20s.

'The book needs but to be read to be appreciated. The illustrations are numerous and well executed, contributing materially to the usefulness of the work. The book is well "got up," handy in size, and will unquestionably prove a valuable companion, whether to the student acquiring knowledge of obstetrics, or to the busy practitioner anxious to keep pace with the times.'
BRITISH MEDICAL JOURNAL.

A MANUAL of MIDWIFERY for MIDWIVES. By FANCOURT BARNES, M.D., M.R.C.P., Consulting Physician to the British Lying-in Hospital, &c. SEVENTH EDITION. With Illustrations. Crown 8vo. 6s.

The EVOLUTION of the DISEASES of WOMEN. By W. BALLS-HEADLEY, MA., M.D. Cantab., F.R.C.P. Lond., Lecturer on Midwifery and the Diseases of Women at the University of Melbourne; Honorary Physician to the Women's Hospital; President of the Section of Obstetrics and Gynæcology at the Intercolonial Medical Congress, Sydney, N.S.W., 1892; late President of the Medical Society of Victoria, &c. With numerous Illustrations. Demy 8vo. 16s.

'The book contains much that is interesting, and a great deal of sound advice on the treatment of gynæcological disease.'
EDINBURGH MEDICAL JOURNAL.
'Should be studied by all who have to deal with the diseases peculiar to women.... It is in our opinion calculated to give the student a clearer insight into perhaps the most difficult branch of medical practice than any other single work on the subject.'
AUSTRALIAN MEDICAL GAZETTE.

A SYNOPTICAL GUIDE to the STUDY of OBSTETRICS: being an Aid to the Student in the Class-room, in Private Study, and in Preparing for Examinations. By ROBERT BARNES, M.D., Consulting Obstetric Physician to St. George's Hospital, &c. Crown 8vo. 3s.

CLINICAL and PATHOLOGICAL OBSERVATIONS on TUMOURS of the OVARY, FALLOPIAN TUBE, and BROAD LIGAMENT. By ALBAN H. G. DORAN, F.R.C.S., Assistant-Surgeon to the Samaritan Free Hospital, formerly Anatomical and Pathological Assistant to the Museum of the Royal College of Surgeons of England. With 32 Illustrations. 8vo. 10s. 6d.

GENERAL and DIFFERENTIAL DIAGNOSIS of OVARIAN TUMOURS, with Special Reference to the Operation of Ovariotomy, and Occasional Pathological and Therapeutical Considerations. By WASHINGTON L. ATLEE, M.D. With 39 Illustrations. 8vo. 20s.

The QUESTION of REST for WOMEN DURING MENSTRUATION. By MARY PUTNAM JACOBI, M.D., Professor of Materia Medica in the Women's Medical College, New York. With Illustrations. 8vo. 12s.

London: SMITH, ELDER, & CO., 15 Waterloo Place.

SMITH, ELDER, & CO.'S PUBLICATIONS.

THERAPEUTICS: its PRINCIPLES and PRACTICE. By H. C. WOOD, M.D., LL.D., Professor of Materia Medica and Therapeutics and Clinical Professor of Diseases of the Nervous System in the University of Pennsylvania. Being the TENTH EDITION of 'A TREATISE on THERAPEUTICS,' Rearranged, Rewritten, and Enlarged. 8vo. 18s.

OCULAR THERAPEUTICS. By L. DE WECKER, Professor of Clinical Ophthalmology, Paris. Translated and Edited by LITTON FORBES, M.A., M.D., F.R.G.S., late Clinical Assistant, Royal London Ophthalmic Hospital. With Illustrations. Demy 8vo. 16s.

A PRACTICAL TREATISE on the DISEASES of the HEART and GREAT VESSELS; including the Principles of their Physical Diagnosis. By the late WALTER HAYLE WALSHE, M.D. FOURTH EDITION, thoroughly Revised and greatly Enlarged. Demy 8vo. 16s.

A PRACTICAL TREATISE on DISEASES of the LUNGS; including the Principles of Physical Diagnosis and Notes on Climate. FOURTH EDITION, Revised and much Enlarged. Demy 8vo. 16s.

AUSCULTATION and PERCUSSION, together with the other Methods of Physical Examination of the Chest. By SAMUEL GEE, M.D. With Illustrations. FOURTH EDITION. Fcp. 8vo. 6s.

HANDBOOK of MODERN CHEMISTRY, INORGANIC and ORGANIC. By the late MEYMOTT TIDY, M.B., F.C.S., Professor of Chemistry and of Medical Jurisprudence and Public Health at the London Hospital; one of the Official Analysts to the Home Office; Medical Officer of Health for Islington; late Deputy Medical Officer of Health and Public Analyst for the City of London; Master of Surgery, &c. &c. SECOND EDITION, Revised and Enlarged. Demy 8vo. 18s.

The ELEMENTS of PHYSIOLOGICAL and PATHOLOGICAL CHEMISTRY. A Handbook for Medical Students and Practitioners. By T. CRANSTOUN CHARLES, M.D., F.C.S, &c., Master of Surgery; Lecturer on Practical Physiology, St. Thomas's Hospital, London; late Medical Registrar, St. Thomas's Hospital, &c. &c. With 38 Woodcut Illustrations and 1 Chromo-lithograph. Demy 8vo. 12s. 6d.

An INDEX of SYMPTOMS as an AID to DIAGNOSIS. By RALPH WINNINGTON LEFTWICH, M.D., late Assistant-Physician to the East London Children's Hospital. Fcp. 8vo. 5s.

⁎ Each Symptom is followed by an Alphabetical List of Diseases in which it occurs.

'So far as we have tested this little book it appears to be remarkably free from errors, and to be likely to be very serviceable in its sugg stiveness . . . altogether a little book of undoubted novelty and utility.'—LANCET.

ELLIS'S DEMONSTRATIONS of ANATOMY: being a Guide to the Knowledge of the Human Body by Dissection. ELEVENTH EDITION. Edited and Revised by G. D. THANE, Professor of Anatomy, University College, London. With 252 Illustrations. Small 8vo. 12s. 6d.

ILLUSTRATIONS of DISSECTIONS. In a Series of Original Coloured Plates, the size of Life, representing the Dissection of the Human Body. By G. V. ELLIS and G. H. FORD. Imperial folio. 2 vols. half-bound in morocco, £6. 6s. May also be had in Parts separately, Parts 1 to 28, 3s. 6d. each; Part 29, 5s.

'With these plates, and such as these, by his side, the learner will be well guided in his dissection; and, under their guidance, be may safely continue his study when out of the dissecting room. With such plates as these, the surgeon will be fully reminded of all that is needful in anatomy when engaged in planning an operation.'—MEDICAL TIMES.

London: SMITH, ELDER, & CO., 15 Waterloo Place.

SMITH, ELDER, & CO.'S PUBLICATIONS.

The DESCRIPTIVE ATLAS of ANATOMY. A Representation of the Anatomy of the Human Body. In 92 Royal 4to. Plates, containing 550 Illustrations. Introducing Heitzmann's Figures, considerably modified, and with many Original Drawings from Nature. By NOBLE SMITH, F.R.C.S. Edin., L.R.C.P. Lond., Surgeon to the City Orthopædic Hospital, and Surgeon to the All Saints' Children's Hospital. Bound in half-leather, 25s.

'Certainly one of the most remarkable publications of the day. The great advantage which it presents is that all the attachments of bones, the arteries, veins, &c., are copiously lettered and described *in situ*; and the arteries and veins are coloured. The book is one of great utility and merit, and reflects credit on the artist, and also on those who have produced it.'
BRITISH MEDICAL JOURNAL.

A HANDBOOK of OPHTHALMIC SCIENCE and PRACTICE. By HENRY E. JULER, F.R.C.S., Ophthalmic Surgeon to St. Mary's Hospital; Surgeon to the Royal Westminster Ophthalmic Hospital; Consulting Ophthalmic Surgeon to the London Lock Hospitals. SECOND EDITION, Revised, with numerous Illustrations. 8vo. 21s.

'Altogether the book is one of which we are able to speak in terms of unqualified approval.'
BRITISH MEDICAL JOURNAL.

'A very good and reliable work, which represents satisfactorily the present state of ophthalmic science and practice.'—LANCET.

VERTEBRATE EMBRYOLOGY. A Text-book for Students and Practitioners. By the late A. MILNES MARSHALL, M.D., D.Sc., M.A., F.R.S., Professor in the Victoria University; Beyer Professor of Zoology in Owens College; late Fellow of St. John's College, Cambridge. With numerous Illustrations. 8vo. 21s.

'The book is welcome, and we do not doubt but that it will obtain the popularity which it so well deserves. The care and accuracy with which it has been written will render it most useful to the student and to the teacher.'
BRITISH MEDICAL JOURNAL.

'Will be extremely useful to all teachers and students of biology . . . an eminently practical treatise.'—NATURE.

A JUNIOR COURSE of PRACTICAL ZOOLOGY. By the late A. MILNES MARSHALL, M.D., D.Sc., M.A., F.R.S., Professor in the Victoria University; Beyer Professor of Zoology in Owens College; late Fellow of St. John's College, Cambridge. Assisted by C. HERBERT HURST, Ph.D., Lecturer in the Victoria University; Demonstrator and Assistant-Lecturer in Zoology, Owens College, Manchester. FOURTH EDITION, Revised by C. HERBERT HURST. With Illustrations. Crown 8vo. 10s. 6d.

'A most successful and important book. . . . The illustrations are excellent, reflecting the greatest credit upon all concerned. . . . It is provided with an exceedingly good index, and presented in a form demanding our sincere thanks.'
NATURE.

A MANUAL of GENERAL PATHOLOGY. By JOSEPH F. PAYNE, M.D., F.R.C.P., late Fellow of Magdalen College, Oxford; Physician and Joint-Lecturer on Pathological Anatomy at St. Thomas's Hospital; Examiner in Pathology in the University of Oxford; late Examiner in Medicine to the Royal College of Surgeons of England, &c. With Illustrations. Crown 8vo. 12s. 6d.

The FUNCTIONS of the BRAIN. By DAVID FERRIER, M.D., LL.D., F.R.S., Professor of Forensic Medicine, King's College; Physician to King's College Hospital; Physician to the National Hospital for the Paralysed and Epileptic. SECOND EDITION, Rewritten, with many new Illustrations. 8vo. 18s.

'No scientific medical man's library can be said to be complete without Dr. Ferrier's book, which contains the records of the author's own work, as well as those of other observers of repute.'—LANCET.

The LOCALISATION of CEREBRAL DISEASE. By DAVID FERRIER, M.D., F.R.S., Assistant-Physician to King's College Hospital; Professor of Forensic Medicine, King's College. With numerous Illustrations. 8vo. 7s. 6d.

London: SMITH, ELDER, & CO., 15 Waterloo Place.

SMITH, ELDER, & CO.'S PUBLICATIONS.

A PRACTICAL TREATISE on TRAUMATIC SEPARATION of the EPIPHYSES; including the Anatomy of the Epiphyses, the Pathological Anatomy, Symptoms, Treatment, and Results of Traumatic Separations. By JOHN POLAND, F.R.C.S., Surgeon to the City Orthopædic Hospital; Visiting Surgeon to the Miller Hospital, and formerly Senior Demonstrator of Anatomy and Surgical Registrar to Guy's Hospital. Royal 8vo. 926 pages, with 337 Illustrations, and SKIAGRAMS. £2. 12s. 6d.

AND BY THE SAME AUTHOR. With 19 SKIAGRAMS. Royal 8vo. 5s.

The SKIAGRAPHIC ATLAS Showing the development of the BONES of the WRIST and HAND for the Use of Students and others.

A SYSTEM of SURGERY: Pathological, Diagnostic, Therapeutic, and Operative. By SAMUEL D. GROSS, M D., LL.D., D.C.L. Oxon. SIXTH EDITION, greatly Enlarged and thoroughly Revised. With upwards of 1,600 Illustrations. 2 vols. 8vo. £3. 10s.

A COURSE of PRACTICAL HISTOLOGY. By EDWARD ALBERT SCHÄFER, LL.D., F.R.S., Jodrell Professor of Physiology, University College. SECOND AND CHEAPER EDITION. With numerous Illustrations. Crown 8vo. 7s. 6d.

'We are very much pleased with Mr. Schäfer's book. It is clearly written, well and originally illustrated, and possesses the merit of being both concise and complete. In conclusion we may say that any student who has gone fairly over the ground covered by this treatise will find that he has not only gained a mastery over the modern methods of microscopical investigation, but a sound knowledge of the several structures of which the body is composed.'—LANCET.

ATLAS of HISTOLOGY. By E. KLEIN, M.D., F.R.S., Lecturer on Histology at St. Bartholomew's Medical School, and NOBLE SMITH, F.R.C.S. Edin., L.R.C.P. Lond., &c., Surgeon to the City Orthopædic Hospital, and Surgeon to the All Saints' Children's Hospital. A complete Representation of the Microscopic Structure of Simple and Compound Tissues of Man and the higher Animals, in carefully executed coloured Engravings, with Explanatory Text of the Figures and a Concise Account of the hitherto ascertained facts in Histology. Royal 4to. with 48 Coloured Plates, bound in half-leather, £4. 4s.; or in 13 Parts, 6s. each.

MANUAL of PATHOLOGICAL HISTOLOGY. By CORNIL and RANVIER. Translated by authority from the New and Re-written French Edition, with the original Illustrations. Vol. I. Histology of the Tissues. Demy 8vo. 21s. Vol. II. Special Pathological Histology. Lesions of the Organs. Part I. Demy 8vo. 12s. Part II. Demy 8vo. 16s.

'We may safely recommend the work as the foremost text-book of its class, and we are certain that it will now be widely studied by many to whom the original was a closed book.'—LANCET.

ELEMENTS of HUMAN PHYSIOLOGY. By Dr. L. HERMANN, Professor of Physiology in the University of Zürich. SECOND EDITION. Entirely recast from the Sixth German Edition, with very copious Additions and many Additional Woodcuts, by ARTHUR GAMGEE, M.D., F.R.S., Brackenbury Professor of Physiology in Owens College, Manchester, and Examiner in Physiology in the University of Edinburgh. Demy 8vo. 16s.

REFERENCE BOOK of PRACTICAL THERAPEUTICS. By VARIOUS AUTHORS. Edited by FRANK P. FOSTER, M.D., Editor of the *New York Medical Journal*, &c. 2 vols. 8vo. £2. 10s.

A GUIDE to THERAPEUTICS. By ROBERT FARQUHARSON, M.P., M.D. Edin., F.R.C.P. Lond., late Lecturer on Materia Medica at St. Mary's Hospital Medical School, &c. FOURTH EDITION, thoroughly Revised. Crown 8vo. 7s. 6d.

London: SMITH, ELDER, & CO., 15 Waterloo Place.

SMITH, ELDER, & CO.'S PUBLICATIONS.

A TREATISE on the THEORY and PRACTICE OF MEDICINE. By the late JOHN SYER BRISTOWE, M.D. Lond., Fellow and formerly Censor of the Royal College of Physicians; Senior Physician to, and Joint-Lecturer on Medicine at, St. Thomas's Hospital; President of the Society of Medical Officers of Health; Examiner in Medicine to the Royal College of Surgeons; formerly Examiner in Medicine to the University of London, and Lecturer on General Pathology and on Physiology at St. Thomas's Hospital. SEVENTH EDITION. 8vo. 21s.

'The busy practitioner will be able by its perusal to keep abreast with the great progress which scientific medicine has made within the past few years, and for which he has neither the time nor frequently the opportunity to consult larger treatises, monographs, and journals. The style of the work is plain and lucid; though condensed, it is never bald. As an accurate and praiseworthy guide it is of the highest order of merit.'—BOSTON MEDICAL & SURGICAL JOURNAL.

An INDEX of MEDICINE: a Manual for the Use of Senior Students and others. By SEYMOUR TAYLOR, M.D., M.R.C.P., Senior Assistant-Physician to the West London Hospital. With Illustrations. Crown 8vo. 12s. 6d.

'Dr. Seymour Taylor may certainly be congratulated on the success of his labours. He has produced exactly what he desired, and the book may confidently be recommended to those for whom it is intended.' LANCET.

CLINICAL MANUAL for the STUDY of MEDICAL CASES. Edited by JAMES FINLAYSON, M.D., Physician and Lecturer on Clinical Medicine in the Glasgow Western Infirmary. With Special Chapters by Prof. GAIRDNER on the Physiognomy of Disease; Dr. ALEXANDER ROBERTSON on Insanity; Dr. JOSEPH COATES on the Throat; Prof. STEPHENSON on Disorders of the Female Organs; and Dr. SAMSON GEMMELL on Physical Diagnosis. THIRD AND CHEAPER EDITION, Revised, with Illustrations. Crown 8vo. 8s. 6d.

The TREATMENT of PHTHISIS. By ARTHUR RANSOME, M.D., M.A. Cantab., F.R.S., Consulting Physician to the Manchester Hospital for Consumption and Diseases of the Chest and Throat; Examiner in Sanitary Science at Cambridge and Victoria Universities. Demy 8vo. 7s. 6d.

BY THE SAME AUTHOR.

The CAUSES and PREVENTION of PHTHISIS. Being the Milroy Lectures for 1890. Crown 8vo. with Charts and Maps, 5s.

RESEARCHES on TUBERCULOSIS. The Weber-Parkes Prize Essay, 1897. Demy 8vo. limp cloth, 2s. 6d. net.

On the PRINCIPLES and EXACT CONDITIONS to be OBSERVED in the ARTIFICIAL FEEDING of INFANTS; the PROPERTIES of ARTIFICIAL FOODS; and the DISEASES which ARISE from FAULTS of DIET in EARLY LIFE. By W. B. CHEADLE, M.D, Physician to St. Mary's Hospital, and Lecturer on Medicine, &c. FOURTH EDITION, Revised. Crown 8vo. 5s.

COLLECTED CONTRIBUTIONS on DIGESTION and DIET. With an Appendix on the Opium Habit in India. By Sir WILLIAM ROBERTS, M.D., F.R.S. SECOND EDITION. Crown 8vo. 5s.

The MINERAL WATERS and HEALTH RESORTS of EUROPE. With Notes on the Treatment of Chronic Diseases by Spas and Climates, and Hints as to the Simultaneous Employment of various Physical and Dietetic Methods. By HERMANN WEBER, M.D., F.R.C.P., Consulting Physician to the German Hospital and to the Royal National Hospital for Consumption, Ventnor, &c.; and FREDERICK PARKES WEBER, M.D., M.R.C.P., Physician to the German Hospital. With a Map. Demy 8vo. 10s. 6d.

'This admirable digest of the principal European Spas and after-cures will now incontestably take the lead in all English works of the kind.... Drs. Weber have placed themselves, in so far as British Balneo-therapeutic works are concerned hors concours.'—QUEEN.
'A most useful and valuable addition to balneological literature.' JOURNAL OF BALNEOLOGY AND CLIMATOLOGY.

London: SMITH, ELDER, & CO., 15 Waterloo Place.

www.ingramcontent.com/pod-product-compliance
Lightning Source LLC
Chambersburg PA
CBHW022113290426
44112CB00008B/657